Saints' Lives in
Middle English Collections

Middle English Texts

General Editor

Russell A. Peck
University of Rochester

Associate Editor

Alan Lupack
University of Rochester

Assistant Editor

Michael Livingston
University of Rochester

Advisory Board

Rita Copeland
University of Pennsylvania

Thomas G. Hahn
University of Rochester

Lisa Kiser
Ohio State University

R. A. Shoaf
University of Florida

Bonnie Wheeler
Southern Methodist University

The Middle English Texts Series is designed for classroom use. Its goal is to make available to teachers and students texts that occupy an important place in the literary and cultural canon but have not been readily available in student editions. The series does not include those authors, such as Chaucer, Langland, or Malory, whose English works are normally in print in good student editions. The focus is, instead, upon Middle English literature adjacent to those authors that teachers need in compiling the syllabuses they wish to teach. The editions maintain the linguistic integrity of the original work but within the parameters of modern reading conventions. The texts are printed in the modern alphabet and follow the practices of modern capitalization, word formation, and punctuation. Manuscript abbreviations are silently expanded, and *u/v* and *j/i* spellings are regularized according to modern orthography. Yogh is transcribed as *g*, *gh*, *y*, or *s*, according to the letter in modern English spelling to which it corresponds. Distinction between the second person pronoun and the definite article is made by spelling the one *thee* and the other *the*, and final *-e* that receives full syllabic value is accented (e.g., *charité*). Hard words, difficult phrases, and unusual idioms are glossed on the page, either in the right margin or at the foot of the page. Explanatory and textual notes appear at the end of the text, along with a glossary. The editions include short introductions on the history of the work, its merits and points of topical interest, and also contain briefly annotated bibliographies.

Saints' Lives in Middle English Collections

Edited by
E. Gordon Whatley,
with Anne B. Thompson and Robert K. Upchurch

Published for TEAMS
(The Consortium for the Teaching of the Middle Ages)
in Association with the University of Rochester

by

MEDIEVAL INSTITUTE PUBLICATIONS
College of Arts & Sciences
Western Michigan University
Kalamazoo, Michigan
2004

Library of Congress Cataloging-in-Publication Data

Saints' lives in Middle English collections / edited by E. Gordon Whatley, with Anne Thompson and Robert Upchurch.
    p. cm. -- (Middle English texts)
 Includes bibliographical references (p.   ) and index.
 ISBN 1-58044-089-4 (alk. paper)
 1. Christian literature, English (Middle) 2. Christian poetry, English (Middle) 3. Christian saints--Legends. 4. Christian saints--Poetry. I. Whatley, E. Gordon, 1944- II. Thompson, Anne, 1939- III. Upchurch, Robert, 1967- IV. Middle English texts (Kalamazoo, Mich.) V. Title. VI. Series.

 PR1120.S37 2004
 821'.1080382700922--dc22

                                                    2004019690

ISBN 1-58044-089-4

Contents

Acknowledgments

Work on this volume was divided up as follows. Anne Thompson edited the texts and wrote the introductions and notes for Chapters IV (St. Thaïs), V(b) (St. Scholastica), and VIII (St. Julian Hospitaller). Robert Upchurch edited the texts and wrote the main drafts of the introduction and notes for Chapters II (St. George) and V(a) (St. Benedict). He also assisted me by preparing preliminary transcriptions, from MS Ashmole 43, of the texts in Chapters I(a) (Martyrdom of St. Andrew) and VII (St. Francis), by checking variants of these texts in several other manuscripts, and in various other ways. My own contribution includes work on the texts, introductions and notes for Chapters I (St. Andrew), III (St. Jerome), VI (St. Austin), and VII (St. Francis), the brief "Language" portions of the introductions to all the chapters, general revisions throughout, as well as this General Introduction and the Select Glossary.

To Robert Upchurch and Anne Thompson I am deeply grateful not only for their excellent scholarly work as co-editors of this volume but also for their patient support during the past few years. Thanks also to Carolyn Lengel, Tom Harford, Christine Rauer, Michael Sargent, Kate Silverstein, Scott Westrem, and Richard Zeikowitz for contributing in various ways to the early stages of the project.

Grateful acknowledgment is made to the curators of various libraries for providing access to their collections and for arranging for permission to print the following texts: Simon Winter's life of Jerome, from Cambridge, St. John's College MS. N. 17 (250), by permission of the Master and Fellows of the College; the *Northern Homily Cycle* legend of Thaïs from MS HM 129 by permission of The Huntington Library, San Marino, California; the legend of George and the Dragon in the *South English Legendary*, from materials held in the University of Minnesota Libraries Collection (MS Z822 N81), with permission; the legends of Scholastica, Benedict, Francis, and Andrew (Martyrdom) from Oxford, Bodleian Library, MS Ashmole 43, by permission of the Bodleian Library, Oxford University; the *Scottish Legendary* versions of the legends of Andrew (Miracle of the Three Questions) and Julian the Hospitaller, from Cambridge University Library MS Gg.2.6, by permission of the Syndics of Cambridge University Library. The legend of Jerome and the Lion is printed from Beinecke MS 317. I am particularly grateful to the staffs of several of the Yale University libraries, including Beinecke, for many courtesies.

The project was aided by several grants from the CUNY Research Foundation's PSC-CUNY awards program, for research and publication costs.

Finally, heartfelt gratitude to Russell A. Peck for encouraging and patiently waiting for this project's completion; many members of the Middle English Texts Series staff assisted in the project: Dana M. Symons and Michael Livingston originally formatted the volume, checked the texts (catching numerous errors), and did full readings of the entire project; Michael Livingston also copy-edited the volume, prepared the Bibliography, and prepared camera-ready copy; N. M. Heckel and Emily Rebekah Huber assisted with read-throughs of a few chapters. Thanks also to Patricia Hollahan and the staff of Medieval Institute Publications for seeing the volume expertly through the press. For any remaining imperfections, *mea culpa*.

This volume is dedicated in memory of a fine scholar of medieval religion and an extraordinary promoter of medieval studies in North America. We would also like to pay tribute here to Sherry Reames, founding President of the Hagiography Society, for her inspiration and leadership in the study of medieval saints and their literature.

Saints' Lives in Middle English Collections

General Introduction

The selection of Middle English saints' lives edited in this volume is designed, like other volumes in the Middle English Texts Series, for relative newcomers to medieval English language and literature (and in this case to hagiography), but it is hoped that the volume will also be of use to more experienced students and scholars seeking to engage more closely with saints' legends whose previous printed editions have provided little or no scholarly apparatus or aids to further research. It will be immediately obvious that the selection here focuses mainly, if not exclusively, on male saints.[1] It was conceived as a complement to another volume of the Middle English Texts Series, devoted solely to female saints.[2] The selection of holy men in the present volume is intended to be broadly representative of saints' lives in Middle English and of the classic types of hagiographic legend as these were presented to the lay public and less-literate clergy of late medieval England. The specific selection and ordering of legends is explained below, after a brief introduction to its larger context. It should be pointed out at the outset that the current selection was not made with any conscious agenda of problematizing the gender of these saints or of staking out a particular position in the burgeoning field of studies in masculinity.[3] It is to be hoped, however, that while they were chosen with other criteria in mind, the legends printed here may prove interesting and relevant to readers pursuing questions of gender in religious narrative, as well as to those interested generally in vernacular hagiography and its sources, and in the vast flowering of Middle English devotional literature in the later Middle Ages.

Saints and Hagiography

While still officially espoused by modern Catholicism, the idea of personal sanctity, as embodied in the spectacularly holy lives and deaths that form the subject matter of Christian

---

[1] Exceptions are Thaïs (IV), a reformed prostitute, Scholastica (V[b]), nun and sister of Benedict (V[a]), and the unnamed, faithful wife of Julian Hospitaller (VIII).

[2] Reames, ed., *Middle English Legends of Women Saints*.

[3] See, e.g., Lees, ed., *Medieval Masculinities*; Hadley, ed., *Masculinity in Medieval Europe*; and Riches and Salih, eds., *Gender and Holiness*.

hagiography ("writings about the saints"),[4] is no longer prominent in Western culture. But in the Christian communities of late antiquity and the Middle Ages it was widely accepted that God from time to time endowed an individual man or woman with special grace to live conspicuously according to the divine will and to wield supernatural power, either from the moment he or she was born, or after a decisive episode of conversion to an intensely committed Christian life as an adult.[5] In this volume, it happens that of those saints whose lives are told in full, the former type (sanctity in birth) is exemplified only in Benedict, the latter (adult conversion) by Thaïs, Francis, and Julian, and, in his own way, by Jerome.

The gift of sanctifying grace was perceived to result not only in the saint's extraordinary degree of moral rectitude, religious zeal, unwavering faith in God, and compelling personal charisma and authority, but also in his or her acts of supernatural power, whether of healing, visionary foresight, exorcism (the ability to detect and expel demons), or, as with the martyr saints, unperturbed resistance to the pain of physical torture and mutilation. After foreseeing and experiencing a death (either by natural causes or by martyrdom) accompanied by further marvels, the saint's soul typically was reported to have ascended joyfully to Heaven where it could be expected to exercise another saintly power: namely, interceding with God in response to the prayers of the faithful. Soon afterwards, or in some cases years later, beginning in the community where the holy body was buried, the death date (*depositio*, lit. "laying to rest") came to be celebrated as an annual feast day of special church services, public festivities, and pilgrimage, and his or her name became a fixture in the festal calendars of churches wherever the saint's memory was revered, which in some cases eventually meant all over Christendom.[6] For example, the cults of saints either buried in Rome or, like St. Andrew, buried in Greece but venerated early in Rome, were carried all over Europe partly by the report of pilgrims and gifts of relics and partly by the widespread adoption, from the seventh through the ninth centuries, of service books reflecting Roman liturgical customs.

In many churches, especially in the more literate monasteries where liturgies were more elaborate and hagiography more assiduously cultivated, it became customary on a celebrated saint's feast day to read selections from a written *vita* ("life") or, for a martyr, from a *passio*

---

[4] Compare Late Latin *hagiographa*, from Greek *agios* ("holy"), and *graphai* ("writings").

[5] See below, p. 7, for some factors contributing to the post-medieval decline of the cult of saints. On early Christian saints and their social significance, see the important collection of essays by Brown, *Society*. On sanctity in the later Middle Ages, see Vauchez, *Sainthood*. For modern ecclesiastical attitudes to sainthood, see Woodward, *Making Saints*. For a comparative perspective, see Kieckhefer and Bond, eds., *Sainthood*.

[6] On the early development of the saints' cults, the classic English study is still that of Brown, *The Cult of the Saints*. See also Wilson, ed. and intro., *Saints and Their Cults*, with valuable early bibliography; and Howard-Johnston and Hayward, eds., *The Cult of Saints*.

("passion," lit., "suffering") recounting his or her torture and execution. Such works were sometimes composed within a generation or two of the saint's death by one of his or her followers or by a professional writer who would interview members of the community for information and anecdotes. In many cases, however, stories constituting the saint's legend might circulate orally for years, even centuries, before being written down.

The variety in the origins of the Latin *vitae* and *passiones* is represented in the present volume, albeit indirectly, in that the legends here are Middle English translations and adaptations, typically abbreviated and abridged in comparison with their Latin sources. Thus the ME legends of the martyrdoms of the apostle Andrew (I[a]) and of George (II[a]) are based closely on well-known anonymous or pseudonymous *passiones* for each saint that circulated widely in the Greek East and soon afterwards in Latin translations and redactions in western Europe and that were frequently copied into the great legendaries or "passionals" maintained by the great religious houses and some smaller churches. The story of George's martyrdom is typical of the *passio* genre in focusing only on the saint's arrest, interrogation, torture, and martyrdom, saying little or nothing about his earlier life and development as a Christian. Like many early *passiones*, that of George is a stylized fictional imagining of the martyrdom, which survives in many different versions, most of which derive from one or more "archetypes" composed in Greek up to two centuries after the putative date of the saint's late-third-century martyrdom proper.

Andrew's Latin *passio*, although it resembles that of George in its present form, was itself based on and extracted from longer "apocryphal acts," detailing his missionary wanderings and career, as well as his martyrdom; these longer acts, thought to have originated among heretical Christian communities, were composed in Greek in the third century close to the very beginnings of hagiographic tradition and exemplify the Christian appropriation of classical literary traditions of epic and romance.[7]

The ME legends of Benedict and his sister Scholastica (the Life of St. Benedict, V[a], and the Life of St. Scholastica, V[b]), on the other hand, are based on the standard *vita* composed in Latin by Pope Gregory the Great in the late sixth century as the second book of his anthology of lives and miracles of recent Italian holy men and women (*The Dialogues*), and the Francis legend (VII) is based on the Latin life by Bonaventure, leader of the Franciscan order in the mid-thirteenth century. Gregory wrote about Benedict and his sister a generation or two after their deaths and had to rely on the oral traditions of communities at Benedict's cult sites. While few today would give total credence to everything Gregory records about Benedict, generally accepted as "historical" is at least the broad outline of Gregory's account of the saint's youthful retreat from urban culture into eremitic solitude, then rural missionary work and the founding

---

[7] MacDonald, *Christianizing Homer*. See also the controversial historical reading of Davies, *The Revolt of the Widows*. The most recent English collection of the "Apocryphal Acts" of the Apostles is in Elliott, ed., *The Apocryphal New Testament*, pp. 227–533.

of many monasteries in central Italy. Likewise, Bonaventure's life of Francis, completed in the 1260s, was based on two or more written *vitae* composed only thirty years earlier (shortly after the saint's death) by members of the Franciscan order who knew the saint well. While the conventions of hagiography encouraged these early biographers to idealize their subject in various ways, and to devote a great deal of space to miracles, their work nonetheless is believed to bring us close to the actual shape of Francis' life.

These written lives served not only to commemorate and glorify the dead saints, and to promote their cults as intercessors (more on this below), but they also frequently served as vehicles for instruction on certain points of doctrine. For example, in the Martyrdom of St. Andrew (I[a]), in the first dialogue between Andrew and his persecutor, the judge Egeus (lines 23–40) seeks to discredit Andrew's faith in the divinity of Christ by charging that Jesus' crucifixion showed His vulnerability and powerlessness. Andrew counters by insisting that, far from being evidence of weakness, His death on the Cross was itself an act of divine power and testified to Jesus' strength of will, since He predicted in advance the time and manner in which His death would happen. A similarly didactic dialogue occurs in John Lydgate's *Saint Austin at Compton* (VI) where an English knight argues vigorously in the archbishop's presence for his right to withhold the tithes demanded of him by the parish priest (lines 186–93). In this case, of course, the entire tale is framed in didactic terms as an exemplum (see below) illustrating the importance of paying tithes, and the dire consequences of withholding them.

It is also often assumed that the lives of the saints themselves were intended to serve as models for virtuous human behavior, and this was doubtless true up to a point, but, given the often superhuman feats the saints are seen performing, it is clear that ordinary Christians could not have been expected to imitate these extraordinary figures literally, but rather to strive for proportionate achievements within their reach. A prayer for the feast of St. Francis in a service-book widely used in late medieval England, the Sarum Missal, does not ask God to endow the congregation with the grace to imitate Francis by becoming wandering, barefoot friars, but rather in a general way asks Him to "grant us to follow his example in despising earthly things and to enjoy everlasting participation in the gifts of heaven."[8] In the *SEL* version of the Life of St. Francis (VII), the poet describes Francis' fondness for visiting lepers, kissing their hands, feet, and mouths, and tells how Francis gave the lepers generously of his possessions, adding that he did so "bi costume" (line 56, "habitually"). The poet then comments:

So aghte, me thencth, ech man   and namelich the riche,
Vor our Lord hath so ofte be iseie   in hor liche (lines 57–58)

---

[8] "Tribue nobis ex eius imitacione terrena despicere et celestium donorum semper participacione gaudere" (Legg, ed., *The Sarum Missal*, p. 331).

4

[So should everyone, it seems to me, and especially the rich; / For our Lord has so often been seen in their (the lepers') likeness.]

The emphasis on the wealthy here implies that the poet expects people to imitate Francis' regular habit of making donations to the lepers, but the exhortation does not appear to be enjoining everyone to be physically intimate with them. More literal imitation of the saint seems to be implied, however, in Simon Winter's exhortations to Margaret of Clarence that in reading *The Life of Saint Jerome* (III[a]) she "may lerne and take ensample to lyve a Cristemannys lyfe in penaunce and straytnes" (lines 13–14). The widowed Margaret is thought to have adopted a semi-monastic lifestyle, which may well have included an ascetic regime similar to that practiced by Jerome, although in the Thames valley she would not experience the scorpions and searing heat suffered by Jerome in the Syrian desert.

In addition to the *vita* and *passio*, another hagiographic genre associated with saints' cults is the *liber miraculorum* ("book of miracles"). The emergence of a saint's cult often was accompanied by (and unlikely to succeed without) the willingness of its sponsors and the surrounding public to believe that the bodily relics of the saint were the source of continuing displays of supernatural power: the power to heal disease, for example, or to avert fires, or to punish the church's enemies, and so on. The saint's spirit, though in Heaven, was believed to remain active among mortals, particularly in response to the explicit prayers or felt needs of the originating community or of individual devotees. The *liber miraculorum*, compiled assiduously by the clerical guardians of the saint's reliquary shrine, contains anecdotes, sometimes brief and simple, and sometimes quite elaborate and lengthy, concerning individual miracles believed to have been performed by God through the intercession of the saint, not only shortly after his death but also in some cases centuries later. Often fascinating for the insights they provide today into otherwise obscurely documented medieval communities, books of miracles became important in the later Middle Ages as documents in support of canonization by the pope, although papal approval was not usually sought before the twelfth century. The local community's acceptance and promotion, through a written *vita* and liturgical commemorations, of their hero's claim to sanctity were usually sufficient proof of its validity. While the present volume, and vernacular saints' legends in general, concentrate mainly on the saints' living acts rather than on their posthumous activities, extracts from such a miracle collection are found below in the chapter on Jerome (III).[9]

---

[9] See Ward, *Miracles and the Medieval Mind*, and Finucane, *Miracles and Pilgrims*. Vauchez (in *Sainthood*) describes the development of the canonization process. Recently edited and translated Latin collections of miracles of individual saints include Sheingorn, *The Book of Sainte Foy*, and Whatley, *The Saint of London*. On the role of the saints' cults in late medieval English parish life, see Duffy, *The Stripping of the Altars*, pp. 155–205.

Better represented in the current volume are individual miracle stories that circulated independently at first and only later became incorporated into a given saint's "dossier." The famous stories of St. George and the Dragon (II[b]) and St. Jerome and the Lion (III), as well as the less-well-known *Saint Austin at Compton* (VI), purport to record miracles performed by the saint in his lifetime, although they were unknown to the earliest hagiographers. Together with the posthumous miracle of Andrew and the Three Questions (I[b]) and the Life of St. Julian Hospitaller (VIII), these stories exemplify the tendency of medieval hagiography to merge at times with literary fiction and entertainment. In addition, the Andrew and Augustine miracles are also prominent examples of the prolific late medieval narrative genre of exempla or illustrative anecdotes, many of which were culled from saints' legends and from the thirteenth century onwards began to be collected for use by preachers to enliven their sermons. The short Life of St. Thaïs (IV) functions as just such an exemplum in the homily from which it is edited here.

From the fourth century to the sixteenth century, the cults of the saints occupied an important place in the developing system of Christian beliefs and rites, and the literary forms associated with them make up a major component of medieval literary production. It is true that the life and death of Jesus, as recounted in the gospels, interpreted in the Pauline letters, and believed to be prefigured and prophesied in the historical and prophetic books of Judaic scripture, remained at the core of the church's teaching. But hagiography came to form a vast supplement to the Bible, reinforcing in stylized, formulaic narratives the belief that God's power and love continued to be active in the world, and that the proliferating holy shrines of His saints offered points of local access to the glittering remoteness of the heavenly Jerusalem. Rarely "biographical" in the modern sense of the term, even when composed, as noted above, soon after the deaths of their subjects, the medieval lives of Christian saints are often closer to myth than history in their profusion of supernatural feats of power and suffering, and in their stereotyped and "unrealistic" portrayal of idealized Christian identity. As has often been pointed out in recent scholarship, the hagiographers sought to describe not the distinctive traits of a unique individual in a particular moment in historical time, but rather his or her likeness to Christ and other saints, and his or her embodiment of the truths of orthodox Christian doctrine and ethical teaching. Each legend was also designed to prove, by recounting miracles and acts of power, its hero's genuine sanctity and worthiness of continued veneration.[10]

---

[10] For an excellent brief overview of hagiography as it affects medieval England, see Reames and Vanderbilt, "Hagiography." For the Latin tradition, with special attention to Anglo-Latin, see also Townsend, "Hagiography." For a historian's recent introduction to hagiography in general and to a substantial chronological selection of hagiographic texts, see Head, ed., *Medieval Hagiography*, pp. xiii–xxxviii (with much relevant bibliography). Among book-length efforts to survey the genre of hagiography are Delehaye's classic (but now dated) study, *The Legends of the Saints*, the structuralist study by Elliot, *Roads to Paradise*, and the insightful but discursive essays by Heffernan in *Sacred Biography*. On the problematic relationship between history, biography, and hagiography, see Stancliffe,

General Introduction

In the early modern period, in northern Europe, the advocates of Protestant reform sought to restore the Bible as the only sacred text worthy of Christian devotion and repudiated the cult of the saints, along with other aspects of medieval Catholicism, as idolatry and superstition. As a result of this Protestant dismissal of hagiographical texts as irreligious, and the rise of the spirit of scientific inquiry and increasingly skeptical attitudes towards the miraculous and supernatural, much of medieval Christian hagiography, especially the legends of the best known apostles and martyrs, has long been deemed unworthy of historical and even literary study except among a few notably energetic Roman Catholic scholars such as the Bollandists.[11] It is only in the past few decades that hagiographic texts have begun to be re-read and re-edited, not so much as flawed or fraudulent biographies but as valuable sources and expressions of the beliefs, values, and preoccupations of the communities and individuals who produced them.[12] Saints' lives and cults have become for historians not simply evidence of religious devotion but also complex "sites" where lines of political, economic, and social force converge and where figurations of gender and power are discernible.[13] Various changes taking place over recent decades in the field of literary criticism have doubtless helped draw critics to the study of this once marginal genre: among the developments is the retreat from earlier preoccupations with formalism and aestheticism, along with the weakening of the idea of a canon of great authors and the broadening of the definition of "literature" and "text" to include modes of writing and communication formerly deemed beyond the pale of literary appreciation. Modern students have begun to read past the ostensibly bland and stereotyped surface of hagiographic narrative, to note the variety of detail and nuance amid the superficial uniformity, and to find different

---

St. Martin and His Hagiographer, and Lawrence, *St. Edmund of Abingdon*. Delehaye's specialized study of the *passio* genre has still not been translated or superseded: *Les passions des martyrs et les genres littéraires*, second ed. The most recent English studies of the *passio* genre comprise gendered readings of the female martyr *passio*, e.g., by Wogan-Browne: "The Virgin's Tale"; see also Wogan-Browne and Burgess, eds., *Virgin Lives and Holy Deaths*, pp. xi–xix.

[11] For descriptions of the history and ongoing projects of the Bollandists, visit their website at http://www.kbr.be/~socboll/.

[12] Examples of the upsurge in the modern study of hagiography are the multi-volume collaborative history in progress under the direction of Guy Philippart, *Hagiographies, Hagiographica*, edited by Claudio Leonardi (founded in 1994), and the magisterial study of early Christian and early medieval hagiography by Berschin, *Biographie und Epochenstil im lateinischen Mittelalter*.

[13] Studies relevant to England include Rollason, *Saints and Relics in Anglo-Saxon England*; Ridyard, *The Royal Saints of Anglo-Saxon England*; Lewis, *The Cult of St Katherine of Alexandria*; and various collections of essays such as Bonner, Rollason, and Stancliffe, eds., *St. Cuthbert*. For the Latin hagiographic background, see Michael Lapidge and R. C. Love, "The Latin Hagiography of England and Wales (600–1550)," in Philippart, 1994–, vol. 3 (2001), pp. 203–325.

kinds of "difference" and *mouvance* in the subtle discrepancies between successive versions of the same legend.[14]

The Selection of Saints

The original plan for this volume aimed at a representation of the chronological history of medieval Christianity through its saints, while showcasing the main categories of saints as they appear in a variety of types and periods of Middle English hagiography, with a special focus on the British Isles in texts composed in the chief dialects of Middle English. As the work proceeded it became obvious that the original plan, calling for over twenty individual texts dealing with more than a dozen saints, was overly ambitious, given the relative lack of existing scholarship and consequent need for much detailed research, and the amount of research required not merely to edit the texts themselves but also to compile the introductions and notes. In the end, to expedite publication after far too long a delay (for which the principal editor is solely responsible), the broad scope of the volume as first envisaged has been reduced, while its basic criteria of selection have been retained.

The texts are arranged so as to constitute a "legendary history" of post-New Testament Christianity in seven parts. Legends such as those printed here, despite their historical unreliability in the eyes of modern scholars, provided generations of medieval people, both lay and clerical, with a stately procession of figures that constituted the Christian past, as well as being still "present" as glorious members of the body of Christ, the communion of saints. Thus the selection of saints in this volume begins with St. Andrew (I), representing the age of Jesus' immediate followers, the missionary apostles of the first century, whose apocryphal "acts" seem to have been composed mainly in the second and third centuries. Following the apostles are, successively, the age of martyrdom and persecution (St. George, II), the late antique age of patristic learning (St. Jerome, III) and of the desert hermits (St. Thaïs, IV), the monastic culture of the early Middle Ages (St. Benedict and St. Scholastica, V), and the conversion of the northern barbarians and establishment of the national churches (St. Austin, VI). The historical sequence then leaps forward many centuries to one of the Church's late bursts of spiritual and pastoral energy, as represented by St. Francis (VII), who in the thirteenth century preached an evangelical revival of apostolic poverty. Chapter VIII (a number that for learned medieval Christians signified the eternal peace destined to follow the end of historical time) features Julian the Hospitaller, an apparently mythical saint (one of several medieval reincarnations of

---

[14] See, e.g., Reames, "Mouvance and Interpretation in Late-Medieval Latin"; Winstead, *Virgin Martyrs*; Delany, *Impolitic Bodies*; Wogan-Browne, *Saints' Lives and Women's Literary Culture*; and Thompson, "The Legend of St. Agnes."

(Œdipus) whose legend is literally timeless in that it lacks any indication of when or where it is supposed to have taken place.

In addition to their historical significance for medieval readers, the saints featured here represent many of the principal types of Christian hero: apostle and martyr (Andrew), martyred layman and soldier (George), doctor of the church (Jerome), abbot and monastic founder (Benedict), virgin (Scholastica), pastoral bishop and missionary (Austin), and a lay founder of an order of mendicant friars who was also a mystic (Francis). Thaïs, the prostitute saint and desert solitary, is classified like Mary Magdalen and Mary of Egypt as "paenitens" (penitent) in the Bollandists' master bibliography of Latin hagiography.[15] Julian Hospitaller fits the same category. However, in terms of the main divisions of saints recognized in the church liturgy, all the saints in this volume fall into one of three groups: apostle and martyr (Andrew), martyr (George), and confessor (everyone else).

The national coloring of the selection is less rich than originally envisaged. Only Austin of Canterbury, founder of the English church (VI), Andrew, patron saint of Scotland (I), and George (II) can be regarded as national saints of the British Isles, the latter two by adoption, since their original cults were in the distant East. Regional variety is, however, deliberately reflected in the mix of ME dialects. Two of the texts — St. Andrew and the Three Questions (I[b]) and the Life of St. Julian Hospitaller (VIII) — are in the Middle Scots dialect of the late fourteenth century. The Life of St. Thaïs (IV) is in an Anglo-Irish dialect of Middle English of the early fifteenth century. Two legends, those of St. Jerome (III) and St. Austin (VI) display different variants (and widely contrasting styles) of the greater London region's dialect in the early and later fifteenth century, while the episode of St. George and the Dragon (II[b]) is from the Northeast Midlands in the late fourteenth century. The remaining texts (Martyrdom of St. Andrew, I[a], and of St. George, II[b]; the Lives of Benedict and Scholastica, V; and the Life of St. Francis, VII) are in the dialect of the Southwest Midlands, the cradle of early Middle English hagiography, from around the turn of the thirteenth century.[16] It will also be evident from this synopsis that the chronological range of the selection, from the thirteenth to the fifteenth century, covers the bulk of the Middle English period of the English language's development.

---

[15] *BHL* 5415, 5439, and 8012.

[16] The earliest surviving ME saints' lives, also from the Southwest Midlands, are the female martyrs' legends in the well-known and much edited "Katherine Group." See, e.g., Millett and Wogan-Browne, *Medieval English Prose for Women*.

The Sources of Middle English Hagiography

Impressive numbers of saints' legends survive from Anglo-Saxon England, composed in Old English verse and prose,[17] and from Anglo-Norman England in Norman French verse.[18] Some of the Old English prose legends continued to be read in some English communities well into the twelfth century, while the saints' legends in French had an English audience from the early twelfth through the fourteenth century since French continued in use, especially as a literary language, among the higher nobility throughout this period. But from the mid- to late thirteenth century, the linguistic and literary scene became more diverse. Just as secular chivalric romances of French origin began appearing in Middle English, so French and Latin devotional texts began to be translated or adapted into various dialects of Middle English with growing frequency. The reasons for this shift are numerous, but among them is the fact that English dynastic ties with Normandy and other parts of France were weakening, and as a result spoken English was becoming more common among the upper classes, especially among the minor nobility and country gentry. From the later thirteenth century, the Church appears to have encouraged the production of Middle English texts as part of its efforts to promote higher standards of religious knowledge and practice among the laity in general.[19] Prominent in newly emerging Middle English religious literature were biblical texts[20] and the lives of saints.[21]

---

[17] Recent surveys are James E. Cross, "English Vernacular Saints' Lives Before 1000 A. D.," in Philippart, 1994–, vol. 2 (1996), pp. 413–27, and E. G. Whatley, "Late Old English Hagiography, ca. 950–1150," in Philippart, 1994–, vol. 2 (1996), pp. 429–99.

[18] See Wogan-Browne, *Saints' Lives and Women's Literary Culture*, for discussion and bibliography relating to Anglo-Norman hagiography. A brief but valuable survey is M. Thiry-Stassin, "L'hagiographie en Anglo-Normand," in Philippart, 1994–, vol. 1 (1994), pp. 407–28. On Old French hagiography in general, some of which circulated in England, see most recently Robertson, *The Medieval Saints' Lives*.

[19] A standard history of the factors underlying the shift from French to English in the thirteenth and fourteenth centuries, but bypassing the influence of the Church, is that of Baugh and Cable, *A History of the English Language*, pp. 126–57. For a searching overview of the political and cultural implications of the emergence of Middle English literature, see Nicholas Watson, "The Politics of Middle English Writing," in Wogan-Browne, et al., 1999, pp. 331–52.

[20] See the survey and bibliography by Lawrence Muir, "Translations and Paraphrases of the Bible, and Commentaries," in *MWME* 2.381–409, 534–52. See also Robert Raymo, "Works of Religious and Philosophical Instruction," *MWME* 7.2255–2378, 2470–82.

[21] Still the best single bibliography of ME saints' lives is that of Charlotte D'Evelyn, "Legends of Individual Saints," in *MWME* 2.561–635. A recent survey of ME hagiography is Manfred Görlach, "Middle English Legends, 1220–1530"; more specialized is Winstead, *Virgin Martyrs*. Heffernan, *Sacred Biography*, includes a good deal of scattered commentary on ME hagiography. A still useful literary-historical survey of Old and Middle English hagiography is that of Gordon H. Gerould, *Saints' Legends*,

The ME saints' legends in this volume are drawn from two different and representative kinds of sources: nine of the twelve distinct items are from large, more or less organized collections of legends, while the remaining three are compositions originally independent of the known collections. This reflects the general pattern presented by the more than five hundred surviving Middle English legends concerning about three hundred saints. Most of them are found in either the *South English Legendary* (*SEL*) the *Scottish Legendary* (*ScL*), the *Gilte Legende* (*GiL*), or Caxton's *Golden Legend* (*GoL*). These large English legendaries in turn form part of a general European trend which begins with the appearance in the thirteenth century of several organized and selective collections of Latin legends. The saints represented in these new legendaries are on the whole only those widely venerated throughout the Western Church, and their legends are provided in considerably abridged and edited form. This combination of abbreviated legends and a selective roster of saints contrasted sharply with the bulky, multi-volume legendaries commonly found in the great monastic houses and larger churches and cathedrals.[22] By far the most successful of the abbreviated collections was the *Legenda aurea* of the Dominican Jacobus de Voragine, finished around 1266.[23] The rapid circulation of manuscripts of the *Legenda aurea*, aided no doubt by the high degree of mobility of the Dominicans, Franciscans, and other new orders of friars, must have helped spur the production of vernacular legendaries of similar types, even when, as is true of the Middle English *SEL*, the *Legenda aurea* was not initially the main source of the vernacular legendary. Vernacular legendaries of this sort were compiled from the late thirteenth to the fifteenth century in languages as diverse as Occitan (Provençal), French, Dutch, Low German, High German, Catalan, Castilian, Czech, and Hungarian.[24] In England and some of the other continental countries, the early vernacular legendaries and individual legends tended to be composed in verse. After the fourteenth century the preferred medium is usually prose.

Other smaller ME collections include the so-called *Vernon Golden Legend*, the *North English Legendary* (itself part of a larger gospel homiliary, the *Northern Homily Cycle [NHC]*), and

---

and the stylistic study by Theodor Wolpers, *Die englische Heiligenlegende des Mittelalters*, unfortunately never translated into English.

[22] The standard survey of medieval Latin saints' legendaries is that of Philippart, *Les légendiers latins*.

[23] Jacobus de Voragine, *Legenda aurea*, ed. Maggioni. See also the modern English translation by Ryan, *The Golden Legend*, and the useful selection by Stace, *The Golden Legend: Selections*. The standard study in English is that of Reames, *The Legenda aurea: A Reexamination of Its Paradoxical History*. For the influence of the *Legenda aurea* on ME hagiography, see Görlach, "Middle English Legends." Two important collections of essays, both edited by Dunn-Lardeau, are *Legenda aurea, sept siècles de diffusion*, and *Legenda aurea — La légende dorée (XIIIe–XVe s.)*.

[24] See, for example, Werner Williams-Krapp, "German and Dutch Translations of the *Legenda aurea*," in Dunn-Lardeau, *Legenda aurea, sept siècles de diffusion*, pp. 227–31.

Osbern Bokenham's "Chaucerian" *Legends of Holy Women*. None of these exhibits the scale or organized design of the larger hagiographic legendaries. Bokenham's, for example, took shape over time and mainly as a series of individual commissions for different patrons among the gentry of East Anglia, and were eventually copied into one manuscript that is now all that survives of the rest.[25]

Most successful of the ME legendaries, at least to judge from the numbers of surviving copies, are the earliest and latest: the verse *SEL* and Caxton's prose *GoL*. *SEL* is extant, more or less complete, in twenty-five manuscripts (dated from the late thirteenth to the mid-fifteenth century), plus nineteen fragmentary manuscripts, with evidence of at least four lost manuscripts.[26] Individual items from *SEL* survive in eighteen other manuscripts. In view of its early date and enduring influence, and also in view of the relative difficulty of its language and the lack of "user-friendly" editions, *SEL* is the most frequently represented source in this volume with six distinct items (chapters I[a], II, V, VII). A more detailed introduction and bibliographical notes to *SEL* follow later in this General Introduction.

Caxton's *GoL*, one of the earliest English printed books, first appeared in 1483 and was reprinted several times over the next forty years. Translated mainly from Jean de Vignay's fourteenth-century French prose translation of the *Legenda aurea*, but with frequent use of the Latin original and other sources, *GoL* is the largest extant English legendary and was intended to be "an authoritative and exhaustive collection."[27] It is not represented in the present volume, however, partly because of space constraints but also because students now have relatively easy access to this famous work.[28] An important model and frequent supplementary source for Caxton was an earlier fifteenth-century prose legendary, *GiL*, compiled in the 1430s, which itself had been in large part adapted from Jean de Vignay's fourteenth-century French translation of the Latin *Legenda aurea*, and supplemented with numerous lives of English saints, some of which were simply taken from *SEL* and rewritten as prose.[29] *GiL* is likewise not represented directly in the present volume, a significant portion of it having just been published for the first

---

[25] Bokenham, *Legendys of Hooly Wummen*, ed. Serjeantson; see also the translation by Delany in *A Legend of Holy Women*.

[26] Görlach, *The Textual Tradition of the South English Legendary*, pp. viii–x.

[27] Görlach, "Middle English Legends," p. 477.

[28] Caxton, *The Golden Legend*, ed. Ellis. Ellis' modern spelling version is now accessible online at http://www.catholic-forum.com/saints/golden000.htm. Another hagiographic collection produced by Caxton, his *Vitas patrum*, containing lives and sayings of the so-called desert fathers, which he left to Wynkyn de Worde to publish (1495), was translated quite closely from a French *Vie des Pères* (1486). The Life of St. Thaïs (IV; see below) derives ultimately from an anecdote in the *Vitas patrum*.

[29] On the complex interrelationships of *SEL*, *GiL*, and *GoL*, see Görlach, *The South English Legendary, Gilte Legende and Golden Legend*.

time.[30] But Simon Winter's prose *Life of Saint Jerome* (III[a]) is similar in its London area provenance and date (fifteenth century, second quarter), as well as in its prose style, to those composed for *GiL*. One of the manuscripts of *GiL* actually incorporates Winter's *Life* in preference to the legendary's indigenous version (which follows the *Legenda aurea* more closely than Winter and includes the episode of St. Jerome and the Lion that Winter omits).[31]

Important for its place in early Scottish literary history, as well as for its intrinsic poetic quality, is *ScL*, a large, unified collection, which was aimed at a lowland Scots audience in the late fourteenth century, but did not apparently achieve wide circulation. From *ScL* are drawn two items in this volume (I[b] and VIII). The *ScL* legends are based mainly on versions in the *Legenda aurea*.

Legendaries such as *SEL*, *ScL*, and their later prose equivalents, are narrative collections designed as private devotional reading and pious diversion for lay people and perhaps also for religious who could not easily read Latin or French. But narratives about saints are also found in compilations of a different, more mixed type. The Life of St. Thaïs edited here (IV) comes from the *Northern Homily Cycle*, a homiliary or book of sermons on the gospel lessons for various kinds of feasts days, Sundays, and even weekdays throughout the year. Linked by modern scholars with the Austin canons, the collection was designed not, apparently, as preaching material, but rather as reading material for the laity; it is a striking example of the late medieval trend by which pious layfolk, while remaining outside the cloister, were encouraged to imitate the habits of reading and liturgical observance formerly practiced only by monastics and other regular clergy and solitaries. The Thaïs legend in the *NHC* serves as an exemplum illustrating various themes in a homily expounding the meaning of a gospel reading for a Monday during Pentecost.[32] More explicitly intended for preaching is the collection known today as *Mirk's Festial*, from the Shropshire region of the West Midlands around 1400. It was intended to provide parish priests with sermons they could preach on the major moveable feasts and principal saints' days throughout the year, and is filled with illustrative anecdotes, or exempla, designed to divert as well as instruct, and often in the form of single hagiographic episodes extracted from longer lives. A somewhat later compilation, also designed for use by priests, but in which the saints' legends are regarded by modern scholars as inferior to those of Mirk, is the *Speculum Sacerdotale*.[33]

---

[30] Hamer and Russell, eds., *Supplementary Lives*.

[31] For more on *GiL* see below, Chapter III, Introduction.

[32] See the Introduction to Chapter IV for further information about the complicated textual history of *NHC*. Another legend from *NHC*, that of St. Anastasia (from a late recension of the collection), is translated into modern English by Winstead, *Chaste Passions*, pp. 44–48.

[33] Mirk, *Mirk's Festial*, ed. Erbe; *Speculum Sacerdotale*, ed. Weatherly. Several of the texts edited by Reames in *Middle English Legends of Women Saints* are from the *Festial* and *Speculum Sacerdotale*.

Finally, a substantial number of Middle English saints' legends were composed and circulated as separate works, although some were then interpolated into organized collections by individual scribes. Thus Simon Winter's *Life of Saint Jerome* (III[a]), as mentioned above, is the version of choice in one of the manuscripts of *GiL*, but Winter wrote the life originally for an individual patron, Duchess Margaret of Clarence, and it circulated in a variety of idio-syncratic manuscript contexts. Similarly, in the later fourteenth century, anonymous stanzaic lives of the fictional ascetic saint, Alexius, the "man of God," were inserted in various manuscripts of *SEL,* despite their obviously different metrical form.[34] John Lydgate's poem, *Saint Austin at Compton* (VI), on the other hand, survives only in manuscripts containing lyric and narrative poetry by Lydgate, Chaucer, and other courtly poets of the era. Lydgate, who composed several long and ambitious saints' lives in addition to shorter ones, typifies the tendency for fifteenth-century men of letters, including Osbern Bokenham and John Capgrave, to devote their poetic energies to hagiography more frequently than their more talented fourteenth-century predecessors, who largely avoided the genre.[35] A celebrated exception, however, is Chaucer's tale of St. Cecilia, preserved in *The Canterbury Tales* as The Second Nun's Tale, but composed independently of, and earlier than, the *Tales* themselves.[36] Most of the surviving individual saints' lives, however, are anonymous.[37]

The South English Legendary

General information about those Middle English compilations from which we have drawn only one or two legends, such as the *Scottish Legendary* and *Northern Homily Cycle*, is pro-vided in the introductions to individual chapters below. But since several legends are edited from one or another recension of *SEL* it seemed more appropriate and more economical to provide a brief introduction to that collection here.[38]

---

[34] See Upchurch, "The 'Goed Fyn' of Saint Alexius."

[35] See most recently Winstead, *Virgin Martyrs*, pp. 112–46, and Görlach, "Middle English Legends," pp. 464–69.

[36] Chaucer's contemporary John Gower included the legend of Pope Silvester and the Emperor Constantine in his *Confessio amantis* 2.3187–3496 (in *The English Works of John Gower*, ed. G. C. Macaulay, 1.216–24). On William Paris' life of St. Christine, see Winstead, *Virgin Martyrs*, pp. 83–85.

[37] There is no separate bibliography of the individual lives as distinct from those composed for inclusion in legendaries. They are all listed together, *seriatim*, in D'Evelyn's alphabetical bibliography, "Legends of Individual Saints," in *MWME* 2.561–635.

[38] The most recent brief introduction is in Wogan-Browne et al., eds., *Idea of the Vernacular*, pp. 195–96. See also Jankofsky, ed., *The South English Legendary*, and the various studies by Görlach cited

SEL is a large collection of Middle English versions of the lives of well-known saints of the Church at large as well as of Britain itself. As far as we know, it was the earliest attempt to provide a comprehensive legendary in Middle English. It survives in dozens of copies, none of which is precisely identical with any other, while many differ considerably not only as to which legends are included but also in some cases as to which version of a given saint's legend is selected. In other words, scribes felt free to adapt the collection to local interests and needs, not only omitting feasts of no importance to them but also adding texts for saints not represented in their master copy.

Despite this textual "instability," there is enough in common between the various extant copies for scholars to have posited the existence of an original core collection, usually designated the "Z" collection, compiled by an individual poet-translator in the Southwest Midlands of England, in the vicinity of Gloucester and Worcester. This unknown poet (sometimes linked with the author of Robert of Gloucester's *Chronicle*)[39] was working probably in the decade after 1270. He writes in rough rhyming couplets, basically iambic in rhythm but with some irregularity as to the number of unstressed syllables before the stressed one in each foot. There are usually seven strong stresses per line (the "fourteener"), with a caesura dividing the line into two parts of respectively four feet and three feet, but sometimes either part may seem "light," i.e., lack sufficient syllables. A random short passage, lines 53–55 from the Martyrdom of St. Andrew (I[a]), will illustrate the flexibility with which the lines have to be scanned for reading aloud.[40] Notice the frequent clusters of weak stresses that were evidently slurred lightly or swallowed altogether, sometimes with elision, as in line 53, where extra syllables proliferate awkwardly in the first four feet, whereas the next line (54), apart from examples of elision before a following vowel ("Andreu," he sede, "ich . . ."), is a perfectly regular iambic line. Trochaic juxtaposition of strong stresses (as in *thou have*, line 55) is also not uncommon.

```
   x  x   / x    / x /  x x x  / x ‖  x  /  x  / x  /
As the Justice sat amorwe in his sige,    to him he was ibroght.

   x   /x  x   /   x / x  /  ‖  x  /  x  /  x  /
"Andreu," he sede, "ich opie wel    that thou be bet bithoght,

   x   x    /   / x /  x /  ‖  x   /   x /   x  /
and that thou have fram folie    thi thoght iturnd to nyght
```

---

in these notes. An older introduction, with bibliography, is that of D'Evelyn, in *MWME* 2.413–18, 556–59.

[39] See, most recently, Pickering, "South English Legendary Style."

[40] In the scansion example below, x and / indicate respectively unstressed and stressed syllables. ‖ indicates the caesura between (normally) the fourth and fifth feet. I have not marked off the individual feet.

The *SEL*-poet deals with each saint in legends that vary considerably in length (some have less than a hundred lines, but the longest, Thomas of Canterbury, is over a thousand). The *SEL*-poet seems to have adapted many of his chosen legends from individual Latin sources or composite sources not yet identified, although the most prolific modern scholar of *SEL*, Manfred Görlach, has always maintained that it must have been a Latin "office breviary" containing abbreviated versions of saints' lives.[41] Görlach, however, could not identify such a breviary among those surviving from late medieval England. Complicating matters somewhat, Görlach discovered that after the poet-compiler had completed legends for the feasts occurring during the first half of the year, he must have acquired a copy of de Voragine's *Legenda aurea* and made use of the *Legenda*'s lives of many saints from later in the calendar (e.g., the legend of St. Andrew the apostle), also using it to revise some already composed.

The *SEL* "Z" collection has not survived complete or uncontaminated. Its *quondam* existence is the widely accepted hypothesis of Görlach, building on the earlier researches of another German Anglicist, Carl Horstmann, who edited what he entitled *The Early South English Legendary* (*ESEL*) from a late-thirteenth-century manuscript. Oxford, Bodleian Library, Laud Miscellany 108 is the earliest surviving *SEL* manuscript and the most important witness to "Z," although it is incomplete and "disorderly." It originally contained about seventy-five legends. Görlach was unable to identify the precise *provenance* (place of origin) of the collection, but on dialectal grounds pointed to the area in and around Gloucester, where various religious houses could have provided the kind of library the *SEL*-author needed if, as it seems, he worked from a variety of hagiographic sources.

Görlach became convinced, after painstaking collation of items in dozens of *SEL* manuscripts, that after the Z compiler had completed a set of saints' legends the collection circulated for some years before it underwent considerable expansion and revision around 1300, probably in the same region, if not at the same center, as Z. This revision stage is known as the "A" collection, represented in several manuscripts of the early fourteenth century and later, containing up to ninety legends. The A reviser not only added legends of saints not included by Z, but he also may be the one to have added readings for both fixed and movable feasts normally associated with the "Temporale," although there are signs that the Z stage included such readings as well.[42] The A reviser also added a new, more elaborate Prologue, and tinkered

---

[41] A breviary is a service book used by monks and other clerics in church services other than the Mass; such books contained not only the special prayers, psalms, chants, etc. for individual feast days, but frequently contained special "lections," or "lessons," to be read during the long night office on a given saint's feast day, abbreviated from longer *vitae* and *passiones* of such saints.

[42] The Temporale cycle includes all the feasts closely associated with Christ, most of them occurring on different dates from year to year, hence the term "moveable" feasts. Among these are Advent Sunday (the fourth Sunday before 25 December, Christmas Day) and Easter itself, along with the Lenten feast Quadragesima, Ascension Day, and Whitsunday (Pentecost), whose dates each year are determined by the shifting date of Easter. Fixed days within the Temporale include Christmas Day, Circumcision (1

with many of the texts originally in Z, adding explanatory and sometimes humorous or satirical comments, as is pointed out where possible in the notes to the texts in this volume. Two of the A manuscripts are the basis of the second and most recent modern edition of *SEL*,[43] which is the basis of the Martyrdom of St. George in this volume (II[a]), while we have used another A manuscript, Oxford, Bodleian Library, MS Ashmole 43, for some others (Martyrdom of St. Andrew, I[a]; Lives of St. Benedict and St. Scholastica, V, and St. Francis, VII). Further revisions occurred to the whole collection as it circulated more widely during the fourteenth century (including a version in the East Midland dialect, compiled around 1400),[44] but its textual evolution seems to have more or less ceased by the end of the century. The largest single *SEL* collection is in another Bodleian manuscript, Bodley 779 (early fifteenth century), containing over 130 legends. Needless to say, a great deal more work remains to be done on the textual transmission of *SEL*.

The few modern scholars to work closely with the poetry of *SEL* are in broad agreement about many of its distinctive characteristics, which include simplification of doctrinal or theological content; use of plain diction, largely devoid of learned poetic figures or elaborate descriptive terms; abbreviation of incidents and longer speeches found in the Latin sources; occasional expansion through authorial didactic explanations and interjections; "dramatization" by means of short passages of lively, often combative dialogue, often replacing third-person narrative in the Latin sources; the use of colloquial rhetorical devices to involve the audience emotionally and sympathetically, and to arouse wonder, indignation, or humor; and plentiful emphasis on native English saints and nationalist sentiments.[45] More recently, one of the editors of this volume, Anne Thompson, looks more closely than previous critics at the differences between the legends retold in *SEL* and their Latin sources, pointing out ways in which the *SEL*-poet lacks the "relentless didacticism" typical of literature aimed by clerics at the laity at this time, and fosters a relationship with his audience, and with the phenomenal, mundane world, that is unusual and unexpected in hagiographic writing.[46]

Still uncertain, however, is the intended audience itself. Modern scholars initially assumed that *SEL*, with its calendar arrangement, was designed for use by the parish clergy or friars during church services for ordinary, mixed congregations, but this view has been challenged

---

January), and Epiphany (6 January). See Hughes, *Medieval Manuscripts for Mass and Office*, pp. 6–12. On the complexities of the Temporale content of *SEL*, see most recently Liszka, "The *South English Legendaries*." Also important is the work of Pickering. See, among his many valuable studies, "The Southern Passion and the Ministry and Passion."

[43] D'Evelyn and Mill, eds., *The South English Legendary*.

[44] See Görlach, ed., *An East Midland Revision of the South English Legendary*.

[45] Jankofsky, "*Legenda Aurea* Materials" and "National characteristics"; Heffernan, "Dangerous Sympathies."

[46] See, e.g., "Shaping a Saint's Life," and *Everyday Saints*.

on the grounds that many of the saints celebrated in the collection (e.g., Mary of Egypt) were unlikely to have feast days at the parish level, that the *SEL* legends vary too greatly in length to be serviceable in a liturgical setting, and that the manuscripts themselves provide no evidence of such use. Neither of the two surviving prologues implies, much less mentions, a liturgical role for the legends, but rather both suggest a collection designed for continuous reading: "Telle ichelle bi reuwe of ham"[47] ("I will relate them one after the other") and "Þei ich of alle ne mouwe nouȝt telle : ichulle telle of some"[48] ("Though I may not relate all of them, I will relate some"). Moreover, the often earthy, lively style and boisterous content seem closer to literary entertainment and satire than liturgical commemoration. Annie Samson has proposed, therefore, that the likely purpose of the collection was to provide Christian reading matter for the lower nobility and landed gentry, but her arguments have yet to be pursued.[49] We hope that the *SEL* texts assembled in this volume will help stimulate further research on this and other aspects of this important medieval legendary, as well as on Middle English saints' legends in general.

Abbreviations

AN	Anglo-Norman
AS	Johannes Bolland et al., eds., *Acta Sanctorum*
BHL	Bollandists, *Bibliotheca Hagiographica Latina*
BL	British Library
CUL	Cambridge University Library
CT	*The Canterbury Tales*
DM	*The South English Legendary*, ed. D'Evelyn and Mill
EETS	Early English Text Society
ESEL	*The Early South English Legendary*, ed. Horstmann
GiL	*The Gilte Legende*
HBS	Henry Bradshaw Society
IMEV	Brown and Robbins, eds., *The Index of Middle English Verse*
LA	Jacobus de Voragine, *Legenda aurea*
ME	Middle English
MED	*Middle English Dictionary*
MWME	Severs and Hartung, eds., *A Manual of the Writings in Middle English*
NHC	*The Northern Homily Cycle*, ed. Nevanlinna
OE	Old English

---

[47] Prologue, line 66, in DM 1:1–3.

[48] Prologue to the Life of St. Fabian, line 5, in *ESEL*.

[49] Samson, "The South English Legendary," pp. 185–95.

OED	*The Oxford English Dictionary*
OF	Old French
ON	Old Norse
PL	Migne, ed., *Patrologia Latina*
ScL	*The Scottish Legendary*, ed. Metcalfe
SEL	*The South English Legendary*
TC	*Troilus and Criseyde*

I(a)

The Martyrdom of St. Andrew in the South English Legendary *(c. 1270–80)*

Introduction

The Cult and Legend of St. Andrew (feast day November 22)

Andrew in the New Testament gospels and book of Acts is, like most of the other disciples, overshadowed by the figures of Peter, Paul, John, and James. Despite his small role in the canonical books of the New Testament, however, he emerges in the fourth century, along with the other apostles, with a widespread cult and a growing legendary tradition of his own. According to this tradition, he preached the gospel in Asia Minor and Greece before being martyred there, at Patras, an Achaian city, which by the mid-fourth century claimed to possess his bodily remains or "relics." From Patras the relics were removed, "translated," to the new imperial capital of Constantinople by Emperor Constantius in 361, where they remained in the great Church of the Apostles. But Andrew's fame, his liturgical feast (November 30), and portions of his relics, had spread to other parts of the Roman world at least by the sixth century, as is amply witnessed by Gregory of Tours in southern Gaul (see below) and by the activities of Pope Gregory I in Rome. The latter, after his stay as papal legate in Constantinople (579–86) received from the Byzantine emperor the gift of the apostle's arm (along with St. Luke's head). Reputedly, Gregory gave Andrew's feast a prominent place in the Roman liturgy (which he helped rewrite) and hence throughout the regions of the Latin West influenced by Roman usage. Gregory's own new monastery in Rome was dedicated to St. Andrew, and the monks whom he recruited from there to carry the gospel to the heathen English (597) also brought with them the cult of Andrew. While the missionaries' first new monastic foundation at Canterbury was dedicated to Sts. Peter and Paul (consecrated after Augustine's death in 604), one of the first major churches built outside Canterbury was that of St. Andrew at Rochester (604).[1] Also dedicated to Andrew was another important early Anglo-Saxon church, built in the North at Hexham (672–78) by St. Wilfred.[2] Not long afterwards Andrew was also on his way to becoming the national saint of Scotland, some of his relics supposedly having been carried to the then-Pictish kingdom of Fife by an Achaian

---

[1] Bede, *Bede's Ecclesiastical History of the English People*, pp. 115, 143, 149.

[2] Eddius Stephanus, *The Life of Bishop Wilfrid*, pp. 44–47. On these and early Anglo-Saxon church dedications to Andrew, see Levison, *England and the Continent in the Eighth Century*, p. 262.

wanderer, St. Rule, in the fifth century (this tradition was probably invented in the eighth or ninth century, or the twelfth).[3] Meanwhile, another Englishman, St. Boniface, the missionary to the Saxons, was consecrated bishop by Pope Gregory II in Rome on St. Andrew's day, November 30, 722.[4] Continued early English interest in Andrew is reflected in the survival of a long Old English poem, *Andreas*, and an anonymous prose homily (in the *Blickling Homilies*), recounting a bizarre legend in which Andrew journeys in a ship piloted by Jesus (in disguise) to the land of the cannibal Myrmidonians to rescue the apostle Matthew, who has been blinded and imprisoned (that's only the beginning).[5] Also among the Anglo-Saxons, the homilist Ælfric produced a prose homily in Andrew's honor drawing on the apostle's *passio*, or story of his martyrdom in Patras, in Achaian Greece.[6] Ælfric's account draws on the hagiographic tradition of the "Acts of Andrew," with which we are concerned here.

The *Acta Andreae*[7] (Acts of Andrew) typifies in various ways the early Christian hagiographical genre of apocryphal acts of the apostles. Works of this type sought to provide diverting and inspiring accounts of the apostles' lives and deaths as a sort of massive supplement to the canonical New Testament book attributed to the third evangelist, Luke, in the second half of the first century and known today simply as Acts (Greek *Praxeis*). The original Greek Acts of Andrew, on which the surviving texts are based, appears to have been composed in the second or third century, like the other principal apocryphal acts, by an unknown author, possibly in Syria or Egypt and probably in a community espousing an "encratic" form of Christianity, that is, one in which sexual continence and a more or less dualistic attitude towards the body and the material creation (associated with the devil) were of special concern.[8] A common motif of the apocryphal acts (and in turn of early martyrdom legends) is the conversion of the wife or daughter of a pagan ruler, e.g., in the Acts of Thomas, where both the Indian noblewoman Migdomia and the queen herself are converted by Thomas' preaching and thereafter shun their husbands' beds.[9]

---

[3] The town of St. Andrews is home to Scotland's oldest university (1411) and one of the world's oldest and most famous golf courses. For a lively survey of the development of the legends about Andrew's cult in Scotland, see Lamont, *The Life of Saint Andrew*, pp. 67–81.

[4] Levison, *England and the Continent*, p. 72.

[5] For the early Christian texts and contexts, see MacDonald, *The Acts of Andrew and the Acts of Andrew and Matthias*; also MacDonald, *Christianizing Homer*. For translations of the Old English versions and their nearest analogues, see Boenig, trans., *The Acts of Andrew in the Country of the Cannibals*.

[6] For the OE text and a modern translation, see Ælfric, *The Homilies of the Anglo-Saxon Church* 1.586–99. The standard edition is now that of Clemoes: *Ælfric's Catholic Homilies*, pp. 507–19.

[7] Although plural in form, the word "Acts" is treated here as a single literary work and therefore as a singular noun.

[8] The most recent edition is that of Prieur, ed., *Acta Andreae*.

[9] For a translation of the Greek Acts of Thomas, see Elliott, *The Apocryphal New Testament*, pp. 479–

Such themes are evident in vivid detail in the extant portions of the Greek Acts of Andrew; for example, in the exciting life of the Christian convert Maxilla (alias Maximilla), wife of the Roman proconsul Aegeas. Her Isolde-like efforts to shun the marriage chamber and spend more time with Andrew and other spiritual friends include bribing a wanton slave girl to be her substitute in Aegeas' bed. In this original Greek version, Andrew's martyrdom is finally ordered by the frustrated and enraged husband, who blames the apostle, with good reason, for the destruction of his marriage.[10] This narrative tradition was, however, substantially complicated and transformed by later censorship and revisions made in reaction, apparently, to the pronouncements of clerics such as Eusebius of Caesarea (in his *History of the Church* 3.25),[11] branding the Greek Acts as heretical. As a result the original collection of Acts, detailing Andrew's missionary journey and adventures from Syria through various Greek and Macedonian cities (Constantinople/Byzantium, Philippi, Thessalonika) to Patras in Achaia, has not survived except in a sixth-century Latin summary (*BHL* 430), thought to be by Gregory of Tours (died 594), and this circulated only among the learned higher clergy.[12] Portions of the original Acts, especially the martyrdom chapter, are extant in rare manuscript copies in Armenian, Coptic, and Greek, but otherwise the apostle's legend was rewritten and purged of its more sensational and "unorthodox" elements by a succession of anonymous Greek and Latin hagiographers. The best known version in the West is the so-called *Letter of the Presbyters and Deacons of Achaea* (henceforth *Passio Andreae, BHL* 428) which poses as an eyewitness account.[13] This expurgated version of the apostle's martyrdom almost completely eliminates the

---

505. For a view of the social context of such works, see Davies, *The Revolt of the Widows*. Medieval English versions of the legend of Thomas of India (who is invoked several times in Chaucer's *Canterbury Tales*, e.g., in The Summoner's Tale, III[D]1980) include that of Ælfric in *Ælfric's Lives of the Saints*, ed. Skeat, 2.398–425, with facing English translation (see especially lines 263–365); and that in *SEL*, DM 2.571–86 (see especially lines 292–366).

[10] For a summary of modern scholarship and translations of the chief extant fragments, see Elliott, *The Apocryphal New Testament*, pp. 231–83.

[11] Eusebius, *The History of the Church from Christ to Constantine*, trans. Williamson, p. 89.

[12] Gregory's summary (Elliott, *The Apocryphal New Testament*, pp. 272–83) was in turn revised and incorporated in the collection of apocryphal acts known today as the *Historiae Apostolicae* of Pseudo-Abdias, which is accessible only in early printed editions. Gregory also devoted a substantial chapter (chap. 30) of his *De Gloria Martyrum* to Andrew. See Gregory of Tours, *Glory of the Martyrs*, pp. 48–51.

[13] The standard edition of the Latin version is that of Bonnet in *Acta apostolorum apocrypha*, ed. Lipsius and Bonnet, 2.1–37 (with Greek parallel text); English trans., "Acts and Martyrdom of the Holy Apostle Andrew," in Roberts and Donaldson, 8.511–16 (electronic versions at http://www.newadvent.org/fathers/ and also at http:// www.ccel.org/fathers2/).

role of Maxilla, along with the sexual intrigue[14] and the encratic material, providing instead a stylized didactic debate between Andrew and the governor, Aegeas, in which the pagan judge voices scepticism about certain aspects of the Christian faith, giving the saint his cue to rehearse some basic tenets of Christian teaching while his audience is involved in the suspenseful anticipation of the violent martyrdom itself. The revised legend preserves little from the original tradition except the apostle's heroic determination to follow his master on the cross and his refusal to be rescued by his irate followers. Notable in all the versions, early and late, of Andrew's death is his elaborate greeting to the cross on which he is to die, a speech that exists in numerous variant forms and that probably influenced other old and famous tributes to the Cross including Fortunatus' *Pange lingua* and the Old English *Dream of the Rood*.[15]

Andrew in the *Legenda aurea (LA)* and the *South English Legendary (SEL)*

Latin versions of Andrew's passion similar to the *Passio Andreae* lie behind the account of his martyrdom included in the second chapter of Jacobus (James) de Voragine's *LA*. Jacobus, however, drew on a wide range of sources, including not only the *Passio* but also the gospels (for Christ's calling of Andrew), Gregory of Tours' summary of the original Acts (probably in the redaction by Pseudo-Abdias, from which Jacobus selects a few of Andrew's adventures prior to his arrival in Patras), and a medieval exemplum or didactic tale in which Andrew, now a saint in heaven, answers three riddling questions in order to rescue a Christian bishop from being seduced by a devil-woman.

The anonymous Middle English version of Andrew's passion printed here was composed in the late thirteenth century as part of the *SEL* (see above, General Introduction). The Martyrdom of St. Andrew is a highly abbreviated, swift-paced version of the apostle's martyrdom, drawing many of its features of plot and phrasing from the version in the *LA,* and other features apparently from the *Passio Andreae* itself, while omitting much that is in both these sources. The *SEL*-poet also seems to have added occasional touches of his own. For example, like the *LA* version, he omits the account given in the older *Passio* of the crowds who come to rescue Andrew from prison, the night before his crucifixion, and who are rebuked by the saint and exhorted to emulate his desire to suffer in patience like Jesus before him. *LA* also omits much of the preliminary dialogue between Aegeas and Andrew the next morning, when the judge in the older *Passio* adopts at first a kindlier tone, hoping that Andrew has changed his mind during

---

[14] Maxilla is mentioned only at the end of the story as the person who arranges for the burial of Andrew's body.

[15] On the Cross in English literary tradition, see Bennett, *Poetry of the Passion*. See also Bestul, *Texts of the Passion*.

the night, and twice offering him his friendship and a happy life if he will give up his foolish beliefs and lead back his Achaian converts to the worship of the gods, who are poised to wreak vengeance otherwise. This finally provokes an angry response from Andrew, who condemns the proconsul as a "Son of death, and chaff made ready for eternal burnings"; *LA* preserves only this part of the lengthy dialogue, where Andrew defiantly bids the judge do his worst, insisting that he (Andrew) will be more pleasing to God the more he suffers.[16] In the equivalent passage of *SEL* (lines 53–64), on the other hand, the poet preserves enough of the old form of the dialogue to suggest the judge's initial conciliatory offers, but omits most of the ensuing dialogue, so that the proconsul's friendly overture is juxtaposed dramatically with the angry response from Andrew. This produces an effect quite different from that in either of the Latin sources, since here in *SEL* Andrew's anger is apparently provoked by the judge's wheedling offer of earthly comforts, rather than by the threat of torture or the vengeance of the gods. The *SEL*-poet throws this extreme viewpoint into high relief by omitting the other ideas that accompany it in the Latin sources. It is possible that he is simply following an intermediate Latin (or French?) version in which the work of conflating different Latin sources had already been done, but this seems unlikely. The poet seems to have browsed among the available versions to find the most dramatic moments, particularly those permitting him to sharpen the encounters between persecutor and martyr with wry personal touches and colloquial idioms.

On the other hand, the *SEL*-poet seems uninterested in much of the Latin versions' doctrinal and didactic materials, which are typical of hagiographic narratives of this sort. For example, in both the *Passio* and *LA* Andrew is allowed to explain to Aegeas in some detail how Jesus foresaw and predicted His Crucifixion, after which the apostle expounds the serial paradoxes of the theology of the Cross. He also explains more than once how important it is for the violence of persecution to be met with patient, non-violent suffering, not with resistance or evasion. Virtually all of this didactic material is omitted from the the Martyrdom of St. Andrew, except for the preliminary give and take between Andrew and Aegeas[17] that precedes the longer didactic passages. The poem concentrates almost exclusively on narrative and dramatic elements, while allowing some space for Andrew's quasi-mystical lyricism (see especially lines 74–80, on the Cross, and 91–92, on Jesus).

A notable difference between the *LA*'s legend of Andrew and the earlier Acts tradition is the former's addition, as a lengthy coda to the martyrdom, of a popular late medieval miracle tale, the story of the Three Questions. The *SEL*-poet also adapts this part of the Andrew legend from *LA*, but for the sake of dialectal and poetic variety, we have omitted *SEL*'s version of the miracle tale, opting instead for the somewhat more complete and less popularized translation

---

[16] "Acts and Martyrdom," trans. Roberts and Donaldson, 8.513 (this passage also preserved in the Hyde Breviary, ed. Tolhurst, *Monastic Breviary of Hyde Abbey*, 4.393); compare *LA*, trans. Ryan, 1.17.

[17] E.g., lines 29–40.

in the late-fourteenth-century *Scottish Legendary* (*ScL*). For the *ScL* text and a separate introduction, see St. Andrew and the Three Questions, I(b), below.

Text

The text of this edition of the *SEL* Martyrdom of St. Andrew is that of Oxford, Bodleian Library MS Ashmole 43 (A), of the first half of the fourteenth century, probably no later than c. 1330. Nothing is yet known of the manuscript's early ownership, but on the basis of the scribe's dialectal usages it has been localized in Gloucestershire in the English Southwest Midlands, where the first version of *SEL* is presumed to have originated. The manuscript preserves many, though not all, individual *SEL* texts more completely than most others, and frequently offers sensible and reliable readings. Although Ashmole is somewhat later than London, British Library MS Harley 2277 (H) and Cambridge, Corpus Christi College MS 145 (C), the base texts of the EETS edition of *SEL* by Charlotte D'Evelyn and Anna J. Mill (DM), and although it has other drawbacks, it is certainly among the best of the manuscripts of *SEL* as a witness to the revised text as it existed in the early fourteenth century, that is, after the early revision labeled "A" by Manfred Görlach.[18] For these reasons, we have selected Ashmole as base text in all but two of our *SEL* selections (see Life of St. George, II, below). A list of the manuscript's contents is in Carl Horstmann's *ESEL*, pp. xiv–xvii, and in DM 3.33–34).

Here in the Martyrdom of St. Andrew, as in other selections, apart from the spelling and punctuation adjustments that are standard in METS volumes, we aim to present the wording of the manuscript faithfully, largely without emendation except where Ashmole is clearly in error. Emendations are identified in the textual notes. Selected variants from London, British Library MS Harley 2277, fols. 174v–176r, 176v; Oxford, Bodleian Library MS Laud Misc. 463 (*SC* 1596), fols. 124v–126r; and the DM edition of the former are occasionally cited in the textual notes to suggest something of the textual variety and instability of this version of Andrew's legend.

Language

Sounds and spelling. The Ashmole scribe (like the C scribe: see below, the Introduction to the Martyrdom of St. George, II[a]) frequently renders the third-person singular pronoun as *is*, dropping the initial *h-*; we have normalized all instances of *is*, without comment, to *his*. The A scribe also occasionally elides syllables in common verbs: *Inele* (line 46) for *Ic ne wole* ("I will

---

[18] Görlach, *The Textual Tradition of the South English Legendary*, pp. 74–75.

not"); *spext* (line 48) for *spekest*; *saistou* (line 27) for *sayest thou*; *wost* (line 27) for *wotest* (i.e., "you know," second-person singular). Among distinctive vowels, the reflex of OE *y/i* is usually, though not invariably, *u*: e.g., *sulf* (line 2, "self"), *wule* (line 9, "while"), *put* (line 22, "pit"). Other spellings disconcerting for modern readers include the frequent use of *v/u* where we expect *f*, as in *vor* and *vorsake* (lines 3, 6) instead of *for* and *forsake*; *deve* (line 26) for *defe* ("deaf"); and *vaste* (lines 67, 83) for *faste*. The modern *sh* sound is usually represented *sch* (e.g., *fischeres*, line 3; *scholde*, line 37), whereas words normally beginning with *wh-* have simply *w-* (e.g., *wule*, line 9; *wat*, line 23, "what"). In accordance with METS editorial policy, the ME letter *ȝ* (yogh), which often indicates the palatal consonant that many phonetics experts represent as [j], but that is usually represented *y* in modern English (e.g., *your*, *year*), has been spelled *g* in our edition in those instances where the word's modern equivalent has *g* (e.g., *give* and *get* and their compounds). Readers should be aware, however, that, especially before front vowels (*e, i/y*), and often before back vowels also, the sound in ME was that of Modern English *y*. Compare Chaucer's comment about the Monk, "He yaf nat of that text a pulled hen" (General Prologue, *CT* I[A]177). Instances in the Martyrdom of Andrew are rare (e.g., *agen* line 35), but common in other texts in this volume.

Pronouns. The most distinctive pronouns are those of the third-person plural: *hi* ("they"), *hem* ("them"), *hor* ("their"). We normalize the second-person singular pronoun *the* to *thee*. The plural forms are *ȝe* and *ȝou*, which we render as *ye* and *you*.

Verbs. The suffix *-eth* is used in the present tense, third-person, both singular and plural, and in the imperative plural: *cometh* (line 5), *hath* (line 23), *beth* (line 26), *worth* (lines 60, 64). The unstressed prefix *y-* (from OE *ge-*) is common not only in the past participle but also as a verb-stem prefix: *igo* (line 23, "gone"), *iturnd* (line 55, "turned"), *isay* (line 4, "saw," third person singular), *isé* (line 36, "saw," first-person singular). Negatives are frequently double or triple, for emphasis, as in Chaucer and modern non-Standard English: e.g., *I ne prechede therof noght* (line 43, "I didn't preach about it at all").

Vocabulary. The *SEL*-poet's vocabulary is native English, with very few recent loanwords from French. As one would expect from a Southwestern work, there is little or no Scandinavian influence. The poet uses numerous words of Old English origin that are now obsolete: e.g., *seththe* (line 10, OE *syþþan*, "after"), *lere* (line 10, OE *læran*, "teach"), *nym* and *nome* (lines 19 and 29, OE *niman*, "to take"), *rode* (line 40, OE *rod*, "cross"), *quath* (line 23, OE *cweþan*, "to say"), *stude* (line 38, OE *stede*, "place"), *herie* (line 49, OE *herian*, "praise"), *worth* (line 60, OE *weorþan*, "become"), *mo* (line 64, OE *ma*, "more"; OE *mara*, our "more," means "greater/bigger"), *swithe* (line 65, OE *swiþe*, "great/greatly"), *yer* (line 91, OE *geara*, "formerly/of yore"). Words such as these were still current in varying forms a century later among cosmopolitan writers such as Chaucer and Gower, unlike other native words found in

SEL: e.g., *yeme* (line 19, OE *gieme*, "care/attention"); *luther* (line 57, OE *lyþer*, "wicked"); *bern* (line 57, OE *bearn*, "young man/child"; compare modern Scots *bairn*); *thole* (line 59, OE *þolian*, "endure/suffer"); *pulten* (line 72, from a putative OE *pyltan*, "thrust"); *afoung* (line 77, OE *onfon*, "receive"; past ppl., *onfangen*); *stei* (line 94, OE *stigan*, "to climb").

French loanwords include: *siwede* (line 7, AN *suer/siwer*, "sue"); *justice* (line 14); *doutede* (line 43); *prechede* (line 43); *joie* (line 44); *false* (line 24); *poynt* (line 38); *vertu* (line 40); *sige* (line 53, "seat"); *folie* (line 55); *torment* (line 58); *pyne* (line 61); *scourgi* (line 66); *croiz* (line 83, "cross");[19] *honur* (line 101); *manere* (line 108).

Possibly of Scandinavian origin is *pasken* (line 8; compare mod. Swedish *paska*, "dabble," as in water).

Indexed in

IMEV 2848.

Manuscripts

London, British Library MS Harley 2277, fols. 174v–176r, 176v.

Oxford, Bodleian Library MS Ashmole 43 (*SC* 6924), fols. 199r–200v.

Oxford, Bodleian Library MS Laud Misc. 463 (*SC* 1596), fols. 124v–126r.

Previous editions

Furnivall. *Early English Poems and Lives of Saints*. Pp. 98–101.

The South English Legendary. Ed. D'Evelyn and Mill. 2.543–46.

---

[19] This form of the word, from OF *croiz/crois*, was more common in Southern usage, whereas *cross* (from ON *kross* from Old Irish *cros*) was more common in the North, supplanting the Southern form by the end of the ME period. See the entry in the *OED*.

I(a)

The Martyrdom of St. Andrew
in the South English Legendary (c. 1270–80),
from Oxford, Bodleian Library MS Ashmole 43, fols. 199r–200v

Seynt Andreu the apostel   was Seint Petres brother.
Our Lord Sulf to Cristendom   him broughte, and non other.[1]
Vor fischeres hi were bothe;   and as hi fischede adai   *For; they; one day*
Bi the se, our Lord com   and hor fischinge isay.   *sea; their; saw*
5   "Cometh," He sede, "after me   and ich you wole make   *I will make you*
Manfischeres," and this other   hor nettes gonne vorsake,   *these others; forsook*
And siwede Him with this word   and ne chose noght amys.   *followed*
Hem was so betere then to pasken   bi the se water, iwis.
Wule our Lord an erthe was   myd Him bothe were[2]
10   And seththe hi wende aboute wide,   Cristendom to lere.   *afterwards; went; teach*
In the lond of Patras   Seint Andreu seththe com;
He turnde ther wel faste   that folc to Cristendom.   *converted*
Chirchen he rerede al aboute   and teighte men therto.   *built; taught (i.e., brought)*
Egeas wyf the Justice   he makede cristene also,[3]
15   Thervore the Justice was wroth   and wende to Patras,
To the cité in gret wraththe,   as Seint Andreu was.   *where*
Cristene men that he ther fond   sone he let hem take,   *at once; had them arrested*
To make hem with his torment   Cristendom vorsake.
Seint Andreu sone to him com: "Sire," he sede, "nym yeme,   *take care*
20   Thou that ert so gret Justice,   seli men to deme.   *wretched; [how you] judge*
The heie Justice of Hevene   thou haddest neode to knowe,
That into the put of Helle   thee schal deme wel lowe."   *pit*

---

[1] *Our Lord Himself, and no other, converted him to the Christian faith*

[2] Lines 7–9: *And followed Him on account of His words, and they did not choose amiss. / They were better off doing this (i.e., following Jesus) than doodling about by the sea, for sure. / While our Lord was on earth, both [of them] were with Him*

[3] *The wife of Egeas the proconsul was also made a Christian by Andrew*

29

          "Wat, artou Andreu," quath the Justise,   "that moni dai hath igo[1]

          And idrawe men to thi false God?   Thou neschalt nevereft mo."[2]

25   "Ich drawe men," quath Seint Andreu,   "to the God that soth is,   *true*

          Ac wrecches and false youre beth   and deve and dombe, iwis."   *are your [gods]; deaf*

          "Wi saistou?" quath the Justise,   "thou wost wel myd alle   *knowest; all along*

          That thou therof loude liest,   hou mighte it so falle.

          Vor the God that thou of tellest   the Giwes wile nome

30   And slowe Him, as He worthé was,   mid pur right of dome."[3]

          "Nai, sire," quath Seint Andreu,   "right was hit noght:

          Thoru His wille, ous to bugge,   He was to dethe ibroght."   *Through; buy (redeem)*

          "Hou mighte hit be," quath the Justise,   "that His wille was therto?

          Vor the Giwes Him with strengthe nome   and Him slowe so."   *by force*

35   "Ich wot to sothe," quath Seint Andreu,   "agen His wille it nas.

          Vor ich was mid Him thulke tyme   and isé hou it was.   *[at] that very time; saw*

          For er wel longe He tolde ous fore   hou it scholde be,   *long before; in advance*

          Tyme and stude and everich poynt,   as we mighte seththe isé.[4]

          Gif thou woldest that sothe ihure,   and yif thou understode,   *hear*

40   Gret vertu ich wole thee telle   of the holi Rode."   *Cross*

          "Ich wole herkny," quath this other,   "ac bote thou do after me,[5]

          In the rode as thi Lord deide   ich wole sette thee."   *On; where*

          "Gif ich doutede," quath this other,   "I ne prechede therof noght,[6]

          Ac theron is al myn hope,   my joie, and al my thoght."

45   "This thou might telle," quath the Justice,   "men that ileveth thee,   *can; believe*

          And vor Inele thee ileve noght   other thing thou shalt telle me.   *because I will not*

          Bote thou bileve on oure godes,   mighti of alle thinge,   *things*

          In the rode that thou of spext   to dethe men schal thee bringe."   *speakest of*

          "Almighti God," quath this other,   "ich herie night and dai.   *praise*

50   Ich bileve on Him and ever wole,   wile ich speke may."   *while*

          The Justise was tho wroth inough.   Seint Andreu he let caste   *then; had [him] thrown*

---

[1] *who has gone around for a long time*

[2] *You shall [do so] never again*

[3] Lines 28–30: *in every respect (lit., however it should befall). / For the God you tell of, the Jews one time seized (Him) / And slew Him, as He deserved (lit., as He was worthy), with a perfectly just sentence*

[4] *Time and place and every detail, as we could afterwards see*

[5] *"I will hearken," said this other, "but unless you do as I say["]*

[6] *"If I were afraid," said this other, "I would not preach about it at all["]*

	In strong prison, and he lai ther the wule it ilaste.	*while it (i.e., night?) lasted*
	As the Justice sat amorwe in his sige, to him he was ibroght.	*next day; throne*
	"Andreu," he sede, "ich opie wel that thou be bet bithoght,[1]	
55	And that thou have fram folie thi thoght iturnd to nyght,	*last night*
	To lyvie with ous in joye gret and leve thin unright."	*leave; give up your wrongdoing*
	"Thou luther bern," quath Seint Andreu, "thou hontest aboute noght.[2]	
	The more torment thou me dost the gladdere is mi thoght.	
	Vor the more turmentz that ich thole her for mi Lord, er ich deie,	*suffer; before*
60	The more worth mi joye with Him in the blisse of Hevene heie.	*shall be*
	Ich doute more of thee then of me, vor mi pyne nele ileste	
	Bote o dai other tweie her, other threo ate meste.[3]	
	Ac the turment that thou schalt have, warto thou schalt wende,	*where; are going*
	In tuenti thousend yer ne mo ne worth ibroght to ende."	*or more; will not be*
65	Tho was the Justice swithe wroth he het is men anon	*ordered; immediately*
	Seint Andreu scourgi so, that him oke ech bon[4]	
	And seththe bynde him honde and fot to the rode vaste	*fast (tightly)*
	With stronge cordes, vor is lif scholde the lengore ilaste	*so that; longer*
	And he the more in pyne be and the more scede of his blode.	
70	The tormentors wel inough his heste understode:	*order*
	Anon to the bon hi bete him verst with stronge scourges and brode.	*first*
	Into the erthe hi pulten faste the tuei enden of the rode.	*drove; two ends*
	Tho Seint Andreu isey the rode adoun he sat akné:	*When; on his knees*
	"Hail beo thou swete rode," he sede, "suetest of alle tre,	*Hail to thee; trees*
75	That thou of my Loverdes lymes ihalwed moste be	
	And of gymmes precious.[5] Wel glad ich thee isé	*gladly I see thee*
	And wel glad ich come to thee, wel glad afoung thou me,	*receive*
	Vor evere seththe mi Loverdes deth iwilned ich have thee.	*since; desired*
	Nym me nou al fram this men, to mi Lord thou most me sende.	*Take; these; must*
80	For al myn hope and my wille is thoru thee to Him wende."	*to go to Him through you*
	Tho he strupte of himsulf his clothes ate bigynnyngge,	*stripped off*

---

[1] *"Andrew," he said, "I very much hope that you have changed your mind["]*

[2] *"You wicked fellow," said Saint Andrew, "you hunt in vain["]*

[3] *I am more afraid for you than me, for my pain won't last / But (i.e., more than) a day or two here, or three at the most*

[4] *[To] scourge Saint Andrew so, that each of his bones would ache*

[5] Lines 75–76: *Because you were permitted to be sanctified with my Lord's limbs / And with precious gems* (see explanatory note)

And bitok the tormentors   that scholde him to dethe bringe.   *handed [his clothes] to*

Vaste bothe vet and honde   to the croiz hi bounde,[1]

The honden beie above the heved,   the fet toward the grounde.   *both; head*

85   That folc com thicke aboute him,   he gan to prechi faste,   *steadily*

Twei dawes and twei nyght,   the wile his lif ilaste.   *days*

That folc thretnede the Justise   and thicke aboute him come

And wolde him have to-drawe,   anon bote he him adoun nome.[2]

The Justice him wolde nyme adoun,   Seint Andreu him vorbed.   *take; forbade*

90   "Inele noght," he sede, "come adoun   er than ich be ded.   *I do not want; before*

Vor ich isé mi suete Lord,   and yer wile ich isei,   *a while ago I saw [Him]*

That abit vorte ich to Him come.   He is her wel ney."   *abides until*

Wen me wolde him nyme adoun,   hem thoghte he wex anhey,[3]

No mon mighte him areche   vor upard he stei.   *reach; upward he ascended*

95   Hor armes wen hi upard reighte   bicome as stif as tre.   *their*

So gret light ther com him aboute   that no man mighte him isé.

Hi hurde him and ne seye him noght.   That light laste iwis   *They heard; lasted*

Vorte the holi soule wende   therwith to Hevene blis.   *Until*

Tho the soule was forth iwend   and the holi bodi levede there,   *When; departed; left*

100   Maximille the Justice wif   and other that ther were

With gret honur hi it neme adoun   and to burynge bere,   *they took it down; bore [it]*

Yut nolde the Justice ileve noght   that he gan him lere.[4]

Therfore amidde the wei,   as he hamward wende,   *in the middle of the road*

He fel ded byvore the men   and his soule to helle kende.   *took its way*

105   Ac Seint Andreu was seththe   hollich ilad iwis   *But; taken in a holy manner*

To the lond of Constantinople   ther as it yut is.   *where it (i.e., Andrew's body) still is*

Swithe glad that lond is   that he evere ther com.

In thisse manere Seint Andreu   tholede martirdom.

[The *SEL* Miracle of the Three Questions, lines 109–236, is omitted; see below, *Scottish Legendary* version.]

237   Nou bidde we Seint Andreu   that he ous so wisse   *guide us in such a way*

And bidde vor ous, that we come   to Hevene blisse.   *pray*

---

[1] *They bound fast both [his] feet and hands to the cross*

[2] *And they wanted to tear him (the judge, Aegeas) apart unless he took him (Andrew) down at once*

[3] *When [the] men wished to take him down, it seemed to them he grew high up (lit., waxed on high)*

[4] *Yet the justice would not believe anything that he (Andrew) had taught him*

Explanatory Notes to the Martyrdom of St. Andrew in the South English Legendary *(c. 1270–80)*

Abbreviations: see Textual Notes.

5   *cometh.* Imperative plural of *come(n)*.

1–7   In the gospels there are several conflicting versions of the calling of Andrew. This simple version, implying that Jesus called Andrew and Peter once and they followed him immediately, is based on Matthew 4:18–19 (also Mark 1:16–17; compare the same incident in Luke 5:10–11, where Andrew is not mentioned). The single calling is also reflected in some surviving late medieval English liturgies, e.g., in one from thirteenth-century Winchester, *The Monastic Breviary of Hyde Abbey, Winchester*, ed. Tolhurst, 4.392–395v, where the gospel for the day is the passage from Matthew. The *SEL*-poet's rather distinctive phrasing at line 7, *And siwede Him with this word*, may echo that of one of the sung responses and versicles (*Mox ut vocem . . . audivit . . . Ad unius iussionis vocem . . .*) and the beginning of the gospel homily commonly preached at the night office for Andrew's feast day: *Audistis fratres karissimi quia ad unius iussionis uocem petrus et andreas relictis retibus secuti sunt redemptorem*, ("You have heard, dearest brothers, that *with a single sentence of command* [lit., the word of one order] Peter and Andrew dropped their nets and *followed* the Redeemer" — *Monastic Breviary*, ed. Tolhurst, 4.394v). In *LA* (trans. Ryan, 1.13), on the other hand, it is explained, in typically scholastic fashion, that the gospels contain three different callings of Andrew, each involving a different kind of vocation: those in Matthew and Luke (which *LA* "edits" to include Andrew) and that in John 1:35–42, in which Andrew is said to have been originally a disciple of John the Baptist.

11   *Patras* is not a *lond* but a city in the portion of central Greece formerly known as Achaia, west of Athens on the southern shore of the Gulf of Corinth. The city of Corinth was the Roman provincial capital, where Paul preached and founded an important Christian community. But although the apocryphal Acts of Andrew claim that he performed miracles and converted people there, Paul makes no mention of Andrew in his two epistles to the Corinthians. Nor is there is any reliable historical evidence that Andrew ever preached in Patras or died there, as was widely asserted

throughout the Middle Ages (according to a more conservative early Christian tradition, he is said to have taken Scythia as his missionary province — Eusebius,
Ecclesiastical History 3.1; trans. Williamson, p. 65).

11–14   Although there is some evidence later (see explanatory note to lines 93–94) that the
poet was familiar with a somewhat fuller tradition, here at the beginning of the story
the ME poet seems to be following the highly abridged *LA* account of the miracles.
Since Ryan's translation (1.16) does not follow the Latin closely here, we provide our
own:

> So blessed Andrew settled in Achaia, and filled the whole region with churches, and con-
> verted (*conuertit*) many people to the Christian faith. Also (*quoque*) he taught (*docuit*) the
> Christian faith to the wife of Ægeas the proconsul and gave her second birth in the sacred font
> of baptism (trans. from *LA*, ed. Maggioni, 1.28).

In the *Passio Andreae* (*BHL* 428) at this point there is no mention of Andrew's church-
building or of the proconsul's wife (later identified as Maximilla). *SEL* also echoes
some of the wording of *LA*: compare *conuertit* with *turnde* (line 12), *quoque* with *also*
(line 14), and *docuit* with *teighte* (line 13).

18   *torment.* The principal medieval Latin versions say that the proconsul ordered or began
to compel the Achaians to revert to paganism (compare *LA*: "As soon as the proconsul
heard this [i.e., that his wife was a convert] he came into the town of Patras and
commanded the Christians to sacrifice to the idols. Then Andrew came to meet him"
— trans. Ryan, 1.16). Only the *SEL*-poet specifies the use of torture: his tendency to
intensify emotion and violence in his legends is commonly noted by modern critics.

19–22   Andrew in *SEL* is more belligerent and wittier than his Latin counterparts. Compare
the equivalent passage in *LA*: "You have earned the right to judge men on earth. Now
what you ought to do is recognize your judge who is in heaven, worship him, and turn
completely away from false gods" (trans. Ryan, 1.16). In general the dialogue that follows in *SEL* is not only racier and more colloquial in tone, but much abridged in
comparison with the Latin versions, in which one can see clearly the didactic intent to
justify Jesus' passive acceptance of crucifixion. The proconsul, in other words, is the
Latin authors' token skeptic.

54–56   *SEL* here seems to follow not *LA*, but the older Latin legend ("Acts and Martyrdom,"
p. 513) or one of the breviary redactions in having Ægeas attempt to sway Andrew with
an offer of friendship and preferment as the alternative to torture and suffering. In *LA*
(trans. Ryan, 1.17), by contrast, the proconsul begins the morning audience immediately in a brusque and threatening manner. See above, Introduction.

57–64   Andrew's speech here is a conflation of two separate speeches in *Passio Andreae*. In the poem lines 61–64 (for which there is no equivalent in *LA*) correspond closely to the Latin: "For I am afflicted about thy destruction, and I am not disturbed about my own suffering. For my suffering takes up a space of one day or two at the most; but thy torment for endless ages [lit., for thousands of years] shall never come to a close" ("Acts and Martyrdom," trans. Roberts and Donaldson, 8.513).

67–71   Compare *LA*: "Aegeus commanded twenty-one men to seize him, flog him, and bind him hand and foot to a cross, so as to make his agony last longer" (trans. Ryan, 1.17). The poet's account depends closely on *LA* here, including the brief rationale for binding rather than nailing (i.e., to delay death and prolong suffering), but not for the somewhat confusing detail about *more . . . blode* (line 69).

72   The phrase *tuei enden* here, along with line 84 ("both his hands above his head"), clearly envisages not the familiar *t*-shaped cross (*crux immissa*) associated with the crucifixion of Jesus, but the *x*-shaped variety (*crux decussata*) found in late medieval depictions of Andrew's martyrdom: e.g., in Jean Fouquet's *Heures d'Etienne Chevalier* (reproduced in Mâle, *Les saints compagnons du Christ*, p. 131). The Scottish flag is a white *x*-shaped cross on a blue background. The only hint of this in *Passio Andreae* is the statement that Andrew was not nailed to the cross but bound hand and foot to it "as if he were stretched out on the rack" (*quasi in eculeo tenderetur* — ed. Lipsius and Bonnet, 2.23–24), implying that his hands are above his head rather than stretched out to either side. Depictions of the "decussate" cross appear as early as the tenth century.

74–80   The *SEL*-poet's version of these lyrical lines is difficult to punctuate with certainty and may be corrupted, although it is obviously based on the following passage from *LA*: "Hail, o cross, you who were consecrated [*dedicata*] by the body of Christ and adorned with his limbs as with pearls. . . . I come to you, therefore, free from care and rejoicing, so that you may joyfully receive me, the disciple of him who hung from you; for always I was your lover and desired to embrace you. O good cross, you who have been endowed with honor and beauty from the Lord's limbs! Long desired, earnestly loved, constantly sought after, and now made ready for my longing heart, take me from among men and return me to my master, so that he may accept me through you, for through you he redeemed me" (ed. Maggioni, 1.31; our trans.).

93–94   The idea that Andrew's body "grew," i.e., was raised out of the reach of the soldiers, seems to be original with the *SEL*-poet. The Latin legends merely tell how the soldiers' arms grew stiff and immobile when they tried to take him off the cross.

106   Andrew's body was said to have been translated from Patras to Constantinople during the reign of the emperor Constantius, c. 361. The *SEL*-poet does not mention the supposed translation of part of the body to St. Andrews in Scotland (see Introduction).

109   See below, I(b), for the Three Questions story from *ScL*.

I(a)

Textual Notes to the Martyrdom of St. Andrew in the South English Legendary *(c. 1270–80)*

Abbreviations: **A** = Bodleian Library MS Ashmole 43 (*SC* 6924), fols. 199r–200v [base text]; **D** = Bodleian Library MS Laud Misc. 463 (*SC* 1596), fols. 124v–126r; **H** = British Library MS Harley 2277, fols. 174v–176r, 176v.

1   Wherever possible, the caesuras in the text follow those marked in A.

6   *Manfischeres.* So A. D: *mannesfisshers.*

23   *"Wat, artou Andreu," quath the Justise.* A: *Wat artou quath the Iustise Andreu.* We adopt H's word order here as the less awkward.

31   *sire.* So A. H: *certes.*

32   *Thoru His wille.* So A. H: *thurf godes wille.* D: *with is gode wille.*

33   *hit.* So H. A: *he.*

39   *understode.* So A. H: *riȝt vnderstode.*

40   *holi.* So A. H: *swete holi.*

45   *ileveth.* So A. H: *luueth.*

50   *ever.* So A. H: *herie.*

71   *brode.* So A. H: *gode.* A's *brode* is more vivid, but H's *gode* makes for a better rhyme: ME open *o,* as in *brod* (from OE *brād*), would not normally rhyme with ME close *o*, as in *rode* (from OE *rōd*).

77   *wel glad ich.* So H. A: *wel ich.*

88   *have to-drawe, anon bote he.* So A. H: *alto drawe anon; bote he* (as printed in DM 2.545). Both versions make good sense, but A's meter, with the caesura immediately after *to-drawe,* is abnormal, yielding three beats in the first half line and four in the second, instead of the regular four and three, as in H (see above, pp. 15–16).

93   *wex.* So A. H: *was.*

99   In order to make sense, *levede* must be construed as the participle dependent, like *iwend,* on *was.* Other manuscripts (e.g., H and D) read *bileuede,* remained.

100–01 These lines are in reverse order in A and H, but in H they are marked to follow the present order, as printed by DM. Other manuscripts agree with this order against A and H.

104   *kende.* So A. H: *sende.*

105   *hollich.* So A. H: *heȝe.*

I(b)

St. Andrew and the Three Questions
in the Scottish Legendary *(c. 1400)*

Introduction

St. Andrew and the Three Questions

As we have indicated in the first part of this chapter, the theme of human sexuality prominent in the original Greek Acts of Andrew is much less evident in the Western redactions, including the *LA* account of the saint's life and martyrdom. Likewise in *SEL*, all that is left of the elaborate story of Andrew's spiritual friendship with Maxilla is her brief appearance near the end of the story to bury Andrew's body (the Martyrdom of St. Andrew, lines 100–01). The sexual-encratic theme of the ancient Acts, however, is revisited in the late medieval Three Questions story, which apparently became attached to Andrew in the thirteenth century and is appended to the martyrdom legend proper in *LA*. Widely represented in medieval Latin collections of stories and exempla of the fourteenth century and later, and in other Middle English versions of Andrew's legend,[1] this story tells how Andrew, disguised as a pilgrim, saves a bishop of hitherto holy life from committing fornication with a devil-woman. The latter has won the bishop's confidence by posing as a young virgin who aspires to the religious life and is a fugitive from an unwanted marriage. During dinner at the bishop's palace, at the moment when the prelate is about to ask the beautiful seductress to have sex with him, an unnamed pilgrim (later revealed to have been St. Andrew himself) knocks at the gate, asking to be admitted to the feast; the temptress tries to ward off the apostle by asking him three riddling theological questions, but he answers them successfully and in the process unmasks her as a demon. The origins of the story are obscure (see below), and it is also attributed, in somewhat different

---

[1] The miracle is no. 214 in Frederic C. Tubach, *Index exemplorum: A Handbook of Medieval Religious Tales*, p. 23, and is listed in Stith Thompson, *Motif-Index of Folk-Literature*, as no. H682. The *LA* version is retold in some detail in Middle English in the Andrew chapters of the *Gilte Legende, NHC*, Caxton's *Golden Legend*, and more briefly in *SEL* and Mirk's *Festial*. The classic modern work on the exemplum genre is that of Welter, *L'exemplum*. For a brief but useful survey in English, see Fleming, *An Introduction to the Franciscan Literature of the Middle Ages*, pp. 142–56.

form, to another apostle, Bartholomew,[2] but it is certainly appropriate to St. Andrew in its emphasis on human sexuality. Whether or not the unknown composer of the tale was aware of the ancient Acts of Andrew, he contrived a virtual reprise of some of the Acts' key motifs, while inverting and undermining others. In the Acts, for example, Maximilla's rebellion against her marital-sexual role is genuine, and she receives help from the itinerant Andrew in pursuing her new celibate vocation, despite the brutal opposition of her worldly, lustful husband; by contrast, in the more typically misogynistic late medieval tale, the chastity that the pilgrim Andrew intervenes to protect is the institutional celibacy of the male cleric, while the female protagonist's rejection of marriage in favor of a spiritual, virginal vocation is completely bogus: fleshly lust is personified here as a diabolical female.

One can see why this story proved popular with late medieval clerical writers and compilers of story collections, given its sympathetic depiction of the devout but fallible male cleric, its thematic focus on the intimacies of the confessional, its central scene of rising sexual tension between the celibate bishop and his newly adopted virgin "daughter," leading into the dramatic intellectual standoff between Andrew and the devil, with the ingeniously integrated questions. The devil-woman in her young aristocratic beauty embodies the lure of earthly life, sexual pleasure, and power, while posing as an ascetic yearning for the corporeal purity which characterizes the official vocation of all medieval clerics, here represented by the bishop. This shared zeal for virginity establishes an immediate, if dubious, rapport between the two. The temptation to lust is all the more subtle and dangerous for being disguised as a militant virginity rebelling against the authority of the fleshly father, yet blatantly and seductively yielding itself to the protection and authority of a new "father," who is the earthly servant and representative of her heavenly spouse. The lust at the heart of the tale is thus not only marked as diabolic but also colored by the dark suggestion of incest that is never wholly absent from the medieval language of divine love.[3] The same involved interplay of opposing bodily and spiritual themes is also a feature of the three questions themselves, each of which is posed in terms of diametric oppositions (great and little, highest and lowest, heaven and earth) and the mysterious interactions of divine spirit and earthly flesh.

---

[2] See *LA*, ch. CCXXIII, trans. Ryan, 2.113–14. For an adaptation of the Bartholomew story, see the Middle English prose *Speculum Sacerdotale*, ed. Weatherly, pp. 193–94, where the pilgrim is the devilish imposter.

[3] The Scottish poet of the version printed below makes such ideas even more evident than in the *LA* version (see lines 905–82 and notes). For a delightful lyric exploitation of the theme of divine incest, see the fifteenth-century lyric, "I sing of a maiden," widely anthologized, e.g., *The Norton Anthology of English Literature*, ed. M. H. Abrams et al., 1.353–54.

The Three Questions and Hagiographic Tradition

As far as we can tell, there is no detailed study of the tale and its origins, and we offer here only a few tentative suggestions as a stimulus to further research. As to its hagiographic genre, the story is, of course, a posthumous *miraculum*, or self-contained miracle tale, not an intrinsic part of the saint's "life" or "acts." Collections of miracle stories relating the posthumous miracles of individual saints, particularly miracles associated with specific shrines and relics, began to be written early in the history of hagiography and became a regular part of a saint's dossier.[4] While many posthumous miracles are relatively simple stories of healings and cures performed at or near the saint's cult site, narrated in a few lines of formulaic prose, others are more complex and consciously artful narratives. An important category of miracle story of this more elaborate type is the so-called Marian miracle, a sub-genre that developed during the early Middle Ages but emerged in its developed form in bulky collections in the early twelfth century, notably in England.[5] The best-known example in the English vernacular tradition is Chaucer's problematic contribution, The Prioress' Tale, in Fragment VII of *The Canterbury Tales*. Typically, a Marian miracle depicts the Queen of Heaven mercifully intervening to rescue one of her devotees in a moment of crisis brought on by human frailty.[6] Frequently, though not always, the protagonist's attachment to the Virgin is expressed in some regular form of ritual devotion or prayer, no matter how perfunctory, doubtless reflecting the strength of medieval belief in the powerful effects of verbal formulas and incantations. Mary's intervention

---

[4] A notable early example is that embedded by Augustine of Hippo in his *Concerning the City of God against the Pagans* 22.8, trans. Bettenson, pp. 1033–47. On medieval miracles and miracle collections, see Ward, *Miracles and the Medieval Mind*; Van Dam, *Saints and Their Miracles*; Sigal, *L'homme et le miracle*; Ashley and Sheingorn, *Writing Faith*.

[5] Southern, "The English Origins of the Miracles of the Virgin." Useful for overviews of the genre and bibliographical references are the following: Gripkey, *The Blessed Virgin Mary as Mediatrix*; Boyd, ed. *The Middle English Miracles of the Virgin*, pp. 3–10; Ward, *Miracles and the Medieval Mind*, pp. 132–65 (especially pp. 155–65, although Ward's focus is less on the literary traditions of the Marian miracles than on the productions of specific Marian shrines); and Whiteford, ed., *The Myracles of Oure Lady*, pp. 8–23, and 96–133 (a catalogue of Middle English miracles of the Virgin). Among the foundational studies of Marian miracle literature are those of Mussafia, "Studien zu dem mittelalterlichen Marienlegenden"; and Poncelet, "Miraculorum B. V. Mariae."

[6] The most notorious of these tells how an abbess became pregnant, but avoided discovery and scandal because she was impersonated by the Virgin Mary (to whom she had been devoted), who fulfilled all her duties while she absented herself from the convent during the last months of pregnancy and the requisite period after delivery. A Middle English prose version is in the mid-fifteenth-century translation of the fourteenth-century alphabetical collection of Latin tales, *Alphabetum Narrationum*: see Arnoldus of Liège, *An Alphabet of Tales*, ed. Banks, 1.11–12.

41

also tends to involve some element of ingenuity or impersonation in addition to her supernatural power, occasionally in contests with the devil.[7] The Andrew miracle has obvious affinities with this class of story in that the bishop, introduced as one who routinely utters a brief formulaic prayer to invoke Andrew's blessing on his daily tasks (see the text below, lines 873–74), proves all too human when the diabolic impersonator attempts to seduce him; the saint arrives, likewise as an impersonator, to rescue the bishop when he is on the point of committing an irrevocable and damnable sin; and the resolution of the problem turns on a duel of wits with the devil and the ingenious solution of metaphysical riddles.[8]

The Three Questions tale as told in *LA* is indexed by Stith Thompson as a folktale and classified among tales involving riddles in the general category of "Tests of Cleverness."[9] The classification assumes that the tale involves answering riddles to escape from the devil. In another standard manual of folk narrative types, that of Antti Aarne, we find several analogous tales in the sub-group, "Man Promised to the Devil" in the larger category of "Religious Tales."[10] The point of reference here is Grimm's fairy tale no. 125, concerning the three soldiers who escape from their Faust-like bargain with the devil by answering his three riddles with the help of a wise old woman.[11]

---

[7] For some typical examples, see the Marian miracles appended by Jacobus de Voragine to his account of the Assumption of the Virgin in *LA* (ch. CXXXI, trans. Ryan, 2.154–58), which includes the very early Marian miracle (a precursor of the Faust story) concerning the cleric Theophilus, in which the Virgin regains possession of a charter recording Theophilus' surrender of his soul to the devil. In another collection, Mary intervenes to prevent an anchoress from abandoning her life of solitude owing to the promptings of a devil disguised as a pious woman (*The Early English Versions of the Gesta Romanorum*, ed. Herrtage, pp. 411–12).

[8] For a story of the devil going to confession, see Robert Mannyng of Brunne's fourteenth-century devotional compendium, *Handlyng Synne*, lines 12507–12626, ed. Sullens, pp. 311–14. For an eastern Christian example, preserved in Coptic, of the devil disguised as a woman, see Amélineau, ed. and trans., *Contes et romans de l'Égypte chrétienne*, pp. 26–42: here the intended victim is a pious widow, Euphemia, who is devoted not only to the memory of her husband but also to St. Michael, whose icon she keeps in a shrine in her house; the devil visits her first disguised as a nun, who attempts, unsuccessfully, to embarrass Euphemia over various points of religious observance. Later, Michael the archangel materializes to rescue Euphemia when the frustrated devil attacks her physically. A distantly related Latin version, concerning a nun Euphemia, is by the early thirteenth-century Cistercian storyteller, Caesarius of Heisterbach, *Dialogus miraculorum*, 5.44, trans. Scott and Bland, 1.377–79. Caesarius' Book 5 (1.313–390) is devoted solely to tales involving devils.

[9] The tale is numbered H543.1 in Thompson, *Motif-Index of Folk-Literature* 3.424–425. See also Tubach, *Index Exemplorum*, nos. 4025–28.

[10] Aarne, *The Types of the Folktale*, pp. 275–76.

[11] See Grimm, "The Devil and His Grandmother," pp. 563–66.

The tale of Andrew, the bishop, and the devil-woman, however, unites a variety of narrative types with the motif of the devil's three questions. For example, it is a seduction story[12] and, as such, part of a large class of religious tales, including many Marian miracles like those noted above, in which someone's virtue and religious devotion arouse the Devil's resentment and prompt him to assume a disguise in order to try to lead the holy person astray, sometimes successfully. One of the earliest examples of this type in the hagiographic tradition concerns an anonymous desert hermit of Egypt, and is told in the life of John of Lycopolis in the *History of the Monks in Egypt*, written in Greek at the end of the fourth century and translated shortly afterwards into Latin by Rufinus of Aquileia.[13] The Andrew miracle also has affinities with medieval secular literature in that the saint's arrival as a stranger at the palace gate, where he demands admission to the feast and provokes debate and discussion within, shows parallels with Arthurian romance, where a stranger knight or damsel often brings a test or challenge or somehow initiates knightly adventure or quest.[14]

One of the most striking parallels to the entire story is found in a famous Hellenistic Greek work of the first century, *The Life of Apollonius of Tyana*, by Philostratus. Here conflict between lust and spirituality takes the form of a confrontation between sensual beauty and reason, in which Apollonius unmasks a flesh-eating Lamia. Philostratus tells how a young man is seduced by a rich and beautiful stranger who offers him both herself and her wealth. His tutor, however, the philosopher Apollonius, comes uninvited to the wedding and under his piercing, rationalist gaze the luxurious bride is metamorphosed into her true self, a revolting serpent, while the palatial house dissolves into nothing. The anecdote was revived in the Romantic era, most notably by Goethe and Keats.[15]

---

[12] It is true that Grimm's "Devil and His Grandmother" is a seduction story of sorts, in that the three soldiers' pact with the devil brings them unlimited wealth for seven years, but they have no choice in the matter (either they agree to the compact or he kills them) and the story allows them to go on enjoying their wealth after the Devil has been discomfited. Any notion of temptation or conflict of values has been lost in the oral secular tradition.

[13] Russell, trans., *The Lives of the Desert Fathers*, pp. 56–57. This anecdote was adapted by the authors of several later saints' lives, including Avitus the hermit, Paternianus, and Romanus of Rouen. See the references in Loomis, *White Magic*, p. 187n140.

[14] Most familiar to students of Middle English is the arrival of the axe-wielding Green Knight in *Sir Gawain and the Green Knight*. A closer parallel to the Three Questions story is that of the Middle Welsh romance, *Culwch and Olwen*, in which the young hero's request for admission to the feast is resisted first by the porter, then by Cei.

[15] For further references on the Lamia of Greek myth, see *The Oxford Classical Dictionary*, ed. Hornblower and Spawforth, p. 812. John Keats' *Lamia*, the story of which he ostensibly read first in Richard Burton's *Anatomy of Melancholy*, is widely available in standard and selected editions of his works, but Goethe's *Die Braut von Korinth* seems to be quite rare, as is the English translation by a contemporary

The closest analogue we have found to the seduction story among hagiographic narratives is in the life of Macarius the Roman, depicted in the murals of the Campo Santo, Pisa, and preserved in the late medieval editions of the *Vitae patrum* ("Lives of the Fathers").[16] The story, which is not in the fifth-/sixth-century *Vitae patrum* collections, was known in the Greek church by the tenth century, and must have been current in the West at least by the thirteenth century. It tells how Macarius, a desert hermit, is tempted by the devil in the guise of the beautiful woman whom Macarius was to have married years earlier but from whom he fled to the wilderness on his wedding day. She comes to his desert retreat (in the Pisan murals she is in pilgrim's garb, with bird's feet protruding below), claiming that she also fled from the world on their nuptial day, desiring like him to lead a life of celibate asceticism. Unlike the bishop in the Andrew tale, however, Macarius has no guardian angel to protect him: the wandering pilgrim and the diabolic seductress, opposing figures in the Andrew miracle, are here merged into one figure. Likewise lacking is the intellectual debate motif, represented by the Three Questions in the Andrew story. But the number three is a factor in the Macarius legend in that the visitor is revealed to the hermit over a three-day period: first he finds a woman's veil outside his cave, next a pair of woman's shoes; having taken both items into his cave without crossing himself, he finds the woman on the third day. After a supper of acorns and conversation, the devil-woman caresses his body, he falls asleep, and during his slumbers they have sex (*in somno me peccatum perpetrasse cognovi*, "I knew that I had committed the sin in my sleep").[17] The morning after, "she" has gone, and he is filled with remorse over his lost virginity. His pet lions help him dig a hole in his cave in which he buries himself up to the neck. Here again the triadic motif is evident, since Macarius exists in this state, living off the grass that grows near his face, for three years, at the end of which the lions dig him up and he feels himself totally healthy and purified. He is rewarded with an ecstatic vision of Christ and His angels in his cave.

Further research is needed to describe better the origins and transmission of the Three Questions episode, as preserved in Jacobus de Voragine's *LA* and other contemporary narrative compendia of the thirteenth century.[18] Jacobus' most recent editor, Giovanni Maggioni, has

---

of Keats, John Auster, in his *Poems, with Some Translations from the German*, pp. 179–238.

[16] *PL* 73.415–26 (*BHL* 5104), especially 422–26, chs. XVIII–XXII. Much of the life, which resembles that of Brendan the Navigator, is taken up with the account of how the supposed authors of the life wandered eastwards in search of the lost Paradise, until they found Macarius and heard his story. For a summary and discussion, with reproductions of the Pisan murals, see Elliott, *Roads to Paradise*, pp. 63–64, 96–102, 108–16.

[17] *PL* 73.424.

[18] For example, see the interesting sixth-century analogue in Gregory the Great's *Dialogues* 3.7, in which the devil tempts Bishop Andrew of Funda to lust secretly after a nun of his household. A Jew, traveling from Campania to Rome, eavesdrops by chance on a company of devils, learns from them of the

identified as Jacobus' immediate source Martin of Troppau (1230–78), a Dominican from Bohemia, active in Rome as papal chaplain (1261–78) and author of a chronicle and a collection of exempla, which is unprinted and survives in a manuscript now in Paris.[19] Whether Martin actually composed the miracle tale in its present form for inclusion in his collection of exempla, or merely adapted it from an existing source, is unclear. Also unclear is whether the tale was attributed to Andrew first, or to Bartholomew, since according to Maggioni the very similar Bartholomew version, included in *LA* chapter CXIX, is taken from a collection of exempla for preachers compiled by another Dominican writer, Étienne de Bourbon (also known as Stephen of Bellavilla, c. 1180/90–1261).[20] In this version, which is briefer and less detailed than the Andrew story, it is the pilgrim Bartholomew who asks the three questions (which differ slightly from those in the Andrew version) and the devil-woman and her intended victim (a learned clerk) who each offer answers. The Bartholomew version is also narrated by Thomas de Cantimpré (c. 1201–71), another Dominican of the same era as Étienne and Jacobus.[21] The similarities and differences between the Andrew and Bartholomew versions of the story imply the existence of a common source that was being passed around and freely adapted in Dominican circles in the middle of the thirteenth century. It is possible that the story was originally told of Bartholomew, since in early Christian apocryphal literature he is depicted specifically as one who asks questions (some of which are similar in scope to those in the miracle tale), of Jesus, the Virgin Mary, and the devil.[22]

---

bishop's temptation, confronts him with his secret, and prompts him to repent. This may be the ultimate origin of the Andrew motif in our story.

[19] *LA*, ed. Maggioni, 1.33n162–222.

[20] *LA*, ed. Maggioni, 2.836–37 (trans. Ryan, 2.113–14). See Étienne's *Tractatus de diversis materiis predicabilibus* I.iv, lines 135–66, ed. Berlioz and Eichenlaub, in *Stephani de Borbone Tractatus de diversis materiis predicabilibus*, pp. 70–71 (1.4, lines 135–66) and note 407.

[21] *Bonum universale de apibus* II, ch. 53, 5: see Vet, *Het Biënboec van Thomas van Cantimpré en Zijn Exempelen*, pp. 162–65.

[22] See the apocryphal *Questions of Bartholomew* (sometimes referred to as *The Gospel of Bartholomew*), in Elliott, *Apocryphal New Testament*, pp. 655–68. Among the questions Bartholomew asks are: "What is the sacrifice which is offered in Paradise?" "How many souls depart out of the world daily?" "What sin is more grievous than all sins?" "What is the sin against the Holy Ghost?" Another early literary context for difficult, riddling questions is that of the so-called *Joca monachorum* (Jests of the Monks) and the closely related OE verse and prose dialogues between Solomon and Saturn. See *The Prose Solomon, and Saturn and Adrian and Ritheus*, ed. Cross and Hill; and Shippey, *Poems of Wisdom and Learning in Old English*, pp. 21–28, 86–103.

St. Andrew

The *Scottish Legendary*

ScL is a late-fourteenth-century collection of hagiographies written in Lowland Scots English, comprising legends of the twelve apostles, plus the evangelists Luke and Mark, to which are added thirty-five legends of other saints, for the most part selected and arranged according to some as yet uncertain design.[23] While no specifically English saints are honored (George is included, however), there are two native Scots saints: Ninian and Machor (numbered XXVIII and XL in Metcalfe's edition). Andrew, of course, was, as we have seen, particularly important in Scotland and not surprisingly receives extended treatment in *ScL*.[24] The poet in his preamble disregards his Latin source to describe Andrew as the meekest man who ever lived and accords him a measure of equality with Peter:

> & to Petir full brothire was,
> as be kynd of manis flesche,
> & in passione evine fere;   *in suffering equal companions*
> for one the cors bath ded thai were.[25]   *on the cross both dead*

The work as a whole survives in one fifteenth-century manuscript (Cambridge, University Library MS Gg.2.6), of uncertain provenance and remarkable only for the fact that it is written in single columns on leaves about 280 mm long and barely 100 mm wide. Little can be said about the identity of the author except that by the time he began work on his collection he was, as he explains in his *Prologue* and elsewhere, avowedly too old and frail to continue his pastoral work as a "mynistere of haly kirke" but is anxious, like Chaucer's Second Nun, to shun idleness, which "giffis novrysingis / to vicis"[26] and therefore he has devoted himself to translating, first the Lives of Christ and the Virgin Mary, and her miracles, and now the legends of the apostles, as devotional reading matter for the higher ranking lay folk and clergy, "þo lordis . . . þat steris landis & haly kirke."[27] Metcalfe, however, the editor of the standard edition, posits multiple authorship for the collection as a whole, since he cannot believe that the frail author of the apostles' lives had the energy or longevity to accomplish the rest.

---

[23] See Charlotte D'Evelyn's introduction to "The Scottish Legendary" in *MWME* 2.419–22, 557–58 (bibliography).

[24] At 1155 lines, the legend of Andrew is the third longest in *ScL*, after those of Mary of Egypt (1490) and Paul (1176).

[25] *ScL De Sancto Andrea*, lines 5–8.

[26] See, e.g., *ScL* Prologue, lines 33–36 and 2–3; compare *The Canterbury Tales* VIII(G)1–2.

[27] *ScL* Prologue, lines 13–14.

Early attempts to attribute the work to the Scottish court-poet John Barbour (c. 1316–95, archdeacon of Aberdeen and royal clerk), are long discredited on grounds of style and language, although the work seems to belong to his time period and is one of the earliest monuments of Middle Scots poetry. The rhyming tetrameter (4-beat) couplets are managed for the most part with fluency, apart from some clumsy inversions of natural word order; the diction, while less dour and prosaic than that of Barbour, is inevitably constrained by its subject matter, lacking the richer variety of their contemporary Chaucer's early poetry or Gower's mature narrative verse. And although the poet sometimes adapts words directly from his Latin source (see below), his language is quite plain in comparison with the "aureate" extravagances and rhetorical exuberance of the fifteenth-century Scottish and English Chaucerians such as Dunbar and Lydgate.[28] On the other hand, while *ScL*'s language is certainly Lowland Scots and requires detailed glossing, even for readers familiar with Middle English, there is little in *ScL* of the Scots colloquialisms and extreme dialectal obscurity of the so-called "low-life verse" cultivated by some later Scots writers.[29]

The Episode of the Three Questions in *ScL*

As Metcalfe points out, *ScL* follows its main source, *LA*, closely, sometimes word for word, although rarely with the effect of stylistic artificiality that slavish translation often achieves.[30] In the absence of detailed studies of his work, it may be instructive to examine the poet's handling of the beginning of the legend, and to compare *ScL* briefly with the equivalent portion of the *SEL* version.

The opening passage displays the poet's habitual combination of fidelity and freedom in the treatment of his source, adopting the concise language and syntax of the Latin where these result in idiomatic vernacular phrasing, but at the same time adding numerous minor touches that clarify the story and help achieve a thoroughly vernacular poetic voice. *LA*'s account begins as follows:

> Episcopus quidam, religiosam agens uitam beatum Andream inter ceteros et supra ceteros sanctos in ueneratione habebat, ita quod in cunctis suis operibus hunc semper titulum preponebat: "ad honorem Dei et beati Andree." (ed. Maggioni, 1.33)

The standard modern English translation manages to be even more concise than the Latin:

---

[28] For a moderate example, see VI, below, John Lydgate's *Saint Austin at Compton*, and the references in the Introduction, note 33. The most famous "aureate" Scottish poem is William Dunbar's "Ane Ballat of Our Lady"; see *The Poems of William Dunbar*, ed. Mackenzie, pp. 160–62.

[29] See Aitken, "The Language of Older Scots Poetry," pp. 18–49, especially 23, 39–43.

[30] *ScL*, ed. Metcalfe, 1.xix.

A certain truly devout bishop venerated Saint Andrew above all other saints and began whatever he was about to do with the invocation, "To the honor of God and Saint Andrew." (trans. Ryan, 1.18)[31]

ScL expands the opening sentence into a leisurely eleven verses, omitting nothing of the Latin's substance, and reusing some of its syntax and language, but also adding various details that subtly alter the cumulative effect and meaning of the passage. For example, "Religeouse lyf liffand ay" (line 864) renders the phrase *religiosam [agens] vitam* word for word; *ScL* also retains the verbal construction of *beatam Andream . . . in veneratione habebat* ("had/held Andrew in veneration"), but translates *veneratio* itself by two different French loanwords: "Sancte Andrew in affecione / Had ay, and in devocione" (lines 865–66), which conveys the quality of the bishop's attachment to the saint in more warmly human terms than the Latin source. Similarly he improves on *inter caeteros [et super ceteros] sanctos* by omitting the redundant *inter caeteros* and adding an intensifying temporal phrase, "Oure all hawlouys that evir ware" (line 867), along with the important reservation, "Outane Goddis modir dere" (line 868), i.e., the Virgin Mary, who in late medieval devotion to the saints occupied the highest place of all.[32] More than a simple pious reflex linking the bishop sympathetically with the great mass of the Christian faithful, this may also serve as a reminder of the hagiographic narrative tradition of the Marian miracles, closely paralleled (as we have suggested above) in the present tale. Finally, the poet offers a more detailed version of the bishop's habit of invoking his patron saint, expanding the Latin's rather vague *cunctis suis operibus* ("in all his works"), into the more specific "Quhen he suld eythir do or say / Or spedful or helplyk thinge" (lines 870–71). Further examples of the poet's translation technique are given in the notes on the text below, but it will be evident from this small sample how the act of verse translation is also, for the anonymous Scots poet, an ongoing process of interpretation and subtle nuancing.

Quite different is the approach of the earlier *SEL*-poet, whose general tendency is to abbreviate the narrative. While *ScL*'s leisurely opening passage occupies twelve verses, the Southern poet conveys the essence of the same passage in only two:

A bischop while an holi man; among holi halewen alle
Mest he louede seint Andreu; so his hurte gan falle.[33]

---

[31] More literally: "A certain bishop, having a religious life, had blessed Andrew, among the rest of the saints, in veneration, so much so that before each of his tasks he would pronounce this dedication: 'to the honor of God and blessed Andrew.'"

[32] See, e.g., Duffy, *The Stripping of the Altars*, pp. 256–65.

[33] "Once upon a time a bishop, a holy man, loved Saint Andrew most of all holy saints, as his heart prompted him"; DM 2.546, St Andrew, lines 111–12.

The rest of the story is told in a mere 129 lines, well under half the Scottish version's total of 290 lines. At the same time as he abbreviates the story, however, the *SEL*-poet is much more inclined than the Scot to add personal commentary, apparently to influence the reader's responses. The most persistent example of this is his habit of branding the devil-woman with a derogatory epithet virtually every time he mentions her: e.g., "false maide" (line 131); "liþere þing" (lines 157, 161, "wicked thing"); "þe screwe" (line 179, "shrew"); "þe devel" (line 194); "þis luþer best" (line 209, "wicked beast"). At one point (lines 143–46) he explodes in vituperation and bitter sarcasm:

Nou liþer þrift vpon hire clannisse; & hire maidenhod also	*ill luck*
Wel felliche heo hire biþoʒte; to make þe gode man misdo	*intended; treacherously*
Whanne wolde hit hire bicome; to beo so god & clene	*befit, suit*
Nou sorewe & sor vpe hire; forte ich hire bymene.[34]	

By contrast, the *ScL*-poet refers to the devil-woman almost always as the "lady" except once, when the word *fend* ("fiend") is used, immediately after the bishop has begun in earnest to lust after the devil-woman, and even here the *fend* seems to refer to the devil as someone external to the woman, manipulating her appearance and behavior (see lines 993–96). The *SEL*-poet's more intrusive style is also evident in his comment on the pilgrim who knocks at the gate. Whereas in *LA* and *ScL* the identity of the clever visitor is withheld from the reader, as from the participants, until after the unmasking of the devil-woman, in *SEL*[35] the poet informs the reader immediately before the pilgrim arrives (lines 163–64):

Seint Andreu, þat he louede; nolde him noʒht vorʒite
Fram heuene he aliʒt adoun; fram sunne him to wite.[36]

In comparing *ScL* to *SEL* (and *NHC*) Gordon Hall Gerould concludes that the poet of the former "had his mind fixed . . . less on the public for which he was writing and more on the legends themselves than the makers of the English collections."[37] Perhaps it would be more accurate to

---

[34] "Now [may] sorrow and pain [fall] upon her before I pity her!"

[35] Similarly in the version printed by Horstmann, *Altenglische Legenden, Neue Folge*, pp. 8–10, from one of the manuscripts of *NHC*, the pilgrim's identity is revealed in advance: "Bot saint Andrew, his faithful frend, / Saw he was ouer-sett with þe fend. / He putted him in a palmer state, / And come vnto þe bisschop ʒate" (lines 413–16).

[36] "Saint Andrew, whom he loved, from heaven he alighted down, to protect him from sin."

[37] Gerould, *Saints' Legends*, pp. 182–83. *ScL* is not discussed in any of the most recent books that deal with Middle English saints' lives. See next note.

say that the *ScL* author is more subtle and restrained than his Southern predecessors in adapting his Latin sources for his intended public. Theodor Wolpers suggests that the narrative style of *ScL*, avoiding the "emotionalism" and dramatic extremes of the more folksy *SEL*, is better suited for a calmly contemplative response, allowing the upper-class, better educated readers for whom the author purports to be writing to meditate on the life of the saint as on a "merroure" of virtuous living, and as an aid to prayer and devotion.[38] Another major difference between the Scottish and English collections, of course, is that the latter apparently had a small circulation and left no evidence of a revised version. Metcalfe considers the core collection of apostles' legends to have been written "with headlong haste" and "want of careful revision."[39]

Language

While we may refer to the language of *ScL* as Scots or Middle Scots as well as "Northern," its author calls it simply "ynglis"[40] and certainly, with due allowance for the typically Northern differences of pronunciation and morphology, his term is accurate. Most modern readers should find our two selections from *ScL* easier going than, say, *Sir Gawain and the Green Knight*, which was written around the same time, but several days' journey southwards.

Vowels. Typical of Northern Middle English in general is the retention of OE long *a* in words like *tha* (line 895, ME *tho*, "those"); *allane* (line 914, "alone"); *nathynge* (line 918, "no"); *hale* (line 923, "whole"); *maste* (line 1032, "most"),[41] all of which are found with *o* in the Midland and Southern dialects. Long *a* may already have begun to be pronounced [e:] rather than [o:], as suggested by such spellings as *fare* (line 884) instead of regular ME *fair*, and *ware* rhyming with *dere* (lines 867–68); or the rhyming of *sa* (for "so") and *fay* (OE *fa*, "foe") in lines 875–76: *sa* is sometimes spelt *say* elsewhere in *ScL*.[42] Just as the long *a* is being raised to [e:], so OE long *o* was being raised to [u:], e.g., *gud* (line 904) for ME *god* ("good"), and spellings elsewhere in *ScL* such as *fwt* for *foot* and *fowd* for *food*.

---

[38] Wolpers, *Die englische Heiligenlegende des Mittelalters*, pp. 275–79, 287–88.

[39] *ScL*, ed. Metcalfe, 1.xxvi.

[40] See the Life of Mary the Egyptian (*Egipciane*), line 1471; *ScL*, ed. Metcalfe, 1.338.

[41] In the N. Midland selection from *SEL* (below, II[b]), the occasional use of the Northern long *a* is scribal, not authorial.

[42] Similarly, the alternating spellings of *gaynand* (line 942) and *ganand* (line 1022), and the spelling *sad* (meaning "said," line 891 and *passim*) from OE *sægde*, which appears elsewhere in ME as a diphthong, *seide/seyde/sayde*. Also the spelling *rednes* (line 1099) for *radnes* (from ON *hrǣddr*).

Consonants. The most unusual Northern variation is the cluster *quh-* instead of *wh-* or *hw-*, as in *umquhile* (line 863, "once") and *quhen* (line 870, "when"). Note that *ch* is used instead of *ȝ* or *gh* before *-t* (*nocht/thocht*, lines 899–900, for *nought* and *thought*); *k* is common instead of medial and final *-ch*, as in *sik* (line 887, "such") and *mekil* (line 915, ME *muchel*). While ME *sh-* usually is spelled *sch-* as in *schou* and *schryf* (line 886, "she," "shrive"), it is reduced to *s* initially in *sal/sall* (e.g., line 959, "shall") and *suld* (e.g., line 870, "should"). Some final and medial voiced consonants are unvoiced: e.g., *haf* (line 892, "have"); *liffand* (line 864, "living"); *schryf* (line 886); *wyss* (line 955, "wisc"). This also affects the dental suffix of the preterite and past participle of many weak verbs, as in *liffit* (line 876, "lived"); *enforcit* (line 878, "enforced"); *transformyt* (line 883, "transformed"), etc.

Pronouns. Medieval Scottish pronouns are already similar to those of Modern English. Third-person plural pronouns (from ON) are: *thai*, *tham*, and *thar*. The familiar second-person singular pronouns are *thu*, *the* (which we have rendered *thee*), and *thi*. Distinctive is the third-person female nominative pronoun: *schow/schou/scho*, of which the oblique form is *hyr/hyre*. The second-person plural forms are *ye/you* and *yore/youre*.

Verbs. Typically, Northern verbs have the present participle suffix *-and*, not *-end* or *-inde/-inge*. Present-tense endings are distinctive: e.g., the suffix *-is/-s* is often (though not invariably) used in present tense second- and third-person singular (*wantis*, line 1019), and first-, second-, and third-person plural (*fyndis*, line 1040; *has*, line 1041), and the plural imperative (*sendis*, line 1030), where other ME dialects would have *-eth* or *-e(n)*. There is some wavering as to the ending of the first-person singular present tense: usually the devil-woman avoids the *-s* (except at line 913: *has* instead of *haf*), as does the bishop initially (lines 892–93), but he says *hechtis* at line 964.

Vocabulary. The poet's diction is largely free of obscure dialect words, freely mingling vocabulary of Old English, Scandinavian, and French origin. The strangeness and difficulty of the work result only partly from its vocabulary, much more so from the peculiarities of Northern/Scottish spelling and pronunciation. Among the words found only in Middle Scots are *increly* (line 949, "earnestly/eagerly"), possibly of ON origin; *grettumly* (line 950, "greatly"), from OE *greatum* (dative plural of *great*) + *-lic* (adverbial suffix); *forferlyt* (line 950, "enchanted"), from OE *færlic* ("sudden/strange/wondrous") + *for* (intensifying prefix); and *forowtine* (line 980, "without"), from OE *forutan*. Other words occurring generally in the Northern dialect include: *but* (line 1009, "without"); *gaynand* (line 942, "suitable"); *ger* (line 880, "cause"), from ON; *till* (line 888, "to"), from ON; *grathly* (line 1087, "properly/well"), from ON; *bad* (a Scots variant of *bode*), as in *but (a)bad* (line 1035, "without delay"); *speryt* (line 1023, "asked"), from OE *spyrian*. Others are mentioned in the notes or explained in the glosses, and most can be further researched in the *MED* and *OED*.

St. Andrew

Text

Our text is based closely on Metcalfe's printed edition of *ScL*,[43] collated with the unique manuscript, Cambridge University Library MS Gg.2.6. In addition to normalizing orthographic variants such as *i/j* and *u/v*, we have also normalized the scribe's occasional (and typically Scottish) use of *w* instead of initial and medial *v*, a variation originally limited to words of French origin. Metcalfe's frequent hyphens are omitted and not all his emendations have been accepted.

Indexed in

IMEV 2650.

Manuscript

Cambridge University Library MS Gg.2.6, fols. 29r–29v. [For the complete *ScL* version, see fols. 21r–32v.]

Previous editions

Horstmann. *Barbour's des schottischen Nationaldichters Legendensammlung.* 1.43–47. [For the complete *ScL* version, see 1.31–47.]

Legends of the Saints in the Scottish Dialect of the Fourteenth Century. Ed. Metcalfe. 1.88–96. [For the complete *ScL* version, see 1.63–96.]

---

[43] *ScL*, ed. Metcalfe, 1.88–96.

I(b)

St. Andrew and the Three Questions
in the Scottish Legendary *(c. 1400)*, lines 863–1156,
from Cambridge, University Library MS Gg.2.6, fols. 29v–32v

	Ane bischope umquhile I herd say,	*one time (once upon a time)*
	Religeouse lyf liffand ay,	*living always*
865	Sancte Andrew in affeccione	
	Had ay, and in devocione,	
	Oure all hawlouys that evir ware,	*Above all saints; were*
	Outane Goddis modir dere.	*Except for*
	And als in custum he had ay,	*also*
870	Quhen he suld eythir do or say	*When; should*
	Or spedful or helplyk thinge,	*Either useful or helpful*
	Ay to say in the begynninge:	
	"In worschipe of God almychty	
	And of Sancte Andro thus do I."	
875	The fals fend thane, our felone fay,	*fiend then; cruel foe*
	Had invy he liffit sa	
	Thankfully to God and mane;[1]	
	Forethi enforcit he hym thane	*Therefore he exerted himself then*
	And for to dissave hym fellounly,	*both to deceive; maliciously*
880	And ger hym fal in lichery.	*cause him to; lechery*
	And that he mycht sa that man wyne,	*overcome*
	And for to ger hym fal in syne,	
	He transformyt hym in hy	*himself in haste*
	In forme of a fare lady,	
885	And come to the bischope in,	*bishop's inn (=palace)*
	Sayand schou wald schryf hir of syne,	
	And to sik man schryfyne be,	
	That till assolye hyr had pousté,[2]	

---

[1] Lines 876–77: *[The devil] resented that he lived so / acceptably to God and man*

[2] Lines 886–88: *Saying she wished to confess her sins [to] / And be shriven by someone / With the power to absolve her*

	That mycht na man, hyr thocht,	*[so] it seemed to her*
890	Sa wel do as he mowcht.	*could*
	Thane answert he, and sad: "Pardé,	*said: "By God["] (par dieu)*
	I haf ministeris undir me,	
	To quham I haff gevine powere	*whom; given*
	Al schriftis halely till here;	*wholly to hear*
895	Tharefor tak thee ane of tha,	*Therefore take to yourself (i.e., choose) one of them*
	And til hym thi schrift thu ma!"	*make*
	Thane sad schow, "Pardé,	*she*
	To na man will I schriffyne be	*confessed*
	Bot anerly to yow, ore nocht	*only; or nothing*
900	Schaw that I haff in thocht."	*Show*
	The bischope than, as innocent,	*as [an] innocent (i.e., without suspecting anything)*
	That misknew al hyr entent	*was ignorant of*
	Sat done thar, and mad hym chifte	*down; ready*
	In gud lasere to here hyr schrift.	*leisure*
905	Thare schow one kneys devotly	*on [her] knees devoutly*
	Sat done and sad mekly,	*said*
	"For Goddis sak I pray thee	
	That thu wil haf mercy of me!	*on*
	Fore I, stabelaste in youthed,	*still very young*
910	As ye ma se, and ye tak hed,	*may; if*
	And fosterit delecatly,	*brought up tenderly (daintily)*
	Of kingis kyne yet am I,	*also*
	Thocht I this symple wed has tane,	*Though I have put on simple clothing*
	And cumyne hiddir one allane.	*alone*
915	Fore my faddir of mekil mycht	
	Wald me haf marryit with a knycht,	*Wished to have me*
	Bot I wald nocht consent thareto,	
	For nathynge he mycht evire do;	
	Fore manis falowschipe haf I	
920	Refoysit evirmare halely,	*Refused (Kept free from); completely*
	And to the Kynge of Hevyne tan me	*taken (i.e., dedicated) myself*
	To lyf ay in virginité.	
	Bot he sa hale set his entent	*so wholly*
	To weddinge to ger me consent	*To make me consent to marriage*
925	That othir worthit me do his will,	*That either it behooved me to*
	And halely my purpos spill,	*thwart*
	Or thole torment gret and fell.	*suffer; cruel*

	Forethi I thowcht I wald nocht dwell,	*stay (hesitate)*
	Bot stal away this prevely,	*thus (so)*
930	Fore me ware levare utrely	
	Be banyste fare owt of myn land,	
	Thane fore to brak to Criste the band,	
	That I hafe mad and paid ay,	
	Of my lif to the last day.	
935	And fore your word is spred wid	
	Of halynes one ilke syd,[1]	
	I chesit you to cum till,	*chose*
	Opand in youre gentill will,	*Hoping (Trusting)*
	That ye in youre gret pitté	
940	In sik distrese wald rew one me;	*such; take pity on*
	For I can fynd place naquhare	*nowhere*
	That to me sa gaynand ware	*suitable*
	As undir your proteccione	
	To luf in contemplacione	*live*
945	And warldly thingis to refuse,	
	And hevinly thing sine to use."	*afterwards to enjoy*
	And quhen the bischope thus tale	*this*
	To the hend had hard hale,	*end; heard wholly*
	He beheld hyr increly	*earnestly*
950	And wes forferlyt grettumly	*greatly amazed*
	That in hyre suld assemblit be	
	Sic nobillay, youthed, and bewté,	*nobility [of birth]*
	And that scho suld yet, nevirthelese,	
	With castité restrenye hyr flesche,	*chastity restrain (subdue)*
955	And oure all hyre wyss spekyne.	*above all; speaking (eloquence)*
	Thane mad he hyr answeringe:	
	"Be sikyr, douchtyr, and dred nocht!	*secure (free from care)*
	For He in quham thu set thi thocht	
	Sall thi helpe and protectore be,	
960	Sene thu til Hym has gevine thee,	*Since; thyself*
	And fore this joy falyeand, thu	*in place of this transitory joy*

[1] Lines 930–36: *To me it would be preferable (lit., dearer) to be utterly banished far out of my land, than ever, to the last day of my life, to break my vow to Christ, which I have made and always kept. And because the fame of your holiness is spread far and wide everywhere*

55

	Aylestand joy has chosine nou.	*Everlasting*
	And I, thocht I symple be,	*although*
	Goddis servand, hechtis thee	*promise*
965	That thu sal hafe thi uphalding	*maintenance (living allowance)*
	With honesté in al thinge	*respectability (dignity)*
	In myn diocé, quhare thu	*diocese*
	Will chese dwelling to mak nou.	*Will choose to make your home now*
	Bot this day with me thu sall ete	
970	Eftyr travel and the hete."	
	Thane sad scho, "Lord, lat be!	
	Of sic thinge requere nocht me	*Do not ask me [to do] any such thing*
	That mycht be hendringe to myn fame,	*harm my reputation*
	And lattinge als to yore gud name	*also a slur upon*
975	For men will lichtly spek ye ill,	*easily slander you*
	Thocht thai haf litill cause tharetill."	
	Thane sad the bischope til hyr sone	*to her at once*
	"Of sic thinge thar thee nocht schone,	*you need not fear*
	For we sal nocht be us ane twa	
980	Converse, forowtine witting ma;[1]	
	That sal al il presumpcione	
	Exclud, and all suspicione."	
	Quhen this wes sad, and mes done,	*said, and [after] mass [was] finished*
	Samyn thai yed to met sone,	*Together; went; dinner (lit., food)*
985	And the lord gert hyr be set	*caused*
	Evene before hym at the mete,	
	Syne the lawe in thar degré	*the rest according to rank*
	War to met set, as thai suld be.	
	Bot ay the bischope in a rane	*continuously*
990	Beheld hyr bewté, and nocht fane	*hostile (averse)*
	[. . . . . .]	
	Quhen his harte wes het within	*heated*
	Of fleschly luste with hyr to syne.	*by*
	And as the fend had persavynge	*perceived*
	That the biscope sic lykyne	*such delight (lit., liking)*
995	Had in hyr farhed, than gerte he	*fairness; caused*

---

[1] Lines 979–80: *For we shall not converse by our selves, just the two of us, without more [people]
knowing (i.e., being present)*

	In hyr appere the mare bewté,	*more*
	Till that the bischope had gret will	
	His fellone lust to fulfil,	*wicked*
	Waittand bot lasare quhen he	*Waiting only for a suitable time (lit., leisure)*
1000	Mycht purchess oportunité.	*grasp*
	Thane come a pylgrime sodanly	
	To the get, and fast cane cry,	*gate; began to*
	"For Goddis sak, entré!" askand.	*entry (i.e., let me in)*
	And fore he sped nocht, with his hand	*And since he had no success*
1005	He knokit faste apone the get,	
	Sayand, fayne he wald haf met	*he very much wished to*
	Before the bischope, ore ellis nocht,	
	Fore tharfor had he thiddir socht.	
	Thane come the portare in but hone	*gatekeeper; without delay*
1010	And to the bischope sad rycht sone	
	That. Quhen the bischope herd that he	
	Askit met in sic degré,	*manner*
	He askit the lady quhat hyr thocht,	
	Gyf he suld haf entré or nocht.	
1015	Scho sad, "Schere, me think resone	*Sir, it seems reasonable to me*
	That ye ask hym sum harde questione,	
	The quhilk gyf he can nocht undo,	*which; solve (answer)*
	That the entré be warnyt hym to,	*refused him*
	For gyf hym wantis sic prudence,	*lacks such intelligence*
1020	He suld nocht cum in your presence."	
	The bischope thocht, and all the lafe,	
	The sentence ganand that scho gafe.[1]	
	Thane speryt thai upe and done	*asked*
	Quha suld mak this questione,	
1025	Bot thar wald no man undertak	
	Sa sle a question for to mak.	*subtle (ingenious)*
	The bischope sad, "Lady, sene ye	*since you*
	Of sle spekine has sutelté	*sly speaking (eloquence); expertise*
	With wisdome thareto at yore wil,	
1030	Sendis the questione hym til!"	*Send the question to him*
	Thane sad scho, "Sir, askis hym in hy	*in haste (quickly)*

---

[1] Lines 1021–22: *The bishop and the rest [of the company] thought / Her verdict appropriate*

57

	Of this warld the maste ferly	*greatest marvel*
	That God in lytil space has wrocht."	
	And to that man quhen this wes brocht,	
1035	He mad answere but abad,	*without delay*
	That the maste mervale that God mad	
	"Is in the visage of the mane;	*the human face*
	That all are lyk and yet, nocht than,	*[In] that; nevertheless*
	In ilke face in sum degré	
1040	Mene fyndis diversyté,	
	Of al mene that evir has bene	
	Sene the warld was, forout wene.	*Since; without a doubt*
	And in the face the wittis all	*senses*
	Of the cors are stedyt, gret and smal."	*body; placed*
1045	And quhen this ansuere wes mad	
	Till al that in the hall abade,	
	Cuth na man fynd till amend	*Could; find [a way] to*
	The answer that wes to tham send.	*sent*
	Yet sad the lady, "Bot I wyll	*said*
1050	Ane uthyre questione send hym till,	*Another*
	Quharein we ma assay his wit;	*Wherein; test*
	And gyf he will answere it,	
	He is worthy till haf entré.	
	Tharefore sperys at hym gyf he	*ask of*
1055	Cane say, quhare the erd heyest is."	*earth*
	And quhen the pilgram had herd this,	
	He sad, "The corse of dere Jhesu	*corpse (body)*
	In hevyne empyre is heyest nou,	*[the] empyrean sphere*
	That sammyne is bath God and man	*simultaneously; both*
1060	In a persone; sa mane we thane	*one; so must we then*
	Trew that the erde in His persone	*Believe*
	Is in the hyeste regione."	
	Thane he that mediatoure had bene,	*messenger*
	And hard this answere all bedene,	*heard; in turn*
1065	Recordyt it to the bischope, all	*Reported*
	As he harde, bath gret and smal.	
	Thane all that in the hall were	
	Ilowit the pilgrame answere,	*Accepted; pilgrim's*
	And sad worthy ware, that he	*said it was fitting*
1070	To the hall suld welcum be.	*should*

	Bot the lady yet sad, "Nay,	
	Anis yet we wil assay —	*Once more*
	And the thred tyme althirebeste —	*third; best of all*
	And wit gyf he doucht to be geste.	*find out; ought (is worthy)*
1075	Fore proponyt till hym sal be	*posed*
	A thinge of gret diffyculté,	
	And myrke, and hard fore to say,	*obscure*
	Gyf his wit gud be til assay;	*To find out if his wit be good*
	And gyve he cane undo that worde,	*if; solve that problem*
1080	He may wele syt at youre awne burde.	*board (i.e., table)*
	Tharefore spere at hym, quhat space is evyne	
	Fra the yerde upe to the Hevyne?"[1]	
	The portare thane this demand mad	
	To the pilgrame, and but abade	*without delay*
1085	Sad to hyme agane, "Thu ga	*[He] said*
	Til hyre that cane this demand ma	*did; make*
	And spere at hyre grathly.	*carefully ask her [to answer]*
	For schow wat it bettyr thane I;	*knows*
	Fore schow met it, quhen scho fell	*measured*
1090	Of the hey Hevine done to Hell.	*From the high; down*
	And fore that I in Hell nevir wes,	
	I cane nocht grathly tel the space.	*readily*
	And say this bischope als, that schow	*to this bishop also*
	That sic demand has mad me to,	
1095	Is the fende in wemanis schape,	
	Hyme with fandinge til umlape."	*To ensnare him with temptation*
	The portare, that hard hym sa say,	
	Come till the hall but delay,	*without*
	Haffand wondir with rednes,	*Feeling amazement and fear*
1100	And tald this til all that thare wes,	
	Quhareof thai had gret ferly.	*astonishment*
	Bot the fend wes away in hy,	*gone in haste*
	Sonare na ony man cuth thynke,	*Sooner than*
	And levit the place full of stinke.	*left*
1105	The bischope thane hymself blamyt,	
	That wes in poynt to have ben schamyt	*about to*

---

[1] Lines 1081–82: *Therefore ask him what distance [it] is even / From earth to heaven*

	Quhene he consentit fore to syne,	
	And fore that cause the fend socht hym.	
	Thane he repentyt hym in hy	
1110	Of his trespace and his foly,	
	And gret with his ewyne rycht sare,	*wept, eyes, bitterly*
	And bad the portare pase but mare	*go out without delay*
	To bringe the pilgram. Bot he thane	
	Away wes went fra sicht of mane.	*gone*
1115	The bischope gert the puple call,	*caused the people to be summoned*
	And word be wourd sad to tham all	*them*
	How that the fend come till his in[1]	
	In wemanis schape to ger hym syne,	
	And commaundit tham fore to pray	
1120	Fore hyme, als walk and fast the day	*also to wake (hold a vigil)*
	Til God, of His debonare will,	*gracious*
	One sum manere wald schau tham til	*show*
	Quha evire wes the pylgram, that sa	*who ever*
	Saffyt hym fra his felone fa.	*malicious foe*
1125	Thane til hymself that nycht but bad	*without delay*
	In visione wes warning mad	
	That Sancte Andro, to God rycht dere,	
	"As a pylgrame apperyt here,	
	To kepe thee fra the fend that, na he,	*if he [had] not*
1130	Had wikitly confundyt thee."	
	And the bischope fra that tym, ay	
	To Sancte Andrew, nycht and day,	
	Wes mare devote, in al thinge	
	Of Sancte Androw in the lowynge,[2]	
1135	To quham wyrschipe and honour be	
	Of alkyne men in al degré!	
	Yet men mycht say mekile thinge	
	Of Sancte Andrew in lowinge	*praise*
	Bot, fore I am alde and swere	*slow (indolent)*
1140	I will say no mare of hym here,	

---

[1] Lines 1116–17: *And told them all in detail / How the fiend came to his palace*

[2] Lines 1131–34: *And the bishop ever from that time forward / Was more devoted to Saint Andrew, night and day, and was glorifying Saint Andrew in every way*

60

	Bot lowis hym gretly, for he wes	*praise*
	Our al the lave of maste meknes,	*Over all the rest*
	And wes the fyrste man of tham al	
	That we "appostil" now can call,	
1145	That chosyne ware with Criste to be,	
	All his derreste and mast privé.	*intimate*
	And syne Sanct Petir, his awn brothir,	
	He broucht to Criste before al uthyre,[1]	
	And syne deit apone the tre,	*died*
1150	As in it deit his mastir fre.	*noble*
	Tharfor he suld haf honowringe	
	That sa thankful til Hevynis Kinge	*so pleasing*
	Was fyrste and laste, and traste is now	*from start to finish; trusted (certain)*
	To bruk that blyse with dere Jhesu	*enjoy*
1155	That ay sal leste but ony end,	*without*
	To the quhilk blyse He us al send![2]	

---

[1] Lines 1147–48: *And except for Saint Peter, his own brother, / He converted more people to Christianity than any other [apostle]*

[2] *May He (Jesus) send us all to the same bliss [as Andrew]*

I(b)

Explanatory Notes to St. Andrew and the Three Questions in the Scottish Legendary *(c. 1400)*

864   *Religeouse*. *Religious* here may mean merely "holy," but the word also often refers to some sort of "regular" regime, i.e., life according to a set "rule" such as those of the Benedictine monks or Austin canons.

888   Priests and bishops were empowered by the Church to confer absolution (God's forgiveness of a person's sins after confession) and to assign a suitable penance.

901–02   The poet's emphasis on the bishop's ingenuousness replaces a less sympathetic word of explanation, *victus* (variant *convictus*, "convinced," "overcome," with a possible pun on the homophonic noun, "companionship/intercourse") in *LA* (ed. Maggioni, 1.33; *convictus* is not translated by Ryan).

905–14   In these lines the "she-devil" coyly prompts the bishop to pay close attention to her youthful appearance (*As ye ma se*, translates *ut cernitis* but *and ye tak hed* is the poet's addition — line 910), while her speech is laden with other innuendoes: e.g., *haf mercy* (line 908) which literally translates the Latin *miserere mei* but in the vernacular belongs as much to the diction of courtly love as to religion; the adjective *delecatly* (line 911, reproducing *LA*'s *delicata*) suggests a kind of pampered softness conducive to the wantonness which is one of the word's other common meanings in ME. See also lines 935–46.

909   *stabelaste in youthed*. Literally, "established/situated in youth." The circumlocution echoes the phrasing of *LA* (ed. Maggioni, 1.33): *in annis puellaribus . . . constituta*. See textual note on this line.

925   This use of the third singular present of OE *weorthan* ("become/turn out") to mean "it behooves [someone]" is a Middle Scots peculiarity. See *OED worth*, vb., B5.

926   *And*. The manuscript reading (see Textual Notes) is *Or*. The syntax is not quite consistent here: *othir . . . or* should mean "either . . . or," but the text has two *or* clauses, the first of which (line 926) fits the context awkwardly. The line would

make better sense if its conjunction were *and*, since by agreeing to marry (her first alternative), the "maiden" would lose her cherished virginity. In *LA*, the choice is simply either to obey her father or suffer punishment (trans. Ryan, 1.19). The Scots poet, in other words, sought to make clear why obeying her father was not an option, despite the alternative prospect of being punished severely for disobedience. It seems best therefore to emend and translate the three lines thus: "So that either I was obliged to do his will, and destroy my goal [of perpetual virginity], or suffer torment great and cruel." The prospect of being cruelly punished by her father for resisting marriage recalls the legendary predicament of virgin saints such as Juliana, whose angry father had her whipped before handing her over to her former suitor for further torture and eventual martyrdom (*LA* chapter 43; trans. Ryan, 1.160–61; also translated in *ScL* 2.424–31 and in DM 1.62–70. Juliana, however, chose to suffer for her ideals rather than run away. The situation here may have reminded some readers of the historical experience of Christina of Markyate (c. 1097–1161): see Talbot, ed. and trans., *The Life of Christina of Markyate*.

942   *gaynand.* The etymology is ON *gegna* ("to meet/encounter") rather than OF *gagner* ("to win"), as asserted by Metcalfe, *ScL* 3.60.

935–46   In the equivalent passage of *LA* the devil-woman's more consciously artful rhetoric makes the bishop's admiration for her "wyss spekyne" (line 955) more understand-able: ". . . I have sought refuge under the wings of your protection, hoping to find a place with you where I might enjoy the secret silence of holy contemplation and avoid the pitfalls [*presentisque uite uitare naufragia*] of [the present] life, and escape from the disorders of the noisy world" (ed. Maggioni, 1.33; trans. Ryan, 1.19). In the Scots version these choice phrases are replaced by the diction of secular love lyrics, as the devil-woman appeals to the bishop's *gentill will* (line 938) and *pitté* (line 939) to *rew* on her *in sik distrese* (line 940).

957–62   Compare *LA*: "Be free from care, daughter, and fear not, because he for whose love you have despised, in manly fashion [*uiriliter*], yourself, your family, and your possessions, will in return bestow upon you abundance of grace in this present life and the fullness of glory in the life to come" (ed. Maggioni, 1.34; my translation). The Scots poet simplifies the Latin here, notably suppressing the adverb *uiriliter*, with which the conduct of holy women, especially early virgin martyrs and early ascetics, was dignified, but which would have clashed here with the poet's ongoing depiction of the relationship between bishop and devil-woman in courtly terms. See Bjerre-Aspegren, *The Male Woman: A Feminine Ideal in the Early Church*, pp. 115–43.

971   Coincidentally, Alison of Oxford uses the same expression to fend off the urgent
       advances of Nicholas the clerk in Chaucer's Miller's Tale (*CT* I[A]3285).

972–76 As if to suggest the development of a more-than-clerical relationship between the
       two, the she-devil affects no concern for the possible immorality of his invitation, but
       only, as befits a figure in a courtly romance, anxiety for their public, worldly repu-
       tations. Notice the flirtatious hint of *litill cause* (line 976), which is the Scots poet's
       addition.

987–88 The bishop would presumably be seated, like any medieval baron, at a table for
       himself and other dignitaries (in this case his new ward, facing him), usually on a
       slightly raised platform or dais, while the other clerics and retainers would be
       arranged according to their ranks at longer tables down the length of the hall. This
       arrangement, and the name "High Table," is still maintained in the dining halls of
       Oxford and Cambridge colleges. *Lawe* or *lave* (line 987) was in common usage in
       OE (*laf*, lit., "leavings/what is left"), but largely confined to Scots in the ME period
       and later.

989   *in a rane.* "Continuously"; the phrase is a Northern expression of obscure origin;
       rane also can mean "a prolonged cry" or "a rigmarole." The poet follows the Latin
       (*LA*, ed. Maggioni, 1.20) in emphasizing the bishop's obsessive gazing at the devil-
       woman's beauty (*Intendit in eam crebro episcopus eiusque faciem non desinit intueri
       et pulchritudinem admirari*, "the bishop gave her continuous attention and did not
       cease gazing at her face and marveling at her beauty" — our translation). Metcalfe,
       however, posits a noun *arane*, "conversation," from OF *aresne*, ultimately from
       Latin *adrationare* (*ScL* 3.68) but this word in ME and Middle Scots is represented
       by *areyne* or *arenyie*, i.e., the legal term *arraign*, "indict/call to account."

990–91 The interruption in sense between *fane* (line 990) and *Quhen* (line 991) suggests that
       two lines are missing between them, as Metcalfe points out (*ScL* 1.91 and 3.69).
       They probably paraphrased part of a sentence in *LA* about how the bishop's heart
       was wounded through his eyes: *Sicque dum oculus figitur, animus sauciatur* (ed.
       Maggioni, 1.34, "And thus when the eye is fixed, the heart is wounded" [our
       translation], a variation on the medieval proverb, *ubi amor, ibi oculus*). The same
       topos, of course, is common in medieval romances of love (e.g., Chaucer's Knight's
       Tale, *CT* I[A]1077–79).

994   *lykyne.* Apparently a shortened form of the verbal noun, *lykynge*, since the rhyme word
       is *persavynge* (compare "spekyne" in line 955). Although the present participle suffix

64

in Scots is *-and*, nouns formed from verbs preserve the OE gerund suffix, *-ung/-ing*, which in ME eventually replaced the present participle suffix *-end*.

1000   *purchess oportunité*. Compare the blander Latin equivalent (*LA* , ed. Maggioni, p. 34): *quando possibilitas se offerret*, "when the opportunity might arise" (our trans-lation). The poet's technique of creative fidelity to his source is nicely illustrated in the subtle differences between the Latin and the vernacular, in that the Latin *possi-bilitas* is directly translated with *oportunité*, but the syntax is altered to make the bishop the active subject. The original meaning of *purchess* in OF and ME is to "seek after," "obtain," or "procure," often nefariously. The word seems carefully chosen here, not only because etymologically it is related to the "chase" (the practice of hunting), which is a common medieval metaphor for erotic desire, but also, perhaps, because one of the meanings of the noun *purchess* in Northern usage is "concubine" (see *OED purchase*, sb., 3b).

1009   *hone*. "Delay," a Northern dialect word of obscure origin.

1010–11 This pedestrian piece of enjambement is one of the poet's rare moments of lazy or unskillful writing.

1019–20 The devil-woman's insinuation, that the bishop should not deign to keep company with dull, ignorant people, adds the temptation of pride to that of lust.

1027–30 It is interesting that here the bishop abandons his habitual way of addressing the devil-woman, using *Lady* (line 1027) rather than "douchtyr" (line 957) and aban-doning the fatherly singular pronoun, appropriate for a bishop addressing a young woman, in favor of the more gallant and courtly plural form (*ye . . . yore*) for the first time, as if acknowledging her as his peer and mistress at this crucial moment.

1036–44 The five "wits" or senses are those of sight, hearing, smell, taste, and touch; the organs of the first four are all part of the "face" in a way, but touch is more usually associated with the hands. The devil-woman's questions, as if she is under some sort of divine compulsion, revolve around the crisis at hand. Thus the answer to the first question is the miraculous nature of the very thing — a beautiful face — that is enticing the bishop to commit the sins of lust and pride. The answer also emphasizes that the face is the location of all the potentially dangerous bodily senses, which up to this point in his life the bishop has successfully disciplined and controlled in his devotion to God and St. Andrew. On the second question, see explanatory note to lines 1057–62.

1057–62   The Christocentric impulse in medieval thought is nicely illustrated in this answer. Not the highest mountain on earth but the human physique of Jesus in Heaven is "where the earth is highest." This second question points specifically away from the beautiful, enticing physicality of the devil-woman to the one body to which the bishop should be devoted, Christ's (*corpus Christi*, the phrase used in *LA*, ed. Maggioni, p. 35, at this point). The pilgrim's answer also invokes the doctrine of the Incarnation, by which Christ is both God and man, divine spirit and human flesh, and which lies at the center of the Christian faith that the devil is seeking to undermine. On the cult of Corpus Christi in the later Middle Ages, see Rubin, *Corpus Christi: The Eucharist in Late Medieval Culture*.

1058   *hevyne empyre.* The "empyrean" (lit., "fiery") is the highest and outermost of the nine crystalline spheres that in Ptolemaic cosmology form the structure of the universe. In Christian thought this sphere of fire became identified with the abode of God and the angels. The word *hevyne* is often used to refer to a cosmic sphere.

1074   *doucht.* Third person singular, past tense (here with present meaning) of *dow*, "to be valid, worthy, profitable, useful"; from OE *dugan*, which became obsolete in the later Middle Ages except in Scotland. Compare Modern English *doughty*.

1081–82   The third question, admirably suited to the context in various ways, continues to thematize the relationship between earth and Heaven that has loomed large in the previous questions and underlies the basic tensions in the story. The question is also apparently much more common in such games of question and answer than the first two. For some of the different answers recorded (e.g., one step, into the grave and up to heaven; or one day, since Christ made the trip in a day), see Thompson, *Motif-Index of Folk-Literature*, H682. Finally, the question allows the pilgrim to go on the offensive, for in affecting not to know the answer and deferring to his opponent's expertise, he is able to reveal the devil-woman's true identity with a sarcastic flourish (lines 1085–96). He is also performing a saintly ritual and hagiographic topos, in that he is not only proclaiming his opponent's identity but also reminding her that she is a damned spirit, defeated by God (compare the encounters of saints and demons in the Lives of Antony and Guthlac and the legend of the Finding of the Holy Cross).

1096   *umlape.* See also textual note. The verb combines the ON prefix *um-* ("around/about"; compare OE *ymb*) and ME *lap* ("enfold/coil"). *Lap* has no known OE or other etymology.
    Fanding, "temptation," is from a common OE word (*fandian*) that remained current mainly in the North in the later Middle Ages.

1099   *rednes*. An orthographic variant of *radness*; Northern dialect *rad* is from Old Norse *hrǽddr*, "frightened/alarmed."

1108   The poet betrays some anxiety as to how to handle this part of the story. In the Latin source there is a brusque statement to the effect that bishop "bitterly reproached himself, and with tears prayed for pardon for his fault" (trans. Ryan 2.20). The Scots poet softens this somewhat by invoking the late medieval distinction between committing a sin in fact (which would have "shamed" the bishop and destroyed his physical chastity) and, as here, *consenting* to it with the will. The implication seems to be that the bishop may have erred but Andrew has saved him from something much worse.

1135 ff. From this point the Scottish author leaves the Latin source (which recounts one more Andrew miracle) and concludes with his own tribute to the saint. His apology for breaking off, namely that he is *alde and swere* (line 1139, "old and slow"), recurs several times in *ScL*, as pointed out by Metcalfe in his note to line 1139 (*ScL* 3.71). The word *swere*, here meaning "reluctant/indolent," from OE *swǽr* (grievous/oppressive), survives in the ME period mainly in the North. See *OED sweer*.

I(b)

Textual Notes to St. Andrew and the Three Questions
in the Scottish Legendary *(c. 1400)*

Abbreviations: **MS** = Cambridge University Library MS Gg.2.6, fols. 29v–32v; **M** = Metcalfe's 1896 ed. of *ScL* (*Legends of the Saints in the Scottish Dialect of the Fourteenth Century*).

863   *Ane.* Space is left for an initial A two lines high.
865   *affeccione.* So MS. M: *affecione.*
868   *Outane.* MS: *Outare.* M's emendation. *Outane*, meaning "except," is the usual form elsewhere in the manuscript. It is the reduced form of *outtane* (*out + tane*, past participle of *ta*, the Northern variant of *take*), lit., "taken out."
870   *he.* Inserted above the line in MS.
872   *to say.* MS: *to þe say.*
873   *almychtty.* So MS. M: *almychty.*
879   *fellounly.* MS: *fellouny.*
909   *stabelaste in youthed.* A later hand has noted the Latin *constituta* in the margin, probably indicating that at least one reader was reading the text against *LA*. See the explanatory note to this line.
911   *fosterit delecatly.* MS: *fosterit is delecatly.* The verb *is*, "written between the lines ... probably by a later hand," is adopted as the correct reading by M, *ScL* 1.89, but it seems redundant in the sentence and clashes grammatically with "am I" in line 912.
925   *his.* MS: *is.* M's emendation.
926   *And.* MS: *Or.* M's emendation. See explanatory note to this line.
928   *Forethi.* MS: *Fore.* M's emendation.
938   *Opand.* MS: *offerand.* The manuscript reading makes little sense and is probably an error for *opand* ("hoping"), as noted by M (*ScL* 3.67), following Horstmann. M leaves the manuscript reading *offerand* in his text, however.
947   *And.* Space is left in the manuscript for an initial A two lines high.
955   *spekyne.* So MS. M emends to *spekynge.*
958   *He.* MS: *Hym.* M's emendation.
964   *servand.* MS: *v* inserted by a later hand.
968   *Will chese.* MS: *will ese chese.*

978   *thar thee.* MS: *ar þe.* M does not emend, but suggests *thar the* as an alternative (*ScL* 3.68). The impersonal verb *thar,* "need" (from OE *thurfan*), takes a dative of respect. *Schone* is the verb "shun," used intransitively in some Northern texts to mean "be afraid."

999   *Waittand.* MS: *wittand.* M's emendation.

1001   *Thane.* Space is left in the manuscript for an initial thorn two lines high. In the right-hand margin, a later hand has written *peregrinus.*

1008   *tharfor.* So MS. M reads *þarefor.*

1030   *the.* So MS. M reads *ȝe.*

1039   *in sum.* MS: *is sum.* M's emendation.

1042   *Sene.* MS: *Send.* M: *Sen.*

1054   *at.* MS: *þat.* M's emendation (the *th-* is marked for deletion by a later hand in MS).

1055   *heyest.* So MS. M reads *hyest.*

1071   *Bot.* Space is left in the manuscript for an initial B two lines high.

1080   *at.* MS: *þat.* M's emendation.

1084   *and.* M: *quha.* M's emendation seems unnecessary. Possibly the word *he* has dropped out at the beginning of line 1085.

1096   *umlape.* MS: *vnlape.* M's emendation.

1100   *And tald.* MS omits *And.* M's emendation.

1116   *tham.* M: *þa.* In MS there is a light stroke over the *a.*

1119   *tham.* MS: *þare.* M's emendation.

1120   *walk.* So MS. M reads *wakk* but the variant spelling *walk* for *wake* is widely attested in Middle Scots.

1150   *mastir.* So MS. M expands as *master.*

II(a)

The Martyrdom of St. George
in the South English Legendary *(c. 1270–80)*

Introduction

The Cult and Legend of St. George (feast day, April 23)

The image of George most familiar to us today, the saint dressed in a white tunic bedecked with a red cross, astride his stallion, and skewering a dragon as he rescues a fair maiden, depends more on a late medieval and Renaissance ideal of this *miles Christi* (knight of Christ) than on his legend in its earlier forms, in which the dragon and the maiden play no part and George's role is one of verbal jousting and violent suffering rather than knightly derring-do. George the martyr was allegedly born in the region of Cappadocia (now central Turkey) and executed by the Persians or Romans (traditions differ) in Diospolis (Lydda), on the road from Jerusalem to Joppa (later Jaffa, now Tel Aviv–Yafo), in the early fourth century. Unlike many other saints in this collection, however, nothing truly historical is known of George and the figure in the legends may be a composite of more than one original saint; only the archeological certainty of an early cult suggests that there probably was a martyr of this name, who was per-haps a soldier.[1] Among this early archeological evidence is the church in Shaqrā, Syria, west of the Sea of Galilee, dedicated to St. George by a Bishop Tiberinus; it is dated by some in the mid-fourth century but by others in the sixth. Certainly by the sixth century the cult's influence had spread not only into Syria, Arabia, Egypt, and Byzantium, but also as far as southern Gaul. By this time, Diospolis/Lydda was the focal point of the cult since the church there claimed to have the saint's relics. Various pilgrims from the early sixth century on recorded their visits to the site, among them the Frankish bishop Arculf, who visited in the late seventh century, according to the Irish hagiographer Adomnan in his *De locis sanctis*, a guide for pilgrims to the Holy Land written near the end of the century. Although Bede knew Adomnan's book well, he and his contemporary Aldhelm are strangely silent about George in their hagiographic writings and elsewhere, perhaps because it was not until the middle of the eighth century, when Pope Zacharias (741–52) transferred what was believed to be George's head from the church of St.

---

[1] For the "soldier-saints" as a group, in addition to the classic study by Delehaye, *Les légendes grècques des saints militaires*, see the excellent website on "Military Martyrs" by David Woods at www.ucc.ie/milmart/.

John Lateran to the church of St. George in Velabro, that the saint began to be culted in Rome and the saint's feast found a permanent place in the Roman service books and their northern offspring. He is celebrated with a couplet in the York metrical calendar, composed probably during the time of Archbishop Ecgberht (754–66).[2]

The Greek legend accompanying the early diffusion of George's cult dates back to the fifth century, and a Latin version of this was apparently circulating in the West by the early sixth century. This version sensationally pushes the genre of the martyr's *passio* to limits even medieval clerics apparently found hard to swallow, for in both Greek and Latin it was subjected to much abridging and revising over the centuries. Our Middle English version of George's martyrdom is based on one of these later abridgements, but it is worth summarizing the earliest form of the legend to give some sense of its bizarrely epic quality, far exceeding the simpler pattern of interrogation, imprisonment, sentencing, and martyrdom that we have observed in the *passio* of St. Andrew.[3]

George, a military leader under Dacian, "king of the Persians,"[4] inaugurates his seven years of torture by boldly coming forward to confess his belief in Christ, as Dacian is preparing to persecute Christians in the area. At Dacian's order, George is stretched out on the rack and ripped to shreds with flesh hooks, harnessed to machines that draw him apart, and then beaten, after which salt is poured into his wounds, which are rubbed with a haircloth. He is then pressed into a box pierced with nails, impaled on sharp stakes, plunged into boiling water, and has his head crushed by a hammer. All to no avail. God comforts George in prison and informs him that

---

[2] See Lapidge, "A Tenth-Century Metrical Calendar from Ramsey," p. 331. Among recent accounts of the archeological evidence for the cult of George in the Near East and the development of the legend is that of Haubrichs, *Georgslied und Georgslegende im frühen Mittelalter*, pp. 224–42, 305–27. See also Walter, "The Origins of the Cult of St. George," especially pp. 314–26, who criticizes some of Haubrichs' data. On the cult in Anglo-Saxon England, see Hill, "Saint George before the Conquest." On the iconographical tradition, see the entry for George in Kirschbaum and Bandmann, eds., *Lexikon der christlichen Ikonographie*, 6.365–90, and Rochelle, *Post-Biblical Saints Art Index*, pp. 115–22. See also the recent study of some medieval English images of St. George by Samantha J. E. Riches, "St George as a Male Virgin Martyr," in Riches and Salih, pp. 65–85.

[3] The Greek tradition of George's legend is examined by Krumbacher, *Der heilige Georg in der griechischen Überlieferung*. The earliest extant Latin versions are represented by *BHL* 3363 and 3367. On the development of the Latin tradition, see the work of Matzke, to which we are much indebted: "Contributions to the History of the Legend of St. George" and "The Legend of St. George: Its Development into a *Roman d'Aventure*."

[4] In the older Greek and Latin versions of the legend, George's persecutor is Dacian, a Persian ruler (*BHL* 3363) who then becomes more vaguely a "king of the pagans" (*BHL* 3367, 3376); in others, the persecutor is the Roman emperor Decius (*BHL* 3384) or a Roman judge, Dacian, under the emperor Diocletian (*BHL* 3386, etc.).

he will die three deaths before entering Paradise. Dacian, confounded, summons the magician Athanasius who shows his mettle by splitting an ox in half and having each half return to life whole. Undaunted, George gulps down two portions of the magician's poison, at which point the magician confesses Christ and is summarily executed by the Persian ruler and George is returned to prison. The next day he is lacerated on a wheel of swords, cut into ten pieces, and thrown into a well that is sealed with a stone. God appears with the archangel Michael to resurrect the saint, at which point the officer in charge, Anatholius, is converted with nearly 1,100 soldiers and one woman, all of whom are immediately executed. Dacian then redoubles his efforts: George is tied to an iron bed, molten lead is poured into his mouth and eyes after which sixty nails are driven into his skull, he is hung upside down over a fire with a stone tied around his neck, and he is shut into the revolving belly of a metal ox which is filled with swords and nails. Yet again at the end of the day the saint goes back to prison. To die his second death, George is sawed in two, boiled to bits, and just before he is buried, God, good to his word, resuscitates him after five days.

In addition to his own resilience, George's miracles include changing thrones into trees, reviving oxen, healing a sick boy, and resurrecting and baptizing men, women, and children who have been dead for centuries.

Despite fastening a glowing iron helmet to the prisoner's head, tearing and burning his body some more, and executing George a third time, Dacian fails to move the saint to sacrifice to Apollo and tries verbal persuasion instead. When George appears to consent, the delighted king invites him to the palace for the night during which the saint surreptitiously converts Dacian's wife Alexandra, who is later executed as a result. George in the meantime goes to the temple of Apollo, whose statue promptly leaves the temple and confesses his fraudulence. The saint stamps his foot, and the ground swallows up the false god. Exasperated, Dacian pronounces George's death sentence yet again. Before his execution, though, George prays and intercedes for those who remember his name and feast day. Having survived seven years of torture and three deaths, he is finally decapitated and gratefully ascends to Heaven.

Such a summary of the legend's gruesome array of tortures is apt to conceal its considerable didactic content. Duncan Robertson has recently described the legend, with its many speeches and prayers incorporating numerous echoes of the gospels and other scriptural texts, as a kind of liturgical dialogue between the reader and the "priest-hero" George, reconstructing the gospel narrative and the redemptive process with each performance of the *passio*.[5] Earlier scholars have scrutinized the spectacular events of the narrative in the light of comparative religion and mythology, and have seen in the chamber of horrors reflections of ancient Near Eastern fertility cults, in which the yearly death and resurrection of gods such as Attis, Tham-

---

[5] Robertson, *The Medieval Saints' Lives*, pp. 44–46.

muz, and Osiris were prominent.[6] Whatever the origins of such narrative forms might be, their obsessive focus on the reintegration and survival of the physical body, and on its triumph over various processes of dismemberment and destruction, reflects perhaps the pervading anxiety among early Christians over the natural fate of the physical body. Recent cultural studies by historians such as Peter Brown and Caroline Bynum have explored the links between these concerns and the rise of cults of martyrs' relics in which the doctrine of the resurrection apparently found dramatic confirmation. The miracles of healing believed to be worked by the fragmentary remains of the martyrs must have appeared as reassuring proof that faith in the Judeo-Christian God, and in His death and resurrection, could bestow upon His faithful the power to overcome the effects of natural physical decay, since in order to perform miracles each particle of the saint's body must in itself be, in a mysterious but real sense, the whole saint.[7] Thus what R. Aubert has called the "fantasmagories"[8] of violent miracles of dissolution and re-integration in the St. George legend may have been a narrative attempt to relieve this underlying anxiety and affirm the faith in Christianity's power to overcome physical change and assure continuity. It is perhaps no coincidence that the cult of relics, and the narrative genre represented here, began to develop while the administrative and economic unity of the Roman empire was itself on the verge of collapse.

Not all Christians were as enamored of the cult of relics as were Jerome and, in his old age, Augustine of Hippo. Some were apparently troubled by the rise of the literary genre which catered so effusively to a hunger for stories of the miraculous triumphs of God's saints over the trials of the flesh. For reasons that are not entirely clear, the early legend of George was condemned as heretical in an early-sixth-century document purporting to be a papal decree of the late fifth century.[9] Precisely what was considered heretical about the George legend we do not know, but possibly the dualistic strains detected by modern scholars were also sensed by some vigilant early Christians, who might have associated them with various heresies of the time. While the decree did little to stem the growing popularity of George's cult and the multiplication of copies of the legend, it may perhaps have helped spur a series of attempts to revise the legend by simplifying and abridging it in various ways, and attempting to "correct" some of its more blatant anachronisms. The textual history of the legend is too complicated to explain here in detail, but we should note that what is today regarded as the first, more sensational type of

---

[6] For summary of and references to older scholarship of this sort, see Fontenrose, *Python: A Study of Delphic Myth and Its Origins*, p. 519.

[7] See Brown, *The Cult of the Saints*, pp. 72–85; Bynum, *The Resurrection of the Body in Western Christianity, 200–1336, passim*, but see especially pp. 59–114.

[8] Baudrillart, Meyer, Aubert et al., eds., *Dictionnaire d'histoire et de géographie ecclésiastiques* 20.633.

[9] See von Dobschütz, ed., *Das Decretum Gelasianum*, pp. 9 and 13; the relevant passage is quoted and translated by Robertson, *The Medieval Saints' Lives*, pp. 44–45.

the legend emerged as the accepted form in the Latin West, although considerably abridged in many of its recensions.

Two main families of Latin manuscripts, *Y* and *Z*, were initially identified by modern scholars (notably John E. Matzke) as descended from a translation of an early Greek version of the legend. Of these, the longer and probably older *Y* version was known in England by the ninth century: for example to the author of the *Old English Martyrology*, a unique compilation of Old English prose summaries of or extracts from Latin saints' legends, which contains entries for George (April 23) and for the Empress Alexandria (April 27) and includes part of the martyr's elaborate final prayer for his devotees.[10] The significantly reduced form of the legend, labeled *Z* by Matzke, held sway in England in the later Anglo-Saxon period and thereafter. This *Z*-recension omits most of the saint's wildly exaggerated tortures, except for the flesh hooks, the brass wheel (which now breaks apart when George is cast upon it), the cauldron of molten lead, and George's decollation. All George's other miracles, including the conversions — most notably the Empress Alexandria's — and his multiple deaths and spectacular resurrections, are missed out.[11] Retained, however, are George's victories over the magician Athanasius and the god Apollo and his worshipers, as examples of George's favor with God. The final intercessory prayer, for those who remember him and his feast day, is preserved, but in shortened form. This reduced version of the legend is the one rendered into Old English rhythmic prose by Ælfric, monk of Cerne Abbey in Dorset (later abbot of Eynsham), in the late tenth century for his *Lives of the Saints*,[12] and after the Norman Conquest it continued to be used to provide lessons to be read in churches on the saint's feast day, as well as for devotional reading among English monastics.[13]

---

[10] *An Old English Martyrology*, ed. Herzfeld, with facing translation; critically edited by Kotzor, *Das altenglische Martyrologium*. On the sources of the entry see Cross, "Saints' Lives in Old English," pp. 45–51.

[11] Among the manuscripts that seem to constitute an "English" family of *Z*-type texts are: Dublin, Trinity College MS 171; London, Gray's Inn MS 3, British Library MSS Cotton Nero E. i, pt. 1 and Cotton Tiberius D. iii (burnt); and Salisbury Cathedral Library MS 221. The most complete assessment and presentation of the textual transmission of the Latin tradition is that of Haubrichs (cited above, n. 2), who has considerably revised the stemma of redactions, but Matzke's work (cited above, n. 3) forms a sufficient background for preliminary study of the legend in its Middle English context.

[12] Ælfric of Eynsham, *Ælfric's Lives of Saints*, ed. Skeat, 1.307–19. On Ælfric's putative source, represented by MS Cotton Nero E.i, see Hill, "Ælfric, Gelasius, and St. George," p. 3.

[13] The feast day, April 23, was of the second highest rank, just below that of the feasts of Christ (Christmas, Easter, etc.) and of the Apostles, the Virgin Mary, and certain special Western saints such as Benedict, Martin of Tours, and Gregory the Great. Equal to George's feast were those of other major saints such as Agnes, Cecilia, Maurice and the Theban Legion, Sebastian, and so on. For some medieval calendars listing George's feast day, see Wormald, ed., *English Kalendars before A.D. 1100*, and *English*

While important throughout Europe in the early Middle Ages, George's cult was further promoted by the crusader knights of the late eleventh and twelfth centuries.[14] However, the oft-repeated claim that George's cult in England was particularly fostered by King Richard the Lionheart during and after the Third Crusade (1191) is no longer to be credited.[15] The special popularity of the cult in England belongs, rather, to the fourteenth, fifteenth, and sixteenth centuries, and beyond, owing to the adoption of George as patron saint by a later generation of warlike English kings, notably Edward III, who founded the chivalric Order of the Garter under the patronage of St. George in 1344–48, and Henry V, under whose influence the feast day was elevated to the first rank (1415) and celebrated as a national holiday. In this late medieval period processions in George's honor and mock battles with the dragon were a common feature of the feast day, as were the curious folk-plays that bear his name, dating from the fifteenth and sixteenth centuries, some of which were still being performed in the nineteenth century.[16] Not only were many late medieval parish churches dedicated to the saint, but he was also adopted as patron by numerous parish guilds, among the most prominent of which was that in Norwich, founded in 1385. Some of these guilds survived the widespread suppression of saints' cults by Reformation Protestants, although the commemoration of George's cult became progressively more secular and variously political in character.[17] In the modern era, six English kings have borne the saint's name, and the official flag of the nation, underlying the Union Jack of the United Kingdom, is to this day the red cross of St. George. The most elaborate literary treatments of his legend are likewise late: those of Alexander Barclay (1515), translated into "rime royal" stanzas from the Latin prose composition of Mantuan scholar Baptista Spagnuoli, and Edmund Spenser's epic poem on George, the "Red Cross Knight" in Book I of *The Faerie Queene* (1597). The climax of Spenser's story is not, of course, the martyrdom but rather the famous battle with the dragon, which, as we observed earlier, is a late addition to the saint's

---

Benedictine Kalendars after 1100. The dismemberment of George's body in his *passio* is paralleled by the dispersal of his relics. For one of several English communities that claimed to possess parts of his body, see Conner, *Anglo-Saxon Exeter*, pp. 180, 194, where an early-eleventh-century relics list includes *Of sanctes Georgies banum þæs mæran Cristes cempan & martyres* ("[some] of the bones of St George, the great champion and martyr of Christ").

[14] See II(b), below, St. George and the Dragon, Introduction.

[15] Laborderie, "Richard the Lionheart."

[16] Chambers, *The English Folk-Play*, pp. 170–85 (to be used with caution).

[17] On the guild processions and the secularization of the feast day, and for further bibliography on St. George's day observances, see McClendon, "A Moveable Feast." On the continued political significance of St. George's feast day in colonial America, see Jones, *Saint Nicholas of Myra, Bari, and Manhattan*, pp. 334–38.

legend, little known until the late thirteenth century, when it appears in the popular *LA*. Since it is absent from the main text printed in this chapter, we will discuss the dragon episode later.

SEL Version

By the late thirteenth century, English libraries contained copies of various forms of the George legend, including not only those handed down from the early Middle Ages, but also the influential later abridgements in Vincent of Beauvais' *Speculum historiale* ("The Mirror of History") and *LA*. It should be noted that while the former follows a *Z*-type shortened text for his account of the saint's martyrdom, the latter, besides inserting the late dragon episode (see II[b], below), incorporates more of the original episodes, including the Lord's appearance to George in prison, the saint's attempt to trick Dacian (here the prefect of the emperors Diocletian and Maximian) into visiting the destroyed temple where he might meet the same fate, and Empress Alexandria's conversion and martyrdom; *LA* also appends, as a posthumous miracle, the story of George's appearance to the Christian armies in Jerusalem.[18] But as we have observed earlier, *LA* does not seem to have been a factor in the composition of the first half of *SEL*, where George's legend occurs. The account of George in most of the extant manuscripts of *SEL* is a shortened version of the legend, probably derived for the most part from Matzke's *Z* tradition. Görlach suggests as a more immediate source the readings for the saint's feast in the widely used thirteenth-century Sarum (Salisbury) Breviary, with which the *SEL* version does show some affinity in its wording and narrative order.[19] Not only does it parallel the *Z* texts in its omission of all the more sensational torture sequences, but like the breviary it also omits the Athanasius episode and the saint's destruction of the pagan temple. However, the Middle English poet provides an expanded version of the final intercessory prayer, lacking in both *LA* and the English breviaries, which suggests that he also had access to a text from the *Y* tradition of the Latin legend.[20]

The *SEL* version thus parallels the Sarum Breviary (or some similarly abridged version) in drastically omitting episodes from the *Z* tradition that demonstrate the saint's role as pious

---

[18] *LA*, ch. LVI (*BHL* 3395), ed. Maggioni, pp. 391–98, trans. Ryan, 1.238–42 (ch. 58 in the older edition of Graesse).

[19] Görlach, *Textual Tradition*, p. 161.

[20] The Sarum Breviary skips the episode of Athanasius the magician, passing directly from George's scourging, salting, and rubbing with haircloths to the bronze wheel torture, while the Exeter Ordinal more closely follows the *Z*-type Latin *passio* and positions the saint's contest with the magician before George's torture on the wheel: *Breviarium ad usum insignis ecclesiae Sarum*, ed. Procter and Wordsworth, 3.257–260 and *Ordinale Exon.*, ed. Dalton and Doble, 3.231.

trickster and agent of divine vengeance (e.g., when George personally wills the destruction of the temple of Apollo, which kills all the priests and worshipers inside it, and when God destroys Dacian and his ministers with fire immediately after the saint's execution). *SEL* presents us instead with a saint who is aggressively uncompromising in his speech, but essentially passive and pacifist in his actions. In keeping with the tone of the *SEL* collection as a whole, the George narrative plays up the verbal jousting between the saint and his persecutor by adding more colloquial and humorous overtones (see lines 27–30), and it is also peppered with the narrator's affective responses to the saint's grievous suffering and martyrdom (see lines 43–46, 71–72).[21] Also apparently original in the Middle English version are Dacian's almost demonic anger at George in the beginning of the narrative and his comical grumbling at Mohammed's idleness toward the end (see lines 15–16, 74–75). In general, with its emphasis on the qualities of patience and non-violence, and its homely, down-to-earth exchanges, this version of the legend seems quite compatible with the Franciscan cultural milieu that has been proposed for the original composition of *SEL*. At the same time, it remains untouched by the chivalric and nationalist associations that would later overwhelm the saint's English image.

SEL Texts of *George*

Of the twenty-four major *SEL* manuscripts identified by Görlach, nineteen contain the legend of St. George, including Oxford, Bodleian Library MS Laud Misc. 108, which is generally regarded as representing the earliest form of the text. Although there are dozens of minor variants among the manuscript copies, some rearrangement of lines, and some shortening of the narrative by a few couplets, there is little substantive variation until the text was expanded in the East Midlands in the late fourteenth century to incorporate the dragon episode (printed separately below in II[b]) from *LA*. For the *passio* or martyrdom proper we have adopted the version printed by D'Evelyn and Mill from an early-fourteenth-century manuscript, Cambridge, Corpus Christi College MS 145, rather than the somewhat later Oxford, Bodleian Library MS Ashmole 43, which is our preference in most other *SEL* selections in this volume. In addition to offering an example of a slightly earlier form of English, and a somewhat different dialect from Ashmole 43, the Corpus text displays some interesting scribal variants resulting from

---

[21] "More important than . . . narrative presentation and setting is the entirely new tone and atmosphere in the [*SEL*]. The mood of compassion and warm human participation in the description of the lives of saints . . . which permeates the entire collection is the result of a more 'realistic' and purposely heightened depiction of the sufferings and joys of the protagonists and of the direct appeal to the emotions and empathy of the audience [often by means of the narrator's emphatic exclamations]. This is . . . the truly important contribution of the [*SEL*] to English literature," Jankofsky, "Entertainment," pp. 710–11.

apparent corruptions and emendations in an earlier exemplar.[22] From dialectal evidence, it has been suggested that the manuscript was copied in the western part of the county of Berkshire (somewhat to the east and south of Ashmole 43's provenance in Gloucester), probably in a large scriptorium like that of the priory of the Augustinian canons at Osney, near Oxford, where Chaucer's carpenter John in The Miller's Tale had business to attend to. By the end of the fourteenth century the manuscript traveled to the East Midlands, where a later scribe, in addition to making some dialectical corrections, added a table of contents and a Life of St. Guthlac at the end of the volume; from there it moved to the Southwest again in the early fifteenth century, to the Augustinian priory at Southwick in Hampshire (where a scribe added the Lives of Judas and Pilate, as well as a conclusion to the Life of St. Thomas of Canterbury). If Görlach's suggestion regarding Osney as the original provenance is correct, this manuscript may have been intended for devotional reading or as a preaching aid for the "black canons" who lived in quasi-monastic communities but also served as pastors in lay society.[23]

Language of the Corpus Manuscript

The Corpus manuscript (C) exhibits typical features of the Middle English speech of the Southwest Midlands in the late thirteenth and early fourteenth centuries. The language is very similar to that of Ashmole 43 (A), as described in our introduction to the *SEL* Martyrdom of St. Andrew the Apostle (I[a]), except that the scribe of C has the expected Southwestern form of OE *siþþen* ("afterwards/after"), namely *suththe*, whereas A, surprisingly, has the form more typical of the Southeastern dialects, *seththe*. C occasionally preserves the distinctive *eo* spellings, typical of the Southwest in early Middle English, supposedly representing a rounded /ö/ sound that developed from the OE *eo* diphthong (e.g., *theos*, line 12; *beoth*, line 13; *eoly*, line 36; *weol*, line 53). But this form may already have been somewhat archaic for the C scribe, who frequently uses simply *e*, forcing D'Evelyn and Mill's textual emendations (lines 27, 37–38, 71–72, 87–88, 92), which we have not retained. The *sh* sound is represented with *ss*, not *sc*, as in *ssame* (line 38, "shame"), *vleiss* (line 46, "flesh").

As in the *SEL* Martyrdom of St. Andrew in I(a), above, we have silently emended instances of *is* to *his*.

---

[22] See, e.g., the humorous variant reading in line 13.

[23] Görlach, *Textual Tradition*, p. 57. In addition to Görlach's description of the manuscript and its affiliations (pp. 77–79), see also that in DM, 3.4–5.

St. George

Indexed in

IMEV 2095.

Manuscripts

Cambridge, Corpus Christi College MS 145, fols. 59r–60r.

Oxford, Bodleian Library MS Ashmole 43 (*SC* 6924), fols. 59r–60v.

Oxford, Bodleian Library MS Laud Misc. 108 (*SC* 1486), fols. 130r–131r.

Previous editions

The South English Legendary. Ed. D'Evelyn and Mill. 1.155–59. [Based on CCCC 145.]

The Early South-English Legendary, or, Lives of Saints. Ed. Horstmann. Pp. 294–96. [Based on Laud Misc. 108.]

Sperk. *Medieval Saints' Legends.* Pp. 107–09. [Based on CCCC 145.]

II(a)

The Martyrdom of St. George
in the South English Legendary *(c. 1270–80),*
from Cambridge, Corpus Christi College MS 145, fols. 59r–60r,
as edited by Charlotte D'Evelyn and Anna J. Mill

	Sein Gorge the holy man, as we vindeth iwrite,	*find written*
	In the lond of Capadose ybore was and bigute.	*Cappadocia; born; begotten*
	The false godes he forsok and tok to Cristendom	
	And lovede wel Jesu Crist and holyman bicom.	
5	Dacian the luther prince that was thulke stounde[1]	
	Alle Cristene men that he vond he let bring to gronde.	*found*
	As he honurede a day his false godes, and other manion,	
	Sein Gorge come and sai it al as he com thervorth gon.	*saw; as he was passing by*
	The signe he made of the Crois and blessede him al about,	
10	And armede him thoru the Holi Gost withinne and eke withoute,	
	And wende him forth wel baldeliche and loude he gan to grede	*exclaim*
	To Dacian and alle his, and theos wordes sede:	*companions; these*
	"Alle false godes beoth develes chikene iwis,	*[the] devil's offspring (lit., chickens)*
	For oure Loverd Hevene made and in the Sauter iwrite is."	*in the Psalter it is written*
15	Tho Dacian hurde this he grennede and femede vaste,	*When; grimaced; foamed fast*
	And lourede with luther semlant,[2] and theos wordes out caste:	
	"Bel amy, wat ertou that so fol ert and bold,[3]	*Fair friend (Fine fellow)*
	That in oure poer and in oure godes such wordes hast itold,	*power; gods' [power]*
	That ne destou us noght one ssame, as we alle iseoth,	
20	Ac oure godes ek, wanne thou seist that hi develen beoth?[4]	
	Tel me sone wanne thou ert and wat is thi name,	*immediately whence*

---

[1] *Dacian, who was the wicked prince at that time (Dacian the wicked, who was prince at that time)*

[2] *And glowered with [an] evil expression*

[3] *"[My] fine fellow, what [sort of man] are you, to be so foolish and audacious?["]* (see explanatory note)

[4] Lines 19–20: *[In] that you shame not only us, as we all see, / But also our gods, when you say they are devils["]*

That derst us segge, and oure godes,   so baldeliche such ssame."[1]

"Gorge ich hatte," quath this other, "Cristen man ich am   *am called*

And of the lond of Capadose   hider to you ich cam."

25   "Bel amy," quath Dacian,   "turn thi thoght anon

And honure here oure godes   other it ssel another gon."[2]

"Be stille thou fol," quath Sein Gorge,   "for thou spext embe noght.[3]

For ich habbe in Jesu Crist   byset al mi thoght."   *firmly placed*

"A, traitor," quath this Dacian,   "woltou take on so?   *behave*

30   Thou sselt in other ribaudie   sone dayes beo ido."[4]

He let him honge up anhei   in a maner rode,   *on high; a kind of cross*

And therto him binde faste naked   mid ropes stronge and gode.

With kene oules there binethe   tormentors ther stode   *sharp flesh-hooks*

And al todrowe his holy limes   that hi ronne ablode.   *tore to pieces*

35   Al hi todrowe his tendre vleiss,   the peces folle to gronde.   *flesh*

Bernynge eoly suththe hy nome   and caste in his wonde.   *oil*

Tho hi hadde him thus todrawe longe   that ruthe it was to se,   *When; pitiful*

Hy bithoghte him of more ssame   and nome him doun of the tre.

With harde scorges leide him on   and wonde up other made.[5]

40   To the bare bon the scorges come   as the oules hadde er iwade.   *where; gone before*

The wonden hi nome and sulte suththe   and that salt thicke caste,   *salted*

And suththe with a clout of here   hi rodde it wel vaste.   *haircloth; rubbed; very hard*

A, Loverd, muche was the pine   that ech up other was there.   *pain; each upon other*

Ruthe it was such pine to se   wo so of ruthe were;   *for anyone possessed of pity*

45   And evere lai this holy man,   as him nothing nere   *as if it were nothing to him*

To sulte so that quike vleiss   and robby with an here.[6]

Tho Dacian isey that he ne mighte   overcome him so,   *saw; might not*

He let binde this holyman   and in strong prison do.

Ther he lay al longe night   to other wowe inowe.[7]

50   The tormentors amorwe   tovore Dacian him drowe.   *next morning before*

---

[1] *Who dare to say to us, and [to] our gods, so boldly such disgraceful (blasphemous) [things]*

[2] *or it (your mind) will have to go another [way]*

[3] *for you speak about nothing (i.e., in vain)*

[4] *["]You shall at once be subject to a different kind of mockery today"*

[5] *They beat him with tough whips and made [fresh] wounds on top of the others*

[6] *To have his living flesh salted and rubbed with a haircloth*

[7] *I.e., to add to his other woes, of which he had plenty*

Hi fondede tho in eche manere   yif hi mighte turne his thoght,   *tried*
Ac hi seie tho wel echone   that it was al for noght.
Dacian let make a weol of bras   so strong so he mighte,   *wheel*
And ssarpe swerdes thicke aboute   theron faste he pighte,   *he firmly thrust therein*
55   And let nyme this holyman   and there above him do,[1]
That the swerdes ssolde his body   rente and todrawe ato.   *rend and tear apart*
Anon so hi this holiman   aboute this weol broghte,   *as soon as they; near to*
That weol tobrak, as God it wolde,   and tobrusede it al to noghte   *shattered itself*
So that this holyman   harmles therof was.
60   Wel wroth was Dacian   so he sei this cas.
A forneis he let nyme of bras   and fulde it fol of led.   *cauldron; filled it full*
A strang fur he let makie inou,   as he nom sone his red.[2]
Tho this was al ymult   and boiled wel vaste,   *melted; vigorously*
He let nyme this holyman   and amidde caste.   *in the middle [of the cauldron]*
65   Sein Gorge nom up his hand   and the Crois bivore him made,
And in wellinde led   wel baldeliche gan wade.   *boiling lead*
Theron he sat wel softe adoun   as him nothing nere,   *as if to him it were nothing*
And lenede him to the brerde[3]   stille as he aslepe were,
And lay as he in reste were,   forte that led attelaste   *until*
70   Was al into the cold iturnd   that boillede er so vaste.
Loverd, much was Thi mighte,   as me mighte ther ise,   *great was Your power; men*
That eny man in welde led   so mighte harmles be.   *boiling hot*
Tho Dacian this isei,   his wit him was nei bynome.   *he was nearly deprived of his wits*
"Mahon," he sede, "hou geth this?   war is thi mighte bicome   *Mohammed*
75   Wanne I ne may this foule theof   overcome in none wise?   *thief*
Ich ssel bynime him sone his lif   ne ssel he nevere arise."   *deprive*
His dome he gan to give anon   that hi Sein Gorge nome   *sentence; should take*
And drou him out thoru al the toun   forte hi withoute come   *until*
And that hi smite of, withoute toun,   his heved attelaste,   *off*
80   And his body there in some voul place   to wilde bestes caste.   *foul*
Tho this dome was thus igive,   it nas noght ilete.   *given; not at all delayed*
Hi lete drawe this holy man   wel villiche thoru the strete   *most vilely*
Forte hi come withoute toun   ther hi wolde is heved of smite.

---

[1] *And gave orders to take this holy man and put him up on top [of it]*

[2] *Exactly according to the strategy he had devised, he ordered [them] to make a fire [that was] fierce enough*

[3] *And leaned against the [cauldron] lip*

Hore arme hi drowe vorth   and wette it kene to bite.[1]
85   "Leve bretheren," quath Sein Gorge,   "an stonde abideth yute.   *abide one moment yet*
Forte ich habbe to Jesu Crist   my preiere ido a lite."   *said for a little while*
His honden he huld up anhei,   adoun he sat akné.   *kneeled*
"Loverd," he sede, "Jesu Crist   that al thing mighte ise,
Grante me, yif it is Thi wille,   that wo so in faire manere   *whoever*
90   Halt wel mi day in Averil,   for mi love an eorthe here,   *holds/observes*
That ther ne valle in thulke hous   no qualm in al the yere,   *fall; pestilence/illness*
Ne gret siknesse ne honger strang   that therof ne be no fere.[2]
And wo in peril of the se   to me bit his bone,   *whoever; sea; offers his prayer*
Other in other stude perilous   help him therof sone."   *Or in another perilous place*
95   Tho hurde hy a vois of hevene   that to him sede iwis,
"Come vorth to me my blessed child.   Thi bone ihurd is."
Tho his heved was of ysmite,   as al that folk ysey,
Angels nome his holy soul   and bar up to hevene an hey,
Ther he is in grete Joye   that last withoute ende.
100   Nou God for Sein Gorges love   us lete al thuder wende.

---

[1] *They drew their weapons forth and sharpened them keenly to bite*

[2] *That there should be no fear [in that house] of great sickness or of a severe famine.*

II(a)

Notes to the Martyrdom of St. George
in the South English Legendary *(c. 1270–80)*

Abbreviations: **A** = Oxford, Bodleian Library MS Ashmole 43 (*SC* 6924), fols. 59r–60v; **C** = Cambridge, Corpus Christi College MS 145, fols. 59r–60r [base text]; **L** = Oxford, Bodleian Library MS Laud Misc. 108 (*SC* 1486), fols. 130r–131r.

2   The C scribe's *bigute* (*biȝute*, "begotten") does not rhyme with *write* ("written"), but in the original *SEL* the rhyme would be *bigite/write* (as in the earliest manuscript, L), since *write(n)* is not subject to dialectal variation in the same way as *bigite(n)*. The scribe's *u* in *bigute* is the typical Southwestern reflex of late West Saxon *i/y*, whereas the *i* form implies the poet's dialect was influenced rather by Midland speech.

13   *develes chikene*. Despite its humorous plausibility in the context, this reading, along with those in many other manuscripts (e.g., London, British Library MSS Harley 2277, *deueles cunne*; and Cotton Julius D. ix, *deuelischildren*; Oxford, Bodleian Library MSS Bodley 779 [*SC* 2567], *deuelis hynen*; and Addit. C. 38 [*SC* 30236], *feendes chikyns*), is undoubtedly a corruption. The closest Latin sources have *Omnes dii gentium daemonia*, "All the gods of the Gentiles are devils," which is a quotation from Vulgate Psalm 95:5 (Septuagint), and a common hagiographic topos. The correct *SEL* reading is preserved in A, *deuelschine*; and L, *deuelschine*, deriving from OE *deofolscin*, "demonic illusion/phantom" (DM 3.46–47).

13–14   Here *SEL* reads very close to the Sarum Breviary: "Cum videret apud impium Dacianum populos multos Christum Dominum blasphemantes et dæmones adorantes: crucis vexillo armatus, Sanctoque Spiritu repletus, in vocem hujusmodi prorupit, Omnes dii gentium dæmonia : Dominus autem cælos fecit." (Procter and Wordsworth, eds., *Breviarum ad Usum Insignis Ecclesiae Sarum*, 3.257–58) ("When [George] saw lots of people in the presence of the wicked Dacian blaspheming Christ the Lord and worshiping demons, he armed himself with the banner of the Cross and, filled with the Holy Spirit, he suddenly shouted out as follows: All the gods of the Gentiles are demons, and the Lord made the heavens"). The phrases *omnis* [sic] *dii gentium demonia* and *Dominus autem celos fecit* are here written in the margin of C (DM 1.156).

15–16　Dacian's rage in the Latin *passio* is rendered less vividly or visually than in *SEL*: *Datianus imperator vehementer exarsit, et intra semet ipsum fremere cepit*, "the emperor Datian grew hot with intense anger, and began to rage within himself" (Matzke, "Contributions," p. 530). There may be echoes here of the Vulgate version of Psalm 2:1 and 13 (Septuagint).

17　　　The French epithet, *Bel amy*, used here and at line 25, was a common expression of derision in early Middle English (compare *CT* VI[C]318, The Introduction to The Pardoner's Tale), but it is possible that the *SEL*-poet is echoing the language of one of his Latin source texts, in which Dacian appears to express regret that George's beauty (*pulchritudinem*) is to suffer such violence under torture (see Matzke, "Contributions," p. 526, where the reading *doles* is probably an error for *doleo*).

19　　　*as*. C: *ac*. DM's emendation.

27　　　*Be*. So C. DM emend to *Beo*. Similar emendations by DM are to be found at lines 37–38, 44, 71–72, 87–88, and 92.

30　　　Dacian means that George's statements against the gods amount to obscene mockery, *ribaudie* ("ribaldry") but that he is now about to become an object of gross humor himself, as a victim of public torture.

31–46　In the margin of C: *Prima tormenta* ("first torment"). In the Latin Z-text, the apparatus is an *eculeum*, or rack for stretching the limbs. The *SEL*-poet freely adapts and expands the following passage (our translation from the Z-text, ed. Matzke, "Contributions," p. 533) so as to render it even more visual and emotive:

> Dacian . . . ordered Saint George to be lifted up on a rack and his body stretched out and lacerated to bits (*membratim*) with flesh hooks (*ungulis*). Then he commanded that his (George's) flanks be torched, so that the insides of his bowels became visible. And when the martyr had endured these pains for Christ, [Dacian] ordered him taken down and thrust outside the city, and there hung up to be whipped and bloodied with all kinds of stripes, and salt was cast into the wounds made by the stripes, and the stripe-wounds were rubbed with a haircloth (*cilicio . . . fricari*).

36　　　In the margin of C: *Secunda pena* ("second torment").

38　　　*him*. C: *hi*.

47　　　In the margin of C: *Tercia pena* ("third torment").

53   In the margin of C: *iiij^a pena* ("fourth torment").

64   In the margin of C: *v^a pena* ("fifth torment").

74   Medieval vernacular writers routinely used the name of the Islamic Mohammed as a pagan god of any era. The *SEL*-poet appears to have invented this outburst of Dacian's, which has no equivalent in any of the sources, although towards the end of the *Y* version, after George has resuscitated a corpse, Dacian bursts his girdle in frustration, falls from his throne, and sadly bemoans the loss of his kingdom.

77   Here *SEL* omits another episode found in the Latin texts in which George seems to yield to Dacian's attempt to cajole him into sacrificing to the idols, but in the temple the next day George secures the destruction of idols, priests, temple, and much of the crowd.

83   In the margin of C: *vj^a pena* ("sixth torment").

II(b)

St. George and the Dragon in the
South English Legendary *(East Midland Revision, c. 1400)*

Introduction

The Dragon Episode in the St. George Legend

The crusading knights of the late eleventh century believed that St. George, with his fellow "soldier-saints," Demetrius, Maurice, and Theodore, had fought alongside them in their battles against the Saracens at places such as Antioch and Jerusalem in 1098–99. Wearing the crusaders' red cross on his white armor, George is said to have been the first to mount the scaling ladders placed against the walls of Jerusalem, promising the Christian solders they had nothing to fear if they followed him as their captain.[1]

It is generally assumed today that it was the crusaders who brought back with them to the West the knightly tale of George and the dragon. Stories of saints encountering and subduing dragons are common enough in Christian hagiography, and it has been suggested that in many of them the conquest of the dragon symbolizes the suppression of a pagan cult.[2] Evidence for this possibility in the present legend includes the emphasis on animal and human sacrifices and the wholesale conversions of the Silenians to Christianity after the dragon's public execution. The underlying story of hero, maiden, and monster, however, may well have its origins deep in the pre-Christian combat myths of Egypt and Greece: for example, in the myth of the Golden Fleece, where the magician Medea helps Jason by using drugs to subdue the dragon guarding the Fleece in its shrine at Colchis; in the myth of Horus, the Egyptian god of good and light, who battles Seth-Typhon, god of evil and darkness (represented in one fifth-century Egyptian bas-relief as a crocodile); and in the myth of Perseus, son of Zeus and destroyer of Medusa, who

---

[1] Matzke, "Contributions," pp. 147–58. See also Robertson, *The Medieval Saints' Lives*, pp. 45–46, for a translated extract from the Old French *Chanson d'Antioch;* for the ladders incident, see *LA*, trans. Ryan, 1.242.

[2] Loomis, *White Magic*, p. 65 and, for references to other dragon-saint encounters, notes 111–17. To Loomis's list might be added the stories of Martha (see below, note on line 108), and Silvester, which is vigorously summarized (from a fifth-century version of the *Actus Silvestri*) by the early English writer, Aldhelm, abbot of Malmesbury (639–709), in his *De Virginitate* (see *Aldhelm: The Prose Works*, pp. 82–83). On dragons and saints, see now Rauer, *Beowulf and the Dragon*.

saves King Cepheus' daughter Andromeda from the jaws of a sea monster to which she has been offered as a sacrifice in order to stop his ravaging of Ethiopia.[3] But when or by whom Horus/Perseus was transformed into George, or Medea "displaced" into the helpless princess, is obscure. The earliest known depiction of the medieval story is from the early eleventh century (Cappadocia in Syria), while the first known narrative version survives in an eleventh-century Georgian text.[4] The dragon episode did not appear in the West until the twelfth century[5] and was not widely known there until it was combined with the standard *Passio Georgii* in Vincent of Beauvais' *Speculum historale* and Jacobus de Voragine's *LA*, which guaranteed its popularity in the later Middle Ages as a literary and pictorial subject.[6]

The Dragon Episode in the East Midland Revision of *SEL*

We have seen earlier that the traditional George legend in *SEL* was composed before *LA* was available. What is surprising is how little impact the *LA* version, with its colorful chivalric addition, had on the later development of the *SEL* version of the George legend. Most of the numerous fourteenth-century manuscripts of *SEL* and even those of the fifteenth century, when George's secular cult was already in vogue in England, continue to recopy the original thirteen-century poem, *sans* dragon; only one manuscript (discussed below) preserves a text, itself fragmentary, of a revision influenced by the *LA* version. Other Middle English collections were less conservative, however: *LA*, with its dragon episode, is the main source (via a French intermediary) of the George legend in the Middle English prose *Gilte Legende* (c. 1438) and William Caxton's *Golden Legend* (1478), along with a verse life in the *Scottish Legendary* (c. 1400), and the prose summary in John Mirk's *Festial* (early fifteenth century).[7]

---

[3] See Cabrol and Leclercq, "Georges (Saint)" in *Dictionnaire d'archéologie chrétienne et de liturgie*, 6.1.636–37, and Hulst, *St. George of Cappadocia*, pp. 15–17 and 17–22; a concise survey, rich in references and insights, is that of Fontenrose, *Python: A Study of Delphic Myth and Its Origins*, Appendix 4, pp. 515–20.

[4] On the earliest eastern text and images (from eleventh-century Georgia), see Walter, "The Origins of the Cult of St. George," 295–326, at pp. 320–22. It has also been suggested that the dragon motif was transferred to the George legend from that of his fellow soldier-saint, Theodore Tiro (Robertson, *The Medieval Saints' Lives*, pp. 51–52).

[5] For the earliest Latin account (*BHL* 3386), see Aufhauser, *Das Drachenwunder*.

[6] E.g., the well-known representations by Albrecht Dürer, Vittore Carpaccio, and Raphaël. For a recent, copiously illustrated study of the dragon episode in art, see Didi-Huberman et al., *Saint Georges et le dragon*. For the version in *LA*, see Maggioni's edition, pp. 391–98, and Ryan's translation, 1.238–42.

[7] For convenient editions of the Mirk and Caxton versions, see Sperk, ed., *Medieval English Saints'*

Introduction to St. George and the Dragon

The fragmentary *SEL* episode of St. George and the Dragon, printed here, is found in University of Minnesota MS Z.822. N.81 (fols. 215v–216v),[8] about whose medieval provenance little is known, except that it was written in the first half of the fifteenth century in the dialect of South Yorkshire (just north of Hull). It comprises a partial copy of *NHC*,[9] a stanzaic version of the life of St. Anne, and the *SEL* legends of St. Bartholomew and St. George. Görlach argues that these two are representatives of what he calls the "East Midland Revision" of *SEL*, partially preserved in a mid-fifteenth-century manuscript (Cambridge University Library MS Additional 3039), but produced originally around 1400 by a writer who modernized the language somewhat and adapted it to the dialect of the East Midlands (chiefly corresponding to modern Leicestershire, Nottinghamshire, and Lincolnshire). He also rewrote sections of some of the *SEL* legends (especially of November/December saints), amplifying them with passages translated closely and rather stiffly from *LA*.[10] For example, he expanded the *SEL* legend of St. Andrew by inserting forty-three verses summarizing two episodes from the apostle's early adventures prior to his arrival in Achaia.[11] The longest addition of this kind, however, is the dragon episode in the legend of St. George, which has unfortunately been lost from Addit. 3039 (along with all the legends for March–April), but which is incompletely preserved in the Minnesota manuscript.

The text begins with lines corresponding to *SEL* Martyrdom of St. George 1–4, after which follows a 126-line rendering of the dragon episode closely following *LA*. The text breaks off on the last folio at the point shortly before the narrative would have rejoined the original *SEL* version at line 5.[12] In comparison with the original *SEL*-poet and the early reviser, the East

---

Legends, pp. 110–12, 118–24; for the *GiL* version, see the edition of Hamer, *Three Lives from the Gilte Legende*, pp. 65–74.

[8] Our text of the dragon episode is based on a fresh collation of the Minnesota manuscript. Previous editions are by Parker, "A Northern Fragment of *The Life of St. George*," and Görlach, *East Midland Revision*, pp. 33–35.

[9] *The Northern Homily Cycle*, ed. Nevanlinna. For more on *NHC*, see below, chapter IV.

[10] Görlach, *East Midland Revision*, pp. 38–45. See also his "Middle English Legends," in Philippart, 1994–, 1.429–85, at p. 457. As Görlach points out (*East Midland Revision*, p. 32), it is not absolutely certain that the Minnesota St. George legend is the work of the East Midland reviser of *SEL*, but the evidence is strong.

[11] *LA*, chapter II, ed. Maggioni, pp. 25–26, trans. Ryan, 1.13–14; for the expanded *SEL* legend of St. Andrew, see Görlach, *East Midland Revision*, pp. 55–62.

[12] Görlach, *East Midland Revision*, pp. 31–35, who also prints the text, supposes (p. 32n23) that no more than ten lines have been lost between the dragon episode and the remainder of George's martyrdom as printed above. Görlach assumes that the East Midland author/scribe would preserve the *SEL* legend of St. George rather than taking pains to rework it to match the *LA* account.

Midland reviser is at times an uninspired, even lazy versifier (e.g., the phrase *hayly man* is used three times in lines 1–5; see also lines 14 and 16 for the repetition of *many a man*), but occasionally he manages to respond more creatively to the story and to recapture something of the energy and emotive power of the older *SEL*-poet. An example is his rendering of the hapless king's first lament at the prospect of sacrificing his daughter to the dragon, which in the Latin of the *LA* is merely as follows: "My dearest child, what have I done to you? Or what shall I say? Am I never to see your wedding?"[13] Compare the English version:

> "Allas, my frely fode,   *noble child (lit., sustenance)*
> That a fowl dragon   sall drynke thi gentyll blode!
> What sall I do or say,   or what tyme sall I se
> That thou to kynge, or kynges son,   sulde rychly spowsed be?" (lines 49–52)

The king's alliterative formulaic epithet for his daughter, *frely fode*, defining childhood in terms of nutrition,[14] appears to provoke a complex series of punning associations, playing sadly with the double meaning of the word *fode* here, and also linking the blood sacrifice, demanded by the dragon, with the king's deep emotional stake in his own blood line, as is evident a few lines later also (64–75), when he has her dressed royally to be *sweloghede* (line 70) by the dragon, and reflects sadly on how he had expected to have brought up (*norischethe*) her children (*knyghtes*) in his palace: *I wende hafe norischethe in my hall knyghtes of thi body* (line 64). Apart from this interesting development (which is partly anticipated in the Latin source),[15] the East Midland *SEL* dragon episode sticks closely to *LA*. The Minnesota rendering is significant not for its poetics, but mainly as the earliest extant English vernacular version of what became such a popular story, and as a rare exception to the relative stability of the *SEL* textual tradition after the fourteenth century.

Language of the Minnesota Manuscript

The dragon episode differs linguistically from the C manuscript's Southwest Midland version of the Martyrdom of St. George (II[a]) in various ways, displaying features typical of the East

---

[13] *LA*, ed. Maggioni, p. 393; trans. Ryan, 1.239.

[14] *Fode*, "food," is used here in the sense "what is fed/a child." See *OED, food*, 6. The formulaic phrase *frely fode* also occurs in Barbour's *Bruce* 3.578. It is not confined to Northern usage: compare the legend of St. Kenelm, line 143: "Alas mi child, mi swete fode, þat ic habbe forþ ibroȝt" (DM, 1.284).

[15] See *LA*, ed. Maggioni, p. 393: . . . *de te filios in regali gremio nutrire credebam* ("I thought I would see sons nursing at your royal breast" — trans. Ryan, 1.239).

Midland dialect (that of the poet who revised *SEL*), and occasionally of a more Northern dialect (that of the Yorkshire scribe of the Minnesota manuscript). For example, many of the present tense verbs in the text exhibit the Midland and Northern *-es* suffix, which would eventually spread to the London area and replace the Southern ME *-eth* suffix in the third-person singular. The *-es* suffix is commonly used in the Minnesota manuscript in the second and third singular (*spekys*, line 43; *gretes*, line 77; *bydes*, line 80; *lokes*, line 85), but it also occurs twice in the plural imperative (*lettys*, line 40; *turnes*, line 119), where the Midland as well as Southern dialects would more usually have *-eth*. The present participle suffix in this text, *-ande* (as in *rennand*, line 8; *gretand*, line 63; *rydande*, line 75), was the regular form in the North and the Northeast Midlands, instead of the familiar *-inge /-ynge* of the Central Midlands and South. Among the other morphological traits of the Minnesota manuscript is the third-person singular feminine pronoun, *scho,* and the third-person plural pronouns, *thai, tham*, and *ther*. In fourteenth-century and earlier texts these would be regarded as Northern traits, but by the fifteenth century their usage had become common further south; only the forms *scho* (for "she") and *tham* (for "them") are still distinctively Midland or Northern. Note that the adverb of place, "there," is, unambiguously, *thor* in this text.

Among the characteristic Northern or North Midland phonological features of the Minnesota text is the simplification of the initial *sc/sh-* fricative (as in *suld*, "should"; *sall*, "shall"). Likewise Northern is the occasional retention of OE long *a* in situations where, further south, this long *a* had "rounded" to an open *o*: e. g., *hayly* ("holy"), *ane* ("one"), *whame* ("whom"), *wald* ("would"), *awne* ("own"), *hald* ("hold"). These last examples probably reflect the speech habits of the Minnesota scribe, not his exemplar, since they all occur within the line, while the end-rhyme pairs, which are usually the surest guide to the language of the original composition, invariably show the rounded *o* (e.g., *ston/wone*, lines 67–68) that one would expect in an East Midland composition. Another Northern orthographical trait is the practice of indicating a long vowel by means of a following *-y* or *-i*: e.g., *hayly*, *boite* ("boot," i.e., "remedy"), *doyne* ("done"), *soyne* ("soon"), *boythe* ("both").

The Minnesota text is sprinkled with words, or forms of words, that were apparently common only in the Anglian dialects of Old English (*bud*, line 24, "behooved"; *gange*, line 60, "walk"; *gretand*, line 63, "weeping"; *mekyll*, line 42, "much/great"; *tyll*, line 29, "to"; *nerhand*, line 9, "near") or that originated in the native speech of the ninth- and tenth-century Scandinavian settlers in the East Midland region (*gerte*, line 62, "caused"; *foyne*, line 35, "few"; *uggely*, line 11, "ugly"; *kavell*, line 29, "cavel/lot"; *caste*, line 29, "cast/throw").

Indexed in

IMEV 2904.

St. George

Manuscripts

University of Minnesota MS Z.822. N.81, fols. 215v–216v.

Previous editions

East Midland Revision. Ed. Gorlach. Pp. 33–35.

Parker. "A Northern Fragment of *The Life of St. George*."

II(b)

St. George and the Dragon in the
South English Legendary *(East Midland Revision, c. 1400),*
from University of Minnesota MS Z.822. N.81 fols. 215v–216v

	Saynt George the gude knyght a hayly man was he	*holy*
	Geten and borne in the lande of Capodse full fre.	*Begotten; Cappodocia*
	All fals goddes he forsoke and toke Crystyndome.	*received Christian baptism*
	He lufede wele Jhesu Cryste, and a hayly man he become.	
5	This hayly man come un a tyme intyll a contré	*came one time into*
	In the provynce of Lyby, thor was a gret cyté.	*Libya, [where] there*
	Gylena the cyté hyght, als we fynde in story.	*was called, as*
	A gret water ther was rennand faste therby,	*close*
	And in the grevys of the banke, ryght nerhand the towne	*cave (hollow); nearby*
10	Thor had wonned many a day a wonder fowle dragone.	*There; dwelled*
	He was both uggely and grete and so lothely to se,	
	Armed men, when thai hym se, away for ferd wald fle.	*fear*
	In that contré wyd abowte he dyde sorow enoghe	
	And with the wynd of hys mowth many a man he sloghe.	
15	To the walles of the cité ylke a day he wente	*each*
	And thorow the blaste of hys mowth many a man ther he schente.	*destroyed*
	The cytesyns toke ther rede when thai thus herd were stede.[1]	
	This dragon spared nother beste ne man no day to he wer fede.	*on any day until*
	Thai ordand emanges tham all ylke a day to take	*ordained amongst*
20	Two schepe to gyffe hym to hys mete, hys males forto slake.[2]	
	So lang thai fede hym with the schepe that thai began to fayle.	*be used up*
	The kynge of the cité and all the folke therof toke consayle,	
	For ther bestes and ther schepe wer nerhand owt spend,	*Because; completely spent*
	Of the folke bud tham nede unto this dragone send.	
25	Forthi thai all, at ane assent, thai ordand thoru the town[3]	

---

[1] *The citizens consulted when they thus hard were pressed*

[2] *Two sheep to give him as his food, to relieve his hunger*

[3] Lines 24–25: *It behooved them, out of necessity, to send people to the dragon. / Therefore they all gave orders, by common consent, throughout the town*

Of the childer ylke a day one   to send to this foule dragon,[1]

With a schep whyles thai myghte laste,   and therto wer thai sworne,

Ryche men childer ne pur,   that none suld be forborne,[2]

Bot ylke a day kavell to caste   and whame so it fell tyll,   *lots; to whomsoever it fell*

30   He and hys schepe sulde be sende forthe,   this dragon forto styll.

Knafe ne mayden sparde thai none,   to wham the kavell fell,[3]

Elles had thai all bene forlorne   with this dragon off hell.   *destroyed by*

So lang tyme thai usede thys   that dole yt was to se,   *they followed this [practice]; sad*

That the childer began to faile   faste in that cité.   *become scarce*

35   A day as thai kavell caste,   for ther was lefte bot foyne,   *One; only [a] few*

Apon the kyngs doghter yt fell,   and he hade bot hyr one,   *alone*

And thorw hys awne ordynance,   and all men of the towne,[4]

Hys doghter was forjugeide   to this dragone.   *forejudged (i.e., sentenced to death)*

Then made the kynge sorow enoghe;   to tham he mad hys mone: *made his lament*

40   "Lettys my doghter," he sayd, "leve,   sen I have bot hyr one.[5]

Halfe my kyngdome I sall yow gyfe   with castell and with towre

And als mekyll as yhe wyll take   of golde and of tresour."   *as much as you*

Thai answerd all with one voce: "Syr kynge, thou spekys for noght.   *in vain*

For thou sall hald the ordynance   that thiselfe has wroght,

45   And owr childer er all spende,   and thou walde now hafe thine![6]

Bot thou do als we hafe doyne,   we sall never fyne   *Unless you do; done; stop*

To we hafe byrnte thi palas   and thiselfe also."   *Until*

Than begane the kynge   to grone and grete all for wo,   *weep*

And to hys doghter he sayde,   "Allas, my frely fode,   *noble child (lit., sustenance)*

50   That a fowl dragon   sall drynke thi gentyll blode!

What sall I do or say,   or what tyme sall I se

That thou to kynge or kynges son   sulde rychly spowsed be?"

Unto the folke doylefully   with sory herte gan he pray

That he myght hafe hyr un lyfe   unto the aghtande day.   *on life (i.e., alive); eighteenth*

55   Thai graunted hym, for he was kynge,   to aghten dayes wer gon.   *until eighteen*

---

[1] *Each day one of the children to send to this foul dragon*

[2] *Neither rich men's nor poor men's children should be spared*

[3] *Neither boy-child nor maiden did they spare, to whom the lots fell*

[4] *By his own ordinance, and by all the townsmen*

[5] *"Let my daughter," he said, "live, since I have only her["]*

[6] *And our children are all destroyed, and you would now have (i.e., keep) yours*

St. George and the Dragon

The dragon to the walles com   and sloghe then many one.

When the dayes wer passede owte   the folke in full grete tene   *anger*

Come to the kynge and sayde   the folke dyed up clene,   *were dying utterly*

All in defawte of hys doghter   that he held so lange,   *in (i.e., because of) the absence of*

60 Forthi hyr bude belyfe   unto the dragon gange.   *So it behooved her at once; to go*

The kynge saghe no nodyr boite,   hys handis gon he wrynge   *no other remedy*

And on hys doghter gerte he do   rych qwenes clethynge   *he had [them] put*

And hailsed hyr full sore gretand   and sayde petusly: *embraced; weeping; pitifully*

"I wende hafe norischethe in my hall   knyghtes of thi body.[1]

65 I wende I sulde with myrth   hafe bede to thi weddynge   *bidden (i.e., invited)*

And calde to thi bridell   prince, duke, and kynge,   *bridal feast*

Thi hall to dyght with clothes of golde   and many of ryche ston   *adorn*

And all maner of mynstralsy   to her within ther wone.   *in their place*

And thou apon thi hede suld have had   full ryall crowne.   *royal*

70 Now thou gose sweloghede to be   of a fowll dragone."   *swallowed*

When he for sorow of hys herte   wordes myght speke no mo,

He blyssyd hyr and kyssed hyr ofte   and forth he lete hyr go.

To the gete thai hyr lede,   and soyne scho was pute owte,   *gate; soon*

And well toward this dragon   in herte scho had gret dowte.   *fear*

75 Als Gode walde, then it befell,   Sayn George com ther rydande   *willed*

And saw that woman that was so fayr   for ferde stode gretande.[2]

"Damsell," quod George,   "why gretes thou? tell me I the pray."

"Lefe yonge man," scho sayd,   "haste the fast away   *Dear*

Or elles thou mon belyfe   here with me be dede."   *must quickly*

80 "Tell me fyrste," quod George,   "whame thou bydes in this stede,   *whom you await*

And have no dred, thou swete thynge,   for I sall note lefe thee[3]

To wyte all thi myschefe,   yfe any helpe may be."   *To experience all your misfortune*

The folke apon the walles stod   full thyke about the town

To se how this maydyn suld be   swalughed with the dragon.   *by*

85 "Whareftyr lokes yonde folke?" quod Gorge.   "Why wonder thai one thee?"[4]

("To wytte what this bemenes   with her sall I be.")   *means*

"Certes, sir," quod scho then,   "ful wele persave I nowe   *perceive*

That thou erte a worthy mane   and herdy herte has thou.

---

[1] *I looked forward to bringing up (lit., feeding) in my palace the boy-children of your body*

[2] *And saw that woman that was so fair standing weeping out of fear*

[3] *And have no fear, sweet thing, for I shall not leave (i.e., abandon) you*

[4] *"What are yonder folk looking at?" said George. "Why do they stare at you?"*

97

Bot lefe yong man, why covetes thou   to dee her with me?   *desirest; die here*

90   Take thi hors belyfe," scho sayd,   "and faste hythen thou fle."   *quickly; hence*

He sayd, "Be hym that ys my lorde,   hythen sall I noght go

To thou hafe me told   the cause of all thi wo."   *Until*

This maydyn tolde hym then   hyr car ylke a dele.   *each part (i.e., all) of her care*

"Drede noght," quod Gorge,   "I sall thee wenge full wele   *avenge*

95   Thorw myght of Jhesu Cryste."   "Nay syr," scho sayd, "I rede

Bettyr it ys that thou fle   then we boythe be dede."   *than*

Als thei thus togyder spake,   this fowll dragon then

Begane to lyfte up hys hede   and ryse up of hys den.

The maydyn whoke for ferde   and bade that George suld fle,   *quaked; should*

100   Bot George umstrode hys hors: agayn this beste rode he,   *mounted; towards*

And hym betoke to Jhesu Cryste   and blyssyde hym wit hys hande.[1]

Agayne the dragon with herdy herte   faste he come rydande,

And a sper to hym sete   and hytte hym full ryghte,   *aimed at him*

And to the erth he bar hym down   als a hardy knyght.   *bore; like*

105   He gafe hym many a depe wonde   and refte hym all hys myght.   *deprived him [of]*

The folke that on the walles lay,   thai saghe this wonder syghte.   *wondrous*

George to that maydyn sayde,   when he had doyn this dede,

"Knyte thi gyrdyll abowte hys neke,   and luke thou have na drede." *Tie; look (be sure)*

When yt was doyn abowte hys neke   then rose this full dragon   *done (i.e., tied); foul*

110   And als a meke honde he folued hyr   furth into the towne.   *meek hound*

George and this maydyn als   into the cyté wente;   *also*

The folke saghe this dragon come: thai wend all hade bene schent[2]

And fled aboute as mad men   and sayde: "Allas this day!

We er dede ylke a man!   We may noght skape away!"

115   Sayne George apon tham cryde   and bade tham hafe no drede:

"No maner of herme he may do yow to: to fle yt ys no nede,   *harm*

For why my lorde Jhesus   send me to this towne   *because*

To delyver yow iwys   of this fowll dragone.   *indeed*

Turnes yow all therfor to Cryste   and baptisede that ye be   *and be baptized*

120   And then sall I this dragon sla,   that ye all may se."   *slay*

The kynge and all hys folke   forsoke ther maumentry   *heathenism*

And crystend wer ilkon   and trowede in Gode haly,[3]

---

[1] *And commended himself to Jesus Christ and blessed him with his hand*

[2] *The folk saw this dragon come: they thought all had been destroyed*

[3] *And each was baptized and trusted wholly in God*

98

And then George this nobyll knyght   hys gude swerde out drogh,
And ther befor all the folke   this foull dragon he sloghe.

125 Acht oxen thai knyte to hym   and drew hym oute of towne   *eight*
Fer intyll a mekyll felde   and ther thai cast hym downe.   *Far; great*
Twenti thusant men that day wer crystynde,   als we in story rede,
Withouten wemen and chylder,   thoru this haly dede.   *Not counting; holy*
The kynge garte rayse a fair kyrke   and craftyly yt dyghte[1]

130 Yn the honour of owr swete Lorde   and Sayn George the knyght.
     (ends fragmentarily)

---

[1] *The king ordered built a beautiful church and artfully decorated it*

II(b)

Explanatory Notes to St. George and the Dragon in the South English Legendary *(East Midland Revision, c. 1400)*

Abbreviations: see Textual Notes.

7 *Gylena.* The city name is apparently a scribal corruption or misunderstanding of *Silena*, in Libya, according to *LA* (trans. Ryan, 1.238), to which the poet refers here, *in story*, and at line 127. This too is suspect, however, since in the earliest Latin version and its Greek source, the city is Lasia in Cappadocia (Aufhauser, *Das Drachenwunder* 182.18–20; see also p. 208).

8 In *LA* the dragon lives in a lake which is said to be "like the sea," presumably for its size: hence the ME poet's *gret water*, but his *rennand* implies a river. Morcovcr, thc poet in the next line gives a different impression of the dragon's lair. Whereas in *LA* it appears to be in the lake (*caput de lacu leuauit*, "the dragon reared his head out of the lake" — ed. Maggioni, p. 393; trans Ryan, 1.239), in the poem the lair is said to be a "grevys," (line 9, "cave") or "den" (line 98) on the bank of the lake or river.

25 The second *thai* is redundant.

46–47 With the people's threat to burn the king and his palace, compare *LA*: *succendemus te et domum tuum*, "We will burn you alive with your whole household" (ed. Maggioni, p. 393; trans. Ryan, 1.239). This is not a feature of the oldest Latin version of the story, where the people merely insist that the princess must die as their own children have done (Aufhauser, *Das Drachenwunder* 184.9–10). The more violent language of the *LA* version may well be intended to recall, although with some complicated inversions of plot, the biblical story of Daniel, Bel, and the snake (*draco*), where the angry people make a virtually identical threat to King Cyrus if he does not hand over Daniel to be executed for killing the snake and overthrowing the cult of Bel. See the Vulgate Daniel 14 (especially 14:28, *Trade nobis Danielem, alioquin interficiemus te et domum tuam*, "Hand Daniel over to us, or we will kill you and your household").

54–55 *aghtande. LA* (ed. Maggioni, p. 393) here has *octo dierum*, "eight days" (i.e., "one week"; trans Ryan, 1.239). Medieval scribes often made mistakes copying numbers.

The poet's numerals in 54–55 (*aghtande*, "eighteenth," and *aghten*, "eighteen") are Northern/Scots forms (compare Old Norse *áttjándi* and *áttjan*, and Danish *atten*). The equivalent Southern or Midland forms are *eyghtethe(o)the* and *eyghtene*.

79   *belyfe*. MS: *be lefe*. The phrase means "quickly," "at once," but literally "by life" (see also line 90), "lively," which is neatly appropriate in the context. Whether by design or not, the poem at this point plays a homophonic game with "lefe" (lines 78, 79, 81). The poet also develops this section (lines 75–96) of the narrative by adding some direct speech (including George's rather theatrical aside, line 86), and modifying narrative details (e.g., the couplet about the spectators on the walls, lines 83–84). Compare the *LA* narrative:

> At this moment blessed George happened to be passing by and, seeing the maiden in tears, asked her why she wept. She answered: "Good youth, mount your horse quickly and flee, or you will die as I am to die." George responded: "Lady, fear not; but tell me, what are all these people waiting to see?" The damsel: "I see, good youth, that you have a great heart, but do you want to die with me? Get away speedily!" George: "I will not leave you here until you tell me the reason for this." When she had told him all, he said, "Don't be afraid, child! I am going to help you in the name of Christ!" She spoke: "Brave knight, make haste to save yourself; if not, you will die with me. It is enough that I die alone, for you cannot set me free and you would perish with me" (trans. Ryan, 1.239).

108   In the earliest Latin version, George asks the maiden to unbind her hair so that he can use the ribbon as a leash for the dragon (Aufhauser, *Das Drachenwunder* 185.25–30). The *SEL*-reviser follows the *LA* account (ed. Maggioni, p. 393; trans. Ryan, 1.239) in having George use the maiden's *cingulum* ("girdle/belt"). *LA*'s author, Jacobus de Voragine, may have altered the story to enhance the parallel with the legend of St. Martha, who subdues a dragon in the Rhône delta region and leashes it with her girdle (trans. Ryan, 2.24).

II(b)

Textual Notes to St. George and the Dragon in the South English Legendary (East Midland Revision, c. 1400)

Abbreviations: **G** = Görlach, *East Midland Revision*, pp. 33–35; **MS** = University of Minnesota MS Z.822. N.81, fols. 215v–216v; **P** = Parker, "A Northern Fragment of *The Life of St. George.*"

39   *sorow*. MS: *srow*. G's emendation.

43   *for*. MS: *fro*. G's emendation.

45   *now*. MS: *new*.

52   *rychly*. So P and G, but the MS reading appears to be *ryohly*, which could be the scribe's mistake for *ryally*, ("royally"), from ME *rial/ryal* (from an OF variant of *real, roial*), as in line 69, below.

67   *dyght*. MS: *digh*. P's emendation.

81   *I sall note*. MS: *sall note*. G's emendation.

87   *persave I nowe*. MS: *persave nowe*. G's emendation.

94   *wenge*. G reads *venge* here (where P reads *wonge*, which makes no sense). But MS appears to read *wenge*, a well attested Northern/Scots variant spelling of *venge*. In *LA*, George says merely, *Filia, noli timere quia in Christi nomine te iuuabo*, "Don't be afraid, child! I'm going to help you in the name of Christ" (ed. Maggioni, p. 393; trans. Ryan, 1.239). Perhaps the poet's more forceful treatment (substituting "avenge" for "help" and "might" for "name") echoes Luke 18:2–8, the parable of the woman who cried out for justice on her adversary (*Vindica me de adversario meo*), which Jesus turns into a prediction of God's salvation of His faithful, as an act of vengeance (*vindicare*) on the adversary. The poet may thus be hinting at the dragon story's underlying simple allegory of salvation through the triumph of good over evil.

97   *togydur spake*. P's emendation, adopted also by G. MS is defective at this point. *dragon*. MS: *dragn*.

101   *betoke*. MS: *betotoke*. G's emendation.

III

St. Jerome

Introduction

St. Jerome (feast day September 30)

Jerome (ca. 340–420) was one of the leading intellectual saints of the medieval church. Born into a Christian family in the Roman empire's Balkan provinces, in a region later overrun by the Goths, he studied grammar, rhetoric, and probably law, in Rome, where he was also baptized, before continuing his studies of Christian and pagan authors in other Western centers of learning such as Aquileia and Trier. By the 370s, after some sort of breach with his family, he left for the East, studying Greek writers in Constantinople and Antioch, still reading widely in pagan and Christian literature but also living for some years as an ascetic in the Syrian desert near Chalcis, where he also began to study Hebrew. He was ordained a priest at Antioch in 379, then returned to Rome to serve as secretary to Pope Damasus, where his work as a biblical scholar began in earnest, and where he participated in and championed the Eastern Christian lifestyle of celibacy and semi-monastism that was finding favor among some wealthy Romans, especially women, with several of whom Jerome formed spiritual friendships. His fervent support of the celibate life and his acerbic satires on corruption and decadence in Roman society won him many enemies, however, and the clerical establishment effectively expelled him from the city in 385 after the death of his patron Damasus. Jerome once more set out for the East, visiting monasteries and scholars in Egypt and Palestine in the company of two close friends and pupils: the patrician Roman widow Paula and her daughter Eustochium, a consecrated virgin. Eventually they settled in Bethlehem, where Paula's wealth founded a complex of four monasteries, three for women, and one for men; here Jerome settled down to work at his biblical translations and other writings. Paula administered and funded the whole community until her death in 404, when her responsibility passed to Eustochium.[1]

---

[1] For Jerome's own biographical eulogy of Paula, in Letter 108 (to Eustochium), see his *Epistulae*, ed. Hilberg, *CSEL* 55.306–51 (*BHL* 6548), trans. in Schaff and Wace, *A Select Library*, 6.195–212. Among the wealth of historical studies on Jerome and his circle are Kelly, *Jerome: His Life, Writings, and Controversies*; Rousseau, *Ascetics, Authority, and the Church*; Clark, *Jerome, Chrysostom, and Friends*; Rader, *Breaking Boundaries*; McNamara, "Cornelia's Daughters"; and Peter Brown, *The Body and Society*, pp. 366–86. The standard study is still that of Cavallera, *Saint Jérôme*.

St. Jerome

Like Ambrose of Milan, Augustine of Hippo, and Pope Gregory the Great, Jerome was celebrated in the Middle Ages as a "Doctor" (i.e., teacher) of the Church, one of the most prolific and influential writers of the patristic age. His translations of the voluminous exegetical writings of the Greek Origen, and his own commentaries on the scriptures, in which he concentrates (unlike his fellow "doctors") on elucidating the literal meaning of the text, would have been sufficient in themselves to secure for Jerome a place of honor in medieval Christian tradition, and every library of standing possessed a set of the commentaries of "Jeronimus," or "Hieronymus," as he appears in the medieval catalogues.[2] But he was also celebrated for having edited and translated, from Hebrew and Greek, the greater part of the Judeo-Christian Bible, producing the authoritative medieval Latin version, the so-called "Vulgate."[3] In addition, he wrote numerous works of Christian apology and anti-heretical polemic, three popular saints' lives (Hilarion, Malchus, and Paul the Hermit), and one of the great early Christian collections of letters, some of which are in themselves important theological and moral tracts (e.g., his famous Letter 22, a defense of virginity addressed to Eustochium).[4]

Unlike his contemporaries, the bishops Ambrose and Augustine, who were the subjects of saintly *vitae* by younger contemporaries, Jerome was not widely recognized as a saint in his own age or for a long time afterwards.[5] The earliest formal *Vitae Hieronimi* now known are two short anonymous works, probably composed in the ninth century, apparently independently of each other. They are usually referred to by their *incipits* or opening words, *Hieronymus noster* and *Plerosque nimirum*, although each was attributed spuriously in medieval manuscripts to respectable ancient authors.[6] While both offer some guidance as to Jerome's career as a writer,

---

[2] For example, the late-eleventh-century book-list of Peterborough Abbey (c. 1100) includes five volumes of Jerome's commentaries on the Old Testament books of Joshua and the major and minor prophets: see Lapidge, "Surviving Booklists from Anglo-Saxon England," p. 77. For a catalogue of extant manuscripts that can be assigned to specific English medieval libraries, see Ker, *Medieval Libraries of Great Britain*.

[3] See Sparks, "Jerome as Biblical Scholar," pp. 517–26.

[4] *CSEL* 54.143–211; also *PL* 22.394–425, trans. in Schaff and Wace, *A Select Library*, 6.22–41. For a bibliographical listing of Jerome's works, see Altaner and Stuiber, *Patrologie*, pp. 394–404, and Quasten et al., *Patrology*, 4.212–47.

[5] His place of burial, "bethlem castello" (in the town of Bethlehem), and the day of his death (Sept. 30) are recorded in the early medieval manuscripts of the so-called Pseudo-Jerome Martyrology, parts of which originated in the fifth century, where he is entitled simply "presbyter." But Bede adds the word "saint" in his brief notice for Jerome in his *Martyrology*. See Quentin, *Les martyrologes historiques*, p. 108; the relevant passage is translated by Felice Lifschitz in "Bede, *Martyrology*," in Head, ed., *Medieval Hagiography: An Anthology*, p. 192.

[6] *Hieronmyus noster*, printed in *PL* 22.175–84, is *BHL* 3869; it was sometimes attributed to Gennadius, fifth-century author of a continuation of Jerome's own *De viris illustribus*. There are two printed versions

quoting copiously from the biographical information which he himself provides here and there in his own writings, the two works simplify and reduce his life and travels drastically, to produce a pattern closer to conventional hagiographic models of sanctity. For example, they omit almost all traces of his long-lasting intimacy with Paula and Eustochium, mentioning them only in passing as recipients of this or that letter. Moreover, the *vitae* represent Jerome as spending only one period of his life in Rome, that of his early education in grammar and rhetoric, living like a monk there, and being widely imitated for his virtues and celibacy; after only three years, he becomes, anachronistically, a cardinal priest (in *Plerosque nimirum*) or is about to be elected pope (in *Hieronymus noster*). At this point, either the Arian heresy (in *Plerosque nimirum*) or the plotting (*insidiae*) of some gluttonous priests (in *Hieronymus noster*) causes him to leave Rome and journey to the East to begin his lifelong settled monastic existence in Bethlehem where he embarks on his great work of translating and commenting on the scriptures. Thus the two Roman periods, and likewise the two Eastern sojourns, are each telescoped into one, which avoids the possible implication that Jerome, having once left Rome for the solitude and purity of the desert, subsequently was induced by the prospect of high office in the church to return to Rome and abandon his desert life of ascetic contemplation and prayer. One of the narrative highlights of *Hieronymus noster* is a more or less verbatim rendering of Jerome's famous account of his dream of being condemned by God as a "Ciceronian" addicted to pagan learning, but the placement of the story in the narrative suggests that Jerome experienced this vision in Rome itself (rather than, as actually occurred, in Antioch during his first visit in the East).[7] The hagiographer thus creates the impression that the dream was part of the process by which Jerome was converted, at an early age once and for all from the life of this world in Rome to the life of the spirit in the East.

The greater portion of *Plerosque nimirum*, however, is taken up with the lengthy and elaborate story of Jerome's encounter with the lion. Originally derived from one of the fables of Æsop, the account in *Plerosque nimirum* is appropriated mainly, perhaps through oral tradition in Rome itself, from an earlier Greek life of an Eastern saint, Gerasimus. Its inclusion in the *vita* is apparently a rather desperate attempt to provide the putative saint with a memorable miracle. But, as Eugene F. Rice suggests, the story might have been read as an elaborate and

---

of *Plerosque nimirum* (Pseudo-Sebastian, because sometimes attributed to one Sebastian of Monte Cassino): the original (*BHL* 3871) is edited by Bonino Mombrizio, *Sanctuarium*, 2.31–36; the other version, in *PL* 22.201–14 (*BHL* 3870), is a clumsy attempt to combine *Hieronymus noster* and *Plerosque nimirum*. A valuable recent account of the medieval hagiography concerning Jerome, to which I am much indebted, is that of Rice, *Saint Jerome in the Renaissance*, pp. 23–48.

[7] *PL* 22:177–78. On the Antioch dream, see Rice, *Saint Jerome in the Renaissance*, p. 3. For the ME version, see the edition below, lines 94–113.

charming allegory of the saint's success in subduing the "beast within."[8] It also depicts Jerome as the benign, tranquil, forgiving, and hospitable father of a traditional all-male monastic community, effectively contradicting the portrait imprinted in Jerome's letters and polemical writings of a prickly, irascible, and vituperative *homme aux femmes*.[9]

This reductive idealized portrait of Jerome was adopted and regularized by important late medieval authors of such standard encyclopedic works as the *Speculum historiale*, by Vincent of Beauvais, and the *Legenda aurea* (*LA*), by Jacobus de Voragine. For example, *LA* synthesizes and abridges the verbose and repetitive early *vitae*, further simplifying and remodeling the saint's story in the hagiographic mold (so that the lion episode now constitutes almost half the whole), while adding a few more details to the construction of Jerome's image as a saint. The most striking of these anecdotes (of twelfth-century origin) explains that the plot (*insidiae*) by which the hostile Roman clergy contrive to have Jerome expelled from the city consists of someone planting a woman's robe next to his bed, so that when Jerome awakens in the middle of the night to attend the service of matins, he absentmindedly puts on the female garment and is thus accused of having had a woman in his bed.[10] The story discreetly acknowledges, while simultaneously discrediting as a malicious slander, Jerome's complex rapport with women, whom desert saints traditionally were supposed to avoid like the plague.

The final phase in the development of Jerome's Latin hagiography occurred in the early fourteenth century, when the dearth of miracles in the available accounts of his life was remedied by an unknown author who produced a collection of forged letters, the first and lengthiest portion of which purports to be a series of accounts of Jerome's life and posthumous miracles by his disciple, Eusebius of Cremona; the other two portions, which appear either together with the Pseudo-Eusebian set or separate from it, are similarly contrived correspondences between bishops Augustine of Hippo and Cyril of Jerusalem, relating the miracles and visions that followed Jerome's death, including many examples of his posthumous powers of intercession. These audaciously fictitious letters were highly successful, to judge by the hundreds of Latin

---

[8] Rice, *Saint Jerome in the Renaissance*, pp. 39–45, gives a detailed account of the sources and possible meanings of the lion story.

[9] In the so-called *Lausiac History* (36, vi–vii) by Palladius, one of the famous fifth-century collections of lives and sayings of the desert fathers, there is a brief but devastating portrait of Jerome:

A priest, Jerome, dwelt in the same place [Bethlehem]; he was a man of good birth and well gifted in Latin letters, but he had such a disposition that it eclipsed his learning. Posidonius [a hermit of Bethlehem] had lived with him a goodly number of days and he whispered into my ear: "The fine Paula who takes care of him is going to die and escape his meanness, I believe. And because of him no holy man will live in these parts. His anger would drive out even his own brother."

Palladius, *Palladius: The Lausiac History*, trans. Meyer, pp. 104–05.

[10] *LA* pp. 653–58; trans. Ryan, 2.211–16.

manuscript copies and the large number of vernacular versions. As Rice explains, the purpose of the forged letters, in which, for example, Jerome's "ranking" in the saintly hierarchy is raised to parity with John the Baptist,[11] and in which Saint Augustine is presented as Jerome's inferior, was initially to promote the cult of Jerome's relics at the end of the thirteenth century in Rome at the church of Santa Maria Maggiore, where the crib of Jesus' nativity was already said to be preserved. The clergy of Santa Maria claimed that Jerome's bones, at the saint's request, had been brought secretly to Rome from Bethlehem around the time when the Mamluk Saracen armies were completing their conquest of Palestine.[12]

Like many other collections of miracle stories, these give voice to various larger themes that were of contemporary concern. George Keiser has drawn attention, for example, to the collection's emphasis, particularly in the Pseudo-Cyril letters, on the doctrine of Purgatory and the Greek church's opposition to it, pointing out the difficulties this disagreement had caused in the papal negotiations with the Greeks (in the second half of the thirteenth century), aimed at reunifying the two churches.[13] The doctrine of Purgatory was also an important instrument of clerical control over the laity in the later Middle Ages, fostering and justifying the expansion of the sacrament of confession, and such intercessory practices as masses and prayers for the dead and papal indulgences. The miracles of Jerome are in some respects typical of the prodigious body of narrative literature, including collections of sermon exempla, produced during the thirteenth and fourteenth centuries, in which the doctrine of Purgatory and its attendant fears are dramatized for the benefit of an impressionable public.[14]

Not only did Jerome's Roman cult prosper during the fourteenth century, but it spread across Europe as the saint was adopted as special patron by remarkably varied groups of devout lay people and clerics, such as the prosperous Bologna law professor, Giovanni D'Andrea (died 1348), or the several religious orders known collectively today as the Hieronymites. Some of these groups were attracted by the way the hagiographic narratives depicted Jerome's austere, penitential mode of life, and some, paradoxically, by his rejection of abstruse higher learning. For while Jerome is acknowledged in his *vitae* as a learned master of languages, his dream-

---

[11] See below, ch. 5 of Winter's ME translation (lines 251–327). The most accessible printed edition of the forged letters (*BHL* 3866–68) is *PL* 22.239–326. For more recent editions and further references, see Henryk Fros' supplement to *BHL*, *Novum Supplementum*, pp. 421–22 (numbers 3866–68).

[12] The end of the Latin Kingdom of Jerusalem is usually dated 1291, when the Mamluks captured Acre. Jerome's cult in Rome and the forged letter collection are discussed by Rice, *Saint Jerome in the Renaissance*, pp. 49–63.

[13] Keiser, "St Jerome and the Brigittines."

[14] Le Goff, *The Birth of Purgatory*, pp. 289–333. On sermon exempla, see most recently Scanlon, *Narrative, Authority, and Power*, and Bremond, Le Goff and Schmitt, *L'"Exemplum."* For a late ME collection of exempla, see Arnoldus of Liége, *An Alphabet of Tales*, ed. Banks.

inspired conversion from the love of pagan, secular literature and philosophy appealed to those who were influenced by the teachings of the more radical Franciscans and hostile to the reviving classicism of the *quattrocento*, as well as to the learned tradition of scholastic theology.[15] Criticism of the latter is implied in one of the Pseudo-Augustine letters, where Jerome chides Augustine for indulging in the kind of speculative metaphysics that characterized the theology of the so-called Schoolmen in the late medieval universities.[16]

While the penitential themes of Jerome's life and writings, as Eugene Rice has shown, helped enhance his prestige and importance among devout readers in the later Middle Ages, it seems likely that his popularity was also fostered in some circles by those aspects of his history that are all but suppressed in the medieval *vitae*, namely his spiritual friendships and intellectual rapport with religious laywomen. Learned clergy, who had access to Jerome's letters and the prologues to his other works, evidently made known to their own female acquaintances more of the facts of Jerome's life than the *vitae* themselves allowed. For example, Jerome is given special attention in the *Revelationes* or visions of St. Bridget (Birgitta) of Sweden (c. 1302–73), where he is praised in two separate contexts as a "lover of widows," *amator uiduarum*.[17] Bridget did learn some Latin after she began to live in Italy later in her life, but it is more likely that her knowledge of Jerome was imbibed from one or other of the learned male counsellors who produced and edited the Latin text of her *Revelations*: particularly Alfonso de Vadaterra (died 1388), a former Andalusian bishop who was associated with a Hieronymite community in Italy and who was Bridget's closest clerical confidant during most of her years in Italy and her literary executor after her death.[18]

The two passages in Bridget's *Revelationes* where the epithet *amator uiduarum* occurs form the nineteenth and concluding chapter of an early-fifteenth-century ME version of Jerome's life and miracles, translated from Latin for a twice-widowed English noblewoman by the Bridgettine monk who was her confessor and spiritual counselor. In some privileged late medieval circles, where religious men and women were mingling with a measure of freedom for devotional and instructional purposes, the relationships of early saints such as Jerome and the widow Paula perhaps provided an inspirational model for later similar pairings, and one that implicitly endorsed not only the education of women but also the act of translating sacred texts into the vernacular.

---

[15] See Rice, *Saint Jerome in the Renaissance*, pp. 73–75, who points to the popularity of the Ciceronian dream as a subject of paintings commissioned by the Hieronymites.

[16] See below, ch. 3 of Simon Winter's *Life of St. Jerome*, lines 147–250.

[17] Bridget, *Revelaciones*, ed. Birger Bergh et al., 4.119 (*Revelationes* 4.20); 6.204–05 (*Revelationes* 6.60).

[18] *The Bridgettine Breviary of Syon Abbey*, ed. Collins, pp. xvii–xviii; Colledge, "*Epistola Solitarii ad Reges*."

Simon Winter's *Life of St. Jerome*

Unlike most of the ME vernacular saints' legends composed in the fourteenth century, which remain anonymous and whose audiences are still uncertain, a considerable number of the fifteenth-century legends are firmly attributed to authors who are now well known, such as John Lydgate, Osbert Bokenham, and John Capgrave,[19] and who wrote for a growing audience of clerics and lay patrons, many of whom were women.[20] Another male author with a devout female audience was Simon Winter, whose ME prose life of Saint Jerome is the subject of this chapter. Winter was one of the first generation of monks of the Bridgettine abbey of Syon on the north bank of the River Thames a few miles west of London. The last of the great medieval English monasteries, Syon was initially founded in 1415 by Henry V as a penitential act of atonement for his father Henry IV's responsibility for the deaths of the deposed king, Richard II (1400), and Archbishop Scrope of York (1405).[21] Shortly beforehand, for similar reasons, he had founded the Carthusian monastery (or "Charterhouse") of Bethlehem of Sheen, on the south bank of the Thames, almost opposite the later site of Syon.

Monasteries founded under the auspices of St. Bridget of Sweden (c. 1302–73)[22] were mixed communities of nuns and monks living in separate quarters but under the direction of one abbess. In addition to the traditional monastic practices of continuous liturgical observance, private prayer and meditation, and chaste living, the Bridgettines also placed unusual emphasis on reading and study. As a result, and doubtless because of its large royal endowment of funds, Syon, along with the Sheen Charterhouse, was to become an important center of book collection, production, and dissemination, and the Syon library was destined to be one of the largest English medieval library collections, the catalogue of which still survives, along with not a few of its books.[23] Unfortunately the medieval catalogue records only the contents of the monks' library, not that of their female counterparts.

Winter and his fellow monks would thus have served as priests, confessors, spiritual advisors, and probably teachers to the nuns who formed the majority of the community's members,

---

[19] See below, Introduction to Chapter VI (St. Austin), pp. 236–37 and note 25, on Lydgate's verse saints' lives and for recent bibliography on Capgrave and Bokenham.

[20] Felicity Riddy points out that "the literary culture of nuns in the late fourteenth and fifteenth centuries and that of devout gentlewomen not only overlapped but were more or less indistinguishable" ("Women Talking about the Things of God," p. 110). Among other surveys of the subject, mainly focusing on female audiences, see Carey, "Devout Literate Laypeople"; Hutchison, "Devout Reading"; Meale, "Laywomen and Their Books."

[21] See Jacob, *The Fifteenth Century 1399–1485*, pp. 1–29.

[22] On Bridget, see below, the explanatory note to line 328.

[23] Bateson, *Catalogue of the Library of Syon Monastery*; De Hamel, *Syon Abbey*.

although most of this relationship was conducted through elaborate partitions contrived to prevent actual physical contact.[24] Among the books Winter himself is known to have contributed to the Syon library are some volumes of Latin sermons that he presumably compiled for his own and his colleagues' use at Sunday services. According to the Syon catalogue, he also appears to have composed commentaries on certain well-known antiphons of the Virgin Mary.[25] It has also been suggested recently that he may have been the author of an important Syon book, *The Myroure of Oure Ladye*, which translates and explains the nuns' Latin liturgical Hours, and their festival Masses and Offices, while also discussing the role of reading and study as the necessary accompaniment of their liturgical celebrations.[26]

In general the Syon congregation's male members were permitted greater freedom of movement, and contact with a larger world, than the strictly enclosed nuns. As a foundation of the king, for example, the abbey was of special interest to the royal family, and, particularly in its early days, to the widowed Margaret, duchess of Clarence. Her second husband, Thomas, duke of Clarence, brother of King Henry V, was killed in the French wars in 1421 (her first husband, John Beaufort, by whom she had six children before he died in 1410, was half-brother to Henry IV and brother to the powerful bishop of Winchester, Henry Beaufort). In the years following Thomas' death, with her two eldest sons living as prisoners of war in France, her daughters growing up, and herself getting on in years, Margaret appears to have taken up residence near Syon Abbey and to have adopted a quasi-religious way of life, obtaining papal permission to receive visits from the brothers of Syon so that they could celebrate Mass in her household, hear her confession, and preach sermons for her benefit. She herself funded some important gifts to the Syon monks' library, including the production of a deluxe manuscript of saints' lives (now in Germany) illuminated by Hermann Schere, one of the leading artists of the day, and the purchase of an older bible.[27] For reasons still unknown, Simon Winter was the Syon priest selected to be the community's liaison with the duchess, serving her spiritual and sacramental needs as counselor, celebrant, confessor, and, evidently, providing her with devotional reading. Winter became ill around 1428 or 1429, when Margaret, praising his zeal as a monk and his spiritual service to her, petitioned the pope for him to be allowed to transfer to a monastery with a less demanding regime, but whether he ever did so or whether their relationship continued, is still

---

[24] On the relevant portions of the *Rule of Saint Savior*, the Bridgettines' code of conduct, see Ellis, *Viderunt eam filie Syon*, pp. 23–24, 32–36.

[25] Bateson, *Catalogue*, pp. 84, 156, 173, 180, 181. See also *Bridgettine Breviary*, ed. Collins, p. xl.

[26] Hutchison, "Devout Reading," p. 220. Collins (*Bridgettine Breviary*, pp. lxxxix–xl) inclines to Thomas Fishbourne, Confessor-General of Syon in the 1420s, rather than Winter. For the text of the *Myroure*, see Blunt, ed., *The Myroure of Oure Ladye*.

[27] De Hamel, *Syon Abbey*, pp. 59–60.

not known. He died in 1448, eight years after the duchess herself.[28] The life of Jerome must have been written at some point between 1422, when the duchess began her relationship with the abbey, and her death in 1439/40.

In his interesting dedicatory Prologue, Winter explains how the duchess, and others who he hopes will obtain copies of the life of Jerome, are to use it to their "goostly profyte" (lines 8–9).[29] What is surprising in this detailed guide to reading the work is Winter's lack of attention to the sanctity of Jerome himself. The whole work is presented as a kind of textbook of lessons for God's "scolers" in the "scole" of earthly existence where they must "use the sharp dysciplyne of this scole" (line 24) and "studye" (line 36) and "lerne . . . to lyve and to dye" (line 21). Thus he says that in the first two chapters, which focus on Jerome's life and death, "we may lerne and take ensample to lyve a Cristemannys lyfe in penaunce and straytnes" (lines 13–14),[30] then in two later chapters he says there are examples of holy dying; but if this "holsum lesson" (line 25) seems burdensome, then in three other chapters (recounting Augustine's accounts of how Jerome posthumously described his life in Heaven),[31] the reader may "see there the greet reward that is gove to them that fervently labour aboute this scole" (lines 26–27). The metaphor of the Christian life as a school in which we study the way to salvation had been a part of monastic tradition since the introduction of St. Benedict's rule, where it permeates the last paragraph of the well-known prologue.[32] It appears to have received special elaboration, however, among the Bridgettines, whose regime, as mentioned earlier, more than those of most female religious orders, encouraged reading and study. The author of the *Myroure of Oure*

---

[28] For the most detailed account of Winter and Margaret, and the importance of the Yale manuscript, see Keiser, "Patronage and Piety," 32–53, especially p. 38. See also Hutchison, "Devout Reading," p. 226. Winter's authorship of the life of Jerome was first suggested in an unpublished work by Ian Doyle, according to Görlach, *South English Legendary*, p. 20n8.

[29] Ian Doyle, discussing ways in which members of religious orders sought to publish their works, sees in Winter's dedication of the prose *Jerome* to Margaret, encouraging her to permit its circulation and recopying, the clearest example of how the process of "publication through dedication" worked. But Doyle remarks that the small number, and monastic milieu, of the surviving copies indicate in this case that Winter's work failed to gain an audience outside religious circles, since even the printed edition by de Worde was probably produced for Syon Abbey itself. See "Publication by Members of the Religious Orders," pp. 116–17.

[30] Chapter 1 is printed below (lines 93–166); Winter's chapter 2, not included here, is adapted from the first of the forged letters of St. Augustine to Cyril of Jerusalem. See the edition by Hamer and Russell, *Supplementary Lives*, pp. 326–28.

[31] Chapters 3 and 5 are printed below (lines 167–327).

[32] "Therefore we must establish a school of the Lord's service . . ."; see Benedict, *The Rule of St Benedict*, trans. McCann, p. 4.

Ladye gives the nuns detailed advice on the practice of reading itself, in a manner that parallels Winter's prologue to the Duchess Margaret, pointing out that certain kinds of reading can "sturre vp. [the] affeccyons to comforte and to hope" in those who may be feeling despondent, while other reading matter arouses love and desire for Heaven or fear of Hell and damnation. In the same work, he refers metaphorically to prayer and the observance of the liturgy as a form of "gostly study," urging the sisters to "inwardly and bysely, & contynewally trauayle in this spyrytuall study."[33]

This Bridgettine emphasis on the religious life as a process of reading and study, learning and contemplation, as well as of prayer and liturgical observance, provides further justification for their attraction to Jerome's cult and life story, a great part of which itself is defined in terms of continual learning and involvement with books.[34] His first and crucial life crisis in the *Legenda aurea* account is the choice between profane and spiritual kinds of reading and study; his second crisis is the frank admission of the struggle against lustful thoughts while coping with the rigors of the ascetic life, a struggle with which many nuns, monks, and celibate layfolk could identify only too well; his later career is expressed mainly in terms of his liturgical compositions and compilations of scriptural readings, and the great linguistic labor of his translation of "holy wryt" and the *Vitas patrum*. Winter includes all this in his first chapter's adaptation of the *Legenda aurea* life, but he simplifies the narrative in various ways by omitting Jacobus' elaborate etymological exegesis of Jerome's name, along with most geographical names, learned allusions, one impish aside in which Jacobus suggests that Jerome may not have been a virgin after all, and another longer passage that makes clear how many enemies Jerome had.

Winter's most striking omission, however, which changes the character of the *vita* considerably, is the lion episode itself, which Winter does not even summarize.[35] In the Yale manuscript (see below), a version of the lion episode has been added after Winter's chapter 19 (the visions of St. Bridget), to form a twentieth chapter. That this additional chapter was not part of Winter's original composition is evident from the surviving copies of his prologue and table of contents, in which the whole work is clearly said to comprise nineteen chapters, none

---

[33] Hutchison, "Devout Reading," pp. 221–22.

[34] The liturgical feast day of Jerome (September 30), while not among the principal feasts at Syon, was celebrated with special reverence, with nine lessons and the grade of "Inferius duplex." See the fifteenth-century calendar in *Bridgettine Breviary*, ed. Collins, p. 11. There is no provision for a proper Office for Jerome in the *Breviary* itself, which reflects the Syon nuns' own liturgical "use." The Syon *Myroure of Oure Ladye* makes it clear that the monks' services, which they sang separately from the nuns, at different times of the day and night, were "after the common vse of the chyrche" (ed. Blunt, p. 24). According to Collins (*Bridgettine Breviary*, p. xv), the monks' office for Jerome would be similar to that in the Sarum Breviary.

[35] The other surviving ME prose life of Jerome, that in *GiL*, does include a version of the lion episode.

of which refers to the lion. Moreover, although the Yale manuscript's text of Winter's *Life of Saint Jerome* clearly derives from a good manuscript family, it has been much interpolated and revised. If the lion story were part of the original Winter text, it would be logical to expect it to have survived as part of chapter 1 of the *Life*, as in the Latin *vita* by Pseudo-Sebastian, and not appended awkwardly to the posthumous miracle collection. It makes more sense to assume that the reason why all but one of the surviving copies lack the lion story is that it was excluded by Winter himself from the outset. And with good reason, since it is quite alien to the portrait of the saint that Winter created. One of the effects of the animal tale, as we observed earlier, is to provide a more balanced portrait of Jerome as a kind old sage in communion with nature, the saintly abbot of a rural monastery, coping with an assortment of mundane problems, including wounded or stolen animals, monks distraught over the daily wood supply, crafty merchants, and the need for oil. But in Winter's version of the *Vita Hieronimi*, perhaps reflecting the idealism of Syon in its early years, nothing is allowed to contradict the image of Jerome as the archetypal scholar and teacher in the "scole" of the penitential life, committed to unrelenting study, asceticism, writing, and prayer:

> And in all these chapitrys, we may see the greet worthynesse and holynesse of hym that was bothe a disciple and a mayster in this scoole, Saynt Jerom, hou holy and strayte he was in lyvynge, and hou myghty and mervaylous aftir his deth, and hou profitable hit is to do aftir hym, to trust hym, and to do hym servyse. (lines 46–50)

Text and Manuscripts

For reasons of space, the following edition of Simon Winter's ME prose *Life of Saint Jerome* includes only the prologue and list of contents, the Life proper (chapter 1), and three chapters (3, 5, 19) from the bulky posthumous miracle collection; to these is added an anonymous ME prose version of the lion episode, which survives in only one of the five extant medieval copies of Winter's work.[36]

---

[36] Winter's *Life of Saint Jerome* was the first of the chapters in this volume to be completed, some years ago. In the interim, two other editions of the text have appeared: that by Hamer and Russell, based on MS Lambeth 72 (see below) as part of their important volume, *Supplementary Lives*, pp. 321–65, 511–13, and containing the life and all eighteen miracles plus the lion episode (from the Yale manuscript), but omitting the prologue and list of chapters; and that by Waters, "Symon Wynter, *The Life of St. Jerome*," pp. 141–63 (translation), 232–49 (edition). Waters' edition is based, like the present one, on the St. John's manuscript; she does not include either the list of chapters or the lion story, but offers a somewhat different and larger selection of miracles, viz., Winter's chapters 2, 5, 6, 8, 9, 14, 16, and 19, abridged in places by omission of selected passages.

Our text of Winter's *Life of Saint Jerome* is based on the earliest manuscript copy, now at St. John's College, Cambridge. Reference is made in the notes to variant readings in the three other manuscript copies and an early printed edition. Following are brief descriptions of the five extant copies.[37]

St John's: Cambridge, St. John's College MS N.17 (250).[38] The manuscript is finely written in an Anglicana book hand of the second quarter of the fifteenth century, and thus probably not much later than the composition of the work (between 1422, when Duchess Margaret, for whom the work was written, began living near Syon Abbey, and her death in 1439/40). It was formerly part of a larger hagiographic collection, which Keiser thinks may have been prepared by a Carthusian scribe from the Charterhouse of Sheen near Syon, at Duchess Margaret's request, for some other member of the royal family.[39] The collection probably existed as one volume as late as the late eighteenth century when the record of sales begins. Other surviving portions of the manuscript, rebound in its now separate parts in the early nineteenth century, are: Cambridge, St. John's College MS N.16 (249), containing prose lives of St. John the Evangelist and John the Baptist (who figures prominently in the miracles of Jerome); Cambridge, Massachusetts, Harvard University MS Richardson 44, containing a prose life of Saint Catherine of Alexandria (which like that of Jerome stresses desert asceticism and the rejection of secular philosophy);[40] San Marino, Huntington Library MS HM 115, containing John Lydgate's *Life of Our Lady*.[41]

Horstmann: London, Lambeth Palace Library MS 432, fols. 1–17.[42] Our variants from this manuscript refer to the edition by Carl Horstmann, to whom the St. John's manuscript (and the other copies) were apparently unknown when he edited the work from Lambeth 432 (third

---

[37] See also Hamer and Russell, *Supplementary Lives,* pp. xxii–xxv.

[38] Described by James, *Descriptive Catalogue of the Manuscripts in the Library of St. John's College, Cambridge*, pp. 285–86.

[39] Keiser, "Patronage and Piety," p. 42.

[40] Gibbs, ed., *The Life and Martyrdom of Saint Katherine of Alexandria*; see the manuscript description in Voigts, "A Handlist of Middle English in Harvard Manuscripts," pp. 64–66. For a modern translation, and a partial transcription of the Harvard text, see Winstead, *Chaste Passions*, pp. 114–63, 184–201.

[41] The manuscript is described in Dutschke et al., *Guide to Medieval and Renaissance Manuscripts in the Huntington Library*, 1.152–53.

[42] The manuscript (a devotional miscellany, which includes a contemplative treatise, *The Abbey of the Holy Ghost*, and a ME prose legend of St. Dorothy found, like Winter's *Saint Jerome*, elsewhere in *Gilte Legende* manuscripts) is described in James and Jenkins, *Descriptive Catalogue of the Manuscripts in the Library of Lambeth Palace: The Medieval Manuscripts*, pp. 599–601. See also Hamer and Russell, *Supplementary Lives*, p. xxv.

quarter of the fifteenth century), described by Görlach as "the most garbled text."[43] Among other shortcomings, it lacks the dedication to Margaret of Clarence and, through scribal omission of a 15-word passage from the prologue, mangles the author's important advice regarding the use and recopying of the text. In addition to numerous other scribal errors and omissions reflected in Horstmann's edition, Lambeth 432 also coyly substitutes "wisdommys" for "widows" in the final chapter's distinctive epithet for Saint Jerome, "lover of widows."[44] A few, but not all, of the other shortcomings of Lambeth 432 are signaled in the notes, with reference to Horstmann's edition. Although still valuable until recently as the only modern edition of the whole work, it is now superseded by that of Richard Hamer and Vida Russell.[45]

Lambeth 72: London, Lambeth Palace Library MS 72, fols. 188v–202r. This copy is included in a recension of the important fifteenth-century English prose legendary, *GiL*,[46] where Winter's *Life of Saint Jerome* replaces the more usual and shorter *GiL* life (a fairly faithful rendering of that in Jean de Vignay's French rendering of *LA*). The Lambeth text of Winter's *Life of Saint Jerome* has been somewhat adapted for inclusion in the legendary, in that it lacks the dedication, prologue, list of chapters, and chapter headings. Otherwise it is very similar to the St. John's text. We have not collated Lambeth thoroughly with the other texts (only two or three of the more distinctive variants from chapter 1 are listed separately in our notes) and readers are referred to the edition by Hamer and Russell, which is based on Lambeth 72 and provides a fuller textual apparatus than the present edition.

Yale: New Haven, Yale University Library MS Beinecke 317, fols. 5r–21v.[47] Keiser believes that this recension, copied near the end of the fifteenth century in a cramped secretary hand, is from Syon Abbey itself.[48] It is valuable for preserving not only the full dedication and prologue but also for identifying Winter as the author (fol. 5r). In other respects, however, the Yale copy is less representative of the work's original form. The scribe, or an earlier reviser, has reworked the text in various places, by adding the lengthy lion episode and other *LA* passages and details omitted by Winter, along with additional reasons (from one of the older *vitae*) as to why Jerome

---

[43] Görlach, *South English Legendary,* p. 20n7. For Horstmann's edition, see his "Prosalegenden," pp. 328–60.

[44] See our edition, lines 10–11 and 343, 346. Compare Horstmann, "Prosalegenden," p. 329, line 4, and p. 359, lines 33 and 38.

[45] See above, note 36.

[46] In addition to Hamer and Russell's description in *Supplementary Lives*, p. xxii, see also Hamer, ed., *Three Lives from the Gilte Legende*, pp. 32–33. See also Görlach, *South English Legendary*, pp. 19–21. The complete *GiL* is being edited by Hamer and Russell for EETS. One possible provenance of *GiL* is St. Albans Abbey, which had close links with Syon Abbey in the later Middle Ages.

[47] See the description by Barbara Shailor, *Catalogue*, 2.120–23.

[48] Keiser, "Patronage and Piety," pp. 43–44.

had to leave Rome; this recension also suppresses part of the saint's revealing account of his sexual fantasies in the desert.[49] It is possible that the lion episode was added to the text during the same stage of expansion and editing. It remains uncertain if the manuscript itself represents a unique text, whose scribe may be the interpolator, or if it is the sole survivor of a more complex textual tradition.

Wynkyn de Worde: [The Lyf of Seint Ierom] [London: Wynkyn de Worde, c. 1499/1500]. The British Library copy (catalogue number IA 55267[50]) seems to be the only extant copy. Although carrying a small printer's device of William Caxton on the last page (fol. D[5]v), the book is known to be an imprint of de Worde's, who continued to use his master's devices for some years after the latter's death, and even his own later devices incorporate Caxton's initials.[51] There is no title page, dedication, or prologue. The table of chapters begins abruptly at the top of the first folio. A small quaint woodcut appears on the second folio, depicting Jerome in his characteristic cardinal's hat, seated in a large chair with a book on his lap and the lion at his feet, one of whose paws he holds carefully in his right hand. The volume comprises twenty-nine unpaginated leaves, with three quires (numbered ABC) of eight folios each (signed on the first four leaves of each quire), and a fourth quire (D) in five (signed on i–iii).

Language

Winter's diction is neither rhetorically ornate nor prosaically simple. He writes a fluent, lucid, and rhythmic prose, alternating quite lengthy complex sentences with short direct statements linked by simple coordinates, such as *and* and *but*, with a tendency to use repetition artfully and melodically.[52] This mixed style is also characteristic of much medieval Latin prose of the time

---

[49] Similarly, the copy of the *Lay Folks' Catechism* in the same manuscript is designated "a significantly reworked text." A. Hudson, qtd. in Shailor, *Catalogue*, p. 121.

[50] The book is numbered 14508 in Pollard and Redgrave, *Short-Title Catalogue*.

[51] De Worde used the same small Caxton device in four other books he produced in the 1490s after taking over Caxton's business. See McKerrow, *Printers' and Publishers' Devices in England and Scotland, 1485–1640*, pp. 2–3 and figure 2. On de Worde's links to Syon Abbey, see Keiser, "Patronage and Piety," pp. 43–45, who surmises that printing the book may have been de Worde's way of developing relations with Lady Margaret Beaufort, granddaughter of the Margaret of Clarence for whom the book was originally written. See also Blake, "Wynkyn de Worde," pp. 132–34.

[52] For Winter's use of repetition, see, e.g., lines 13–23 of the Prologue, and lines 175–84 of chapter 3. For examples from another Bridgettine work, see the passage quoted by Ann Hutchison from *The Myroure of Oure Ladye,* p. 64. See above, note 26.

(e.g., Jacobus de Voragine's Life of Jerome). Given Winter's generally lucid style, we have not found it necessary to gloss very many whole sentences or phrases.

Nor is Winter's vocabulary as a whole much of an obstacle to comprehension. A glance through our glosses reveals that he uses few words that are obsolete today. These include *mowe* (line 9, "be able"), *wene* (line 123, "think/expect"), *woot* (line 17, "knows"), *leffull* (line 256, "allowed, lawful"), *kon* (line 18, "know how to"), *or* (line 33, "before"), *clepe* (line 268, "call"), *behote* (line 33, "promise"), *evenyng* (line 314, "equating"), and *heyghneth* (line 269, "raises"). Most of the slight difficulties of the work's language arise from the Middlesex scribe's spelling and pronunciation (e.g., *latte* for *let* in line 11, *dew* for *due* in line 293, *lyche* for *like* in line 60, *hit* for *it* in line 8, *yyf* for *if* in line 24, *gove* for *given* in line 26, and the frequent spelling of the preterite and participial suffix as *-yd* instead of *-ed*, and of noun plurals as *-ys* instead of *-es*). A potentially confusing feature is the consistent dropping of final *-n* in the past participle of verbs, even where it is retained today (e.g., *be* for *been*, *do* for *done*, *drawe* for *drawn*, *knowe* for *known*). This parallels the equally consistent absence of the final *-n* commonly found in the infinitive and present plural of verbs in Midland English. As is typical of Midland English in the fifteenth century, Winter's personal pronouns are virtually the same as in modern English, even in the plural, except for an occasional appearance (lines 39 and 69) of the native English *hem* instead of the Scandinavian import *them* (*hem*, of course, survives unaspirated in colloquial English: e.g., *Give 'em a break*). The characteristic plural possessive of Chaucer's English, *hire/hir/her/here* is almost completely replaced in Winter's usage by *theyr(e)*.[53]

The language of the lion story in the Yale manuscript (here III[b]), although copied half a century or more later, is very similar to that of St. John's. Stylistically, however, the translator is less sophisticated than Winter, and more closely dependent on his Latin source, but for the most part his translation is fluent and idiomatic, only occasionally marred by stiffly Latinate phrasing, as in *enjoyned . . . this offyce* (lines 12–13) and *entendyd of herte to hospytalyté* (64–65).[54]

Indexed in

---

[53] For a group of texts, known to have been copied in either London or the adjacent areas of Middlesex and Surrey, displaying forms and spellings of common words very similar to St John's (though none of them identical in every respect), see McIntosh, Samuels, and Benskin, eds., *A Linguistic Atlas of Late Mediaeval English*, 4.298–306, 493–500.

[54] For specifics, see the notes to the text of these lines.

St. Jerome

Manuscripts

Cambridge, St. John's College MS N.17. [Base text; formerly MS 250].

London, Lambeth Palace Library MS 72, fols. 188v–202r.

London, Lambeth Palace Library MS 432, fols. 1–17.

New Haven, Yale University Library MS Beinecke 317, fols. 5r–21v.

Previous editions

Hamer and Russell, eds. *Supplementary Lives in Some Manuscripts of the Gilte Legende*. Pp. 321–65, 511–13. [Based on Lambeth Palace Library MS 72.]

Horstmann. "Prosalegenden." Pp. 328–60. [Based on Lambeth Palace Library MS 432.]

Waters, Claire. "Symon Wynter, *The Life of St. Jerome*." Pp. 141–63 (translation), 232–49 (edition). [Based on St. John's College MS N.17; see note 36, above.]

de Worde. [The Lyf of Seint Ierom.] [London: Wynkyn de Worde, c. 1499/1500.] *Short Title Catalogue* no. 14508.

III(a)

The Life of Saint Jerome, *by Simon Winter (c. 1430),*
from Cambridge, St. John's College MS N. 17 (250), fols. 1r–35v

[Prologue]

The prologe into the lyfe of Saint Jerom drawe into Englyssh to the hyghe Prin-
cesse Margaret duchesse of Clarence.

Ryght noble and worthy lady, and my fulle reverent and dere gostly doughtir in
oure Lorde Jhesu, I have mynde hou on Seynt Jeroms day, that is the morwe after
Myghalmas day, aftir I had toolde you somwhat of the lyfe and myraclys of Saint
Jerom, I sayde that wyth oure Lordys help, when I had laysere, I wolde wryte his
lyfe and myracles on Englysh to the praysynge and worshep of oure Lorde and of
hym; and that not oonly ye shulde knowe hit the more cleerly to youre goostly
profyte, but also hit shulde mowe abyde and turne to edificacion of other that
wolde rede hit or here hit. Wherfore I desire that hit shulde lyke youre ladyshype
first to rede hit, and to doo copye hit for youreself and syth to latte other rede hit
and copye hit, whoso wyl. For ther is thynge therynne ful needfull to be knowe,
and had in mynde of alle folk. For in the first and secounde chapitres we may
lerne and take ensample to lyve a Cristemannys lyfe in penaunce and straytnes.
And in the vii. and ix. chapitres we may lerne to dye. And what ys more necessarye
to ony man or womman in erthe, then to conne lyve and dye. Sothly alle folke lyve
and dye and yche man that lyveth woot wel he shal dye, but fulle fewe ther be that
kon lyve and dye. What ys hit to konne lyve and dye but to lyve soo that we be
alway redy to dye, so to have oure hert and oure soule redy unto God, that we
abyde deeth as the comyng of a loved frende that we desyre to goo wyth, from
wrecchednes unto delytes. Thus lerne we to lyve and to dye, for hit is to greet a
dulnesse not to konne doo, nor be aboute to lerne that thynge that every man
doeth and moste nedys doo.

1 **drawe**, translated; **to**, for. 3 **gostly**, spiritual. 4 **morwe**, morrow (next day). 9 **hit shulde
mowe . . . other**, it might remain available and be used to edify other people. 10 **lyke**,
please. 11 **latte**, let. 12 **is thynge**, are things; **knowe**, known. 14 **Cristemannys**,
Christian's; **straytnes**, discipline. 16 **conne**, know how to. 17 **woot**, knows. 18 **kon**,
know how to. 21 **to greet**, too great. 22 **dulnesse**, folly. 23 **moste**, must.

119

25 But yyf hit seme over hard to use the sharp dysciplyne of this scole wher we shulde lerne this holsom lesson, then we may loke in the iii., iiii., and v. chapitres and see there the greet reward that is gove to them that fervently labour aboute this scole.

And yyf the counfort of oo greet reward make not oure harde hertys to melt, thenne may we see in the viii. and x. chapitres the strayt doom that we goo to and 30 the greet paynes that be put aftir this lyf unto alle trewantys, that the beholdynge therof may breke oure dulnesse and hast us to goo lerne and travayle in this scole of penaunce.

And yyf we behote oureself longe lyfe, thenkynge that hit wil be long or this reward or paynes come, and so waxe wery to abyde so longe in straytnesse and 35 tribulacion wythoute counfort, and therfore begynne to play wanton among the lustys of the world and of the flesh whyle we schulde studye in this scoole, then loke we in the vi., xii., xiii., xiiii., xv., xvi., xvii., and xviii. chapitre and there we schall mowe see how mercyfully oure Lord, aftur He hath suffred His scolers to be chastysed a lytil while, anoon He helpeth hem and delyveryth hem from theyre 40 disese nat oonly at theyre deeth but also in this present lyfe. And ayeynward hou ferefully He betechyth alle trewantys as wele wyth temporall vengeaunce, as wyth endlees paynes. And so begynneth in this lyfe bothe His reward and punyshynge that we shulde outher for love of joye, or for drede of payne temporall or everlastynge, stably and hastly sette us to entre and to abyde in this scole to lerne 45 to lyve and dye. And for we schulde be the better wylled hereto, at the last in the xix. chapitre oure mercyfull Lady geveth hire blessynge to alle suche scolers. And in alle these chapitrys, we may see the greet worthynesse and holynesse of hym that was bothe a disciple and a mayster in this scoole, Saynt Jerom, hou holy and strayte he was in lyvynge, and hou myghty and mervaylous aftir his deth, and hou 50 profitable hit is to do aftir hym, to trust hym, and to do hym servyse.

Thus ys this werke divided into xix. chapitris, that ye shull not ben over wery to rede hit, whyle ye may at yche chapitris ende have a restynge place, and oon tyme rede oon, another tyme anothir, yyf ye have leyser to rede no moo at ones.

The first chapitre is of the lyf of Saynt Jerom as hit is take of *Legenda aurea*. 55 The ii. is of his lyffe also as Saynt Austyn wryteth in his epistell.

The iii. is how Saynt Jerom apperyd to Saynt Austyn in greete joye and swetnesse the same houre of his deeth.

---

24 yyf, if. **26 gove**, given. **28 oo**, one. **29 strayt doom**, strict judgement. **30 trewantys**, truants. **33 behote**, promise; **or**, before. **38 mowe**, be able. **40 ayeynward**, on the other hand. **41 betechyth**, teaches. **43 outher**, either. **44 stably and hastly**, firmly and quickly. **45 for**, in order that. **53 moo at ones**, more at one time.

The iiij. is how iiij othere men had a mervelous vision of Saynt Jerom the same houre that he dyde.

60 The v. is how Saynt John Baptist and Saynt Jerom arayed bothe lyche apperyd to Saynt Austyn.

The vi. is how by meritis of Saynt Jerom iii. men were areryd from deeth to lyfe in destruction of an heresye.

The vii. is of a mervaylouse and a feerfull deeth of a hooly man clepid Eusebie 65 and how Saynt Jerom apperyd to hym and comfortid hym in the houre of his deeth.

The viii. is how the sayde iii. men that were areryd toolde of the paynes of Helle and of Purgatorye.

The ix. is of the dyynge of the same iii. men and how Saint Jerom helped hem 70 in thayre dyynge.

The x. is how the soules of the same men aftir theyre deeth stood to fore the doom and hou Saynt Jerom lad them to see the joyes of Hevene, the paynes of Purgatory and of Helle, and syth baad them goo ageyn to theyre bodyes.

The xi. is of ii. myracles of Saynt Euseby that were doo or his bodye were 75 buryed.

The xii. is hou an heretyke called Sabyman was mervaylously hevedyd and a bysshop clepid Sylvan delyvered from deeth by help of Saynt Jerom.

The xiii. hou the fend apperyd in the lyknesse of the same Archebysshop Syl-van and sclaundryd hym mervaylously and how Saynt Jerom help hym.

80 The xiiii. hou Saynt Jerom savyd ii. hethen men that come to visite hym from thefys and from deeth.

The xv. hou Saynt Jerom saved ii yonge men from deeth that come from Rome to visite hym.

The xvi. is hou an abbay of nonnes was distroyed for symonye and for covetyse 85 and hou Saynt Jerom savyd oon of thoo nonnes that was not gylty in that synne when alle that other were kyllyd by vengeaunce.

The xvii. how iii heretykes were mervaylously puneshyd for offence agenst Saynt Jerom.

The xviii. is how Saynt Jerom delyveryd a man out of pryson from oo lond to 90 anothir on a nyght.

The xix. is hou oure Lady preyseth Saynt Jerom as hit is wryton in the *Revelacions* of Saynt Birgytt.

62 **areryd**, raised. 72 **lad**, led. 74 **or**, before. 76 **hevedyd**, beheaded. 81 **thefys**, thieves.

The liff of Saint Jerom as hit is take of *Legend aurea*. Capitulum i.

Saynt Jerom come of a noble kyn and in his childhood he was sende to Rome to lerne and there he lerned Grewe, Latyn, and Hebrew, and on a tyme as he wryteth
95 hymself to the hooly mayde Eustache when he studyed bysyly nyght and day in bokes of poetys and of philosophres by cause they savouryd hym bettir then bokes of holy scripture, hit happed that about mydlent he was smyte wyth a sodeyn and a fervent fevir in so moche that all his body was deed and coold unto the hert. And when they were bysye to dispose for his buryinge sodeynly he was
100 ravyshyd tofore the doom of God. And there he was askyd what man he was and he answeryd that he was a Cristenman. Then sayde the Juge, "Thow sayst not soeth, for thou art an hethen man and nought a Cristenman; for where thy tresour is there is thy hert. And thy hert is more uppon worldly bookys then uppon holy wrytt." Saynt Jerom coude not onswere. But anoon the Juge bade bete hym hard.
105 And then he cryed and sayde, "Have mercy uppon me Lord, have mercy uppon me." And they that stood bysyde prayde that he myght have forgyfenesse for he was but yonge. And then Saynt Jerom swore tofore the Juge almyghty God, and sayde, "Lord, yif evere Y have ony seculer or wordly bookys or reed uppon them hereafter, then forsak me for a Cristenman." And by this ooth he was late goo,
110 and anoon he lyvyd ageyn and fonde hymself alle bewept, and his body sore and full of woundes of the betynges that he suffred tofore the Juge and from thensforth he studyed and redde al busily uppon holy bokes as he had doo tofore uppon wordly bokes. Then he made hymself a monk and there he lyvyd so holyly, chastysynge the luste of the flesh and wythstondynge the desyres of the world
115 that he caused other that were holy religious to be the better for his ensample. When he was xxxix. yeere of age he was maad a cardinal prest in the chirche of Rome. And after the pope was deed, alle folk cryed and sayde that Jerom was worthy to be pope. But for as moche as he had used to blame the flesshlynesse of mysgovernance of clerkes and religious peple, they wyth grete indignacion lay in
120 wayte to do hym repreef. And on a nyght when Saynt Jerom shulde ryse to Matyns as he was woned, he dyde uppon hym a wommannys cloth and so went to the chirche wenynge hit had be his owne, whiche his enemyes had layd besyde his beddes side to make folk wene that he hadde hade a womman in hys chambere and so to scorne hym. And whanne he sawgh thayre malice he fledde thens and

94 **Grewe**, Greek. 99 **dispose**, arrange. 100 **doom**, judgement seat. 102 **soeth**, truthfully. 108 **wordly**, worldly. 111 **woundes of**, wounds from. 119 **mysgovernance**, evil living. 120 **do hym repreef**, harm his reputation. 121 **woned**, wont; **dyde**, put; **cloth**, garment. 122 **wenynge**, thinking.

125 come unto Constantynenople and there he comened wyth the byshop of holy
scripture and syth went into desert. And there he suffred grete penaunce and
dissese iiii yeere togedir. Wheroff he wryteth unto the sayde holy mayde Eustace
and sayth, "When I was in desert in that greet wildernesse, where ys a full horribil
dwellynge place al tobrent wyth the sonne, me thought Y was amongst the delytes

130 of Rome. All my body was deformed and clad in sakke and my skyn made blak
lyche an Ethyope or a man of Ynde. Every day wepynge, every day waylynge,
and when sleep come uppon me unnethe Y wolde suffre my drye bones to reste
uppon the bare erthe. Of mete and drynke Y speke not, when they that be seek
use there but coold water and hit semed glotonye to ete eny thyng sooth. I was

135 felaw of scorpyons, and of wilde bestys, and yeet in this coolde body and in my
deed flesh Y felt brennynges and sturynges of unclennes. (And therfore sith they
fele suche temptacions that so dispyse thayre bodyes and fyght oonly wyth thayre
thoughtes, what suffre they, men or wommen, that lyve in delites? Soothly as the
apostel sayth they lyve in body but they are deed in soule.) But oure Lord ys my

140 wytnes that aftir many wepyngis full often tymes me semed that I was amongst
the companyes of angels."

Aftir he had lyved thus in desert iiii. yeere he went ageyn unto Bethleem, and
there offred hymself as a wyse beist to abyde by the crybbe of oure Lorde. And
there he gadrid many disciples and founded a monastery and lyved under the rule

145 of the apostles and lv. yeere and an half he travaylid about translacion of holy
wryt and unto his ende he lyvyd a virgyne. Also he wrote the lyvys of hooly
Faders in a book that ys called *Vitas patrum*. He was also wyse that what man had
askyd hym ony question he shuld anoon wythoute taryinge geve hym a resonable
and a sufficient answere.

150 And when ther had yet nevere as unto that tyme be sette no maner servyse in
hooly chirche, but yche body sang and radde what he wolde, the emperour prayed
the pope that he wolde ordeyne som wyse man to sett divine servyse. And for the
pope knewe wel that Saynt Jerom was parfyte and moost excellent in Latyn tonge,
Grew, and Hebrew, and in al wysdom, he commyttyd unto hym that office. And

155 thenne Seynt Jerom devydid the Sautere into nocturnes and assigned to yche day
in the woke a propure nocturne and ordeyned that *Gloria Patri* schulde be sayd

125 **comened**, conversed; **of**, about. 127 **dissese**, distress. 129 **tobrent**, burned up. 131
lyche, like. 132 **unnethe**, scarcely. 133 **seek**, sick. 136 **brennynges**, burnings; **sith**,
since. 147 **also**, so; **what**, whatever. 150–51 **And when . . . hooly chirche**, And because,
prior to that time, no regular form of divine worship had been drawn up for use in holy
church. 151 **yche body**, everybody. 156 **woke**, week; *Gloria Patri*, Glory be to the
Father.

123

atte the ende of every psalme. He ordeyned also pisteles and gospelles for al the
yere and other thynges that longe unto divine servyse, and sent tham from Bethleem
unto the pope, which he and his cardinals resceyved and apprevyd and auctorized
160   forevere. Then wyth abstinence and labour he wex so wery and feble that when
he lay on his bed he myght not aryse but as he pullyd up hymself wyth a roop
teyghyd unto a balk, for to goo do the servyce that longed to be doo in the monastery. After this he made hymself a grave in the mouth of the cave where oure
Lord laye when he was bore, and therafter he had lyvyd foure score yeere and
165   xviii. and vi. monthis, he dyed and was buryed, the yeere of oure Lord CCC. and
xviii.

[Selections from the posthumous miracles: Pseudo-Augustine/Pseudo-Cyril
correspondence. The first miracle, Chapter 2, is omitted].

Hou Saynt Jerom the same houre that he dyede appered unto Saynt Austyn. Capitulum iii.

That the meritis of moost hooly Jerom be not hid I shal telle that byfell me
thorow Goddis grace the same day of his passynge. For the same day and houre
that hooly Jerom dyede of the cote of filthe and unclennes and was clad wyth the
170   clothynge of joye and of undeedlynes, whyle I was in my celle thynkyng bysili
what glorye and myrthe was yn the blissid soules that joye wyth Crist, desyrynge
to make therof a short tretys as I was prayed, I toke penne and ynke to wryte a
pistelle therof unto moost hooly Jerom, that he shulde write ageyn to mee what he
felt in this matiere. For I knewe well that in so hard a question I myght not be
175   lerned so evidentlye as of hym of no man on lyve. And when I began to write the
begynnynge of my lettre sodaynly an unspekable lyght wyth a mervelous swetnes
of swete smell entred into my celle att Complyn tyme. And when I sawe hit I was
so greetly astonyed that I loste al my strength bothe of herte and of body. I wist
not yeet then that the mervelous hond of God had enhaunsyd His servaunt Jerom,
180   makynge his mervaylys knowe to muche puple. I wist not that God of His wont

158 longe, belong. **161 but as**, unless. **162 balk**, beam; **longed to be doo**, was customary. **169 dyede of**, took off. **172 was prayed**, had been asked. **175 lerned . . . lyve**,
instructed by anyone alive as clearly as by him. **179 yeet**, yet; **enhaunsyd**, exalted. **180
knowe to muche puple**, known too many people; **wont**, customary.

mercys had dissolvyd His trewe servaunt Jerom from corruption of the body and arayed hym so hyghe a sete in Hevene. But for my eyen had never saw suche a lyght, my smellyng had nevere felt suche a savour, I was gretly astonyed at so unherd mervayles. And while I thought in myself what hit myght be, anoon ther
185 souned a voyce out of the light sayinge these wordes.

"Austyn, Austyn, what sekest thou? Trowest thou that alle the see shalle be putt in a lytelle vesselle or wenest thou to close all erthe in a lytil fyst, or to lette the firmament from continuel movynge, or to lette the see from his wont cours? That nevere mannys ye myght see, shalle thyn see? Or thyn eere huyre that nevere
190 mannys herd? Wenest thou to mowe undirstonde that nevere mannys hert undirstood, nor myght thynke? What shalle be the ende of an endles thinge? What shal be the mesure of thynge that may not be mesured? Rather shalle al the see be speerd in a litelle pitt, rather shal all the erthe be hoold in a lityllle fist, rather shal the see ceese of ebbynge and flowynge then thow schuldist undirstonde the leest
195 part or portion of the joyes and blisse that blessed soules in Hevene have wythouten ende, but yyf thou were taught by experience and tastynge of the same blisse as I am. Therfore travayl thou not to do thyngys that be impossible til the ende of thy lyfe be come. Seche thou not here tho thynges that may not be knowe but of hem that be in blisse. But rather travayle thou to do suche dedys that thou may be in
200 possession ther of suche thyngys as thou desyrest to knowe here. For they that ones entyr thyder goo nevere out ageyn."

Then I all astonyed for drede, and wythoute strengthe of herte, tok to me a lytel booldnes and sayde, "Who art thou that droppest so swete wordes into my throte?" "I am," he sayth, "Jerom preist to whom thou hast begonne to wryte a pistelle. I
205 am his soule that this same houre in Bethleem, levynge the birden of the flesh, am joyned unto Crist and, felawed wyth alle the companyes of Hevene clad in lyght and arayed wyth the stoole of undeedly blisse, goo unto the everlastynge kyngdom of Hevenes. And from hensforth I abyde no lassyng of joye but morynge, when I shal be joyned ageyn to the body that shal be glorified and the glory that I have
210 now aloone I shal have thenne wyth the body in the day of Resurrection, when alle mankynde shal aryse and oure bodyes shal be chaunged from corrupcion and we shal be ravyshed up into the eyre to mete wyth Crist, and so we shul alway be wyth oure Lord."

181 dissolvyd, set free. **182 arayed**, prepared for; **for**, because. **185 souned**, sounded. **187 wenest thou**, do you think (hope); **lette**, prevent. **189–190 That . . . . herd**, "Do you think to see what man's eye (**ye**) has never seen, or hear what his ear has never heard?" **192 Rather**, sooner. **193 speerd**, confined. **196 but yyf**, unless. **198 but of**, except by. **207 stoole**, robe; **undeedly**, immortal. **208 lassyng**, lessening; **morynge**, increase.

125

Then I, Austyn, not cessyng to wepe, answeryd and sayde, "O thou worthiest
215   of men, wolde God Y myght be worthy to be thy footman. But have mynde on thy
servaunt, thoughe I be moost unworthy, whom thou lovedist in the world wyth so
greet affeccion of charité, that by thy prayeres I may be clensyd of synne, by thy
governaunce I may goo wythoute stomblyng in the ryght way of vertu, by thy
bysy defence I may contynuely be defendid from myn enemyes, and by thyn holy
220   ledynge I may come to the havene of helthe. And now lyke hit thee to answere me
to som thyngys that I schal aske thee."

Then sayde the soule, "Aske what thou wylt, knowynge that Y shal answere to
thy wylle al."

Then Y sayde, "Y wolde wyte yf the soules that be in Hevene may wylle enythyng
225   that they may not gette."

The soule answerid, "Austyn, knowe thou oo thyng: that the soules in that
hevenly blys are made so seure and stable that ther is no wille in thaym but Goddis
wille. For they may wille nothynge but that God wille. Therfore they may gete
what thay wille, and what they wille God wille and fulfyllyth hit. Noon of us is
230   defraudid of oure desyres ageinst oure wille, for noon of us desyreth onythynge
but God. And for we have God alwaye, as we wylle oure desyres are alway fully
fulfyllyd, for we abyde perfytly in God and He in us."

O fadir Cirille hit were to longe to write in this short pistelle alle thyngys that
that glorious soule answerid and made knowe unto me. But I hope wyth Goddys
235   help aftir fewe yeeres to come to Bethleem to visite his hooly reliques, and then to
declare more openly that I herde and have write. If Y shulde speke with the
tongys of alle men, Y myght in no wyse worthyly expresse hou sotylly, hou opynly,
and hou mervaylously that hooly soule abydynge wyth me many houres expressid
unto me the unité of the hooly Trinité and the trinité of Unité, and the generacion
240   of the Sone of the Fader, and the goynge forth of the Hooly Goost from the Fadir
and the Sonne, and tho ierarchies and ordres of angellys and of blessed spiritis
and thayre mynystracion and the blessid joyes of hooly soules and other thyngys
profytable and hard to mannys undirstondynge.

And aftir this the lyght vanysshyd from myn eyen, but the swete smelle abode
245   many dayes aftir. How mervaylous is this man, doynge so many mervayles and
shewynge to men so unwont wondres. Therfore to hym crye we and joye we and
geve we glorye unto his praysyng, for certaynly he is worthy all praysynge and
we are not sufficient to prayse hym, for he is entryd into the hous of oure Lord,

220–21 **lyke hit thee to answere me to,** may it please you to answer for me. **222–23 to
thy wylle al,** everything you wish. **228 that,** what.

126

bryght and moost fayre, where wythouten doute he hath an everlastynge sete
250 amongst the hyghist mansions of blisse.

[chapter 4 omitted; chapter 5 follows]

Hou Saynt John Baptist and Saynt Jerom aperid to Saynt Austyn in a vision. Capitulum Quintum.

No man thynk that I am so boold to say that Saynt Jerom is better then Saynt John Baptist, for as oure Saviour berith wytnes, noon ys more then he. Nor that Jerom is in the blys of Hevene tofore Petir and Poule and other apostelis that were specially choose and halowid of Crist Hymself. Yeet though reson forbede to say
255 that Jerom shuld have more glorie in Hevene then thay, I see no resons why hit shulde not be leffull to say that Jerom is even in blys wyth thaym whyle he was not discordynge from them in hoolynes. And syth God is not acceptor of persones but He discernyth the meritis of yche persone, He geveth to yche all that they deserve. If hit seme that Jerom shulde have lasse joye then John Baptist and
260 othere apostelis, yeet the meritis of his hoolynesse, the grevys of his labours, the bokys of his wrytynge, the translacion of bothe lawes, the ordinaunce of divine servyce, the frutis and profytis of goodnes that he dyde not oonly to alle that be now, but also to them that be to come, seme to preve that Jerom is even to them in blis.
265 But lest that I make a snare of scornynge of somme that wolde deme that for carnal affeccion — wherthorough a man may lyghtly erre from trouthe — or for unkonnyng of myself I lykned glorious Jerom to Saynt John Baptist or other apostelis, I clepe God to witnesse that I shal telle a thyng that Y lernyd nevere of man but by revelacion of almyghty God that heyghneth and magnifyeth His chosyn.
270 The iiii. nyght aftir his passynge, when I thought desyrously uppon the praysyng of moost blest Jerom and began to wryte a pistil therof unto thee, about mydnyght, when sleep come uppon me, ther byfille me a mervelouse vision. There come unto me a grete multitude of angels and amongst them were two men wythoute comparison brighter then the sonne, so lych that ther semed no difference, saaf that

251 thynk, should think. **256 leffull**, allowable. **257 discordynge from**, unequal to; **acceptor**, respecter. **260 grevys**, hardships. **263 even**, equal. **266 lyghtly**, easily. **267 unkonnyng of myself**, my own ignorance. **268 clepe**, call. **269 heyghneth**, raises. **273–74 wythoute comparison**, incomparably. **274 lych**, alike.

275   oon bare iii. crownes of goold sett fulle of precious stonys on his heed and that
other but ii. Bothe they were clad wyth mantellis moost white and fayre al wofe
wyth goold and preciouse stonys. They were so fayre that no man may ymagyne
hit; they bothe come neere unto me and stood still in scilence. Then he that had iii.
crownys sayd unto me these wordys: "Austyn, thou thynkyst what of trouthe
280   thou shuldest say of Jerom and aftir longe thynkyng thou woost nevere; therfore
we be come bothe unto thee to telle thee his blys. Sothly this my felaw whom
thou seest is Jerom, which is even unto me in all wyse in glorye as he was even to
me in lyvynge. That I may, he may; that I wylle, he wylle. And as I see God, so
seeth he God, knoweth God, and undirstondeth God, in whom is al blessidnes of
285   sayntes; nor no saynt hath more or lasse blis then othir but in as moche as oon
hath more cleere contemplacion and sight then another, of the fayrnes of God.
That crowne that I bere more then he is the aureol of martirdom by which I endid
my bodily lyff. For, though Jerom, for the travaylis and dissesis, penaunces and
affliccions, wordes and repreves, and other grevous thyngis whiche he suffred
290   joyfully for Crist and so beyng a verry martir, hath not loost the reward of
martirdom; yeet for he endid not his liffe by the swerd he hath not the aureol that
is geven in token of martirdom. The ii. other crownes that bothe he and I have are
the aureols that are dew oonly to virgyns and doctours by which they are knowe
from other."

295   Then answerid I and sayde, "Who art thou, my lord?" He saide, "I am John
Baptist that am come down to teche thee of the glorie of Jerom, that thou telle hit
to other puple. For knowe thou that the worship that is doo to ony saynt is doo to
alle sayntys. For ther is noon envye ther, as is in the world where yche man
seketh rather to be above then undir. Not so in Hevene, but there yche soule is als
300   glad of otheres joye and blys as yyf he had hit hymself. Wherfore the joye of yche
ys the joye of alle. And the joye of alle ys the joye of yche."

        When these thyngys were sayde that blessid company went theyre wayes and I
awook of that swete slep and felt in me so grete fervour and brennynge of love
and charité that I felt never so moche afore. And from thensforth was ther noon
305   appetite in me of envye or of pryde as was tofore. God is my wyttnes, that ther is
so moche fervour of charité in me that I joye more of anotheres good then of
myne. I desire more to be undir alle then above ony. I say not this for to gete me
vayn praysyng, but for no man shuld wene that these were vayn dremys, wherby

276 **wofe**, woven. 280 **woost nevere**, do not know at all. 287 **aureol**, golden crown. 293
dew, due (proper). 296 **telle**, should tell. 297 **doo**, due. 308 **for**, so that.

310 we are ofte scorned, but a trewe vision by the whiche we are otherwhyle taught of God.

Prayse we therfore God in this saynt, prayse we moost hooly Jerom that dyde grete thyngis in his lyf and hath resceyved greet thyngis in his deeth. A man oweth not to be slawfull to prayse hym whoom God hath magnifyed. Ne wene no man to do wrong to Saynt John and to the apostellis, evenyng Jerom unto thaym. 315 For they wolde gladly, yf they mygth, geve hym of theyre glorye. Therfore thou that worshippist Saynt John and the aposteles, worship also Saynt Jerom for he ys even unto them in alle thyngys. Sykirly therfore, wythoute drede, knawleche we wyth devocion that Jerom is even unto John, for yyf we say that he is lesse then John we do derogacion unto John.

320 This tretys of the praysyng of Jerom I sende unto thee, fadir Cirille, prayinge that thou scorne nat my litylle wytt, but that thou wylt rede these praysyngys that I have write of charité. If alle tongys of alle men shuld prayse hym, they were not sufficient. Worshipfulle fadir have mynde on me, synnere, when thou stondist in that place where the body of Jerom lyyth and commende me wyth thy prayerys. 325 For noo man doute, whatever Jerom desyre in Hevene, he may gete hitt. For he may in noo wyse be defraudid of his desyre.

Farewelle, fadir, and pray for me.

Here endyth the pistel of Saynt Austyn unto Cirille and begynnyth the pistel of the same Cirille bisshop of Hierusalem unto Saynt Austyn of the myracles of Saynt Jerom. And first hou iii. deed men were areysid and an heresye destroyed by Saynt Jerom. Capitulum sextum.

[Chapters 6–18 omitted; chapter 19 follows]

Hou oure Lady commendyth Saynt Jerom in the *Revelacions* of Saynt Birgytt. Capitulum undevicensimum.

When Seynt Birgit was on tyme in hir prayere she sayde unto oure Lord, "Blessid be Thou, my God, that art iii. and oon, iii. in persones, oon in nature. Thou art

309 otherwhyle, sometimes. **313 oweth**, ought. **313–14 Ne wene no man . . . evenyng Jerom unto thaym**, No one should think it injurious to Saint John and the apostles to compare Jerome to them. **317–18 knawleche we**, let us acknowledge. **322 of charité**, charitably (indulgently). **325 doute**, should doubt that. **328 on tyme**, once.

330   verrey goodnes and verrey wisdom. Thou art verry fayrnes and power. Thou art
verry ryghtwisnes and trouthe, by whoom alle thyngis lyve and have thayre beynge.
Thou art like a floure growynge syngulerly alone in the feeld, of whiche floure alle that
neygh therto resceyve sweetnes in thayre tastynge, relevyng in thayre brayn, delecta-
tion in thayre syght and strengthe in alle thayre membris. So alle that nyghe unto Thee

335   are made the fayrere by levynge of synne, wysere folewynge the wyl of Thee and
nought of the flesshe, more ryghtwys folewynge the profyte of the soule and the
worship of Thee. Therfore, moost pytefull God, graunt me to love that that plesyth
Thee, myghtyly to wythstonde temptacions and to despise alle wordly thyngys, to
hoold Thee busyly in myn mynde."

340   The moder of God, oure Lady, answerid, "This salutacion gate thee that good
Jerom by his meritis, that went from fals wisedom and founde trewe wisedom, that
dispysed erthly worshep and wan God Hymself. Blessid is that Jerom and blessid are
they that folew his techyng and lyvynge. For he was a lovere of wydewis, a myrrour
of alle that profyte in vertu, and a doctour and techere of alle trouthe and clennes."

345   And another tyme oure Lady sayde to Saynt Birgitt, "Doughtir, have thou in mynde
how I toolde thee that Jerom was a lovere of wydous, a folewer of perfyt monkis and
an auctour and defensour of trouthe, that gate thee by his meritis that prayere that
thou saydest? And now I adde to and say that Jerom was a trompe by whiche the
Hooly Gooste spake. He was also a flaume inflaumyd of that fyr that come uppon me

350   and upon the appostelis on Pentecost day. And therfore blessid are thay that here this
trompe and folew therafter." Explicit.

     Iste est qui ante deum magnas virtutes operatus est et omnis terra doctrina eius
repleta est. Ipse intercedat pro peccatis omnium populorum. Amauit eum dominus et
ornauit eum. Stola glorie induit eum.

355   Deus qui uobis per beatum Jeronimum confessorem sacerdotemque tuum, scripture sancte veritatem et mistica sacramenta reuelare dignatus es, presta quesumus vt
cuius commemoracionem agimus eius semper et erudiamur doctrinis et meritis
adiuuemur. Per christum dominum nostrum. Amen.

330 **verrey,** true. 333 **neygh,** come near. 335 **levynge of,** abandoning. 340–41 **This salutacion
. . . Jerom,** Jerome obtained for you this greeting. 341 **went,** turned (converted). 352–54
Iste est . . . . glorie induit eum, This is he who has wrought mighty miracles in the presence
of God, and the whole earth is filled with his teaching. May he intercede for the sins of all
peoples. The Lord has loved him and adorned him. He has clothed him with a stole of glory.
355–58 **Deus qui uobis. . . . Amen,** God, you who have deigned to reveal to us, through
blessed Jerome, your confessor and priest, the truth of holy scripture and the mystic sacra-
ments, grant, we pray you, that as we celebrate his feast day we may continually be instructed by his teachings and assisted by his merits. Through Christ our Lord. Amen.

III(a)

Explanatory Notes to The Life of Saint Jerome, *by Simon Winter*

Abbreviations: see Textual Notes.

4   *Seynt Jeroms day*. September 30, in the ecclesiastical calendars the day for commemorating the saint's death.

5   *Myghalmas day*. September 29, the feast day of the archangel Michael; an important seasonal day in medieval and modern England, traditionally the beginning of the autumn "term" when the London law courts, and Oxford and Cambridge colleges, are in session.

9   *mowe*. *Mowe*, "to be able to," "have power to," is one of the forms of the infinitive of *may*. See *MED mouen*, v.(3) 2a, where all the examples, however, are of its finite use as an auxiliary.

51   *xix. chapitris*. Of the nineteen chapters, the following are printed in our edition: 1, 3, 5, 19. For the rest, see Hamer and Russell, *Supplementary Lives*, pp. 323–65 and H's edition of the text of L.

84   *symonye*. The buying or selling of ecclesiastical offices or orders, as here where the nuns charge fees for admission to their convent. For the origin of the name, see Acts 8:9–24.

93–166   The life of Jerome in *LA* (chapter 146 in Ryan's translation, 2.211–16) is the basis of Winter's chapter 1; in the notes we have indicated his occasional omissions and additions.

93–94   *Saynt Jerom come . . . on a tyme*. All the copies except Y abbreviate *LA*'s description of Jerome's parentage and education, omitting especially the proper names that are numerous in this section of the narrative. The occurrence of the names in Y exemplifies an inconsistent pattern of interpolation and revision by the Y copyist or his exemplar (e.g., the interpolation at lines 125–32). Winter's work is ostensibly intended for laypeople, for whom the Roman names might be assumed to have had little meaning or devotional value. Following is the Y version of the opening passage (note the insertion of the statement that Jerome went to Rome before he was christened, a detail not supplied in *LA*):

> Seynt Jerom come of noble kyn. & he was born yn a town callyd Strydon that is betwyx ii. contreyes of which that oon ys callyd Dalmatia, that other Pannonia. His fadres name was Eusebius, & yn his childhade he was sent to Rome to lerne [er] that he was crystenyd, & lernyd grew, latyn, & Ebrew. His master yn gramere was Donatus & yn Rethoryk Victorinus, & on a tyme . . .
> (fol. 5v)

95   *Eustache*. Eustochium, consecrated virgin and daughter of the devout Roman widow, Paula. They (and other patricians, including the widow Marcella) befriended Jerome during his second period in Rome and followed him into exile in the East in 385. Paula founded and administered the monastic settlement in Bethlehem in which Jerome lived and worked during the latter part of his life. Hence the epithet for Jerome recorded in Saint Bridget's visions: "lovere of wydewis" (*viduarum amator*), quoted in Winter's chapter 19 (line 343). Jerome's long letter (no. 22) to Eustochium, the tract on virginity, includes his famous account of his "Ciceronian" vision, and also his account of his experiences in the Syrian desert. All the medieval *vitae*, and in turn Jacobus de Voragine in *LA*, draw on the letter for these two episodes. See *LA*, trans. Ryan, 2.213 and, e.g., Pseudo-Sebastian, *PL* 22.203–04, 205–06; for the letter itself, see Jerome's *Epistulae*, in *CSEL* 54.152–54 (the desert episode), 189–91 (vision); *PL* 22.398–99, 416–17; trans. in Schaff and Wace, *A Select Library*, 6.24–25, 35–36. On Jerome and his circle of friends (and enemies), see above, Introduction and note 1.

102–03   *where thy tresour . . . hert*. Compare Matthew 6:21: *Ubi enim est thesaurus tuus, ibi est et cor tuum*, "For where thy treasure is, there is thy heart also."

113–15   *Then he made hymself . . . ensample*. This passage is adapted by Winter not from *LA* but from the Pseudo-Sebastian life of Jerome, *PL* 22.203: . . . *probatissimorum quoque monachorum habitum factumque imitatus est . . . voluptatemque corporis . . . frangens, plerosque bonorum religiosorum, meliores fore suo docuit instituto*.

116   *cardinal prest*. Jerome was actually ordained priest not in Rome but in Antioch, Syria, during his first long period of study and hermit life in the East. The term "cardinal priest," originally meaning a priest licensed to conduct services in churches other than where he was ordained, became current in Rome in the eighth century, and is applied to Jerome in the Pseudo-Sebastian life (ninth century); the office did not acquire high ecclesiastical dignity until the eleventh century, when the cardinal

priests of the major Roman churches became the pope's senior advisors and administrators. Jerome is often depicted in late medieval art wearing the distinctive red hat of the Roman cardinals. See Rice, pp. 35–37.

120–24　　*And on a nyght . . . so to scorne hym.* This humorous "transvestite" anecdote, which Winter translates closely from *LA*, is apparently first told in the mid-twelfth-century *Vita Hieronimi* now attributed to Nicholas Maniacoria (*PL* 22.186). See Rice, p. 28. Maniacoria plausibly links the trick played by Jerome's enemies to suspicions aroused by his friendship with Paula and other women. While there is no historical basis for the episode or the accusation, Jerome's departure from Rome was in part occasioned by public criticism of his relationship with the patrician widow Paula. See Kelly, *Jerome*, pp. 113–14.

121　　　　*Matyns.* The service or "office" of Matins, comprising mainly the chanting of groups of psalms and readings from homilies and saints' lives, was sung by medieval monks and cathedral clergy in the middle of the night, starting usually around 2:00 a.m. This type of service, clearly formulated in the rule of Benedict in the sixth century, was already taking shape in Roman churches served by monks in the century after Jerome (Van Dijk and Walker, *The Origins of the Modern Roman Liturgy*, p. 17), but the episode as told in the life of Jerome is anachronistic.

125–32　　*and there he comened wyth the byshop . . . when sleep come uppon me.* After his first sojourn in the desert communities of Syria, Jerome studied Greek and biblical exegesis with the theologian and opponent of Arianism Gregory of Nazianzus (died 390), who was briefly archbishop of Constantinople. Like *LA*, Y (fol. 6r) supplies Gregory's name (which Simon Winter omits), but also goes on to interpolate several lines justifying Jerome's departure from Rome as an act of divine providence. The passage, which also touches on Jerome's authorship of the life of the captive monk, Malchus, is adapted not from *LA* but from one or other of the Latin lives (compare *PL* 22.178–79 and 204–05):

> & ther he comynd with the bisshop of the cyte of holy scriptur whos name was Gregorius nazanzenus. But his fleynge out of Rome was not only do be the malyce of his pursuers, but be the mercyfull prouydence of god, that the chirch of Rome thorough his laboure shulde haue holy wryt translatyd ynto latyn out of the trouth of Ebrewe tonge. Wherethorough the iewes sholde no lengyr scorne crystyn peple for lakke of knowynge of holy wryt. And the grekys, which mayntenyd hem that we had holy wrytt only of hem, shulde knowe that thorough Jeromes labour we haue [holy writ] more clerly out of the welle of Ebrewe than they hemsilf. But aftir seynt Jerome had studyed holy scripture

with the seyd holy bysshop he went ynto Cyrye & ther he wrot the lyf of the monke that was take prisoner ynto hethenesse & aftirwarde he went ynto wyldernesse to do penawnce as he had longe desyryd & so gladly he wente therto that he semyd rather to fle than to go [i.e., to fly or float than to walk].

After this the Y scribe or his exemplar resumes Winter's narrative of Jerome's life at *and ther slep come vpon me* (compare our edition, line 132: *and when sleep come uppon me*), thus omitting several lines of Winter's narrative proper (125–32).

126   *desert*. Here an abstraction, connoting the condition of solitude sought by hermits in desolate places.

127   *Eustace*. For "Eustache" and the source of this episode, see note on line 95, above.

130–31   *blak lyche an Ethyope or a man of Ynde*. Jerome's comparison of his sun-blackened skin with that of an Ethiopian is in *LA* (*Ethiopice carnis*: ed. Maggioni, p. 1004; trans. Ryan, 2.213), but not the Indian allusion. However, in a late-fifteenth-century manuscript of *GiL* (BL Add. 35928, fol. 125r), adapted independently from the fourteenth-century French *Legende doree*, we find the Indian comparison, in identical wording, but without the Ethiopian: "blak lyk a man of Ynde." Caxton, in his adaptation of the same material, has "black like to the skin of a Morian" [i.e., Mauretanian] "or an Ethiopian" (*Golden Legend*, ed. Ellis, 5.202). For fanciful medieval acccounts of Ethiopia and India, see Mandeville's *Travels*, pp. 117–18, 120–26.

134   *sooth*. Here meaning "boiled,"or "cooked," it is a variant of *sothe(n)*, past participle of ME *seethe*. The desert ascetics scorned to eat cooked food (*aliquid coctum — LA*, ed. Maggioni, p. 1004; trans. Ryan, 2.213), even when sick. The word is misunderstood by W and H, who print it (plausibly enough) as an emphatic adverb *soth(e)*, "truly," beginning the next sentence.

136   *Y felt brennynges and sturynges of unclennes*. Winter tones down the more graphic imagery of the *LA* account by omitting Jerome's confession that he often fantasized that he was surrounded by dancing girls: *saepe choreis intereram puellarum* (*LA*, ed. Maggioni, p. 1005; trans. Ryan, 2.213).

136–39   *And therfore sith they fele . . . they are deed in soule*. The moralizing parenthesis, including the quotation from St. Paul (1 Timothy 5:6), is not based on *LA*, but closely adapted from Jerome's own comment on his temptations in the desert in his Letter 22. Winter, however, aims the warning at a more general audience, *men or wommen*, in place of the single *puella* Jerome has in mind. See Jerome's *Epistulae*, *CSEL* 54.154; *PL* 22.399; trans. in Schaff and Wace, *A Select Library*, 6.25.

144–45   *rule of the apostles*. Winter again departs from his source here (*LA* does not mention an "apostolic" rule, or even the founding of a monastery as such), apparently drawing on one or other of the medieval *vitae*: compare *PL* 22.206: . . . *monasterium construxit. In quo statuta ab Apostolis regula degens coepit . . . cum fratribus habitare.* In the later Middle Ages, some of the newer orders (e.g., the Augustinians and Franciscans) invoked the *vita apostolica* as purer and more authentically biblical than the customs of the Benedictines.

145–46   *translacion of holy wryt and unto his ende he lyvyd a virgyne*. Winter here omits Jerome's own admission, mischievously quoted in *LA* (trans. Ryan, 2.213), that he was not in fact a virgin. Winter also omits at this point the famous story of Jerome and the lion, which follows immediately in *LA* (trans. Ryan, 2.213–15). He supplies two brief passages in lieu (see next two notes), culled from different portions of the other medieval *vitae*, before resuming the *LA* narrative with an account of Jerome's liturgical compositions.

147   *Vitas patrum*. Jerome in fact wrote only three lives of desert saints (Hilarion, Malchus, and Paul the Hermit), but in the later Middle Ages the great collection known as the *Vitae patrum* (translated by various writers into Latin from Greek in the fifth to sixth centuries) was commonly attributed to him, e.g., in the Pseudo-Gennadius life, *PL* 22.183: *Plerasque Eremitarum Patrum vitas insignium veracissimo eloquio texuit historiae*. For modern translations of the *Vitae patrum*, see The Life of St. Benedict (V[a]), Introduction, note 3, below.

147–49   *He was also wyse . . . and a sufficient answere*. This passage, not in *LA*, occurs in Pseudo-Sebastian, *PL* 22.207 (*ut undecumque interrogatus fuisset, paratum haberet et competens sine aliqua dilatione responsum*); it was borrowed not only by Winter here but also by the Y copyist in his additions to the lion episode. See below.

152–60   *And for the pope knewe wel . . . apprevyd and auctorized forevere*. This apocryphal story anachronistically attributes to the late Roman era the initiatives for liturgical uniformity taken by the Frankish emperor Charlemagne (who commissioned Alcuin to revise the mass books). However, a system of chanting all the psalms each week (so many each night of the week at the service of Matins, which comprised three successive "nocturns") had gradually emerged in the larger Roman churches by the sixth century and is also reflected in the Benedictine rule. For the Psalter divisions, see Taft, *The Liturgy of the Hours in East and West*, p. 136. Although Jerome himself was not responsible for this system, he did prepare three editions of the Psalter: in 383 ("Roman"), 385 ("Gallican"), and 405 ("Hebrew"). By the eighth century, he was also being falsely credited with preparing a lectionary of readings from the gospels and epistles for use at Mass: see the forged letter *Ad Constantium* (*PL* 30.487–88, 501–03) discussed by Vogel, *Medieval Liturgy*, pp. 320, 393; and Rice, p. 46n72, for further references.

161–63   *a roop teyghyd unto a balk . . . in the monastery.* The story of the pulley, which figures prominently in the iconography of Saint Jerome, is not in *LA*. Winter adapted it from Pseudo-Sebastian, *PL* 22.214, where it follows the preparation of the grave at the cave mouth. Winter here omits a long passage in his source quoting testimonials in Jerome's favor by famous authors such as Augustine and Sulpicius Severus, along with general comments on Jerome's embattled career (*LA*, trans. Ryan, 2.215–16). Some of this material forms the conclusion to the lion episode added by the Y scribe. See below.

164   *foure score.* Represented in S, H, and Y by *xx* over *iiii*; W simply has *lxxx*. Jerome's age is thus said to have been ninety-eight and a half, as in many copies of *LA* (ed. Maggioni, p. 1008; trans. Ryan, 2.215).

165–66   *CCC. and xviii.* All the extant copies have this corrupted date of 318. The sixteenth-/seventeenth-century hand in the margin of S notes the date given in *LA* as 388, perhaps an error for 398, as in a variant recorded by Maggioni (p. 1009), and reflected in Ryan's translation (2.216). The correct date is generally agreed to be 420.

172   *as I was prayed.* According to Winter's Latin source, the Pseudo-Augustine epistle (*PL* 22.283–84), the person who asked Augustine to write this treatise was Sulpicius Severus (author of the Life of St. Martin of Tours).

177   *att Complyn.* The brief liturgical office of Compline was the last of the "hours" of the liturgical day in medieval monasteries, usually around sunset just before the monks went to bed.

186–87   *Trowest thou . . . . a lytell vesselle.* The forger of the letter here casts Augustine as the misguided rationalist intellectual, the archetypal Schoolman chided by Jerome for being distracted from genuine devotion by abstruse questions of metaphysics and logic. The first of the examples of pointless, impossible projects alludes to a tale (first told concerning an anonymous Parisian theologian by Caesarius of Heisterbach in the late thirteenth century) that appears in various late medieval collections of preachers' exempla and was commonly associated with Augustine by Renaissance artists: it tells how Augustine, musing on his great treatise on the Trinity during a walk on the sea-shore, came upon a child scooping sea water into a small container and claiming he was trying to empty the whole ocean into the vessel. When Augustine told him this was impossible, the child (really an angel or Jesus himself) replied that Augustine's own efforts to explain the mysteries of the Trinity were even more futile. See the published summary of an untitled 1955 paper by H.- I. Marrou, in *Bulletin de la Société Nationale des Antiquaires de France*, 1954–55, pp. 131–35.

189–90   *That nevere mannys . . . . nevere mannys herd.* Compare 1 Corinthians 2:9: "That eye hath not seen, nor ear heard: neither hath it entered into the heart of man, what things God hath prepared for them that love him."

192   *mesure . . . mesured.* Compare Matthew 7:2: "For with what judgment you judge, you shall be judged: and with what measure you mete, it shall be measured to you again." In W, the first *mesure* falls at the end of the verso of leaf (A5); but the order of the following two leaves has been inadvertently reversed, so that the sentence actually continues at the top of (A7) recto, not (A6).

203   *so swete wordes into my throte.* Winter's source, *tam dulcia eloquia gutturi meo* (*PL* 22.284–85) in turn echoes Psalm 118:103 in the Vulgate: "How sweet are thy words to my palate! more than honey to my mouth."

207   *stoole of undeedly blisse.* With Winter's rendering of his source (*PL* 22.285: *illo induta immortalitatis deaurato vestimento*) compare the Wycliffite *Lay Folk's Catechism*: *[crist] wyle clothe oure sowlys . . . with the stole of vndedlynesse* (ed. Simmons and Nolloth, p. 73, line 1115). See also below, line 354, and the explanatory note to lines 352–58.

210–13   *day of Resurrection . . . be wyth oure Lord.* Migne's edition of Winter's source reads *rationis die*, "day of reckoning," but the text printed by Klapper has the reading corresponding to Winter's: *resurrectionis die* (Johann von Neumarkt, *Schriften*, ed. Klapper, 2.266.22–23). After the word *Resurrection*, Winter adds a few phrases of his own (*when alle mankynde . . . wyth oure Lord*) echoing the language of 1 Corinthians 15:51–53 ("We shall all indeed rise again. . . . For the dead shall rise again incorruptible. And we shall be changed. For this corruptible must put on incorruption: and this mortal must put on immortality"), and 1 Thessalonians 4:17 ("Then we who are alive, who are left, shall be taken up together with them in the clouds to meet Christ, into the air: and so shall we be always with the Lord").

226–32   *Austyn, knowe thou . . . . and He in us.* By attributing these ideas to the spirit of Jerome, the author of the Pseudo-Augustine epistle ingeniously implies that Augustine's famous account of life in Heaven near the end of the *City of God* was dictated to him by Jerome! See *City of God* 22.30, especially the following: "I shall be everything that men can honourably desire . . . 'so that God may be all in all' (1 Corinthians 15:28). He will be the goal of all our longings" (trans. Bettenson, p. 1088, and see *PL* 22.285).

233–43   *O fadir Cirille . . . to mannys undirstondynge.* This passage is another, more blatant instance of the tendency of Winter's source to imply that Augustine did not compose his most important theological treatises himself, under the inspiration of the Holy Spirit, but rather that the spirit of Jerome dictated them to him. See also above, note on lines 226–32.

248–50   *for he is entryd . . . amongst the hyghist mansions of blisse.* Winter combines his source's image of Jerome's heavenly seat (*sete*, line 249), with an allusion to the well-known passage from John 14:2: *in domo Patris mei mansiones multae sunt* ("in my Father's house are many mansions"). But Winter's phrase *hyghist mansions* (line 250) also introduces the idea of Jerome's ranking in the celestial hierarchy, a topic explored further in Winter's chapter 4 (not printed here), where "Austin" reports a vision seen by Sulpicius Severus at the moment of Jerome's death, confirming that "he is of the hyest Ceteceyns of heuenly Jherusalem; and no-man dout but that, as his will is more nere to goodis will, so he may gitt there what he will, rather than other" (H, p. 338, lines 15–18; compare Hamer and Russell, *Supplementary Lives*, p. 333, lines 329–31). This last remark reveals an underlying purpose of the Pseudo-Augustine letters, namely to promote the idea of Jerome's power and influence in Heaven, as a way of enhancing his appeal as a patron saint and intercessor on earth. This theme continues in Winter's chapter 5, below.

252   *noon ys more then he.* See Matthew 11:11 ("there hath not risen among them that are born of women a greater than John the Baptist"); Luke 7:28 ("Amongst those that are born of women, there is not a greater prophet than John the Baptist").

257   *acceptor of persones.* Winter's source, Pseudo-Augustine, here echoes Acts 10:34 (*non est personarum acceptor Deus*, "God is not a respecter of persons") where Peter is proclaiming the doctrine that God saves people regardless of their nationality or

social standing, provided they fear him and live righteously. Compare 2 Chronicles 19:7 (*non est enim apud Dominum Deum nostrum iniquitas, nec personarum acceptio, nec cupido munerum*, "for there is no iniquity with the Lord our God, nor respect of persons, nor desire of gifts") and Galatians 2:6 (*Deus personam hominis non accipit*, "God accepteth not the person of man").

261   *bothe lawes*. The Old and New Testaments.

265   *snare of scornynge of somme*. Winter seems to have had some trouble with this passage and renders it in a painfully literal manner. The basic meaning of the Latin source (*PL* 22.287: *ne aliquibus deridendi laqueum injicere videar*) is "Lest I incur the risk of being scorned by some people." The text is corrupt in H, who omits *snare of*, and in W (*suaar of*). Y is almost identical with S.

267   *unkonnyng of myself*. Winter's rendering seems to mean something like "my own ignorance" but the sense of the Latin is more "my insane stupidity" (*PL* 22.287: *vesanae mentis imperitia*).

269   *heyghneth*. For other examples of this verb, in similar contexts, see *MED heinen* (a), "to raise, exalt, honor." It is variously rendered or misunderstood in the other copies: Y: *heryeth*; W: *hiheth*; H: *honoureth*. Compare *PL* 22.287: *qui suos exaltat . . . et magnificat*.

285   *more or lasse blis*. Compare the ME *Pearl*, lines 601–04: "Of more and lasse in Godez ryche / . . . lys no joparde / For þer is vch mon payed inlyche / Wheþer lyttel oþer much be hys rewarde" (ed. Andrew and Waldron, *The Poems of the Pearl Manuscript*, p. 82). See also lines 298–301 and the explanatory note, below.

287   *more then he*. I.e., John's third crown: Jerome has only two (see lines 275–76).

        aureol. "Little golden crown," from *corona aureola* (see Exodus 25:25), denotes the disk-like head-adornment of a saint, commonly depicted in medieval and renaissance art, and now displaced in common usage by the words *halo* or *nimbus*. The emphasis on the *aureola* is anachronistic in this context, since it did not become a familiar Christian image until centuries after the age of Augustine and Jerome.

293   *virgyns and doctours*. Various different ways of classifying the saints existed side by side in the Middle Ages. The oldest system, reflected in early medieval service books and in some early legendaries, recognized *apostles*, *martyrs* (male and fe-

male), *virgins* (i.e., virgin females who were not martyred), and *confessors* (all other male and female saints), the latter category including ecclesiasts such as Augustine and Jerome. For a typical medieval discussion of the types of saints, see that of Jacobus de Voragine in *LA*, chapter 162 (trans. Ryan, 2.272–80). The author of the Pseudo-Augustine letter offers an alternative grouping, designed to give special prominence to the sub-category of confessors to which Jerome belonged, namely *doctors*, meaning "teachers," distinguished for their contributions to Christianity as a body of doctrine. Special pleading is a factor here, however, in that John the Baptist would not normally be classified as a doctor and Jerome would not normally be considered a virgin.

296   *that thou telle.* I.e., present subjunctive, "that you should tell" (Latin *nunties*: *PL* 22.288).

298–301 *For ther is noon envye ther . . . joye of alle ys the joye of yche.* Compare Augustine, *City of God* 22.30 (trans. Bettenson, p. 1088): "no inferior will feel envy of his superior." Augustine's argument in the final chapter of his great work rests on the doctrine of the communion of the saints, in that, although they differ in honor, all are as members of one body in which all are content with their place: "the finger does not wish to be the eye." Each has the gift of contentment with what he has. Clearly, however, Jerome's devotees are not at all content that he should remain inferior to even the highest saints. Pseudo-Augustine alludes to the communion of the saints here in order to justify his claim that Jerome deserves to be glorified equally with the apostles and martyrs, since they all participate in each other's glory.

309   *scorned.* I.e., mocked, deceived. The Latin text has *quibus saepe deluditur mens nostra* (*PL* 22.288). On true and false dreams in Antiquity and the Middle Ages, see Kruger, *Dreaming in the Middle Ages*, pp. 17–34.

311–12   *that dyde grete thyngis . . . in his deeth.* Winter's source reads: *quoniam in vita sua magnifice fecit . . . . Quapropter magnus est in medio nostri*, audaciously praising Jerome in the language Isaias uses to praise God's glorious deeds (Isaias 12:5–6): *Cantate Domino quoniam magnifice fecit . . . quia magnus in medio tui sanctus Israel* ("Sing ye to the Lord, for he hath done great things: shew this forth in all the earth. Rejoice, and praise, O thou habitation of Sion: for great is he that is in the midst of thee, the Holy One of Israel").

327   *Farewelle, fadir, and pray for me.* This short valediction was added by Winter, whose source ends at *defraudatur desiderio* (*PL* 22.289).

Chapters 6–18 are omitted here. For their contents see above, lines 62–90. For an edition based on L, see H, pp. 340–59. See also Hamer and Russell, *Supplementary Lives*, pp. 336–61.

328   *Seynt Birgit.* Bridget (Birgitta) of Sweden (1303–73), a noblewoman of Upland, and for a time lady-in-waiting to Queen Blanche, wife of King Magnus II, bore eight children to the wealthy Ulf Gudmarrson, whom she had married when fourteen years of age. But while at court in the 1330s she began to experience visions and a call to a life of penitence and pilgrimage, visiting the shrines of St. Olaf in Norway and St. James in Spain. When she was widowed (1343), she withdrew into religious seclusion and three years later founded at Vadstena the mother house of what became known as the Order of the Most Holy Savior, or Bridgettines (nuns and monks sharing a common church, but living in separate quarters, under the authority of an abbess). From 1349 Bridget lived mainly abroad in Italy or on pilgrimage elsewhere, supervising the growth of her order, and experiencing and recording her numerous visionary experiences. On the Bridgettine convent founded outside London by Henry V, see the Introduction, above. Winter's chapter 19, which forms a Bridgettine appendix to the lengthy collection of miracles from the Pseudo-Augustine and Pseudo-Cyril letters, comprises a rather flatly literal translation of two separate passages from the massive Latin collection of Bridget's *Liber celestis* (or *Revelaciones*) 4.21 and 6.60. See the modern edition, *Revelaciones* 4.119 (ed. Aili) and 6.204–05 (ed. Bergh). Neither editor makes use of a huge manuscript, London BL MS Harley 612, copied in 1427 from a Swedish exemplar in Vadstena by Syon Abbey monks (for the passages corresponding to Winter's extracts, see fol. 43, col. 166, and fol. 89, col. 349; however, it appears that Winter's chapter 19 was translated from a text more like that edited by Aili and Bergh: see the explanatory note to line 330). There are several Middle English versions of Bridget's *Liber*, two of which have been published. One of these, the abridged rendering in BL MS Cotton Claudius B. i., shares a few similarities of phrasing with the text of Winter's extracts but for the most part the two versions differ considerably. Winter's is, for the most part, more learnedly faithful to the Latin. See *The Liber Celestis of St. Bridget*, ed. Ellis, 1.278, lines 5–22, and p. 448, lines 11–19.

330   *Thou art verry fayrnes and power.* This corresponds to *Tu ipsa pulchritudo et potestas* in the Aili/Bergh edition of Bridget's *Revelaciones* (4.119), but is lacking in Harley 612, implying the latter was not Winter's immediate source.

331   *alle thyngis lyve and have thayre beynge.* Compare Acts 17:28: *In ipso enim vivimus et movemur et sumus* ("for in him we all live and move and are"), by which Winter

must have been influenced in adapting Bridget's words: *per quam sunt omnia, viuunt et subsistunt* (*Revelaciones*, 4.119).

332–33   *of whiche floure alle that neygh therto resceyve sweetnes in thayre tastynge.* This literally translates *omnes appropinquantes flori optinent suauitatem in gustu* (*Revelaciones*, 4.119).

333   *relevyng in thayre brayn.* This translates *alleuiationem in cerebro* (*Revelaciones*, 4.119); today we might say "relief of tension."

340   *salutacion.* This word is made clearer in the Virgin's second speech (below, lines 345–51). It means here Bridget's prayer, to which the Virgin is responding; i.e., Bridget did not compose the preceding prayer solely by her own efforts but rather she was inspired to utter it through St. Jerome's "merits," i.e., his saintly virtues, which have become available after his death for Christ to use to secure for other Christians various kinds of heavenly blessings. On the doctrine of "merits" as used here, see *New Catholic Encyclopedia* 12.972.

343   *lovere of wydewis.* I.e., Jerome was the spiritual friend of devout widows such as the Roman patrician Paula, whose life offered many parallels to that of Bridget of Sweden.

345   *And another tyme.* See *Liber Celestis* 6.60 (*Revelaciones* 6.204–05), which is mainly about the doctrine of the Assumption of the Virgin Mary but closes with the brief passage that Winter translates here.

350   *Pentecost day.* This closing allusion is to the idea that the Virgin Mary was present with the apostles when they received the gift of the Holy Spirit in the upper room at Pentecost. Although she is not mentioned specifically in Acts 2:1–4, it is easy enough to infer from Acts 1:14 that she could have been present with the twelve. In medieval artistic depictions of Pentecost before the twelfth century, Mary is only occasionally seen with the apostles, but in the later Middle Ages, her presence is more and more taken for granted, although some modern commentators attribute this to her typological identification with *Ecclesia*, i.e., she is not present in person, but as a personification of the Christian Church, which was established at Pentecost. Bridget's visionary affirmation of the Virgin's personal reception of the gifts of the Holy Spirit refutes the typological rationale and implicitly validates the visionary experience of women like Bridget herself. Shortly after the events in the upper room, Peter is said to have repeated the eschatological prophecy of Joel (2:28) that the charismatic gifts of the Holy Spirit would be bestowed on men and women alike (Acts 2:16–18).

352–58   *Iste est . . . Amen.* The Latin coda, comprising a set of Latin liturgical texts for singing or reciting on St. Jerome's feast day, occurs after chapter 19 in S, H, and W, and in Y after the added chapter 20. All identify the text beginning *Deus qui* (lines 355–58) as an *Oracio* or prayer, here specifically the one (often called the *Collecta* or Collect) recited at the beginning of Mass and of certain of the "hours" of the liturgical Office. H and W identify the first text, *Iste est* (lines 352–54), as an anthem (*Antiphona* or *Antifona*), which was originally a refrain or responsorial chant accompanying the singing of a psalm, but the term came to be used of various kinds of refrains or responsorial chants sung during Office and Mass; it usually takes the form, as here, of a linked pair of short texts, each sung, as in a dialogue, by different parts of a church choir, before and after a *lection* or reading. W identifies the second anthem, *Amavit eum*, as a verse or versicle (*versus*), which might refer to the responsorial chant sung with or after the Alleluia, before the reading of the Gospel at Mass, but the terminology of responsorial texts fluctuates and overlaps. See Hughes, *Medieval Manuscripts for Mass and Office*, pp. 33–34, 39–41. W (fol. D5v) adds an alternative and longer set of texts (omitted here). The Collect for Jerome's day, *Deus qui*, is represented widely in medieval service books in England and abroad: it is edited, with a list of sources, in the monumental *Corpus Orationum*, number 1821, ed. Moeller et al. (*Corpus Christianorum Series Latina* 190B.51–52. While this prayer was written with Jerome in mind, the other liturgical pieces are from the "Common," i.e., they are taken from a repertoire of similar optional texts available for singing at prescribed junctures in the services for the feast of any confessor saint (but especially a churchman). The texts selected for Jerome, as often, echo scripture: e.g., *ante deum magnas virtutes operatus est* (line 352) probably recalls Wisdom of Solomon 8:7, *labores huius magnas habent virtutues* ("her labors have great virtues"); with *Stola glorie induit eum* (line 354), compare Baruch 5:1, *exue . . . stola luctus et vexationis tuae et indue te decore et honore eius quae a Deo tibi est in sempiterna gloriae* ("Put off, O Jerusalem, the garment of thy mourning, and affliction: and put on the beauty, and honour of that everlasting glory which thou hast from God"). The image of the *stola* is especially appropriate in this context since it is one of the vestments (a sort of scarf) priests wear to celebrate Mass; as such it was also associated figuratively with the "Angelyk doctryne" of "doctors" like Jerome and Augustine, as in John Lydgate's poem *The Interpretation and Virtues of the Mass*, 153–55:

> The stoole also, strechyng fer in leyngth
> Ys of doctors the Angelyk doctryne,
> Mawgre herytykes to stonde in his streyngth,
> Fro Crystes law neuer to declyne.

See *Minor Poems*, ed. MacCracken, p. 94. See also line 207, and note, above.

III(a)

Textual Notes to The Life of Saint Jerome, *by Simon Winter*

Abbreviations: **H** = Horstmann; **L** = London, Lambeth Palace Library MS 72, fols. 188v–202r; **S** = Cambridge, St. John's College MS N.17 [base text; formerly MS 250]; **Y** = New Haven, Yale University Library MS Beinecke 317, fols. 5r–21v; **W** = Wynkyn de Worde printed ed., London, 1499/1500 (*Short Title Catalogue* no. 14508).

36   *we.* So H, Y. S omits.

94   *Hebrew.* S: *Hebrewȝ.* H, W, Y: *Ebrew.* L: *Hebrewe.*

95   *in.* So H et al. S: *iij.*

96   *bokes of poetys and of philosophres.* Y (fol. 5v) adds: *that is to say of Tullius & of Plato.*

         savouryd. So S et al. H: *sauoure.*

97   *holy scripture.* Y (fol. 5v) adds: *whych him semyd were not eloquent.*

108   *seculer.* So H et al. S: *sedules.* Compare *LA* (ed. Maggioni, p. 1003; trans. Ryan, 2.212): *codices seculares.*

114   *chastysynge the luste . . . of the world.* So S et al. H: *chastising his body with the lust þerof.*

119   *mysgovernance of clerkes.* So S. H et al.: *misgouerned clerkes.*

120   *repreef.* So S et al. L: *represse.*

125   *comened.* S. H: *comende.* Others: *communed* or *commyn(e)d.* See explanatory note to lines 125–32 for Y's variant version of this passage.

130   *clad.* So S et al. L: *clothyd.*

132   *Y.* So H et al. S omits.

134   *sooth.* So S. Y: *sodyn.*

136   *Y.* So H et al. S omits.

151–52   *the emperour prayed the pope.* So S. Y is more faithful to *LA*: *The Emperor theodosius prayed þe pope callyd Damasus.*

157   *gospelles.* So L. H: *gospellis.* Y: *gospellys.* S: *gospelle.*

179–81   *Jerom, makynge his mervaylys . . . . trewe servaunt Jerom.* Omitted accidentally in W.

181   *mercys.* So Y, H. S: *meritis.* Compare the Latin source, *PL* 22.284: *Deus antiquae miserationis* (i.e., "God of enduring mercy").

182   *my eyen.* So S (in margin *yyn*) and W. L: *myne eyen.* H: *myne yghene.* Y: *myne eyȝene.*

183	*lyght.* So H, W. L, Y: *syght.*
186	*sekest thou.* So Y, H, L. S and W omit *thou.*
189	*huyre.* So S (in margin: *here*).
201	*entyr.* So Y, H. S: *euere.* W: *euer entre.*
207	*undeedly.* Y (fol. 8v) omits.
208	*morynge.* So S et al. H: *mornyng.*
220	*havene.* So H et al. S: *heuene.* The majority reading is corroborated by Winter's source, *PL* 22.285: *salutis attingam portum.*
227	*seure.* In the margin of S (fol. 9v) a contemporary hand has written *sure.*
230	*defraudid.* So Y, W, H. S: *descaudid* (in margin: *descayued*). Compare *PL* 22.285: *fraudatur.*
240	*Sone.* So H et al. S: *Same.* Compare *PL* 22.285: *Filii a Patre generationem.*
245	*man.* So H et al. S: *mannys.* Compare *PL* 22.285–86: *Quam mirabilis ergo iste est, faciens tot mirabilia.*
255	*resons.* So S, Y. W, H: *resone.*
260	*grevys.* So Y et al. S: *greuous.* Winter's source (*PL* 22.287) reads *illius laboris gravia.*
265	*deme that.* So Y et al. S omits *that.*
273–74	*wythoute comparison.* So S et al. H: *incomparable.*
293	*dew.* So H et al. S: *dewly.*
304	*afore.* So S (corrected in the margin to *tofore*), H. Y: *before*; L, W: *tofore.*
313	*slawfull.* So S. H: *slewfull.* Y: *sloughfull.* W: *slenthfall.* In S, the *a* is the single-bowled type, very rare in this manuscript, and could be a poorly-formed *o*. With the exception of W's garbled effort, all these are spelling variants of the late ME word *slowfull* ("slack," "sluggish"), deriving from the adj. *slow* rather than the n. *slough* or *sloth*, although this has influenced W's typesetter or exemplar.
314	*the apostellis.* So H et al. S omits.
315	*mygth.* So S (in margin: *myght*).
320	*unto.* So H et al. S: *un.*
329–30	*Thou art verrey goodnes.* H omits *Thou art verrey.*
338	*wordly.* So S et al. H: *worldly* (also Hamer and Russell); but the spelling *wordly* seems to have been quite common. Compare above, line 108.
350	*Pentecost day.* So S et al. Y: *Whit sonday.*
	this. So H et al. S: *his.* The majority reading is supported by the equivalent phrase in the Latin *Liber Celestis* (see explanatory note to line 328, above): *hanc tubam.*
353	*pro peccatis.* So H et al. S: *pro pitio.*

III(b)

St. Jerome and the Lion,
from New Haven, Yale University MS Beinecke 317, fols. 20r–21v

How be the byddynge of Seynt Jerom a lyon was keper of an asse and of the wysdom and pacyence of Seynt Jerom. Capitulum 20.[1]

Seynt Jerom prest and relygiows man whan he dwellyd yn Beethlem, which is vi. myle fro Jerusalem on the south syde, on an even as he sat with his bretheryn and herde the holy lesson of here collacyon, there come sodeynly a lyon haltynge ynto the monastery and whan the bretheryn see hym they ran awey for drede. But Seynt Jerom
5   went ayenst hym as ayenst a gest to receyve hym. Than the lyon shewde his foot that was hurte to Seynt Jerom. Wherfore he callyd his brederyn ayen and badde hem waisshe the lyons foot and seke bysily where the sore was and so they dyd and they fonde that the sole of his foot was as hit had be woundyd and kut wyth knyves. And after they had do cure and leyde medycynes therto hit wex hoole and the lyon, levynge
10   all his wyldnesse and fersnesse, dwellyd amonge theym as a tame best. Than Seynt Jerom, seenge that God had not sent that lyon to theym oonly for helynge of his foot but also for theire profyghte, be cownseyle of his bretheryn he enjoyned the lyon this offyce: that he sholde dryve to pasture and kepe an asse which thei had to fecche home wode fro the parke. And the lyon obeyed, for every dey yn maner of a shipherde,
15   he had out the asse to his pasture and abode with hym contynually as his felow and defensour, and such tyme as the asse was wont to be brought home for to laboure, the lyon brought hym home bothe for to fette his owen mete and for to brynge home the asse.

2 **even**, evening. 3 **collacyon**, evening reading; **haltynge**, limping. 4 **see**, saw. 5 **ayenst**, against (towards). 7 **bysily**, carefully. 8 **fonde**, found; **be**, been. 9 **do cure**, done (taken care); **wex hoole**, grew healthy. 12 **be**, by; **enjoyned**, laid upon. 13 **kepe**, protect. 14 **parke**, private forest. 17 **fette**, receive.

---

[1] Although the unique manuscript copy in New Haven, Yale University, MS Beinecke 317, presents this text as "Chapter 20" of Winter's *Life of Saint Jerome*, for reasons outlined above in the Introduction to Saint Jerome's legend, we have treated the lion episode as a separate composition, with its own line numbers and separate endnotes.

St. Jerome

20 But on a day hit happyd that while the asse was yn his pasture the lyon felle sore
aslepe and marchawntys that come be the wey, and see nothynge but the asse, stale
the asse and had here forthe with theym. And whan the lyon awooke and fonde not
his felow, he roryd and went abowte rorynge and whan he fonde hym not he turnyd
home soryly to the yatys of the monasterye. But he thurft not entyre as he was wont,
for shame. Whan the bretheryn of the hows see that he come latter than he was wont
25 to doo, and that he brought not the asse with hym, they wende that for hungire he had
ete the asse and therfor they wolde not yeve hym his mete that he was wont to have,
but they seyde unto hym, "Goo and ete that other dele of the asse as thou hast begonne,
and fulfylle thi glotenye." Nevertheles, for they were yn doute whedire the lyon had
do such trespas, they went ynto the pastoure and sought alle aboute yef they myght
30 have fownde eny token of the asse that he had be slayn; and whan they cowde ryth
nought fynde, they turnyd home and tolde Seynt Jerom alle that was doo. Than Seynt
Jerom had theym put the lyon to the same offyce that the asse was wonte to use and
so they dyd. They hewgh wode and leyde hit upon the lyon as they were wont to do
upon the asse and he suffred and bare hit pacyently. On a day whan the lyon had do
35 his laboure, he went out yn to the felde and ran abowte fro place to place, as yef he
wold have wyst what had befalle of his felaw the asse. And thus sone he see aferre
how the marchawntys come with theire camelys lade and the asse goynge before
hem. For the maner of that contré ys, that whan they goo ferre with theire camelys,
they make an asse go before hem with a rope abowte his nekke, to lede hem the ryght
40 wey. But whan the lyon knewe the asse he ran upon theym with a gret rorynge and
alle the men fledde and ran awey for drede. Than the lyon ferfully cryenge and rorynge
smot the grownde strongly with his tayle and made alle the camelys, as they were lade
with marchawndyse goo before hym home to the abbeye. Whan the bretheryn see
this, they tolde Seynt Jerom and he bad that they shulde waysshe theire gestys feet,
45 that is to say the camelys feet, and yeve hem mete and abyde the wyll of oure Lorde
therupon. Than the lyon ran abowte the monasterye and with glad and faunynge chere
he felle down prostrate at eche brotherys feet and waggynge his tayle he semyd to
aske foryefnes of the trespas, that he had not do as he sholde have do; or ellys more
veryly he made joye for the fyndynge of his felowe. But Seynt Jerom knowynge yn
50 spiryt what was to come, bad his bretheryn make redy that was necessarye for gestys

20 come be the wey, came along; stale, stole. 23 yatys, gates; thurft, dared. 24 latter,
later. 25 wende, guessed (believed). 26 yeve, give. 27 dele, part. 29 yef, [to see] if. 30–
31 ryth nought fynde, find right nothing (find nothing at all). 33 hewgh, hewed
(chopped). 36 wyst, known; sone, soon. 37 lade, laden (loaded). 44 bad, bade (gave
order). 46 with glad and faunynge chere, with a display of joy and affection. 50 that,
what.

that were comynge. And while he was spekynge ther come a messengere to hym and seyde that men were come to the yate that wolde speke with the abbot. Seynt Jerom wente unto hem and they felle down prostrate at his feet and askyd hym foryefnesse for stelynge of the asse. But he benyngly lyfte hem up and bad hem ryse and toke hem
55 ynto the abbey and shewyd hem gret charyté and humanyté. And afterwarde he delyvered theym theire camelys with all theire marchawndyse and bad them take theire owen and stele noon other mannys. Than they prayed Seynt Jerom that he wolde take half the oyle that they had yn herc caryagc yn thc wcy of charytć, but he wolde not assente. Nevertheles they compellyd hym so ferforth that unnethe he bad
60 his bretheryn take hit. And they behyghte that they wolde yeve so moche oyle eche yere to his bretheryn and to charge theire eyrys with the same for evyre after.

In this is shewde gret charyté of Seynt Jerom that he had yn kepynge of hospytalyté, for not only he receyvyd men but also bestys to his charyté, and therfor he wrytith hymself and sayeth thus, "In my monasterye," he sayeth, "we entendyd of herte to
65 hospytalyté, for we receyve alle with glad chere and waysshe theyre feet, saf only heretykys." And as the holy man Severe wrytyth of hym, he was so excellent yn connynge of Latyn, Grew, and Hebrew, that yn all connynge noon was lyke unto hym. For whatsoever was askyd of hym he had redy a competent answere withoute eny delay. And yef ther were take hym a book of Grew he wolde rede hit forthwith yn
70 Latyn. And a Latyn book ayenward as redily yn Grew withoute stomblynge, as yef the same langwage had be wryte before hym that he redde. He translatyd the Book of Danyel out of the tonge of Caldé, and the Bok of Job out of the tonge of Arabyke ynto Latyn. And therfor sayeth Seynt Austyn that hys wysdom and eloquence shone as the sonne out of the east ynto the weste. And oo thynge he laboryd ever yn all his studye:
75 that the enemyes of Crystys chirche shulde alwey be his enemyes. And therfor he had contynualle werre agenst wykkyd lyvarys and mysbelevars. And therfor heretykes and Lollardys hated hym because he impugnyd theire heresyes so myghtyly and wysly that noon myght withstonde hym. Clerkys also hatyd hym for he sparyd not to blame theire ynsolent lyvynge and theyre synnes. But alle good folke lovyde hym and had
80 hym yn worship. And how pacyently he took all detraccyon and persecucyon that was doo ayenst hym, he showyth hymsilf yn a pystyll that he wrot *ad Gallam* where he wrytyth thus. "I thonke God," he sayeth, "that I am fownde worthi to be hatyd of

---

54 benyngly lyfte, graciously lifted. **58 caryage**, baggage. **59 unnethe**, reluctantly. **60 behyghte**, promised. **61 charge . . . after**, legally impose upon their heirs in perpetuity the obligation to make the same annual gift. **64–65 entendyd of herte to hospytalyté**, gave our attention to hospitality from the heart. **65 saf**, save (i.e., except for). **69 take**, given. **72 Caldé**, Chaldee. **76 werre**, war; **wykkyd lyvarys**, evil-doers. **79 ynsolent**, extravagant.

the worlde, for they calle me a wykkyd doare. But I kan goo to the kyngdom of Hevyn be ynfamye and be good fame, be sklawndire and be good loos. And wolde God that

85   for the name of my Lord and for His ryghtwynesse alle the myslyvarys of the worlde shulde pursewe me. Wolde God that all the worlde shulde ryse agenst me to my repref so that I mote deserve to be preysid of Cryst and that I mote hope to have the mede of his behest. For hit is an acceptable and a desiderable temptacyon, whereof mede and rewarde is hopyd to be had of Cryst yn Hevyn. And cursynge and sklawndire is not

90   grevous whan hit is chawngyd for the preysynge of God. And that trybulacyon is joyfull and pacyently to be suffred which getyth grace here and endles blys hereafter." To the which grace and blys oure lord Jhesu brynge us, thorough prayers and desertys of this gloryows Seynt Jerom. Amen.

Here endith the lyf of the holy doctoure Seynt Jerom.

---

84 good loos, fair renown. **85 myslyvarys,** unbelievers (evil-doers). **86 to my repref,** to accuse me. **87–88 the mede of his behest,** his promised reward. **88 desiderable temptacyon,** desirable trial.

III(a)

Notes to St. Jerome and the Lion

Abbreviations: **Y** = New Haven, Yale University Library MS Beinecke 317, fols. 20r–21v [base text].

1   *prest and relygiows man.* In many medieval calendars and liturgical books, Jerome's traditional cognomen was simply *presbyter* (priest), or, later, *presbyter et doctor.* The addition of *relygiows man* here specifically identifies him also as a monk. The insertion of such an introductory epithet here (lacking in *LA*) may be another indication that this translation of the lion story was originally self-contained and separate from Winter's work.

1–2 *Beethlem . . . south syde.* This detail, not in *LA*, is in *Plerosque nimirum* (Pseudo-Sebastian), *PL* 22.206: *Bethleem . . . . quod ab Jerosolymis sex milibus separatur contra meridianam plagam.*

3   *collacyon.* Anglicized form of Latin *collatio,* conference (lit., "bringing together"). In monastic usage, it meant the gathering of monks after supper to hear and discuss a reading from the early Christian lives and maxims of the desert fathers (*Vitae patrum*) or from the *Conferences* of Cassian (early fifth century).

7   *waisshe.* In Y, *was* is awkwardly corrected above the line in a contemporary hand, perhaps the original scribe's.

12 *profyghte.* A late ME variant, influenced by Latin *profectus,* of ME *profit* (from OF *profit*).

12–13 *enjoyned . . . this offyce. Hoc injunxit officium,* "assigned a duty to the lion" (*LA,* ed. Maggioni, p. 656; trans. Ryan, 2.214).

17 *fette.* Literally "fetch," but here "get" or "receive." The lion was used to being fed by the monks each evening.

21 *here.* This is the only time the ass is referred to as female.

23   *thurft.* Preterite singular of the ME preterite-present verb *thurven,* "to need" (from OE *þurfan*); here, however, it means "dared," through a common ME confusion with *durren,* "to dare." See *MED thurven* 8(c).

46   *faunynge chere.* Translator's addition (*LA* merely has *laetus,* "glad"). *Faunynge* means physically showing affection and delight as dogs and other animals do (OE *fægnian,* "rejoice"; compare the now archaic English word *fain,* "glad," and see *OED, fawn,* vb.[1]).

48–49   *or ellys . . . his felowe.* This last clause seems to be the translator's addition, perhaps with a hint of sarcasm at the first explanation.

61   *evyre after.* The lion story proper thus ends with a gesture of formal lay charity, typical of the medieval era. The anonymous Syon author of the translation of the lion episode now departs from his source in *LA,* apparently to avoid repeating material already included in Winter's original translation of the life of Jerome. He provides the lion episode with a coda by reworking other material, omitted by Winter, from the closing section of the *LA* life. This material is skillfully linked to the end of the lion story through the motif of Jerome's charity. Although the lion episode proper ends with the considerable enrichment of Jerome's foundation by the oil merchants' bequest, the English translator borrows a short quotation from a later passage of the *LA* chapter, and thereby deftly refocuses the reader's attention on the charity the monastery gives to outsiders, implying that whatever wealth the monks have gained has been earned for them by their master and the customs he instituted.

64–65   *we entendyd of herte to hospytalyté.* A stiffly literal rendering of *hospitalitati ex corde intendimus,* "we extend hospitality from the heart" (*LA,* ed. Maggioni, p. 658, trans. Ryan, 2.215).

68–69   *whatsoever was askyd . . . eny delay.* Not from *LA,* but Pseudo-Sebastian, *Plerosque nimirum, PL* 22.207 (Mombrizio, p. 32, lines 44–45: *et undecumque interrogatus fuisset paratum haberet et competens sine aliqua dillatione responsum*).

69–71   *yef ther were take hym a book . . . that he redde.* This passage is not in *LA.* In Pseudo-Sebastian's *Plerosque nimirum* the equivalent material, which the English translator follows fairly closely, occurs shortly after the passage quoted in the previous note, long before the lion episode. See Mombrizio, p. 32, lines 54–58: *Tanta namque utriusque linguae peritia fungebatur ut quoscumque libros æolicos in manibus acciperet: latine sine offensione transcurreret: iterumque latinos attico sermone legeret: ut crederetur hoc sermone conscriptum hic esse scriptum quod eius os inoffensa velocitate fundebat.* Compare *PL* 22.207.

72   *Caldé . . . Arabyke.* This information is not in *LA* but occurs in Pseudo-Sebastian, *Plerosque nimirum,* somewhat earlier than the passage quoted in the previous note. Mombrizio, p. 32, lines 38–39 (also *PL* 22.206): *Daniellem quoque prophetam Chaldæo stillo locutum* [var. *sermone prolocutum*] *et Job justum Arabico, in romanam linguam . . . mutavit.* The ultimate source is Jerome's prologues to his editions of Daniel and Job in the Vulgate Bible (see Weber et al., eds., *Biblia sacra,* fourth ed., pp. 731, 1341); the prefaces are translated in Schaff and Wace, *A Select Library,* 6.491–93. "Chaldee" is an old name for classical or imperial Aramaic, a Semitic language closely related to Hebrew and widely used in the Babylonian and Persian empires. The Book of Daniel, as extant, is composed partly in Aramaic, and partly in Hebrew. Pseudo-Sebastian exaggerates in implying the Book of Job was written in Arabic; Jerome in his preface describes it as a mixture of Hebrew, Arabic, and Syriac. More accurately, its Hebrew vocabulary is richly idiosyncratic, with numerous loanwords from the neighboring Semitic languages, including Arabic, Akkadian, and Aramaic. See Buttrick, ed., *The Interpreters' Bible,* 3.892.

73–74   *And therfor . . . weste.* With this passage, the translator returns to the collection of "testimonies" in *LA* (trans. Ryan, 2.215).

75   *his enemyes.* In *LA* (trans. Ryan, 2.215) this passage, on Jerome's defense of the Church against heretics and the attacks he suffered in return, is carefully adapted from Sulpicius Severus, *Dialogues* 1.8, in which two characters (Postumianus and Gallus) offer somewhat different views of Jerome. See the translation by Hoare, *Western Fathers,* pp. 77–79.

77   *Lollardys.* *LA* merely has *haeretici*; the Lollards, who preached Church reform and espoused various unorthodox theological positions, were fifteenth-century England's best-known heretical sect.

81   *ad Gallam. LA* (ed. Maggioni, p. 1009, trans. Ryan, 2.216) has *ad Asellam,* to whom Jerome wrote his Letter 24, defending himself against the Roman clergy and pro-testing their mistreatment of him, in 385. Asella was an elderly Roman woman of great humility, who lived "enclosed," i.e., in voluntary solitude. *Gallam* doubtless is due to textual corruption.

84   *be ynfamye . . . good loos.* The second pair of opposites is the translator's addition; compare *LA*: *scio ad regnum pervenire per infamiam et bonam famam*, "I know how to get to heaven, whether others think well or ill of me" (ed. Maggioni, p. 1009, trans. Ryan, 2.216).

88   *desiderable temptacyon.* A near-literal rendering of *LA*'s "desirable . . . trial" (*desideranda* [var. *desiderata*] *tentatio*, ed. Maggioni, p. 1009; trans. Ryan, 2.216), explaining, as a test of his capacity for patient suffering, the hostility and vituperation Jerome often incurred (in reality, he often failed the test). ME *desiderable* is a learned formation (now obsolete), from Latin *desiderabilis*, alongside ME (and OF) *desirable*.

94   *Here endith . . . Jerom.* Immediately following in Y, but omitted here, are the same Latin liturgical anthems and prayer that are found in the other copies after the end of Winter's chapter 19, printed above.

IV

The Life of St. Thaïs in the Northern Homily Cycle *(early 1300s)*

Introduction

The Whore Who Became a Saint: The Cult and Legend of St. Thaïs (feast day October 8)

Thaïs is one of a small and select company among the ranks of the saints. Along with Mary Magdalene, Mary of Egypt, and Pelagia (to name the most well known), she is distinguished not for her zealous guarding of virginity, ordinarily the most cherished attribute of the female saint, but for the repentance to which she is moved following a life of sinful sexuality.[1] Her October 8 feast day, which she shares with Pelagia, is mentioned in Greek menologies but she is not named in the standard Roman martyrologies.[2] Although no liturgical cult ever formed around Thaïs, her legend enjoyed widespread popularity throughout the Middle Ages. Numerous early versions of the legend of Thaïs and her converter, Paphnutius, exist in Greek, Syriac, and Latin, but the basis for all the later medieval redactions and disseminations is the *Vita Thaisis,* a sixth- or seventh-century Latin translation (traditionally attributed to Dionysius Exiguus or Dennis the Little) of an earlier Greek life. This in turn may have been based on an anecdote, concerning the Egyptian abbot Serapion and an unnamed courtesan, in the *Sayings of the Fathers (Apophthegmata Patrum).*[3] The *Sayings* circulated during the Middle Ages sometimes separately but often as part of a larger collection of fourth-sixth-century hagio-

---

[1] For modern translations of the medieval lives of the prostitute saints, see Ward, *Harlots of the Desert.* On sinner-saints in general, see Dorn, *Der Sündige Heilige.* Not only are the sinner-saints few in number, they are allocated in a time and place safely distant from the later Middle Ages. See Weinstein and Bell, *Saints and Society*, p. 105, who see the church and hagiographers for the most part requiring life-long virtue as a necessary if not sufficient basis for sainthood.

[2] An early printed edition (Cologne: Greven, 1515) of the martyrology of Usuard has the following entry for Thaïs on August 28: *Taysis, quondam peccatricis, quam sanctus Pafnucius abbas convertit et in cella arcta inclusit, ubi in maxima poenitentia exactis annis tribus, postea quievit in pace* ("[The feast of] Thaïs, formerly a sinful woman, whom St. Paphnutius converted and enclosed in a narrow cell, where, after spending three years in profoundest penitence, she rested in peace"); quoted in *PL* 123.411.

[3] Ward, *The Sayings of the Desert Fathers*, pp. 226–27. For other close analogues of the Thaïs legend, see Ward, *Harlots of the Desert*, pp. 77–79.

graphic and ascetic writings, the *Lives of the Fathers* (*Vitae Patrum*), about the desert monks and hermits of Egypt and Palestine. Various individual lives of desert saints, including Antony, Paul the Hermit, Mary of Egypt, and Thaïs, were also incorporated into *Vitae Patrum* manuscripts. The most comprehensive version of this collection is the first modern scholarly edition, by the humanist scholar Heribert Rosweyde.[4]

In her *Vita*, Thaïs is portrayed as an Egyptian courtesan whose beauty has reduced many young men to a state of abject poverty in attempts to buy her favors. Hearing of the bloodshed caused by quarrels among the would-be lovers of Thaïs, a monk named Paphnutius decides to visit her, with the following result:

> He handed her a silver piece as the price for committing sin. She accepted the price and said, "Let us go inside." When he went in, he sat down on the bed which was draped with precious covers and he invited her, saying, "If there is a more private chamber, let us go in there." She said, "There is one, but if it is people you are afraid of, no one ever enters this room; except, of course, for God, for there is no place that is hidden from the eyes of divinity." When the old man heard this, he said to her, "So you know there is a God?"

When Thaïs answers in the affirmative, Paphnutius expresses amazement that her belief does not fill her with fear and regret with regard to the loss of her own soul, as well as those of the young men she has led to damnation. Overwhelmed by the monk's words, Thaïs bursts into tears and asks for a suitable penance which Paphnutius obligingly supplies. After publicly burning all her worldly goods, Thaïs is sealed into a monastic cell and when she asks the monk where she is to urinate he charitably responds, "In the cell, as you deserve." Thaïs accepts this, along with further humiliation, as her just deserts, but after three years Paphnutius himself becomes a little anxious and seeks advice from St. Antony. A vision soon follows indicating that Thaïs has been forgiven; she is removed from the cell and dies fifteen days later.[5]

---

[4] Heribert Rosweyde, ed., *De vita et verbis seniorum libri x, historiam eremiticam complectentes* (Antwerp: Plantin, 1615). The short title by which the collection was known in the Middle Ages, *Vitae Patrum*, was added in the second edition, 1628. The whole is reprinted in *PL* 73–74. For the *Vita Thaisis,* see note 5, below.

[5] The translated excerpt here is taken from Ward, *Harlots of the Desert*, p. 83. For the Latin text of the *Vita Thaisis* (*BHL* 8012) in the *Vitae Patrum*, see *PL* 73.661–62 (also *AS* Oct. 4.225). The most significant early texts in Syriac, Greek, and Latin, have been collected and printed by Nau, "Histoire de Thais." For an alternative view of the early development of the legend, see Freire, *A versão latina*, 1.18–24. The iconographical tradition is described in Kirschbaum and Bandmann, eds., *Ikonographie der Heiligen*, p. 428, and Rochelle, *Post-Biblical Saints Art Index*, p. 228. The most recent and exhaustive study of all aspects of the development of the Thaïs legend is by Gloria Ann Capik, "La Vie de Thais: Prolegomena."

What germ of historical truth, if any, lies behind this dramatic story? St. Antony, the desert father, is real enough, and a monk by the name of Paphnutius is mentioned in the life of St. Antony. The name "Thaïs" is identical to that of the famous courtesan who was associated with Alexander the Great. But nowhere do we find historical evidence for the association of these names with the narrative events just summarized or, indeed, for anything like the events themselves. At the beginning of the twentieth century a sensation was caused when the Egyptologist Albert Gayet announced that the mummified remains of Serapion and Thaïs had been discovered in Egypt. These remains were placed on display at the Musée Guimet in Paris, and in a stunning display, Gayet staged the resurrection and entombment of Thaïs before the eyes of his enchanted audience. In his published account of the results Gayet takes a more cautious attitude: responding to the criticism that he was said, on one day, to have identified the legendary Thaïs with the remains he had uncovered, only to deny this claim the next day, he writes, for the record, "I have no convincing document that would allow me to identify the bodies exhumed from the necropolis with the historical Serapion and Thaïs. Neither do I have any authorizing me to claim the opposite; under these circumstances, loyalty forbids me to pronounce."[6] Nonetheless it is clear where his own heart lies and the remainder of his essay seeks to establish grounds for believing in the possibility, at least, of the identification. Towards the conclusion he takes the audience on what might today be called a "visualization," a recreation in heightened romantic prose of the site as it would have been perceived by Thaïs and Serapion in the fourth century: "Who was this Serapion?" wonders Gayet, ". . . . Without doubt, one of those unknown solitaries, withdrawn into the ideal mountain of dreams which is the mountain of Antinoë, so hollowed out with grottoes that one might call it one immense beehive."[7]

This is great stuff, almost as good as the story of Thaïs herself, with Gayet exerting a charismatic power to compel belief reminiscent of nineteenth-century mesmerists. History, alas, has not been kind to either, and an essay published in 1903 by Pierre Battifol convincingly reduces Gayet's work to the "art of faking mummies." Battifol not only casts doubt on Gayet's most fundamental assumption, that the name recorded on the sepulchre is actually that of Thaïs, he further builds an excellent case for the legend of Thaïs having arisen in the late fourth century as an entirely fictitious morality story. In the eyes of the most ascetical monks at this time, he explains, Christians who sinned after having received baptism could not receive remission for their sins. A memoir written by the Egyptian bishop Ammonios records a message sent by St. Antony whose purpose was to counter this extreme theological position (which had already been officially repudiated by the church): "Those who after their baptism have fallen into sin, as happens nearly everywhere, if they beg for divine mercy, if they lament their faults sincerely, they are mercifully received in grace by God, and all their sins are remitted." The city

---

[6] Gayet, *Antinoë et les sépultures de Thaïs et Sérapion*, pp. 35–36 (our trans.).

[7] Ibid., p. 40.

of God, in other words, was not just a city of the perfect and the pure, but a city of penitents and the creation of the legend of Thaïs became a way of confirming at the popular level the words of St. Antony.[8]

True or not, the legend, with its message that no sinner is beyond the reach of God's compassion, has inspired a variety of rewritings, including a Latin play, *Pafnutius*, by the tenth-century canoness Hrotsvit of Gandersheim.[9] One of six dramas composed by Hrotsvit in rhymed rhythmic prose, *Pafnutius* aims, while imitating the style of the Roman comedian Terence, to offer a holy alternative to works in which "the shameless acts of lascivious women" were portrayed.[10] While scholars remain undecided as to whether Hrotsvit's plays were ever actually performed, their sophistication is not in doubt. Typical of her elaboration of the allegorical potential of the figure of the harlot are the words Paphnutius uses to describe Thaïs to the abbess whose protection he solicits on her behalf:

> I have brought you a half-dead little she-goat, recently snatched from the teeth of wolves. I hope that by your compassion its shelter will be insured, and that by your care, it will be cured, and that having cast aside the rough pelt of a goat, she will be clothed with the soft wool of the lamb.[11]

More recently, Thaïs' story has given rise to a novel by Anatole France (1891), an opera by Massenet (1894), a Broadway play (1911), and a Hollywood film (1918).[12] The first of these offers an extraordinary inversion of the prostitute's salvation at the hands of the monk. For France, the prostitute is the heroine, priestess of the life-affirming religion of love, and Paphnutius is the lascivious villain whose life-denying asceticism is both wrong-headed and a sham. In refusing Thaïs' love he loses his chance at a kind of existential salvation, a choice he

---

[8] Battifol, "La Légende de Sainte Thaïs," 207–17. Battifol's position is affirmed by H. LeClercq in Cabrol and LeClercq, eds., *Dictionnaire d'archéologie chrétienne et de liturgie*, 1, pt. 2.2337–40, and somewhat more hesitantly by Capik, "La Vie de Thais," p. 40.

[9] Hrotsvitha, abbess of Gandersheim, *Opera*, ed. Homeyer, pp. 328–49. *Pafnutius* is available in English (*Paphnutius*) in *The Plays of Hrotsvit of Gandersheim*, trans. Wilson, pp. 93–122. For other Latin versions and epitomes of the Thaïs legend, including a poem by the twelfth-century poet Marbod, see *BHL* 8012–19. Capik, "La Vie de Thais," pp. 13–24, has the most complete listing and discussion of Latin versions (pp. 13–24), and of translations into medieval French (pp. 46–66) and Middle English (pp. 67–87), as well as Bohemian, Dutch, German, and Italian (pp. 88–97).

[10] Hrotsvitha, *Plays of Hrotsvit*, trans. Wilson, p. xi.

[11] Hrotsvitha, *Plays of Hrotsvit*, trans. Wilson, p. 112. For a good discussion of Hrotsvit's use of allegory and symbolism see Charlotte Thompson, "Paphnutius and the Cultural Vision." Thompson notes (p. 115) that in the tenth century the converted harlot was gaining popularity as a figure for the Church and the sinning soul rescued by grace.

[12] Capik, "La Vie de Thais," pp. 132–55.

regrets for the rest of his life.[13] If much of France's highly original interpretation seems ludicrously anachronistic, he does raise a question that may have occurred to more than one reader, medieval as well as modern: just how pure are the motives of a monk who frequents a brothel? Is it not, in fact, possible that a secret lust has been deflected by the embarrassing perceptiveness of the whore who knows that there is no place God does not see? While no medieval version shares France's underlying conviction that belief in God is merely an illusion, the complex set of responses which the legend itself enables can be seen as one of the sources of its continuing fascination.

Thaïs in the *Northern Homily Cycle*

Unlike many of the sources for the saints' lives gathered together in this collection, the *Northern Homily Cycle* (*NHC*) is not a legendary. Extant in twenty manuscripts and three distinct recensions, the *NHC* is in essence a sermon collection: the prologue announces the author's intention to provide vernacular versions of the Gospel lections for Sundays (although other days are also provided for), in order to supplement sermons for laymen who go to church regularly but do not understand Latin or French. Beginning with Advent, each item offers a paraphrase of the day's gospel, followed by an explanation in part dependent on patristic exegesis and concluding in some (but not all) cases with an illustrative tale. Along with narratives of saints and monks, the tales offer bits of folklore, risqué fables, and accounts of miraculous beasts. Originally composed in a Northern dialect at the beginning of the fourteenth century, perhaps by an Austin canon, the collection is clearly aimed at a popular audience but often reveals a greater level of sophistication and erudition than its near contemporary, the *South English Legendary*.[14]

---

[13] Anatole France, *Thaïs*, trans. Douglas. For an interesting analysis of the reasons for the popularity of France's novel in its own time, as well as its subsequent decline, see Booth, "Irony and Pity Once Again."

[14] *NHC* is known variously to scholars as the *North English Homily Collection*, the *Northern Homily Collection*, and, as here and in the standard edition (see below), the *Northern Homily Cycle*. There is as yet no description of the *NHC* that is at once comprehensive and easy to follow. Despite its outdated nature, J. E. Wells' *Manual of the Writings in Middle English*, which includes the *NHC* under the heading of "Homilies and Legends" (pp. 287–92), may be the simplest place to begin (see also Gerould, *Saints Legends*, pp. 164–76). The revised version of the *Manual* contains no parallel listing in the section on saints' legends, though individual legends of saints, including Thaïs, are included in the bibliographical section (Charlotte D'Evelyn, "Saints' Legends," in *MWME* 2.313–39, 556–635). A recent brief guide is Morey, *Book and Verse*, pp. 323–30, useful for further references and especially for its list of the gospel pericopes from Nevanlinna's edition. Still valuable, however, is Carl Horstmann's detailed discussion and

St. Thaïs

The Gospel passage for which the *NHC* Life of St. Thaïs serves as illustration is John 3:16–21, a text which was assigned to the Monday following Pentecost and part of which I quote below:

> Because the light is come into the world and men loved darkness rather than the light: for their works were evil. For every one that doth evil hateth the light and cometh not to the light, that his works may not be reproved. But he that doth truth cometh to the light, that his works may be made manifest: because they are done in God.

The *NHC*-poet's exposition of this passage skillfully elaborates the metaphors of light ("Criste that lufly lyght") and darkness ("syne that es gastely myrkness"), concluding with a vividly concrete simile of the robber who works in the dark:

He braydyth on the thefe that hatith lyght	*resembles*
And doith his robry on the [n]yght;	
He dredith more man is syght	*man's*
Tha[n] God is that seith al his plyght.[15]	*God's; sees; condition*

These words lead directly into the tale, where the homily's thematic linkage with Paphnutius, who seeks ever a place more withdrawn from public sight, and Thaïs, who knows that God sees everywhere, soon becomes apparent.

Unlike the other five Middle English adaptations of the legend of Thaïs, the *NHC*-poet finds only the first part of the story relevant for the purpose of illuminating the gospel passage from John.[16] The single scene elaborated by him is the initial encounter between Thaïs and Paphnutius for which he creates some lively dialogue. The second and for many redactors more significant component of the tale, which details Thaïs' imprisonment and suffering along with her final release, is reduced to a mere eight lines. Although this is not one of the *NHC*-poet's more original or imaginative efforts, by limiting his narrative in this way, he does achieve a stronger thematic focus: first, on the impossibility of concealing evil from God and, second, on the will to repentance as itself definitive.

---

description of the contents of the different *NHC* manuscripts, *Altenglische Legenden*, pp. lvii–lxxxviii. Informative though more specialized discussions can be found in the following: Heffernan, "Orthodoxies Redux," 75–87; *NHC* 1.1–4; Heffernan, "The Authorship of the 'Northern Homily Cycle.'"

[15] San Marino, Huntington Library MS HM 129, fol. 114r; see below and note 20.

[16] For the other versions see: Arnoldus of Liège, *An Alphabet of Tales*, ed. Banks, 1.2–4; *Jacob's Well*, ed. Brandeis, pp. 22–23; *ScL*, 2.215–22; the 1438 *Gilte Legende* (not printed); William Caxton, *The Golden Legend*, ed. Ellis, 5.240–44.

According to Ruth Mazo Karras, the story of Thaïs, of all the medieval English representations of prostitute saints, places the most emphasis on money. The Church taught that women bore the major responsibility for a sexuality viewed primarily in negative terms, and it was lustfulness and sexual immorality which chiefly defined the prostitute; the connection with financial exchange, though less significant, nonetheless brought with it the further taint of venality.[17] The twelve pence which Paphnutius offers Thaïs in the *NHC* are more than the typical price of a prostitute in the fourteenth century,[18] and thus draw attention to the commercial nature of the transaction, but generally speaking it is difficult to see anything uniquely English about this version, which follows the *Vita Thaisis* found in the *Vitae Patrum* very closely. More significant, perhaps, is the author's selection of this particular legend to illustrate his gospel pericope. The words of Jesus as quoted by John are, after all, concerned with wrongdoers who hide from the light, a category which potentially includes just about any sinner one might care to name. Yet the metaphor of furtive concealment does perhaps have a specific and powerful affinity with the image of sexual sin for medieval writers and audiences, as suggested, for example, by St. Augustine's emphasis on the shameful need, in brothels and marriage-chambers alike, for secrecy and privacy in sexual intercourse, or what Shakespeare's Edgar would call "the act of darkness."[19]

NHC Texts of Thaïs

Sixteen of the twenty extant manuscripts of the *NHC* belong to the original early fourteenth-century recension whose primary home was in the North of England, perhaps in Yorkshire. The first of the two major expansions is represented by the Vernon and Simeon manuscripts, dating from the late fourteenth century, which render the collection in a Midland dialect, and add new homilies particularly for each day in the octaves of Easter and Pentecost. The second major expansion is found in two fifteenth-century manuscripts, Cotton Tiberius E. VII and Harley 4196. Like the first recension, this version is composed in a Northern dialect; distinguishing features include the introduction of fresh material from the Vulgate into the previously composed homiletic material, expansion of narrative items, though without greatly changing them, and the addition of a series of saints' legends as readings for Christmas week. Our text, taken from a manuscript copy of *NHC* in the Huntington Library in San Marino, MS HM 129,

---

[17] Karras, *Common Women*. See Chapter 6, "Saints and Sinners," pp. 102–30, and especially p. 125 for a discussion of Thaïs.

[18] Karras, *Common Women*, pp. 80, 125.

[19] See Augustine's *De Civitate Dei* 14.18, trans. *Concerning the City of God against the Pagans*, pp. 579–80. See also Shakespeare's *King Lear* 3.iv.84.

belongs to the original unexpanded version. The Anglo-Irish provenance of this early-fifteenth-century manuscript (see below) suggests the widespread popularity of a collection that began to be dispersed throughout England by the end of the fourteenth century.[20]

Language

As one might expect of a late copy of a work that had circulated widely in different parts of the country, HM 129's text of the Life of St. Thaïs displays a variegated linguistic profile, partly preserving the original Northern dialect of *NHC*, but also revealing features identified by Michael Benskin and Angus McIntosh as characteristic of the English-speaking parts of southern Ireland.[21] The original dialect of *NHC* is evident in the retention of some mainly Northern words such as *till* (line 12, "to"), *kythe His brethe* (line 30, "show His ire"), and *grete* (line 35, "wept"). On the other hand, *graythyd* (line 15, "arrayed"), although not uncommon in Northern texts, is more widespread in the South (its rhyme-word *said* [line 16], however, suggests that the original form here was the Northern form *graid*, preserved in Vernon, *greide/seide*, and Harley 4196, *graid/said*). The Northern present-indicative suffix is found in *lyis*, rhyming with *Tayis* (lines 1–2), and in *dedys/ledys* (lines 25–26).[22] By contrast, within the line, where rhymes are not affected, the scribe uses the South English and Midland form of the third-person present singular, as is usual for Medieval Hiberno-English (MHE): *-eth/-th*, as in *seith* (line 22) and *doth* (line 28) (compare Add. 38010, *sees* and *duse*). The apparently Northern/Northwest form of the feminine singular pronoun, *scho*, might also be the choice of the Anglo-Irish scribe of HM 129 rather than deriving from a genuinely Northern exemplar. Also typical of the Anglo-Irish provenance established by Benskin and McIntosh is the combination of traits observable in the following examples: *and* (line 2), a back-spelling of *an*, resulting

---

[20] For a full description of MS HM 129, see Dutschke, et al., *Guide to Medieval and Renaissance Manuscripts in the Huntington Library*, 1.164–73. For the most recent and accurate listing and categorization of *NHC* manuscripts, see *NHC* 1.2–4, and Heffernan, "Orthodoxies," p. 81n8. Existing printed versions of the Thaïs story in *NHC* are: 1) the original unexpanded version, London, BL MS Add., in Rosenthal, "Vitae Patrum," pp. 158–59; 2) the Vernon Manuscript (Oxford, Bodleian Library MS Eng. poet. A.1), in Horstmann, "Die Evangelien-Geschichten," p. 279; 3) the expanded version, BL MS Harley 4196, in Rosenthal, *Vitae Patrum*, pp. 159–60, and Nevanlinna, *Northern Homily Cycle* (who also prints the biblical text and homily which preface the legend), 2.229–33. Of these the closest to HM 129 is the Vernon text.

[21] Benskin and McIntosh, "A Medieval English Manuscript of Irish Provenance." See also McIntosh and Samuels, "Prolegomena to a Study of Medieval Anglo-Irish."

[22] See also the same couplet in the Northern manuscript Additional 38010, printed in Rosenthal, "Vitae Patrum," p. 158.

from the tendency of MHE to drop the *-d* from the consonant pairs *-nd* and *-ld*; doubling of consonants: *gaff* (line 7, "gave"), *gyff* (line 19, "if"), *whare off* (line 28, "where- of"), *yyff* (line 32, "if"), and *casst* (line 31, which is also characteristic of Middle Scots). The striking form *whare* (line 44,"were") is typical of texts from the counties immediately north and west of Dublin in the fifteenth century.[23]

Indexed in

IMEV 40.

Manuscripts

Cambridge, University Library Gg.5.31, fols. 91r–91v.

London, British Library MS Add. 38010, fols. 96r–97r.

London, British Library MS Harley 4196, fols. 96v–97r.

Oxford, Bodleian Library, Eng. poet. A.1 (*SC* 3938), fol. 195v. [The Vernon MS.]

San Marino, Huntington Library MS HM 129 [*olim* Phillipps 20420], fols. 114r–114v. [Base text.]

Previous Editions

Horstmann. "Die Evangelien-Geschichten." P. 279.

Rosenthal. "The Vitae Patrum." Pp. 158–59. [BL MS Add. 38010.]

---

[23] Benskin and McIntosh, "A Medieval English Manuscript of Irish Provenance," p. 129.

IV

The Life of St. Thaïs
in the Northern Homily Cycle (early 1300s),
from San Marino, Huntington Library MS HM 129, fols. 114r–114v

	And a gode litill tale her lyis	
	Off and hore that heght Tayis —	*Of a whore that was named*
	Hir fairhede folis to foly drow,	*beauty drew fools*
	And many sowilis with syn scho slow —	*souls with; destroyed*
5	And an hermyte that heght Pafniyzy	
	That made hyr leve thus hyr foly.	*leave (abandon)*
	He come and gaff pennyis twelfe	
	And sayd, "I woll syn with thee myselfe."	
	And into chamyr scho hym led	*[a] chamber*
10	And schowyd hym a fayr bed,	
	And bade hym, "Stey and do thi will,"	
	And he answerd and sayd hyr till:	
	"This sted is noght privey inoghe."	*place; private*
	And in a nidyrmor chamyr scho hym droghe,	*lower room*
15	Into a chamyr honestely graythyd	*respectably (neatly) arrayed*
	And suche wordys to hym scho said:	
	"In this sted may no thynge us se	
	Bot God fro whom noght hyd may be."	
	And he askyd gyff scho trowyd ryght	*if she believed*
20	That noght is hyd fro Godis syght.	
	And scho sayd, "Ye, well trow I	
	That He seith all as Allmyghty."	
	And he sayd, "Than is grete ferly	*marvel*
	How thou art so bold and hardy	
25	To do byfor Hys eyin thase dedys	*before His eyes those*
	That man to pyn off Hell ledys,	*pain*
	As lechery and spousbrek	*[Such] as; adultery*
	Whare off the fyre of Hell doth wrek.	*For which; punish*
	So lange may thu thi Loueryd wrethe	*Lord anger*
30	That on thee woll He kythe His brethe,	*manifest His wrath*

	And into Hell fyre thee casst	
	Bot yyff thou leve thi syn in hast."	*Unless*
	That hore was aferd of the pyne off Hell	
	And to the hermyte fete scho fell,	
35	And sore scho grete and eskyd mercy	*wept*
	And sayd scho wold leve hyr folly.	
	"I am," scho sayd, "a synful caytyfe,	*wretch*
	And with penauns I woll mend my lyfe;	
	Thou have, leve fadyr, mercy of me	*Dear father, have mercy on me*
40	And gyfe me leve to folow thee."	
	To wildernys scho with hym yede	*went*
	And bet with penauns hyr mysdede.	*atoned by penance [for]*
	I may noght of hyr penauns tell	
	For lange hit whare in to dwell;	*would be*
45	Bot to yow schortely for to speke,	
	Scho toke on hyr body suche wreke,	*inflicted; punishment*
	That hyr sely gost to God yold scho,	*blessed spirit; yielded*
	And so gyff God that we may do.	*God grant*

IV

Notes to The Life of St. Thaïs
in the Northern Homily Cycle *(early 1300s)*

1–2   *And a gode litill tale . . . heght Tayis.* The beginning of the Life in HM 129 is indicated by a marginal Latin abbreviation for the word *narracio*. Only Vernon, with its Latin incipit — *Conversio Taysis meretricis* ("the conversion of Thaïs the prostitute") — makes explicit reference to a conversion. Where our manuscript begins by using the vernacular *hore* (line 2) to describe Thaïs, other versions name her a *woman of ill fame* (BL Add. 38010), a *comun woman* (BL Harley 4196), or simply a *woman* (Vernon; CUL Gg.5.31). On the doubled consonant in *Off* and the redundant *d* in *and*, see the Introduction.

1–6   *And a gode litill tale . . . hyr foly.* Harley 4196, which contains the "expanded" version of the *NHC*, adds ten lines overall to the Life of St. Thaïs. Most of the changes are not substantive, except near the beginning where the story is said to take place "in þis land" and a couplet is added, explicitly linking the prostitute with an urban location as well as making the monk's virtuous intention more apparent. The first twelve lines are as follows (ed. Rosenthal, *Vitae Patrum*, p. 159; our punctuation):

> Sum tyme bifell so in þis land
> A comun woman was dwelland
> In a cete and vsed hir syn
> And spared nowther more ne myn.
> Hir fairhede foles to foly drogh
> And many sawles with sin scho slogh.
> So it bifell opon a tide
> A haly hermit þar biside
> Thurgh þe grace of god mighty
> Gert hir forsake hir foly.
> He went to þe cete on a day
> Þis woman for he wald assay.

The last two lines here are a little closer to the *Vitae Patrum* which says of Paphnutius: *sumpto habitu saeculari et uno solido, profectus est ad eam in quadam Ægypti civitate* (*PL* 73.661; *AS* Oct. IV.225a).

5   *And an hermyte*. *And* coordinates with "Off and hore" (line 2), i.e., the tale is of a whore and a hermit. Lines 3–4 constitute a parenthesis. But other manuscripts, whose scribes apparently found the syntax odd, introduce a finite verb in the next line to complete the sense: e.g., Vernon: *And an hermyte, . þat hiȝte pasmid, / Made hire hit leue . And hire folwid* (ed. Horstmann, "Die Evangelien-Geschichten," p. 279). Other versions supply the verb *wo(n)ned* (dwelled), as in *Ane hermyte wonned thar ner herby* (CUL Gg.5.31; compare BL Additional 38010, in Rosenthal, *Vitae Patrum*, p. 158).

     Pafniyzy. The hermit's name varies widely among the different versions (although neither Thaïs nor the monk is named in Harley 4196). The most common spelling in the manuscripts is *Pan(n)onye*, as in Gg.5.31 and Add. 38010. The form *Pafniyzy* (most likely the *z* is pronounced *s* or *ts*) seems to derive quite regularly from the medieval Latin *Paphnutius*, also rendered *Pafnuce* elsewhere in ME.

10   *fayr*. So HM 129, Vernon. Harley 4196, Add. 38010 read *burely*. Metrically, *burely* seems more likely to be the original reading, but at some stage in the transmission of the text, a scribe has dropped the Northern adjective in favor of *fayr*, presumably for the benefit of readers in the South of England.

14   *And in a nidyrmor chamyr scho hym droghe*. This metrically "heavy" verse is possibly corrupt in the manuscript. While *nidyrmor* may well be a Northern variant of ME *nethermore* ("lower"), the resulting five-beat, eleven-syllable verse is unusual in *NHC*, as is the duplication of "chamyr" in lines 14–15. Vernon and Harley agree on a quite different rendering: *And Innore more þo heo hym drouh* (Vernon) and *Inermare þan scho him drogh* (Harley), while Add. 38010 evades the issue with *Than by þe hande sho hym droghe*.

15   *graythyd*. Vernon, Harley: *graid*. See above, Introduction.

25   *thase*. HM 129: *that*.

27   *spousbrek*. The literal meaning of the term is "the breaking of marriage vows." The last recorded usage of this colorful word, according to the *OED*, was in 1637, if we except James Joyce's 1922 allusion, in *Ulysses*, to a dog "got in spousebreach." All the *NHC* manuscripts I have examined refer explicitly to lechery and adultery, whereas the *Vita Thaisis* makes no mention of particular sins, referring only to Thaïs' general responsibility for the damnation of men's souls as well as her own: *Cur tantas animas perdidisti, ut non solum pro tuis, sed et pro illorum criminibus reddita ratione damneris?* (*PL* 73.661; *AS* Oct. IV. 225a) ("Why are you causing the loss of so many

souls so that you will be condemned to render an account not only of your own sins but of theirs as well?" trans. Ward, *Harlots*, p. 83). The other Middle English versions, as well as *LA*, which served as an additional source for some of them, likewise follow the *Vita*'s more generalizing language. The *NHC*-poet's dramatic allusions to hellfire and an angry God represent a further expansion of the Latin text.

30   *brethe*. A variant form of *brathe*, from ON *brœði*.

37   *caytyfe*. Our scribe uses here the Norman form of the Old French word for captive. Compare Chaucer's use of the same word in The Pardoner's Tale, in the self-description of the Old Man as "a restelees kaityf" (*CT* VI[C]728), and in The Parson's Tale, in the description of the damned: "For, as seith Seint Gregorie, 'To wrecche caytyves shal be deeth withoute deeth' " (*CT* X(I)213).

40   *leve to folow thee*. Several versions add the following lines to Thaïs' speech here: "To do pennaunce for my synne / That I sa lang has dwelled in" (CUL Gg.5.31).

44   *lange hit whare in to dwell*. This would appear to be the *NHC*-poet's way of signaling his radical abbreviation of the second half of the legend.

48   *gyff God that we may do*. The Vernon manuscript adds the following prayer, the language of which (e.g., the end-rhyme of the first couplet, implying *holi gost* was originally *hali gast*) suggests it originated in the North, not in the scribe's own region:

Lord, send vs . þe holi gost	
And ȝif vs grace . vr synnes (to) wast,	*purge*
þat we ne drede . wo ne wandreth	*distress*
But ȝif vs mekenesse . and Meth,	*temperance*
And bring vs . to þat ilke blis	
Ther meke men . wiþ Crist is. amen.	

V(a)

The Life of St. Benedict
in the South English Legendary *(c. 1270–80)*

Introduction

The Cult and Legend of St. Benedict (feast day March 21)

Like St. Jerome and St. Thaïs, St. Benedict died not as a martyr but of natural causes, and was venerated in the medieval church calendar as a "confessor." Also like Jerome, he was an ascetic and a monk. But whereas Jerome, although born a Latin, is associated like Thaïs with the Eastern desert tradition, Benedict embodies and represents the newer monasticism of the West. He and Jerome are also different in that Jerome's life is very well known to us from a variety of sources other than the hagiographic legends composed to promote his cult, whereas Benedict's life as "father of monks" is known almost exclusively from his legend: the Life of Benedict written in 594 by Pope Gregory the Great, half a century or so after Benedict's death.[1]

Gregory's Life of Benedict imitates the hagiographic traditions of the East, which Jerome himself helped transmit to the West, in that it is part of a larger work, the *Dialogues*, devoted to the miracles and visions of many saints of a specific region, in this case Italy.[2] The *Dialogues* is, among other things, a Roman imitation of and response to the widely read books of lives, sayings (*apophthegmata*), and miracles of Eastern desert saints, known collectively as the *Vitae patrum* or *Lives of the Fathers*. Although composed in Greek, most of these were available in Latin translations from the fifth century.[3] A major difference between the *Dialogues* and the

---

[1] The precise date of Benedict's death is unknown, but it was apparently around the middle of the sixth century.

[2] Gregory the Great, *Dialogues*, ed. Adalbert de Vogüé. Book 2, the Life of Benedict, forms vol. 2 of de Vogüé's edition. In the Bollandists' list of hagiographical texts, *BHL*, it is numbered 1102. For an English translation of Book II that includes a commentary by de Vogüé, see Gregory the Great, *The Life of St. Benedict*, trans. Costello and Bhaldraithe. More widely available now is the translation by White, in *Early Christian Lives*, pp. 165–204, 218–20.

[3] De Vogüé (*Dialogues* 1.118, 119) makes this point in some detail: "After two centuries, [Gregory's] country finally will possess, thanks to him, a hagiographic collection comparable to that of Egypt. By him alone, there will be for Italy a Rufinus, an Athanasius, and a Palladius. . . . With [the *Dialogues*] his country had not only a grand biography, capable of rivaling that of Antony, but also an abundance of

Lives of the Fathers lies in Gregory's emphasis, especially in his Life of Benedict, on the cultivation of a disciplined, orderly, communal life (cenobitism) within the walls of a monastery proper.[4] In the *Lives of the Fathers* the monks are generally depicted as pursuing more individualistic and specifically eremitic goals, even when their cells are physically close together and they are ostensibly under the authority of an abbot. Gregory's Benedict may begin his spiritual odyssey as a youthful hermit and ascetic living in solitude, but he spends most of his life as the founder and builder of a great abbey, as the leader and corrector of its monks, and as its protector against human, demonic, and natural enemies.

Another of the *Dialogues'* departures from the Eastern model is its use of frequent dialogic interludes between narrative episodes, in which Gregory the "author" is questioned by his disciple, the deacon Peter, giving Gregory a chance to comment on and interpret some of the implications of the narratives themselves. Gregory probably adapted this dialogic device from Sulpicius Severus, whose lengthy supplement (404–06) to his Life of Martin of Tours was cast in dialogue form,[5] although the dialogue was common enough in Latin literature in general.

Gregory's account of Benedict, which forms book 2 of the *Dialogues*, is regarded by many modern scholars as historically reliable in its biographical outline, even if much of its detailed substance is taken up with the saint's miracles. Benedict was born in Nursia (now Norcia, near Spoleto, northeast of Rome) to wealthy parents who sent him to Rome to be educated. Put off by the immorality of his fellow students, Benedict found more congenial company in a religious community at Affile (present-day Effide). When his first miracle (using prayer to mend a broken sieve) drew unwanted attention, he retreated to a cave near a lake at Subiaco, just north of Effide. He emerged three years later to govern a nearby community of monks, but when they

---

hagiographical events comparable to that of the *Vitas patrum* in Egypt." On Gregory's reasons for writing the *Dialogues*, see also Markus, *Gregory the Great and His World*, pp. 62–66, and Petersen, *The Dialogues of Gregory the Great*, pp. 56–58. There is no complete modern edition or translation of the *Vitae patrum* (*PL* 73–74) as a whole, but some of the separate works of the collection can be found in Waddell, *The Desert Fathers*; Ward, *The Sayings of the Fathers*; Russell, *The Lives of the Desert Fathers*; Palladius: *The Lausiac History*, trans. Meyer; Athanasius, *The Life of Antony*, trans. Gregg. See also White, *Early Christian Lives*, which includes Athanasius' Antony, and Jerome's lives of Paul of Thebes, Hilarion, and Malchus, as well as the lives of Martin and Benedict. For a historical survey of Eastern monasticism, see Chitty, *The Desert a City*.

[4] For a historical overview of Western monasticism, and for further bibliography on the subject, see C. H. Lawrence, *Medieval Monasticism*. Still the classic work on Benedictine and Cistercian monastic spirituality is that of Leclercq, *The Love of Learning and the Desire for God*.

[5] Trans. Hoare, *Western Fathers*, pp. 68–144. The dialogue form is not unknown in the Eastern tradition, of course, but it is more commonly found in doctrinal and devotional treatises than as a narrative frame, as in Sulpicius, or as a commentary on narrative, as in Gregory. See, for example, John Cassian, *Conferences*, written in Latin in southern Gaul a generation or so after Sulpicius.

reacted against his strictness by trying to poison him, Benedict returned to his solitary life at Subiaco. When the fame of his holiness gave him more and more followers, he organized them into twelve separate communities of twelve monks each. He eventually settled with his closest disciples at Monte Cassino,[6] midway between Rome and Naples, and there built the monastery where he spent the rest of his life and wrote his famous rule. Benedict's death is variously dated in 543 or 547, although Gregory does not specify this or the saint's birth date (probably c. 480).

That Benedict's cult as a saint began to flourish immediately following his death (or even before), at least in central Italy, is evident from certain details in Gregory's Life of Benedict that could easily be affirmed or contradicted by his contemporaries (e.g., his statement in *Dialogues* 2.1.2 that "everyone could see" the miraculously mended sieve hanging "for many years . . . above the doors of the church [of Effide]" until the Lombards took over the Spoleto region in 576),[7] as well as from the living testimony of certain of Benedict's followers who apparently were carefully cultivating the memory of his sanctity and of the places associated with him.[8] But in the century and a half following his death, Benedict's local cult had become international, as Pope Gregory's own stature as an ecclesiast and writer ensured the publication of the Life in the *Dialogues* all over Christian Europe, and especially in the northwest, where Gregory's own cult was flourishing by the late seventh century.[9] In the early eighth century, his Life of Benedict was quoted and imitated by the Insular hagiographers who wrote the early

---

[6] The imposing mountain site is still occupied by the Benedictines, although the present buildings date only from 1964. The monastery, in a strategic location commanding an important north-south route, has been sacked, destroyed, and rebuilt five times in all, beginning with the Lombards who destroyed Benedict's foundation in 585 (see *Dialogues*, ed. de Vogüé, 2.17.1–2). It was the object of fierce fighting between the Germans and the Allies in 1944.

[7] *Quod annis multis illic ante oculos omnium fuit, et usque ad haec Langobardum tempora super fores ecclesiae pependit* (*Dialogues*, ed. de Vogüé, 2.130). That a sieve was on display over the church doors does not authenticate the miracle, of course, but it attests to the persistence of local belief in the miracle.

[8] *Dialogues*, ed. de Vogüé, 2.1.2. Although Monte Cassino had been abandoned by the monks in the face of the invading Lombards who sacked it, Subiaco, the site of Benedict's cave-hermitage and the first community he established, was evidently in Gregory's day actively fostering the saint's memory (the "cell" or small monastery there was headed by Honoratus, one of Gregory's informants). See the story of the madwoman in Benedict's cave (*Dialogues* 2.38.1), the only posthumous miracle Gregory recounts.

[9] The earliest clear English reference to Benedict as a notable saint is that of Aldhelm of Malmesbury in his *De Virginitate* (see below, note 20), which is dated in the last quarter of the seventh century. Aldhelm was schooled at Canterbury, under Archbishop Theodore and Abbot Hadrian, who were no doubt responsible for encouraging Benedict's cult. On the early cult of St. Gregory in England, see Thacker, "Memorializing Gregory the Great."

Latin lives of, for example, Cuthbert, Columba, and Guthlac,[10] and some of the oldest surviving manuscripts of the *Dialogues* are of Anglo-Saxon provenance.[11]

The *Old English Martyrology*, a ninth-century compilation of Old English prose summaries of and extracts from saints' legends, draws on the *Dialogues* for its lengthy tribute to Benedict, and near the end of the century Bishop Wærferth of Worcester, at King Alfred's request, translated Gregory's *Dialogues* into Old English as one of the books "most necessary for all men to know."[12] In the later tenth century, Ælfric of Eynsham composed an OE prose life of Benedict, based on the *Dialogues*, as one of his Second Series of *Catholic Homilies*, intended for preaching to the laity.[13] By this time, Benedict's feast day, along with that of Gregory himself (March 12), was in the calendar of national holidays.[14] In the monastic calendars, another important feast day was that of Benedict's "translation" (July 11), commemorating an event that was widely believed to have occurred in the late seventh century: namely, the removal of Benedict's body, with that of his sister Scholastica, from their joint tomb amid the ruins of Monte Cassino, to the abbey of Fleury on the River Loire in Merovingian France. The monks who later rebuilt Monte Cassino vehemently denied that the body had been moved, but by the late ninth century, the cult of Benedict's relics at Fleury (Scholastica's were taken to Le Mans)[15] was flourishing, as witness a substantial collection of Benedict's posthumous Fleury

---

[10] Felix, *Felix's Life of Saint Guthlac*, ed. Colgrave, chapter 35, pp. 110–13, 186; in Colgrave, ed., *Two Lives of Saint Cuthbert*, see the anonymous Life of Cuthbert III, 2 (pp. 96–97, and the note, p. 326) and Bede's Life of Cuthbert, chapters 11, 14, and 19 (pp. 192–93, 202–203, 222–23, and the notes on pp. 347 and 350); Adamnan of Iona, *Life of St Columba*, trans. Sharpe, pp. 146 and 305n189.

[11] For example, Stuttgart, Württembergische Landesbibliothek MS Theol. et Philos. Qu. 628 is believed to have been copied in Northumbria, or on the Continent by an Anglo-Saxon scribe, at the turn of the seventh century. See Gneuss, *Handlist of Anglo-Saxon Manuscripts*, p. 144 (no. 937.3).

[12] For an accessible edition of the OE text and a modern translation, see *An Old English Martyrology*, ed. Herzfeld. For the OE *Dialogues* see Wærferth of Worcester, *Bischofs Waerferths von Worcester Übersetzung der Dialoge Gregors des Grossen*. On the place of the *Dialogues* in the Alfredian canon, see Bately, "Those Books That Are Most Necessary for All Men to Know."

[13] Ælfric of Eynsham, *Ælfric's Catholic Homilies: The Second Series*, ed. Godden, pp. 92–109.

[14] This is evident not only from Ælfric's inclusion of Benedict's feast in the cycle of *Catholic Homilies*, which covered only the major feasts celebrated in all churches (not just the monasteries), but also from other sources, including an OE poem on the major feasts, *The Menologium*, in which the following verses (37–44) occur: "On the eleventh night [of March], the holy Gregorius hastened into God's protection, renowned in Britain. Also Benedictus nine nights later sought out the Savior, the brave and strong-hearted one, the Ruler's servant, who is praised by men learned in written lore, soldiers faithful to the rule." See Dobbie, ed., *The Anglo-Saxon Minor Poems*, p. 50 (translation EGW).

[15] See the Life of St. Scholastica (V[b]), below.

miracles, published in 870 by Adrevald of Fleury, who also wrote a popular account of the removal of the relics from Monte Cassino. All this helped ensure Fleury's prosperity and importance in the reform movement of the time, and its customs and culture were profoundly influential on the reform-minded English monks of the mid- to late tenth century.[16] From this point on, in England, as well as in France and elsewhere in Northwest Europe, Benedict's place as one of the most important saints in the Church calendar was assured.[17]

The wide veneration of Benedict as a saint, while promoted by the Life in Gregory's *Dialogues*, and the cult of his relics at Fleury and Monte Cassino, was also due to the prestige and authority of his rule.[18] Written in simple and at times colloquial Latin, and indebted to earlier cenobitic codes,[19] it comprises a set of rules governing the daily routines and ideals of monks living and worshiping God as a disciplined community owing strict obedience to one abbot. Their communal purpose is to perform the daily liturgy in God's praise, *opus dei* ("the work of God"). Their individual goal is to win salvation through denial of all worldly, and especially sexual pleasures, humility, and the subordination of individual needs and desires to those of the community, in obedience to the abbot. Indeed the emphasis is as much on communal discipline as on spirituality. Eventually this rule would become the best known and most influential guide to monastic organization in the Middle Ages, but its effect was by no means instant or uniform in the early medieval period. Even among the Anglo-Saxons, whose conversion to Christianity was begun by Augustine of Canterbury and other missionaries sent by Benedict's biographer, Gregory the Great, at the end of the sixth century,[20] Benedict's *Rule*

---

[16] See Nightingale, "Oswald, Fleury and Continental Reform."

[17] For a sampling of post-Conquest English calendars, see Wormald, ed., *Benedictine Kalendars after 1100*. Of the several extant liturgies, secular and monastic, for Benedict's feast day see, for example, *Ordinale Exon.*[Exeter], ed. Dalton; *The Hereford Breviary*, ed. Frere and Brown, 2:129–30; *The Monastic Breviary of Hyde Abbey, Winchester*, ed. Tolhurst, 4.232r–234v; *Breviarium ad usum insignis ecclesiae Sarum*, ed. Procter and Wordsworth, 3.225–34.

[18] See the translations of Benedict, *Rule*, by Fry, *RB 1980*, and McCann, *The Rule*.

[19] E.g., an earlier, anonymous *Rule of the Master* and Rufinus' translation of the rule of St Basil. On the former, see Knowles, *Great Historical Enterprises*, pp. 137–95; on Basil's rule, see Lawrence, *Medieval Monasticism*, pp. 9–11.

[20] This is not to deny the early importance of Benedict's rule in Anglo-Saxon England. One of the oldest surviving copies (Oxford, Bodleian Library MS Hatton 48) was written in England in the eighth century. St. Wilfred (634–709) boasts of first bringing the rule to Northumberland (see Eddius Stephanus, *The Life of Bishop Wilfrid*, ed. Colgrave, chs. 14 and 47, pp. 30–31, 98–99). Aldhelm of Malmesbury (d. 709) in the metrical version of his *De Virginitate* glorifies Benedict, erroneously, as the first to provide a rule for monastic life. See Aldhelm, *Aldhelm, the Poetic Works*, trans. Lapidge and Rosier, p. 122. But the typically early Anglo-Saxon (and Frankish) double monasteries of men and women can hardly be termed "Benedictine," nor is there any precedent in the rule or in the Life of Benedict for Wilfred's and Aldhelm's

was only one of a number from which monastic founders could pick and choose, and "mixed rules" (sometimes blending Celtic and Roman traditions) were the rule rather than the exception for centuries.[21] Benedict's great work was "never imposed as a code," insists David Knowles,[22] but it was invariably an important standard of reference wherever there were attempts to achieve reform and a greater measure of discipline and regularity amid the wide fluctuations in monastic fervor in the West.

In one such reform period, in England in the late tenth century, for example, Benedict's rule was not only frequently copied and glossed but was also translated by Bishop Æthelwold of Winchester into the vernacular in two recensions, one for monks, the other for nuns, which were still being copied in the twelfth century.[23] From the later Middle Ages, no less than five separate translations are extant, beginning with the early ME prose version (adapted from the OE) from the nunnery of Wintney, in Hampshire.[24] Although the Wintney translation may have been necessitated solely by the results of linguistic change (the vocabulary and syntax of the OE version having finally become too difficult for people to understand), it is equally possible that it was prompted by developments in the larger ecclesiastical world. For the early thirteenth century also saw the beginning of the efforts of some leading clerics, under the influence of the reforming popes, to bring a greater discipline and uniformity of practice to the country's numerous older abbeys. It was during this period for the first time, following the important Fourth Lateran Council in 1215, that abbots of the leading monasteries were required by papal decree to meet together in periodic councils, called "chapters," to enact legislation that would be binding on all the member institutions. It is only from this period on that one can properly speak of the independent English monasteries (those that professed some form of allegiance to the rule of Benedict and were not Cistercian or Premonstratensian) as constituting an "order."

---

simultaneous enjoyment of monastic and episcopal careers. The tendency of English monks to become bishops persisted, and is especially noticeable between c. 950 and 1200.

[21] On the mixed rule of Benedict Biscop at Bede's Jarrow and Wearmouth, see Blair, *The World of Bede*, pp. 197–201, and Knowles, *The Monastic Order in England*, pp. 22–23. There was a similar arrangement at Lindisfarne under Cuthbert, according to the anonymous Life of Cuthbert, III, 1: *Two Lives*, ed. Colgrave, pp. 94–97.

[22] "The Rule of St Benedict" in Knowles, *Saints and Scholars*, p. 8.

[23] Æthelwold, bishop of Winchester, *Die angelsächsischen Prosabearbeitungen der Benediktinerregel*, ed. Schröer. See the list of Latin and OE MSS of Anglo-Saxon provenance in Gretsch, "Æthelwold's Translation of the 'Regula Sancti Benedicti,'" pp. 126–27. Passages from the rule were supposed to be read aloud at specified times in the reformed monasteries, according to Æthelwold's *Regularis*, ed. and trans. Symons, pp. xl and 17. On Anglo-Saxon monasticism in general, see Knowles, *Monastic Order in England*, pp. 16–82.

[24] See Charlotte D'Evelyn, "Instructions for Religious," in *MWME* 2.460–63, 654–55.

The emphasis on the *ordre* of St. Benedict in the *SEL* Life of St. Benedict (e.g., lines 10 and 55) may well reflect these developments.[25]

SEL Version: The Life of St. Benedict

The earliest ME account of Benedict, found in sixteen of the extant manuscripts of *SEL*, is an abbreviated and highly selective version of the life in Book 2 of Gregory's *Dialogues*.[26] For the poet's more immediate source, Manfred Görlach posits "an unknown epitome."[27] The chapter on Benedict in *LA* (BHL 1113)[28] contains all of the episodes used by the *SEL*-poet, omits the moralizing pieces of dialogue that often follow individual episodes in the *Dialogues*, and also omits some of the same episodes as the *SEL* Life (e.g., the diabolical kitchen fire that is the sequel to the immovable stone episode in *Dialogues* 2.10.1–2).[29] But Görlach points out that the *SEL* Life of St. Benedict includes details absent from *LA* and adopts a different ordering of episodes. It is also much shorter. On the other hand, the *SEL* version does not correspond significantly, except in length, with that in any of the medieval English breviaries,[30] so the poet may well have been working creatively with more than one source, including possibly *LA*.

Of the thirty-eight chapters of Book 2 of the *Dialogues* or the twenty-seven chapters covered by *LA*, twelve are employed in the Life of St. Benedict. The following table compares the order of the ME episodes with that of the *Dialogues* and presents the chapter numbers of the original according to their position in the Life of St. Benedict.[31] Note that the ordering tabulated in the last column is, as far as we can tell, original to the *SEL*-poet:

---

[25] See Knowles, *The Religious Orders in England*, 1.9–27.

[26] In addition to the version edited here, there is a second *SEL* Life of St. Benedict (discussed briefly below, note 33), as well as later prose versions in the *Gilte Legende* and Caxton's *Golden Legend*. See D'Evelyn, "Saints' Legends," in *MWME* 2.571.

[27] Görlach, *Textual Tradition*, p. 155.

[28] *LA*, ed. Maggioni, 1.309–20; trans. Ryan 1.186–93.

[29] See the text below, lines 59–62; compare *LA*, trans. Ryan, 1.189. In both cases the fire episode is omitted and the narrative proceeds immediately to the stone wall episode (*Dialogues* 2.11).

[30] Görlach, *Textual Tradition*, p. 155.

[31] Lines not accounted for in the table are considered to be original to *SEL*. Other original lines, which have been integrated into an episode from the *Dialogues*, will be discussed in the endnotes.

SEL Life of St. Benedict, Episodes	*SEL* Lines	*Dialogues*, Book 2, Chs.
Benedict leaves Rome for the wilderness	1–6	Prol., 1.1
Benedict resists sexual temptation	11–24	2.1–2
Easter feast followed by preaching	31–50	1.6–7
Benedict establishes Monte Cassino	51–54	8.10–11
Devil disrupts building work by sitting on a rock	58–62	9
Benedict resuscitates monk crushed beneath a wall	63–73	11.1–3
Monk distracted from prayers by demon	77–92	4.1–3
Devil tempts pious layman to break fast	93–114	13.1–3
Jester in king's clothing tries to fool Benedict	115–22	14.1–2
Servant hides keg of wine meant for Benedict	123–34	18
Monks fret about lack of food during famine	135–44	21.1–2
Unblessed monk's body will not remain buried	145–58	24.1–2
Benedict predicts the day of his death	161–66	37.1–2
Monks' vision of Benedict's highway to heaven	169–74	37.3

The *SEL*-poet's originality can be seen first in the way he streamlines the narrative by re-ordering the events of Benedict's early career. By reversing the order of Benedict's temptation and the Easter feast, omitting any mention of his community at Subiaco, and skipping directly to the calling of the saint's disciples to Monte Cassino, the *SEL*-poet has Benedict's life mirror Christ's withdrawal into the wilderness, his temptation, and the beginning of his ministry (see Matthew 4:1–21). Apparently with the latter in mind, the poet represents Benedict as an itinerant preacher (*SEL* Life of St. Benedict, lines 48–50), a role more commonly associated with the Franciscans or Dominicans than the Benedictines.[32] In the *Dialogues*, on the other hand, Benedict is never seen to "wander about" preaching, and only after he founds Monte Cassino does he begin "calling all the surrounding people to the faith by his continual preaching" (*Dialogues* 2.8.11), whereas here in *SEL* it is made to appear that as a result of his successful ministry Benedict is led by God's grace to Monte Cassino.

Second, unlike the authors of *LA*, the breviaries, or the other *SEL* version (see below), whose narratives move from miracle to miracle without explanation or comment, this poet provides a rationale for the *SEL* narrative by adding transitions between events or sets of miracles. For example, because Benedict is so steadfast in his prayers in the wilderness, the devil tempts him (*SEL* Life of St. Benedict, lines 7–10); because the saint observes Lent faithfully and is nourished at Easter, he is able to begin preaching (lines 47–48); because the devil envies Benedict's success, he strives to thwart the building of his monastery (lines 58–59); because Benedict

---

[32] See Görlach, *Textual Tradition*, p. 49, and Wolpers, *Die englische Heiligenlegenden des Mittelalters*, p. 239.

176

rebuffs Satan's repeated assaults, the devil turns his attention to the saint's monks (lines 75–76); because Benedict's holiness enables him to anticipate the devil's wiles, he repeatedly displays his gift of prophecy (lines 115–74), which is shown to be increasingly far-reaching. Each of the subsequent four miracles of prophecy testifies to the magnitude of the saint's power and propels us toward the climax of Benedict's prediction of his own death and the angelic confirmation of his glorious reception in Heaven.

Third, in addition to demonstrating Benedict's power as a saint and ultimately as an intercessor, the *SEL*-poet seems at times to reinforce the saint's benevolence throughout the story. For example, when a servant hides a cask of wine for himself that is intended for Benedict and his brethren, the *SEL* adds that he is not poisoned by the snake awaiting him inside the cask because Benedict did not wish it (lines 133–34), and when the monks fret about the shortage of food at the monastery, Benedict comforts them (lines 140–41) instead of trying to "correct their timidity with mild reproof" (*Dialogues* 2.21.1). Finally, when Benedict hears of the monk whose body will not remain in its tomb, the saint himself goes to bless the body (*SEL* Life of St. Benedict, lines 153) rather than remaining at his monastery and sending a consecrated host to be placed on the monk's chest as he does in the *Dialogues* (2.24.2).

It remains to be seen, however, if the *SEL*-poet's selection and reordering of episodes from Benedict's life are his own, original work, or influenced by one or more of the numerous medieval retellings of the *Dialogues* account.

Text

As with all but two of the *SEL* legends in this collection, we have chosen the text of the early-fourteenth-century manuscript, Oxford, Bodleian Library MS Ashmole 43 (A) for our edition (see I[a], Introduction). A's version of the Benedict legend is the same as that found in fifteen of the twenty-five major manuscripts of *SEL*; four others preserve a shorter version, apparently unrelated to the A version and structured in a less obviously skillful fashion.[33] It has not yet

---

[33] Görlach in his apparatus (*Textual Tradition*, p. 154) distinguishes the longer and shorter versions of *SEL*'s Life of St. Benedict as be and !be respectively. The shorter version is printed from the copy in the Vernon manuscript (Oxford, Bodleian Library, Eng. poet. A.1. [*SC* 3938]) by Justin McCann, "Early English Verses on St Benedict," pp. 53–56. After a rather repetitive preamble (lines 1–8), in which Benedict is credited (line 2) with being the founder of the *white monkes* (i.e., the Cistercians), and after describing Benedict in rather vague terms as the leader of a community of ascetics dwelling in the *wildernesse* and performing many miracles (lines 9–18), the narrator goes on to relate five miracle episodes which together present a quite different (and much briefer) picture of Benedict from that in A's Life of St. Benedict. Three of the stories are in both versions (compare the above table of episodes): viz., Benedict resists sexual temptation (Vernon, lines 19–34; compare A, Life of St. Benedict, lines 11–24);

been determined which was written earlier, but neither is found in Oxford, Bodleian Library, MS Laud Misc. 108 (L), representing the earliest layer of the collection, although a short legend for Benedict's sister, Scholastica, is (see the second part of this chapter, V[b]). The existence of the two separate *SEL* lives of Benedict remains a conundrum deserving closer study; suffice it to point out here that it suggests (but does not prove) the absence of a life of Benedict from the earliest layer of *SEL*. Although the shorter version is confined to a small group of manuscripts affiliated with L, they are all late manuscripts from outside the Southwestern dialect area in which *SEL* originated. The shorter version also seems to lack the poetic quality of the main *SEL* corpus as well as of the longer Life of St. Benedict, and may well be a later composition.

According to Görlach, among the manuscripts preserving the longer version edited here there are many minor variants and instances of abridgement, though most amount only to a few couplets. We have not attempted to collate A fully with the numerous other witnesses, but the endnotes provide occasional variants from Cambridge, Corpus Christi College, MS 145 (C) edited by D'Evelyn and Mill.[34] In a few instances, we have used C readings to emend what seem to be clearly mistakes in the A copy, although for the most part A's text seems somewhat superior to C's. In addition to the usual minor modifications required by the format of the Middle English Texts Series, we have supplied initial *h* where it is frequently omitted by this scribe from the possessive pronoun *his*.

For a sketch of the main linguistic features of the A manuscript, see above, I(a), Introduction. Some additional linguistic information is provided in the notes below.

Indexed in

IMEV 2860.

---

monk distracted from prayers by demon (Vernon, lines 35–42; compare A, Life of St. Benedict, lines 77–92); servant hides keg of wine meant for Benedict (Vernon, lines 63–74; compare A, Life of St. Benedict, lines 123–34). The remaining episodes are: a raven helps Benedict detect poison in bread sent by a jealous priest, Florentius (Vernon, lines 43–62; compare *Dialogues* 8.2–3, trans. White, p. 176); a novice monk (Placidus) is saved from drowning by a monk (Maurus) walking on water (Vernon, lines 75–88; compare *Dialogues* 7.1–2, trans. White, p. 175). These two episodes from the shorter *SEL* Life of St. Benedict were added on additional leaves, by a Cheshire scribe in the mid-fifteenth century, to a late-fourteenth-century text of the longer version, London, BL MS Egerton 2810 (M). See Görlach, *Textual Tradition*, pp. 91, 154, and 270n86.

[34] DM 1.122–27.

Manuscripts

Cambridge, Corpus Christi College MS 145, fols. 46r–48r.

Oxford, Bodleian Library MS Ashmole 43 (*SC* 6924), fols. 46r–48v.

Previous editions

The South English Legendary. Ed. D'Evelyn and Mill. 2.543–46.

McCann. "Early English Verses on St. Benedict." Pp. 48–53.

V(a)

The Life of St. Benedict
in the South English Legendary *(c. 1270–80),*
from Oxford, Bodleian Library MS Ashmole 43, fols. 46r–48v

	Seyn Benet was ibore in the lond of Nursie.	*born*
	To Rome he was wel yong isend to lerny of clergie.	*sent; get an education*
	His norise he hadde ther with him, that him wel wuste.	*nursemaid; knew*
	Fram hire he stal aday wel stillich, that heo it nuste,	
5	And bilevede his scole and ek hyre, and al that were him sibbe,[1]	
	And wende him into wildernesse, in penaunce vorte libbe.	*for to (i.e., in order to) live*
	Honger and chele he hadde ther and no conford he nadde.	*cold; comfort*
	Stablich he was in his beden; swithe strong lif he ladde.[2]	
	Siker me may be that the devel to him envye hadde.	*men (i.e., one) can be sure*
10	Of the ordre that he make scholde swithe sore he dradde.	
	At on tyme, as this gode mon in his orisouns him nom,[3]	
	In fourme of a threstelcok the devel to him com,	
	And flei al aboute his eien, that he scholde his mighte do[4]	
	Vorte chatche this vaire fowel and bileve his beden so.	*chase (hunt); abandon*
15	This holi mon nom never yeme, ac to God his herte sette.	*took; heed*
	The devel flei vorth his wei, tho he ne mighte him noght lette.	*when; hinder (disturb)*
	Tho he sei that thulke art nas noght, another doghede he nom.[5]	
	In fourme of a vair womman sone to him he com.	*fair (lovely); soon*
	With vair speche and fol semblaunt, in such fondyng heo him broghte[6]	
20	That he bilevede his orisouns: go vorth with hire he thoghte.	*to go forth; intended*

(margin note: devil as thrustlecock)

---

[1] Lines 4–5: *From her he stole away one day very quietly, [so] that she knew it not, / And forsook his school and also her, and all [those] who were related to him*

[2] *Steadfast he was in his prayers; [a] very severe life he led*

[3] Lines 10–11: *He (the devil) dreaded very much the [monastic] order that he (Benedict) was destined to found. / One time, when this good man took himself into (i.e., was engrossed in) his prayers*

[4] *And flew all around his eyes so that he (Benedict) would exert himself*

[5] *When he saw that kind of trickery was all for nought, he tried another "noble deed"*

[6] *With fair speech and wanton demeanor, by such temptation she brought him*

The gode mon sone ofthoghte his thoghte;   to amende he was cof.[1]

Thoru signe of the verei Crois   the devel awei he drof.   *Through; true Cross*

Himsulf he strupte naked anon,   among thornes he wende   *stripped*

And breres, and turnde him her and ther,   that al his flesc torende.

25   Thulke sunne he boughte dere inough,   as we scholle oure myd righte.

The devel agen him never eft nolde with thulke sunne fighte.[2]

Vor wen he mai a mon overcome   with a sunne, with his lore,

Vonde he wole myd thulke sunne   ever the leng thc more.

Ac gif the man wole fight agen,   ofscamed he is so sore

30   That never eft he nele, myd thulke sunne,   fonde him vor fore.[3]

At Ester feste our Lord com   to a prest ther biside.   *feast of Easter; nearby*

"Thou makest," he sede, "mete inough   agen this heie tyde,[4]

And my seriaunt in wildernesse   is in much pyne,   *servant; pain*

Vor he nath nother mete ne drinke.   Parte myd him of thyne."   *has neither; share*

35   This prest, as our Lord him het,   to wildernesse he gan gon;   *commanded*

Mete and drynke he nom with him,   Seyn Benet he vond anon.   *found at once*

"Seyn Benet," he sede, "ichabbe thee here   mete and drinke ibroght   *I have*

That schost bothe ete and drinke,   vor vaste ne schaltou noght."   *That you should*

"Yuse, sothes," quath this gode mon,   "tyme it is to vaste,

40   Me and ech Cristeneman,   the wule Leynte ilaste."[5]

"Nai," sede the prest, "nost thou noght   that Leynte is al ido,   *knowest; done (finished)*

"And the heie tyme of Ester   is nou icome us to?"   *solemn feast*

"Seistou soth?" quath this holi mon,   "Our Lord ous lete him queme.[6]

Wat Crist, ich wende it were Leynte: ne nom ich never yeme.

---

[1] *The good man soon repented his thought; to make amends he was quick (eager)*

[2] Lines 24–26: *And briars, and turned himself here and there, so that all his flesh was torn to shreds. / He paid dearly for this sin, as we must [pay for] our own, and rightly so. / The devil would never again fight against him with this sin (i.e., sexual temptation) [as his weapon]*

[3] Lines 27–30: *For when he (the Devil) may overcome a man with a sin, by means of his prompting (lit., teaching) / Tempt [the man] he will with that [same] sin ever more and more. / But if the man will fight back (lit., again), ashamed he (the Devil) is so sorely / That never afterwards will he, with that [same] sin, tempt him (the man) on account of fear (i.e., of being shamed)*

[4] *"You make," he said, "food enough in preparation for this solemn feast["]*

[5] Lines 39–40: *"Yes, surely," said this good man (i.e., disagreeing with the priest), "it is time to fast, / [For] me and all Christians, as long as Lent lasts"*

[6] *"Are you speaking the truth?" said this holy man. "May our Lord let us please him (i.e., give us grace to do right)*

45	Me thincth it were a quinte man, bote he couthe of gramerie,
	That scolde stele a day of Leynte. Sugeth yif ich lie."[1]
	Seyn Benet et tho wel, and dronk, and thonkede Godes sonde,
	And suththe he wende wide aboute and prechede in the londe.
	To God he turnde much folc and to Cristendom,[2]

50	So that to the hul of Casyn thoru Godes grace he com.	*hill*
	Maumets he vond ther vele, and men of luther lawe.	*Idols; many; wicked belief*
	That folc he turnde to Jhesu Crist, the maumets he gan todrawe,	*to break in pieces*
	Of Seyn Jon the Baptist a chirche he let rere,	*had [men] build*
	Ther men honoured Jhesu Crist, that hethene er were.[3]	
55	The ordre of Blake Monekes verst he made there.	*first*
	Mony gode men come to him that the abit bere.	*who donned the [monk's] habit*
	The verst abbei he let ther rere that was in eny londe.	
	To him and to his word also the devel hadde gret onde.	*envy*
	A ston hi vounde swithe vair, to hor wal good and clene[4];	
60	Al that folc that ther was ne mighte it hebbe up ene.	*lift; once (i.e., at all)*
	Seyn Benet isei the devel him holde, he blessede the ston,	*saw; him (i.e., it)*
	The devel orn tho awei; a man it bar anon.	*ran; one man carried it*
	Another tyme, tho this worc was heie imad of stone,[5]	
	The devel com to Seyn Benet as he sat alone.	
65	"Benet," he sede, "thou hast worcmen. Icholle loke hou hem spede.[6]	
	I ne com noght nei hem mony a day. Ich mot ofservy my mede."	*must earn my pay*
	Seyn Benet sende his worcmen word and bed hem iwar be;	*bade; aware (wary)*
	He sede hor fo hem wolde lette, thei hi ne mighte him isé.	*their foe; hinder; though*
	Ar the messager sede his ernde, the devel was wel yare,	

---

[1] Lines 44–46: *Christ knows, I thought it was Lent: I wasn't paying attention. / It seems to me, it would take a very clever man (i.e., cleverer than I), unless he had mastered higher learning, / To steal a day of Lent. Say if I lie"*

[2] Lines 47–49: *Saint Benedict ate well then, and drank, and thanked God's providence / And afterwards he went all over the countryside preaching. / He converted many people to [faith in] God and Christianity*

[3] *Where men honored Jesus Christ, who heathen before were*

[4] *They found a very fine stone, good and clean (i.e., just the right shape) for their wall*

[5] *On another occasion, when the stone "work" (i.e., building under construction) had already been built to a considerable height*

[6] *"Benedict," he said, "You have workmen. I'll go see how they are getting on["]*

70   and that worc velde up to doun: hi ne mighte hem be so ware.[1]

A yong child, that monek was,   was offalle there.   *monk; killed (crushed)*

Gret deol his bretheren vor him made   and bivore Seyn Benet him bere.   *lament; bore*

This holi mon thoru Godes grace   rerede him fram dethe to lyve.   *raised; life*

The devel nadde never eft no power   his worc so to drive.[2]

75   Ac tho he nadde power non   his worc to lette more,   *although he had no power; hinder*

He fondede bringe his monekes   in to luther lore.   *tried to; wicked ways*

Ther was monek that he ne might noght   with his bretheren dure

— As him thoght, vor feblesse —   his service to hure,

Ac al dai eode out of the quer.   His felawes it bispeke,

80   Seyn Benet hi tolde vore,   leste he his ordre breke.[3]

This gode mon bihuld at matyns,   yif he it mighte leve.   *watched; if he would leave it*

He sei a lute, blac, pollede grom   nyme the monek bi the sleve[4]

And ladde him out fram his felawes.   Seyn Benet yeme nom;   *took heed*

Bihynde he siwede afterward   and to the monek com.   *followed*

85   A lute he smot him with a yerd,   and a lute bigan to chide,   *little; smote; switch*

The pollede boie flei anon,   he ne dorste no leng abide.   *dared; longer*

"Merci, sire," this monek sede,   "I ne mighte it habbe bileved

Vor feblesse, thei me wolde   habbe ismyte of myn heved."[5]

"No," sede this holi mon,   "al to prest thou were   *you were far too amenable*

90   "To the devel that thee ladde vorth.   He ne schal nan more thee lere."   *guide*

This monek eode in to his felawes   and ever eft stable was.   *steadfast*

Never eft nadde the devel mighte   to bringe him in that cas.   *power; situation*

A good, seli mon biside   ofte hadde in wone   *virtuous; from nearby; was accustomed*

To Seyn Benet vastyng wende,   to herie Godes Sone.

---

[1] Lines 69–70: *Before the messenger said his errand (message), the devil was well ready / And hurled* (lit., *felled*) *that work upside down; they were not able to be wary enough*

[2] *The devil never again had power to overthrow his (i.e., Benedict's) building*

[3] Lines 77–80: *There was a monk who could never bear to stay to hear the whole of the divine office with his brother monks — on account of weakness, as it seemed to them — / But every day he would leave the choir; his fellows complained, / Told about it in the presence of Saint Benedict, lest he (the monk) violate his order (i.e., his obedience to the rule of the order)*

[4] *He saw a little, black, close-cropped boy take the monk by the sleeve*

[5] Lines 87–88: *"Thank you, sir," this monk said, "on account of my feebleness of will, I was unable to forsake it (i.e., this habit of leaving church) even if I were to be beheaded (i.e., no matter what I did)"*

95 A dai as he was thuderward, a man come bi the weie[1]
 And sede he wolde with him go, wondri aboute and pleie. *wander; joke around*
 "Bred," he sede, "ichabbe ibroght: it is good that we ete,
 Leste we be feble bi the wei, vor defaute of mete." *lack of food*
 "Nai, sothes," this other sede, "I nele noght my fast breke *certainly; will not*
100 Ar ic habbe thoru godes grace with this holi mon ispeke." *Before; spoken*
 Another dai bi thulke weie, this felawe com efsone, *on that same road; again*
 And bed him ete vor feblesse, ac he nolde noght do his bone. *bade; grant his request*
 The thridde tyme as this gode mon toward Seyn Benet eode, *third*
 His felawe com yut to him, and gret love him gan bede. *yet again; friendship; offered*
105 He ladde him in to a wel vair med of floures and of gras, *very fair meadow*
 A cler welle theron amydde, a swithe vair stude it was. *in the middle of it; place*
 So vaire he spak tho with him, vor this murie stude, *in favor of; pleasant*
 That this gode mon sat adoun and et, as he him hadde ofte ibede.
 Ac tho he com to this holi mon, Seyn Benet anon sede, *when*
110 "Gode mon, thou nere noght iwoned to don er this dede.[2]
 The devel thee hath ifonded thrie, to bringe thee to this rede. *tempted thrice; decision*
 At the thridde tyme he thee overcom in thulke false mede.
 Hit nas no med, thei it thoghte so; he wolde him narwe thenche
 Hou he mighte man best bitraie, his godnesse to quenche."
115 This holi mon wuste of alle thing, thei he ne seie it noght,[3]
 So that the tidinge of this wonder to the kynge was ibroght. *As a result; miracle*
 That sothe he wolde therof fonde. His beste robe he tok there[4]
 And clothede therwith a jogulour as thei he kyng were. *minstrel (fool)*
 Noblich he eode to Seyn Benet: kyng he was, he sede. *Nobly (i.e., in a stately manner)*
120 "Leve sone," quath this holi mon, "do of other monnes wede.[5]
 Kynges clothes thou hast on, vor he dude the hider sende, *he (i.e., the king) did*
 Ac a fol thisulf thou hider come, and a fol thou schalt hom wende." *fool*
 A gentil man ther biside twei costres myd wyne

---

[1] Lines 94–95: *To travel to Saint Benedict, fasting [on the way], in order to praise God's Son. / One day as he was traveling thither, a man came along the road*

[2] *"Good man, you were not wont (accustomed) to do this kind of thing before now"*

[3] Lines 113–15: *["]It was no meadow, although it seemed so; he (i.e., the devil) wanted to plan carefully / How best he might betray mankind and destroy his piety." / This holy man had knowledge of events even when he did not see them*

[4] *The truth about this he wished to put to a test. His best robe he took there*

[5] *"Dear son," said this holy man, "take off other men's garments*

Sende a day Seyn Benet,   bi on of his hyne.

125 Ac this messager was unhende.   That on costret vorth he ber;[1]

That other he hudde bi the wei,   to nyme it hamward ther.   *hid; take; from there*

He eode vorth with the on costret   and dude his presaunt blithe.[2]

"Leve sone," quath this holi mon,   "thonk thi lord swithe,   *thank; very much*

Ac of that costret ne drink thou noght   that thou hast bileved bihinde.   *left*

130 Ac ar thou drinke, loke wat   thou might therinne fynde."   *before; what*

This hyne was ofschamed sore,   ac tho he com withthoute toun,[3]

A neddre he vond in his costret   swymme up and doun.   *snake*

That was vor wreche thuder icome   him to aposny there;

Ac, vor al his gile, Seyn Benet   nolde that he apoisined were.[4]

135 In a dere yer it bivel   that Seyn Benetes covent   *year of dearth (scarcity); monastery*

Vor defaute, as many othere,   hadde ofte gret turment.[5]

As hi were a day, sore afyngred,   to the bord isete,

Hi nadde bote vif smale loves,   hi alle, to the mete.[6]

Ech monek was sori in his herte,   ac nothing hi ne sede.

140 "Wi beth ye sori?" quath Seyn Benet.   "Of nothing nabbe ye drede.   *do not have*

Habbeth gode hope to Jhesu Crist,   vor he is good and hende   *in; gracious*

Ar tomorwe this tyme,   inou he wole you sende."   *before this time tomorrow, enough*

In hor gerner, that empty was,   amorwe hi fonde and nome   *granary; next day; took in*

Two hondred sak vol of gode wete,   hi nuste wanne it come.

145 A monek wende out in a day,   ac so ne aughte he noght do,[7]

Withthoute leve of Seyn Benet   and withthoute his blessynge also.

He wende to speke with his frend,   as he dude er ilome,   *went; friends; often before*

And among his frendes he deide ther,   ar he agen come.

---

[1] Lines 123–25: *One day, a nobleman [who lived] near there sent, with one of his servants, two flagons of wine to Saint Benedict. / But this messenger was ill-mannered. So [only] one flask he took all the way*

[2] *He went forth with the one flask and offered his present graciously*

[3] *This man was sorely ashamed, but then he went outside the town*

[4] Lines 133–34: *It had come thither to poison him in revenge [for his theft], / But despite his falsehood, Saint Benedict did not want him to be poisoned*

[5] *Because of a shortage [of food], as [did] many others, often had much hardship*

[6] Lines 137–38: *When one day they, very hungry, were seated at the table, they had only five small loaves, altogether, for their meal*

[7] Lines 144–45: *Two hundred sacks full of good wheat, they did not know whence it came. / A monk went out on a day, but as he ought not to have done*

Me dude bi him as me aughte do,   and burede him wel vaste,[1]

150   Ac the erthe, anon so he was iburede,   up agen him caste.   *as soon as*

Hi burede him enes and efsones,   ofte and fele sithe,[2]

Ac the erthe him caste up agen.   His frend were wel unblithe.   *unhappy*

Seyn Benet hurde herof telle: thuder he gan gon.   *heard tell of this*

He blessede this wrech bodi   and het it burie anon.   *ordered it to be buried*

155   This men in the erthe it burede: stille anon it lay.   *these*

Ech mon hadde therof wonder,   that this miracle isay.   *was amazed; saw*

The erthe him nolde avonge,   vor he iblessed nas   *would not receive; for*

Of this holi mon Seyn Benet.   Nas this a wonder cas?[3]

The vaire miracles that of him were,   no tonge telle ne may.

160   Tho he was old and feble inou,   his ending he say.   *When; quite weak; foresaw*

The tyme he told of his deth,   ther bivore then sevethe day.   *foretold; the seventh*

Tho son him nyme a strong fevere: bote six dawes he ne lay.

Then sixte day he lette his bretheren   to the heie aughter him lede.

And there he let him houseli   and his orisouns he sede.[4]

165   To our Lord he huld up his honde   and thonkede his swete sonde,   *providence*

And ther righte deide at the weved,   bitwene his bretheren honde.[5]

In the vif hondred yer,   and in the eightethe yere,   *In the 580ᵗʰ year*

After that God an erthe com,   Seyn Benet deide here.   *on earth*

Twei monekes thulke nyght,   that in diverse stude were,

170   Seie, hem thoghte, on metynge,   as the angel hem gan lere.[6]

Hem thoghte hi seie a wel vair wei,   with floures swote and brighte,

Fram Seyn Benetes celle,   estward, swithe lighte,[7]

---

[1] Lines 148–49: *. . . before he had a chance to return. / Men dealt with him as men ought to do and buried him very securely*

[2] *They buried him once and a second time, often and many times*

[3] *Was this not a miraculous situation*

[4] Lines 162–64: *Soon after, a strong fever seized him: he lay [sick] for only six days. / On the sixth day he had his brethren (i.e., fellow-monks) lead him to the high altar. / And there he had them give him the Eucharist and his prayers he said*

[5] *And straightway died at the altar, between (i.e., supported by) his brethren's hands*

[6] *Saw, it seemed to them, one and the same dream, in which an angel instructed them*

[7] Lines 171–72: *It seemed to them that they saw a very fair road, with flowers sweet and bright, / [Extending] from Saint Benedict's monastery, eastward, brightly shining*

Into Hevene tille the other ende,[1]   and the angel hem sede:

"Thervorth Seyn Benetes soule   to Hevene we gonne lede."   *Along that way; did lead*

175   Nou God, vor the love of Seyn Benet,   ous lete then wei wende,   *let us travel that road*

And to the joie that he is inne,   to him come aten ende.[2]

---

[1] *Towards Heaven at the other end*

[2] *And let us come at the end to the joy that he is in*

V(a)

Explanatory Notes to the Life of St. Benedict in the South English Legendary (c. 1270–80)

5   *and al that wer him sibbe*. The poet's independence of *LA* is indicated here at the outset. Whereas Jacobus de Voragine says only that Benedict left his school and then his nurse, the ME version, in mentioning also Benedict's *sibbe*, appears to echo Gregory's *Dialogues* 2 Prologue 2: "and leaving his father's home and property," trans. White, p. 165. The ME poet, of course, has conflated Benedict's successive departures from the school and the nurse into one episode, omitting the miracle of the broken sieve (*Dialogues* 2.1.1–2). The *wildernesse* (line 6) to which Benedict retreated was a cave near Subiaco, in hilly country to the east of Rome.

7–10   *Honger and chele . . . swithe sore he dradde.* In these lines the poet gives a different impression of Benedict's wilderness experience from that in the Latin tradition, where there is no specific mention of him suffering cold or hunger, but rather we are told that various helpers made sure that he had a regular, if surreptitious, supply of bread from a local monastery and a comfortable feast on Easter Day. Moreover, the devil's hostility in the *Dialogues* is explicitly directed at Benedict's personal asceticism, not, as here, at the order that he would found (see *Dialogues* 2.2.4–7). The ME poet thus provides a larger motive for the ensuing, ongoing battle between Benedict and his disciples, on the one hand, and the devil on the other. See also below, note on lines 25–30.

12   *threstelcok*. Male thrush. The Latin sources describe it as "a small black bird, commonly called *merula*." Although *merula* means "blackbird," both the OE versions of this episode, like the *SEL*-poet, identify the bird not as an *osle* (ME *ousel, ouzel,* "blackbird"), but as a *throstel*, the song-thrush, a brown bird with a speckled breast, about the size and shape of an American robin. Dr. Christine Rauer informs us that the English blackbird and thrush belong to the same ornithological family, *Turdus*, of which *throstel/thrush* is the common English name (see *Webster's Deluxe Unabridged Dictionary*, second ed. [New York: Dorset and Baber, 1983], p. 1904, "thrush," with illustration). In all likelihood, therefore, *threstelcok* could just as easily mean today's "blackbird" as "thrush." De Vogüé in his edition of the *Dialogues* (2.137n1) notes the relevance of Matthew 13:4 (see also 13:19), and the fact that in hagiography demons frequently take the form of black birds.

188

15   *holi mon.* In the *Dialogues* and *LA*, Benedict drives the blackbird away with the sign of the cross, which the ME poet omits, transferring it to the episode immediately following. See next note.

17–25   *Tho he sei that . . . we scholle oure myd righte.* The poet makes significant changes to this episode, apparently to enhance Benedict's asceticism, and heighten the drama of the incident, but also to draw a moral different from that in the *Dialogues*. In the Latin version, it is implied that the blackbird is merely a sign that the devil is at hand, preliminary to the onslaught of a powerful erotic fantasy; but the *SEL*-poet treats the bird as a separate and different kind of temptation (*thulke art* — line 17), involving not just the joy of the chase, but also, presumably, the anti-ascetic prospect of a tasty little meal. The *SEL* Benedict, however, is so intent on his prayers to God, he does not even have to make the sign of the cross for the tempter to fly away discomfited. The second ploy, sarcastically termed a "noble deed" (*doghede* [line 17]: variant *dogheþe*, from OE *duguþ*; see *MED douth*), is also subtly different here from its sources. In the Latin *Dialogues*, the devil produces before Benedict's mind's eye (*ante ejus oculos mentis*) the silent image of a woman he had once seen, i.e., a memory of her. But in *SEL* the devil takes the actual form of a beautiful woman, enticing the lonely ascetic with her "fair" body and "fair" speech. This vivid bodily presence makes Benedict's momentary lapse more understandable, while his recovery is presented, with an emphatic piece of internal "rhyme rich," more as a triumph of individual will (*The gode man sone ofthoghte his thoghte* — line 21) than the result of divine aid (*Dialogues* 2.2.2: *superna gratia respectus ad semetipsum reversus*, "suddenly he was touched by heavenly grace and came to himself once more" [trans. White, p. 168]). In the Latin, Benedict's naked plunge into the briar patch is the *means* by which he frees himself forever of his temptation, a violent form of reflex conditioning, by which Benedict seeks (successfully) to associate the desire for sexual pleasure with the experience of extreme pain. Here in the *SEL* version, however, it is with the sign of the *verei* cross that Benedict *drof awei* the demonic erotic illusion, as if it were something more external than internal (line 22). The briar patch is now the *consequence* of, or *penalty* for, his sin (desire for sex and a return to the world), as the poet emphasizes with the metaphor of payment (*boughte dere* — line 25). The English poet's reinterpretation of this episode in penitential terms is characteristic of the pastoral theology of the thirteenth and fourteenth centuries. See, e.g., Pantin, *The English Church in the Fourteenth Century*, p. 192.

19   *fol semblaunt.* The variant reading in C (*fair semlant*) recalls the name of one of the arrows of Love, *Biaus Semblaunt* ("Fair Seeming"), in the well-known Old French dream-vision of Guillaume de Lorris and Jean de Meun, *Le roman de la rose* (thirteenth century); see the translation by Dahlberg, p. 43.

25–30   *Thulke sunne he . . . fonde him vor fore.* These lines have no specific parallel in the *Dialogues* and represent the longest addition among several that are aimed to teach readers why and how the devil attacks Christians and how to resist him (see also lines 9, 58, and 112–14). The discussion between Gregory and Peter at the equivalent point in the *Dialogues* (2.2.3–5) turns into an exegetical commentary on Numbers 8:24–25, on reserving positions of authority in the church for those old enough to have outgrown sexual temptation.

31–47   *At Ester feste our Lord com . . . Seyn Benet et tho wel, and dronk.* The Christian season of Lent (ME *leynten*, from OE *lencten*, "spring") lasts for forty days from Ash Wednesday to Easter Saturday, during which time all medieval Christians were required to fast in imitation of Jesus' forty days of fasting and temptation in the desert (Matthew 4:1–11) and also as ritual purification and penance in preparation for Easter's celebration of Christ's death and resurrection (it was also a time when winter food stocks, especially meat, were usually running low). This episode of Benedict's Easter visitor is based on *Dialogues* 2.1.6–7, where it occurs earlier than the temptation episodes involving the bird and briar patch. As pointed out in the Introduction to this chapter, the poet has rearranged the order of episodes as found in the Latin versions, the better to represent Benedict as imitating the life of Christ. The original episode is a gently humorous reflection on Benedict's isolation from society and his absorption in his ascetic solitude: he has lost track of time, not realizing that Lent is finished, and Easter has arrived (most would be hungrily counting the days). But God sends a local priest to him, so that Benedict will be able to share in the great and joyful Easter feast like everyone else. The episode is also a subtle reminder that God expects even holy ascetics to gratify their appetite for food and drink on solemn occasions, such as the day of the Resurrection. The ME poet increases the humorous content somewhat by having Benedict at first resist the priest's request that he end his fast, whereas in the Latin sources Benedict cheerfully accepts the priest's news at once. Moreover, there is further humor in the way the poet has Benedict, after realizing his mistake, protest that he is not ingenious or learned enough to have deliberately tried to "steal a day of Lent," i.e., appropriate an extra fasting day for himself, by recalculating the date of Easter (at least, this seems to be the meaning of the rather enigmatic lines 43–46).

47   *sonde.* A colloquial word for God's providence, literally "sending," what God sends. Compare Chaucer's The Man of Law's Tale: "She kneleth doun and thanketh Goddes sonde" (*CT* II[B¹]523).

50   *hul of Casyn.* Monte Cassino (modern Cassino, about 100 km southeast of Subiaco). In order to shorten his tale and give the impression that Monte Cassino (the mother

house of the Benedictine order) was Benedict's first monastery, the *SEL*-poet omits several episodes from the *Dialogues* after the briar patch incident: e.g., Benedict's first (abortive) abbacy of a local monastery, whose monks he abandoned after they tried to poison him (2.3.1–5); his subsequent founding of twelve monasteries and the growing attractiveness of his way of life to the noblemen of Central Italy, among whom were his well-known disciples, Placidus and Maurus (2.3.13–14); the hostility of the priest Florentius (2.8), which forces Benedict to leave his own monastery (thought to have been at Subiaco) to establish a new monastic site (Monte Cassino) for himself and his immediate disciples. The *SEL* version, on the other hand, makes it appear that Benedict happened upon Monte Cassino in the course of his travels as an itinerant preacher.

51   *Maumets*. From OF *Mahumet*, a common medieval form of the name of the Islamic prophet, Mohammed. Owing to the widespread misconception that he was worshipped as a pagan god, the name came to be used, as here, for any pagan idol. See also, e.g., the *SEL* Martyrdom of St. George, line 74 (I[a], above).

51–53   *Maumets he vond ther . . . a chirche he let rere*. Gregory (*Dialogues* 2.8.10–11) identifies Cassino as a *castrum* or fortified site half way up the mountain, with an ancient shrine (*fanum*) and temple of Apollo, and sacred groves of trees (*luci*). He explains how Benedict reconsecrated the temple as a Christian church dedicated to St. Martin of Tours, but smashed the statue of Apollo, overturned the god's altar and replaced it with a shrine or chapel (*oraculum*) in honor of John the Baptist. Gregory recommended similar procedures to his missionaries in England (see Bede, *Ecclesiastical History* 1.30), as is summarized memorably in the ME poem *Saint Erkenwald*, ed. Clifford Peterson, lines 15–19.

55   *ordre of Blake Monekes*. Benedict's famous rule was written at Monte Cassino, but the poet's language here is otherwise anachronistic. On the slow evolution of the Benedictine order, see the Introduction, above, and Knowles, *Saints and Scholars*, p. 8. The term "black monk," referring to the customary black robe or "habit" (see next note) did not come into regular use until the twelfth century, after the rise of the Cistercians, who wore a white habit. Not until the fourteenth century were those who followed the Benedictine rule actually called "Benedictines."

56   *abit*. "From earliest times the symbol of 'conversion,' of becoming a monk, was the reception of the habit, which publicly indicated an intention of living the life of a monk." Benedict, *RB 1980*, trans. Fry, Appendix 5, p. 449.

bere. The regular preterite plural of ME *bere(n)* (from the OE strong verb, *beran*). The preterite singular is *bar*, as below (line 62). The vowel of *bore*, the Modern English preterite, was transferred or "leveled" from the past participle, *-bore(n)*.

57   *verst abbei he let ther rere that was in eny londe*. The poet's claim that Monte Cassino was the first monastery in the world (understandable in view of the prominence of the Benedictines in the history of the Western Church) is, of course, historically untrue, and is indirectly contradicted elsewhere in *SEL* itself. The *SEL* St. Jerome, for example, has abundant details of life in the Bethlehem monastery of which Jerome was abbot (DM 2.428–34; see also above, III[b]). That text (line 157) dates Jerome's death (erroneously) in 334 in the twelfth year of Theodosius the Great, so his monastery is clearly said to predate Benedict's by almost 200 years, since *SEL* dates Benedict's death (again erroneously) in 580 (see below, Life of St. Benedict, line 167). See also the *SEL* St. Martin (lines 95–98), where Martin is clearly depicted as builder of a substantial abbey of monks, and later (line 267) said to have died in 466 (DM 2.486, 492), over a century before Benedict.

66   *ofservy my mede*. We adapt the reading of C (*of serui mi mede*) rather than that of A (*of hem servy my mede*), which does not correspond to any recorded usage of *serve* and produces a metrically heavy line. It is possible, however, that the A scribe's exemplar had *of hem ofservy my mede*, "earn my pay from them" (the rare verb *ofserve*, "earn, deserve," is explained in *OED* as a "half-translation" of OF *deservir*, English *of-* rendering French *de-*). The devil's darkly humorous remark here is the poet's own addition. The Latin version (*Dialogues* 2.11.1) says only that the devil taunted (*insultans*) Benedict and told him he was off to visit his workmen.

71   *offalle*. From OE *offeallan*, to fall upon, kill, destroy.

74–76   *The devel nadde never . . . in to luther lore*. The resuscitation miracle (adapted from *Dialogues* 2.11), which ends here, forms the climax of the episodes skillfully selected and arranged by the *SEL*-poet to demonstrate Benedict's personal conquest of the devil and his imitation of Christ. Next the poet relates a pair of episodes showing how the devil, after failing with the saint himself, seeks easier victims among Benedict's monks and laymen friends. The first of these episodes (lines 77–92) is moved from a point much earlier in the *Dialogues* (2.4) than the resuscitation miracle, while the second (lines 93–114) is taken from somewhat later (*Dialogues* 2.13), but they fit naturally together in the new arrangement.

77–92   *Ther was monek . . . in that cas.* In the equivalent episode of *Dialogues* (2.4.1–3), the monk has difficulty devoting himself to silent prayer with the rest of the brothers after the end of the *psalmodia* of the Night Office or Matins. The *SEL*-poet, on the other hand, clearly states that the monk's problem was that he could not endure *his service to hure* (line 78), i.e., the long office of Matins itself (line 81).

80   *leste he his ordre breke.* The poet here uses *ordre* not to mean "constituted body or association," but virtually as the equivalent of "rule," i.e., the regulations governing the conduct of monks in the Benedictine *ordre*. For the poet's use of the same expression in his life of Benedict's sister, see the Life of St. Scholastica, line 42 (see V[b], below), and with regard to the Franciscan Rule, see the *SEL* Life of St. Francis: "he halt noght his ordre, ich wene" (line 164; see VII, below).

82   *lute, blac, pollede grom.* This topos, whereby a sin, such as lust or monkish "instability," might be caused by, or embodied in, a demon in the form of a little black boy or "Aethiopian," derives from earlier hagiography. De Vogüé in his edition of the *Dialogues* (2.152–53n2) cites several examples from the lives of the Desert Fathers, including that of Saint Antony. ME *grom* (boy, man-child, man, servant) is of uncertain etymology, and is apparently unrelated to OE *grama* (anger, envy, demon).

87–90   *"Merci, sire . . ." ". . . schal nan more thee lere."* In the *Dialogues* (2.4) Benedict and the monk do not exchange words after the saint beats the monk with a rod and the demon flees. The *SEL*-poet's added dialogue seems intended to clarify the significance of the incident, but the translation is uncertain. Our footnote gloss represents one possibility, but it is also feasible that the monk means that he would never, for the life of him, have left the service on account of mere physical weakness ("feblesse," line 78). Benedict's response completes the explanation: on the contrary, he says, the problem was the monk's susceptibility to demonic temptation. While the episode continues the theme of diabolical assault on Benedict's monastic project, it also implies that monkish recalcitrance can be cured with a dose of old-fashioned discipline. Corporal punishment was, of course, provided for in the rule (e.g., chapters 23 and 27; Benedict, *Rule of St. Benedict*, trans. McCann, pp. 34 and 36), as in all walks of medieval life. With the monk's expression, *thei me wolde habbe ismyte of myn heved* (line 88), compare the familiar ME oath, "mawgree my hed," as in Chaucer's *Book of the Duchess*, line 1201.

91   *stable.* The word is not casually chosen. As well as connoting the physical act of standing still in the abbey choir during the long night office, it also evokes the time-honored monastic concept of *stabilitas* (physically staying put within the confines of

one's monastery, resisting wanderlust, and mentally preserving unwavering commitment to the strict ideals of the monastic life). See above, line 8.

96   *wondri aboute and pleie*. In the Latin sources, the newcomer does not announce himself as so evidently frivolous, but merely offers his fellow-traveler food.

101   *Another dai*. In the *Dialogues*, the three attempts on the pious layman's resolve are made during the same journey on the same evening, whereas here in the Life of St. Benedict the devil, apparently in the same form each time, tries on three separate days.

106–07 *swithe vair stude . . . murie stude*. These phrases, and especially the second ("pleasant place"), translate *locus amoenus* in *Dialogues* 2.13.2, evoking the classical literary topos of the "pleasance." See the discussion by Curtius, *European Literature and the Latin Middle Ages*, pp. 192–93, 195–200. The literal demonization of the classical topos recalls the early antipathy between the Greco-Roman literary tradition and Christian culture. For another reflection of the same conflict, see the castigation of Saint Jerome's classicism in Simon Winter's *Life of Jerome*, above, III(a).

115–16 Several of the demonic temptation episodes in *Dialogues* 2 depend on Benedict's gift of miraculous "sight" for their resolution. The *SEL*-poet, on the suggestion of *Dialogues* 2.13.4–14.1, now makes this "gift of prophecy" explicit as the theme of the next several episodes. The king in the present episode is the Ostrogoth, Totila (541–52), the most effective of the successors of Theodoric (490–526, whose rule over Italy effectively signaled the end of the Roman Empire in the West). Totila's visit to Benedict, argues De Vogüé in his edition of *Dialogues* (2.181n1), took place in 546. He died in battle against the Byzantine emperor Justinian's troops under the command of Narses.

120–22 In *Dialogues* 2.14.1–2, the impersonator is not a "jogulour" (line 118), minstrel, or fool, but Riggo, one of King Totila's guards. The change allows the *SEL*-poet to make Benedict's verbal unmasking of the impostor more pungent and amusing than in the Latin, where Benedict simply says, *Pone, fili, pone hoc quod portas: non est tuum.* ("Take off what you are wearing, my son, take it off. It does not belong to you," trans. White, pp. 182–83). Here, Benedict puns on two meanings of the word *fol*: namely, "foolish one" and "the king's fool," whose job was to provide jokes, music, and entertainment in a medieval court. The basic expression (a fool is the same, coming and going) is apparently proverbial. See Whiting F392.

123   *costres*. DM (3.48) gloss this OF word as "bottle," although De Vogüé translates the equivalent word in *Dialogues* 2.17, *flascones*, as "barillets" (2.195), i.e., small kegs. The *SEL*-poet is evidently envisaging some sort of large flask or small barrel.

135   *dere yer*. I.e., when food is scarce and very "dear," expensive. Compare Modern English *dearth*, "lack." De Vogüé cites contemporary sources to pinpoint 535–39 as years of widespread famine in Italy. See the note on *Dialogues* 2.21.1 in his edition (2.198–99).

138   *vif smale loves*. Compare Matthew 14:17. The biblical miracle of the five loaves and two fishes initiated a popular hagiographical topos. Early examples are cited by De Vogüé, in his notes to *Dialogues* 2.21.1–2 (2.199).

145–58 In *Dialogues* 2.24.1–2, the truant monk is a young boy, *puerulus monachus*, "who loved his parents more than he should have" (trans. White, p. 192). The *SEL*-poet may have felt the original version of the story to be a little severe, at least for lay readers, and produced this blander version instead. The story, unlike those immediately preceding it in the Life of St. Benedict, which concern Benedict's special powers of vision or prophecy, demonstrates his authority beyond the grave through the "merit [he] possessed in the eyes of our Lord" (trans. White, p. 192). Even the earth rejects someone who had died in a state of disobedience to Benedict. For another episode illustrating Benedict's power over the dead*, see Dialogues* 2.23.2–6; this and similar stories are discussed below in the context of excommunication (Introduction to VI, below).

159   *no tonge telle ne may*. With this commonplace apology, the *SEL*-poet dismisses the next dozen chapters of the life of Benedict in the *Dialogues*, including the famous last encounter with his sister, Scholastica, which is the subject of a separate legend of *SEL* (see V[b], below).

164   *houseli*. The term is from OE *huslian*, to give or receive the *husl*, i.e., Communion or Eucharist; but the pre-Christian meaning was simply "sacrifice."

167   Confusion over dates is common in medieval texts, partly through faulty calendars and chronology, partly through scribal errors in transcribing Roman numerals. The date the poet gives here is off by about forty years, but no one knows the exact year of Benedict's death, only the date, March 21. Gregory gives no specific information in the *Dialogues*, and the year 518 offered by Jacobus de Voragine in *LA* does not refer to Benedict's death, but to the time when he was in his prime, *floruit* (ed. Maggioni, p. 320).

171   *with floures swote and brighte.* The Latin versions do not mention flowers along the
      heavenly road, but describe it instead as "spread with cloaks and shining with innumer-
      able lights" (*strata palliis atque innumeris corusca lampadibus via*: *Dialogues* 2.37.3;
      trans. White, p. 203). Upon Jesus' entry into Jerusalem the crowds "spread their gar-
      ments on the road" (*straverunt vestimenta sua in via*, Matthew 21:8). It is hard to see
      why the *SEL*-poet sacrificed the biblical parallel.

176   *aten ende.* I.e., *at then ende*, in which *then* is the oblique case of the definite article, as
      in line 161, "then sevethe day," and 175, "then wei."

V(a)

Textual Notes to the Life of St. Benedict in the South English Legendary *(c. 1270–80)*

Abbreviations: **A** = Oxford, Bodleian Library MS Ashmole 43 [base text]; **C** = Corpus Christi College, Cambridge MS 145.

1   *Nursie*. A: *Mursie*. C: *Nuirsie*. A's mistaken rendering of Nursie/Nursia (modern Norcia, near Spoleto in Umbria, Italy) is also found in the Hereford Breviary (*Fuit vir vite venerabilis, benedictus nomine, ex prouincia mirsie exortus*), but the two texts share little else in common.

8   *his*. A: *is*. I have made this regularization throughout the text.

9   *me may be*. So A. C: *ic ne mai noȝt be*.

13   *scholde*. C: *ssolde*. A: *schode*.

14   *chatche*. A variant form (from Southern AN *chachier*) of *catch* or *chase*, the forms and meaning of which are frequently confused in the early ME period. C has *cacche*.

15   *holi mon*. So C. A: *holi*.

19   *fol semblaunt*. So A. C: *fair semlant*. See explanatory note to this line.

20   *orisouns*. A: *orisous*.

30   *eft*. So C. A: *ef*.

    vor fore. So A. C: *more*. The "harder" reading of A makes sense if we take *fore* as a Southern variant of *fere*, "fear." Compare *SEL* St. Katherine, line 241: "ȝoure maumetȝ ich forsake; y ne bileue for no fore" ("Your idols I forsake; I will not remain [or "believe in them"?] for any fear [i.e., whatever you threaten me with]), ed. DM 2.541.

31   *At Ester feste*. So A. C: *ac efter feste*.

38   *schost*. A contraction of *scholdest*.

66   *ofservy my mede*. So C (*of serui mi mede*). A: *of hem servy my mede*. See also the explanatory note to this line.

68   *hor fo*. So A. C: *hou he*.

88   *feblesse*. So C. A: *febesse*.

115   *wuste*. So A. C: *thohte*.

125   *unhende*. So C. A: *unhede*.

126   *he hudde*. So A. C: *leuede*.

133   *icome.* So A. C: *icrope.*

        there. So C. A: *nere.*

161   *The tyme.* So C. A: *To tyme.* The reading in A is a recognized idiom, but it normally
        means, "forever" or "until the time when," neither of which makes good sense here,
        whereas C's reading seems right.

170   *Seie.* So A. C: *Beie.*

V(b)

The Life of St. Scholastica
in the South English Legendary (c. 1270–80)

Introduction

St. Scholastica (feast day February 10) and the Female Benedictine Tradition

Scholastica (480–543) was the sister of St. Benedict of Nursia, and is revered as the patron saint of Benedictine nuns. She is said to have established a convent at Piumarola in Italy, in accordance with the principles of the monastic rule established by her brother at nearby Monte Cassino. Artistic representations often depict her as a youthful Benedictine abbess, wearing black and holding in her hand a book or a dove.[1] Everything that is known of her comes from the *Dialogues* of Gregory the Great who, in Book 2, chapters 33–34 describes a meeting between the siblings and the subsequent death of Scholastica.[2] There is little outside the *Dialogues* that attests with certainty even to the existence of this saint and at least one scholar has suggested that Gregory invented her, following the rhetorical tradition which provided so many of the early saints with sisters to serve as a foil for their more virtuous brothers.[3] Accounts of the seventh-century translation of Benedict and Scholastica to Fleury and Le Mans do little to prove the case either way, but early calendars and place-names in the Monte Cassino region offer independent evidence of a modest nature for the historical reality of Scholastica.[4]

Since there were few organized monastic communities for women in early-sixth-century Italy, Scholastica, if she did indeed exist, was in all likelihood a consecrated virgin, alone or with a few companions, perhaps in her family home in a kind of "house monastery."[5] Nevertheless, her

---

[1] Kirschbaum and Bandmann, eds., *Lexikon der christlichen Ikonographie*, 8.315–16; Rochelle, *Post-Biblical Saints Art Index*, p. 211; Kaftal and Bisogni, *Iconography of the Saints*, p. 907.

[2] Gregory the Great, *Dialogues* 2.33–34, ed. de Vogüé, 2.230–235; trans. White, *Early Christian Lives*, pp. 198–200.

[3] Cusack, "St. Scholastica," 145–59.

[4] For a full account of the evidence regarding the translation of both saints, see Beau, *Le culte et les reliques de Saint Benoît et de Sainte Scholastique*.

[5] For the history and development of female monasticism from earliest times to the present day, see McNamara, *Sisters in Arms*, with chapter-by-chapter bibliographies. On Scholastica, see pp. 100 and 147.

perceived significance to future generations as the first "Benedictine nun" gives her an honorary place in the history of female monasticism, as well as pointing up the need to understand a little of that history on its own terms. The Benedictine rule, which ultimately held sway for so many centuries as the rule par excellence for both men and women, was not the first formal attempt to codify a communal monastic life (see the Introduction to V[a], above). It was preceded, inter alia, by a rule designed specifically for women, that of Caesarius of Arles. Caesarius composed his rule (c. 512–534) for his sister, Caesaria, whom he had helped to establish in the monastic life. In addition to the three great vows of chastity, poverty, and obedience, common to all rules for both sexes, Caesarius recognized that "many things in monasteries of maidens seem to be different from those of monks," in particular the need for complete claustration: "If anyone, having left her parents, wishes to renounce the world and enter the holy fold . . . let her never leave the monastery until her death, not even into the church, where the door can be seen."[6] This emphasis on absolute removal from the world, it should be noted, was occasioned at least in part by the violence of life in a society under constant threat of barbarian invasion and the consequent need to protect the lives of female religious from attack.[7]

Stability of place is also a feature of the rule of St. Benedict, which, however, makes no distinction with regard to gender, stating in chapter 66 that "the monastery should . . . be so arranged that all necessary things, such as water, mill, garden and various crafts may be within the enclosure, so that the monks may not be compelled to wander outside it, for that is not at all expedient for their souls." Wandering monks (*gyrovagi*) were castigated (Chapter 1) and monks who presumed to "leave the enclosure of the monastery, or to go anywhere, or to do anything at all, however trifling, without the permission of the abbot" (Chapter 67) were to be punished.[8] Nevertheless these recommendations did not seek to achieve strict claustration,[9] and during the earlier Middle Ages, as the rule of St. Benedict came to serve, informally, as the

---

[6] Amt, ed., *Women's Lives in Medieval Europe*, pp. 221–31 (extracts). For a complete translation and a study of the Caesarian rule in relation to its sources, see Caesarius of Arles, *The Rule for Nuns*, trans. McCarthy.

[7] The dangers facing women in the sixth century are exemplified in the history of Queen Radegund, who was captured and forced to marry the polygamous Clothar I, but who finally gained release from her marriage vows and went on to found the monastery of Sainte Croix in Poitiers: McNamara and Halborg, *Sainted Women of the Dark Ages*, pp. 60–105. For information on the theory and practice of enclosure for women, see McNamara, *Sisters in Arms*, *passim*, and Schulenberg, "Strict Active Enclosure." See also McNamara and Wemple, "Sanctity and Power," pp. 90–118.

[8] Benedict, *Rule of St. Benedict*, trans. McCann, pp. 5–6, 74–75.

[9] See above, the Life of St. Benedict, lines 145–54, where the monk's sin was not so much in having gone to visit his friends outside the monastery, as in having failed to ask the permission of Benedict, his abbot.

guideline for monks and nuns alike, this latitude allowed initially for considerable female influence both within and without the walls of the monastery.

In England, which saw the first great expansion of Benedictine monasticism, Hild, the seventh-century abbess of Whitby, founded several monastic institutions and presided over a synod of bishops who had gathered to debate the virtues of Celtic versus Roman practice. Abbesses ruled over communities of men and women, and offered advice to secular rulers. Nuns such as Leoba and Tecla furthered the work of missionaries like Boniface by leaving their English convents to help establish monasteries abroad or, like Abbess Eadburg of Minster-in-Thanet, by contributing books, money, and altar cloths. As teachers and scholars, gifted administrators, organizers of building campaigns, the contributions of these women to the learning and culture of early medieval Europe constituted, relatively speaking, a golden age for female monastics.[10]

During the later Middle Ages, as ecclesiastical authority became more and more concentrated in the hands of a celibate male clergy, an ever increasing emphasis on enforced claustration for women led to a concomitant diminishment of their power. In 1298 the bull *Periculoso* of Pope Boniface VIII declared that all religious women everywhere must be cloistered, stressing, as JoAnn McNamara puts it, "the peril of men's inability to resist raping women and women's natural inability to refrain from tempting men."[11] Caesarius, who had recognized early on the difficulties that strict enclosure would pose for nuns with regard to the recommendation that monastics should provide for themselves by the labor of their own hands, endowed his sister's foundation with his own money. The paradox remained, however, and women's foundations, always poorer than their male counterparts, continued to struggle with the problem of how to raise money for their convent without leaving it. The prohibitions with regard to enclosure, moreover, helped to fuel an image, gleefully embraced by male writers, of sex-starved nuns, frantic to get out from behind those walls. In the thirteenth-century English *Land of Cokaygne*, a comic burlesque of the literary topos of the earthly paradise, nuns are satirically portrayed as taking off for a day on the river (which is of "swet milke") and going for a swim once they are out of sight of the nunnery:

Hi makiþ ham nakid forto plei
And lepiþ dune in-to þe brimme.
And doþ ham sleilich forto swimme.

---

[10] McNamara and Wemple, "Sanctity and Power," pp. 96–100; Schulenberg, "Female Sanctity." Stephanie Hollis, *Anglo-Saxon Women*, while painting a rather darker picture overall, acknowledges the significant role played by monastic women in the early Anglo-Saxon church; see especially her introduction, pp. 1–14.

[11] McNamara, *Sisters in Arms*, p. 317.

Þe ȝung monkes þat hi seeþ:
Hi doþ ham vp, and forþ hi fleeþ.
And commiþ to þe nunnes anon. (lines 155–61)[12]

[They strip themselves naked to play and leap down into the water and begin swimming about skillfully. The young monks see this: they jump up and rush forward and come to the nuns at once.]

Though sexual scandals doubtless occurred,[13] a problem exacerbated by the tendency to treat convents as a dumping ground for women (whose options were increasingly limited in the later Middle Ages), most convents continued to house women who respected their vows, even if they did leave the monastery precincts for relatively innocent social reasons or in their effort to support themselves.

The Cult of Scholastica in England

The existence of Scholastica's cult in England is attested by the inclusion of her feast day, February 10, in all Anglo-Saxon calendars where, moreover, its growing importance can be seen by the high rank order Scholastica achieved in a number of litanies.[14] The seventh-century poet Aldhelm wrote about her in both the prose and verse sections of his *De Virginitate*, and in the late tenth century Ælfric of Cerne (later of Eynsham) included her in his homily on St. Benedict. Not surprisingly, given the focus of his own work, Aldhelm stresses Scholastica's purity throughout, though Gregory did not comment specifically on this aspect of the saint. The brief prose narrative explores the spectacular nature of the miracle she achieves rather than the relationship between sister and brother. In the more expansive verse treatment Aldhelm deduces Scholastica's learned qualities from her name, says that "she gained golden rewards by her vow of virginity" and nicely pulls the emphasis away from Benedict, even blackening him a little with the comment that not only did he refuse to stay in response to Scholastica's pleading, but he "showed scorn of his holy sister." The prominence accorded Scholastica in Aldhelm's poem

---

[12] Bennett and Smithers, eds., *Early Middle English Verse and Prose*, p. 143. The poem is thought to have been composed in Ireland: see the editors' introduction, p. 138.

[13] The most celebrated scandal (paralleling that of Peter Abelard and Heloise) is that of the Gilbertine nun of Watton in the mid-twelfth century, which attracted the attention of the Cistercian abbot and writer Aelred of Rievaulx (died 1167): see Golding, *Gilbert of Sempringham*, pp. 33–38.

[14] Ortenberg, *The English Church and the Continent in the Tenth and Eleventh Centuries*, pp. 180–81n184; Lapidge, ed., *Anglo-Saxon Litanies of the Saints*. For medieval calendars listing Scholastica's feast day, see Wormald, ed., *English Kalendars before A.D. 1100* and *English Benedictine Kalendars after 1100*.

perhaps owes something to its dedication to the Abbess Hildelith and her nuns, one of whom was named Scholastica.[15] The bond between Benedict and Scholastica very likely suggested itself as a model to the eighth-century hagiographer Felix, who in his life of the hermit Guthlac similarly emphasized a spiritual relationship between brother and sister which transcended physical separation.[16]

The *SEL* Version

The *SEL* is unique among medieval English legendaries in allowing Scholastica an independent existence, that is, in giving her a legend all to herself. Other Middle English versions, e.g., in the 1438 *Gilte Legende* and Caxton's *Golden Legend*, follow Gregory's practice and include Scholastica in their lives of Benedict, but the sixty-four lines of the *SEL* version are found, on their own, in the place appropriate to her feast day, February 10.

Manfred Görlach has speculated that, in its earliest stages, the *SEL* was heavily dependent on a liturgical collection. Given the widespread observance of Scholastica's feast day, as noted above, a breviary text, like that found, for example, in the uses of York and Exeter (which follow Gregory's text very closely), could have served as a source for the *SEL* legend. But, as Görlach has further noted, the *Legenda aurea* of Jacobus de Voragine, which influenced many *SEL* legends, appears to have had little or no influence on legends of saints whose feast days, like that of Scholastica, occur in the first half of the year. A comparison of the *SEL* with these various Latin versions confirms the fact that the *SEL* has retained many details from Gregory found neither in Jacobus' severely curtailed narrative (which does not even name Scholastica), nor in the breviaries.[17] Indeed, the *SEL*'s expansive treatment of the legend, as well as the many original touches that distinguish it from all other extant versions, make it impossible to

---

[15] *Ælfric's Catholic Homilies: The Second Series, Text*, ed. Godden, pp. 106–7; Aldhelm, *Aldhelm, the Prose Works*, trans. Lapidge and Herren, p. 113; Aldhelm, *Aldhelm, the Poetic Works*, trans. Lapidge and Rosier, pp. 147–48, and see p. 259n36 for Lapidge's speculation on the connection between the saint and her Barking namesake.

[16] Hollis, *Anglo-Saxon Women*, pp. 284–293, who also mentions the long-standing intimacy of Boniface and his kinswoman, Leoba, as described in Rudolf of Fulda's Life of Leoba.

[17] *LA*, ed. Maggioni, pp. 319–20, trans. Ryan, 1.192–93; Görlach, *Textual Tradition*, pp. 144–45. For the York and Exeter breviary lections for Scholastica's feast day see *Breviarium ad Usum Insignis Ecclesie Eboracensis*, ed. Lawley, 75.195–97; *Ordinale Exon.*, ed. Dalton and Noble, 3.207. Among the details from Gregory's *Dialogues* not found in either York or Exeter are the clear weather before Scholastica's prayer and the night spent in happy communion after Benedict is forced to remain.

determine its source with certainty. The following extract from Chapter 33 of Gregory's *Dialogues* will provide a foundation for the interpretive remarks that follow.

> [Benedict's] sister, whose name was Scholastica, had been dedicated to the almighty Lord since her very infancy. She used to come to see Benedict once a year and the man of God would come down to meet her at a property belonging to the monastery not far from the gate. Now one day she came as usual, and her venerable brother came down to meet her with his disciples. They spent the whole day praising God and in holy conversation, and when night's darkness fell, they ate a meal together. While they were seated at table, talking of holy matters, it began to get rather late and so this nun, Benedict's sister, made the following request: "I beg you not to leave me tonight, so that we might talk until morning about the joys of heavenly life." Benedict answered, "What are you saying, sister? I certainly cannot stay away from my monastery." The sky was so clear at the time that there was not a cloud to be seen. When the nun heard the words of her brother's refusal, she put her hands together on the table and bent her head in her hands to pray the almighty Lord. When she lifted her head from the table, such violent lightning and thunder burst forth, together with a great downpour of rain, that neither the venerable Benedict nor the brothers who were with him could set foot outside the door of the place where they were sitting. For the nun, as she bent her head in her hands, had poured forth rivers of tears on to the table, by means of which she had turned the clear sky to rain. That downpour began just as her prayer finished — in fact, the coincidence between the prayer and the downpour was so precise that she lifted her head from the table at the very moment when the thunder sounded and the rain came down exactly the same moment that she raised her head.
>
> Then the man of God realized that he could not return to his monastery in the midst of the thunder and lightning and the heavy downpour of rain. This upset him and he began to complain, saying, "May the almighty God forgive you, sister. What have you done?" To which she replied, "Look, I asked you and you refused to listen to me. I asked my Lord and He heard me. Go now, if you can. Leave me behind and return to your monastery." But being unable to leave the building, he had to remain there against his will, since he refused to stay there voluntarily. And so they spent the whole night awake, satisfying each other's hunger for holy conversation about the spiritual life.[18]

This episode, occurring near the end of St. Benedict's life, is narrated by Gregory, in response to a question put by his disciple, Peter, to show that the desires of saints are not always fulfilled. In this one instance, explains Gregory, Scholastica justly thwarted her brother's wishes by the greater strength of her love.

In addition to the interpretation offered by Gregory himself, modern scholars have read the episode in a variety of ways: for example, to show that Benedict is passing from the active to the contemplative life, or that gender oppositions are reconciled in God, or as an act of sympathetic magic echoing older pagan rites, or as a signal that the death of Benedict himself is at hand. Most interesting, perhaps, are the parallels with other saints' lives in which a brother and

---

[18] Trans. White, *Early Christian Lives*, pp. 198–99.

sister figure and which, according to one critic, may have provided the inspiration for Gregory's narrative. There is a core of thematic similarity in all such narratives whereby the sister is the weaker of the pair, giving way to emotion, and allowing for the brother to show not only his affection but his superior strength and virtue. More than one critic has seen a further parallel with Luke's account of the anointing of Jesus's feet at the house of Simon the Pharisee (Luke 7:36–50), a scene which has in common with the Scholastica episode a supper, a woman's tears, and the justification of excessive love.[19]

The *SEL*-poet, in telling the story of Scholastica separately from that of her brother, has, not surprisingly, added much in the way of psychological and narrative detail without, however, changing the basic form of the story. Most notable, perhaps, in distinction to the interpretations outlined above, is the focus on her materiality as a "real" human being. Whatever meanings may emerge from this version of her legend, the *SEL* Scholastica cannot simply be seen as a way of figuring some aspect of her more important brother's life. Among the poet's original touches is the emphasis on Scholastica's great age and feebleness, which increase her desire to see her brother since she is afraid this may be her last opportunity. In addition, Benedict is more rude and disagreeable, Scholastica more appealing, not just because she is old and infirm, but because of the humorous asperity of her remarks.

One of the most interesting aspects of the Scholastica narrative is the way the question of enclosure plays out in the different versions. While the claustration of women was, in historical terms, a far more pressing concern than that of men, the focus in Gregory's narrative is on Benedict's wish to get back to his cell by nightfall. Since Gregory was an active promoter of the Benedictine rule and claustration, it is hardly surprising that he takes the opportunity to underline this point. The fact that there is no similar emphasis for Scholastica may suggest either that she was not, strictly speaking, a nun, or simply that Gregory was less interested in her. What is perhaps a little more surprising is that all the later versions deriving from Gregory continue to focus exclusively on Benedict's determination not to spend the night outside his monastery, while disregarding the fact that Scholastica is in a similar position. The increasing stridency in the later Middle Ages of pronouncements that women remain within their monastery walls at all times finds no reflection in these narratives; it is impossible to tell whether this disregard stems from respect for the authority of Gregorian tradition or the relatively insignificant role of Scholastica within the legend of Benedict. The *SEL* alone seems to have attended to (contemporary) historical reality as well as to tradition: brother and sister are both Benedictines, both concerned with keeping their vow of enclosure. But, Scholastica says, God will forgive them for this breach because of their "good intention" (line 24). This em-

---

[19] Wansbrough, "St. Gregory's Intention"; de Vogüé, "La rencontre de Benoît et de Scholastique," trans. in "The Meeting of Benedict and Scholastica"; Morrissey, "Scholastica and Benedict"; Cusack, "St. Scholastica."

phasis avoids the hysterical focus on the threats posed by women's sexuality and the need to preserve female chastity, by making enclosure equally important for brother and sister. The fact that the *SEL* Life of St. Scholastica appears to be the first instance of her legend appearing in the vernacular unattached to Benedict's, that the collection, in its earliest form (MS Laud 108), contains the legend of Scholastica but not that of Benedict, and that the legend begins with the comment that Scholastica would rather be a nun than a wife, suggests for one critic an intended audience of nuns.[20] The question of *SEL*'s audience is complex and remains unresolved, but it seems fair to say that the legend of Scholastica demonstrates a willingness on the poet's part to present a legend which would certainly appeal to nuns as well as others.

SEL Texts of Scholastica

The sixteen major *SEL* manuscripts identified by Görlach as containing the Life of St. Scholastica show little variation in the text. As with the majority of *SEL* selections in this volume MS Ashmole 43 has been used to provide a base text of this edition. For more on the selection of Ashmole, see the Introduction to I(a), above.

Indexed in

IMEV 3052.

Manuscripts

Cambridge, Corpus Christi College MS 145, fols. 22r–22v.

Oxford, Bodleian Library MS Ashmole 43 (*SC* 6924), fols. 23v–24r.

Previous editions

The South English Legendary. Ed. D'Evelyn and Mill. 1.59–60.

Early South English Legendary. Ed. Horstmann. Pp. 197–99.

---

[20] McMahon, "Scholastica — Not a Wife!," pp. 18–28.

V(b)

The Life of St. Scholastica
in the South English Legendary *(c. 1270–80),*
from Oxford, Bodleian Library MS Ashmole 43, fols. 23v–24r

Seyn Scolace the holi maide,   holi was of lyve,
Levere heo hadde nonne be   then be iwedded to wyve.[1]
Seyn Benet hire brother was,   that verst the reule bivond   *established*
Of blake monkes and of nonnes   that me halt into al that lond.   *that is observed*
5   His soster Seyn Scolace   blac nonne he lette make
And taughte hire penaunce to do,   to vaste, and eke to wake.   *fast; keep watch*
This to holi creatures   ech yer hadde ane wone   *these two; custom*
To come togadere some tyme   and telle of Godes Sone.   *God's Son (i.e., Christ)*
Ac hor nouther in otheres abbei   bileve come ne mighte,
10   Ne wende bileve vor nothing   out of hor celle bi nyghte.[2]
Tho this gode holi maide   ibroght was in gret elde,   *When; great age*
Hire longede with hire brother speke   vor feblesse that heo velde.   *felt*
Tho heo hadde to him isend,   togadere hi gonne wende,   *sent [a message]*
And tolde of Godes priveté   al then day to ende.   *mysteries until that day's end*
15   Of the joie of Hevene —   hou holi men hor lif ladde —
Therof al hor joie was   that hi bitwene hem hadde.[3]
Sori were this holi thinges bothe   tho it was eve;   *these holy creatures*
Seyn Benet to his soster sede   that he ne mighte noleng bileve.   *no longer remain*
Sori was this maide tho.   "Brother," heo sede, "thin ore!   *have mercy*
20   This holi wordes so murie beth,   yut we mote telle more.
Wen we in Godes service beth,   ne dorre we our ordres breke.   *dare; vows*
Icham so feble that I ne wene   never eft with thee speke;   *I am*
Bileve we togadere this one nyght,   vor Him that ous dere aboghte.[4]

---

[1] *She would rather be a nun than be wed as a wife*

[2] Lines 9–10: *But neither of them could come to stay overnight at the other's abbey, / Nor would [they] think of staying out of their cells at night for any reason*

[3] *All the joy they experienced with each other came from this (i.e., these conversations)*

[4] *Let us remain together this one night, for the sake of Him who dearly redeemed us*

Ichot He wole it ous vorgive,   vor we doth it in gode thoghte."   *I know*

25   "Be stille," quath Seyn Benet,   "loke wat thou dost telle;[1]

Wel thou wost that I ne may   bi nyghte be fram my celle."   *by night be away from*

Tho this maide isei that it ne huld   to bidde hire brother more,[2]

Hire heved heo gan to honge adoun   and wep swithe sore.   *head*

"Lord," heo sede, "Thou art fol   of milce and of ore;   *full of mercy and compassion*

30   Let me, yif Thi wille beo,   hure more of Thi lore.   *hear*

Ne let noght my brother tonyght,   Lord, fram me wende,

Ac let ous with tales of Thi blisse   this night bringe to ende."

As this maide lokede up,   tho heo hadde ido hire bone,   *made her request*

That weder that was so cler and vair   bigan to chaungi sone.

35   Hit gan to snywe and thondri,   lighte, and eke reyne,   *to flash lightning*

That ver withynne nyght it was   ar that weder wolde fyne.

That wel was ech quic best   that was in eny inne.[3]

Nou was this a maister maide   that such weder couthe awynne!

Tho ne mighte Seyn Benet   for weder thenne wende,

40   "Soster," he sede, "wat hastou do?   Thou fondest me to scende!

Yif it my Loverdes wille nere   wel ne dudestou noght;

That ich schal myn ordre breke   so nadde ich never ithoght."[4]

"Leve brother," the maide sede,   "ich bad thee swithe yerne   *beseeched; earnestly*

To bileve her thus nyght,   and ever thou dust werne.   *remain here this; did refuse*

45   Ich bad mi Lord another bone   and He me herde anon.

Ches wether thou wolt bileve,   other henne gon.   *or go hence*

Bilef me al one yif thou wolt,   vor no thonk ne can ich thee;[5]

Ich thonke God of Hevene   that so sone hurde me."

Tho hi ne mighte departi noght   al nyght togadere hi woke,   *watched (stayed awake)*

50   And tolde of the swetnesse that was myd God   in tale and eke in boke.

The nyght hem thoghte swithe scort,   and sori aten ende

---

[1] *"Be quiet," said Saint Benedict, "take care what you say["]*

[2] *When this maid saw that it was of no avail to entreat her brother more*

[3] Lines 36–37: *The night would be well advanced before the bad weather ended. / It was well for every living creature who found shelter*

[4] Lines 39–42: *Then Saint Benedict could not on account of the weather go thence, / "Sister," he said, "what have you done? You are trying to destroy me! / Unless it (your prayer) was my Lord's will, you did not do well; / I never thought that I would break my vows["]*

[5] *Leave me all alone if you like, for I do not owe you any thanks*

Hi were, tho hi seie dai,   that hi moste ato wende.[1]

Hi ne dorste no leng togadere be   ac wende to hor celle;   *longer*

Sori hi were for hi ne mighte   no leng togadere telle.   *converse*

55   Tho the maide was hom icome   sore sek heo lay,

And as our Lordes wille was   heo deide then thridde day.

As Seyn Benet in his celle eode   his soster soule he sei   *walked about*

In forme of a culvere wit   fle to Hevene an hei.   *white dove fly*

Hevene openede hire agen,   the colvere gan in fle.   *to her (at her approach)*

60   Glad was this holi man   that this mighte isé.

Amorwe he and his covent   thuder wende sone,   *The next day; convent (community)*

And burede this holi maide,   as right was to done.

So God leve that we mote   with Cristenemen be   *grant*

Ibured at our ende day   and to Hevene fle.

---

[1] Lines 51–52: *The night seemed very short to them, and they were sorry at the end [of it], when they saw daylight, that they must go their separate ways*

V(b)

Notes to the Life of St. Scholastica in the South English Legendary *(c. 1270–80)*

Abbreviations: **A** = Oxford, Bodleian Library MS Ashmole 43 [base text]; **C** = Cambridge, Corpus Christi College MS 145.

3–5   *Seyn Benet hire brother . . . he lette make.* On Benedict's rule, see the Introduction to the *SEL* Life of St. Benedict (V[a]), above. On the late medieval custom of distinguishing the Benedictines from other orders by the color of their "habit," see the explanatory note to the *SEL* Life of St. Benedict, line 55. The earliest *SEL* manuscript, Oxford, Bodleian Library, Laud Miscellany108 (ed. Horstmann, *ESEL*, p. 197, chapter 34, lines 5–6) adds the following couplet between lines 4 and 5 of the present text: *Of blake Monekus at Duyn : An Abbeye he let a-rere, / him-sulf þe Abite furst he nam : þe ʒongore for-to lere.* The puzzling *Duyn* here is perhaps a variant form of *dun*, hill; the site of Benedict's monastery at Cassino was on a mountain, which was often incorporated into the place-name, as in the modern Monte Cassino. Compare the *SEL* Life of St. Benedict, line 50: "the hul of Casyn."

14   *then.* Acc. masc. sing. of ME definite article (compare OE *þone*).

14–16   *tolde of Godes priveté . . . hi bitwene hem hadde.* Compare Gregory the Great, *Dialogues* 2.33.2, *in dei laudibus sacrisque conloquiis* ("praising God and in holy conversation" — trans. White, p. 198), which is echoed variously in the breviaries. But Jacobus de Voragine in *LA* (chapter XLVIII, ed. Maggioni, p.319), does not specify the subject of their conversation, nor even the fact they talked at all.

17   *Sori were this holi thinges bothe tho it was eve.* That both saints regret the end of their day together is *SEL*'s addition here, echoed again later (see lines 51–54).

22   *never eft.* So C. A: *neuerſt.*

19–24   *Sori was this maide tho . . . in gode thoghte.* The implication of these lines is that although monks and nuns should not break the rules of their monastic order (in this case, by spending the night away from their monasteries), Scholastica's age and infirm-

210

ity lead her to wish for an exception, since she fears she will never see her brother again. The poet has already clearly explained in line 10 that Benedict and Scholastica would not normally think of spending the night away from their respective abbeys. But on this occasion the thought of cutting short their blissful conversation at day's end is particularly hard to bear, and when Benedict says it is time to part, Scholastica begins to appeal to him to let their meeting continue (19–20). However, there may be a textual problem in line 21, where Scholastica's flat statement that those who serve God dare not break the rules of their order fits uneasily into the surrounding context, in which she is arguing that God will forgive them for prolonging their stay. The Laud manuscript reading for this line makes better sense: *ȝwane we In godes seruise beoth : we ne doz nouȝt ore ordre breke* (Horstmann, *ESEL*, p. 198, line 23), i.e., we are not violating our rule, as long as what we do is part of serving God. This anticipates her statement in lines 23–24 of the present edition, where Scholastica assures her brother that Christ will forgive them their infringement of the literal rule because their intention is *gode* (line 24). None of Scholastica's reasoning is found in Gregory's *Dialogues* at this point, where Scholastica simply asks Benedict not to leave so that they might go on talking all night. The *SEL* version adds human pathos to the scene and depth to Scholastica's character here, while also rendering explicit what is implied in Gregory's account, i.e., that Scholastica, like many saints, has foreknowledge of her own death, which occurs three days later. Since Benedict himself dies not long after his sister, the episode as a whole serves a doubly prophetic purpose.

34   *weder that was so cler and vair bigan to chaungi sone.* Compare Gregory's *Dialogues* 2.33.3: *Tanto uero erat caeli serenitas, ut nulla in aere nubes apparet* ("the sky was so clear at the time that there was not a cloud to be seen" — trans. White, p. 199), the gist of which also occurs, though shortly afterwards, in *LA* (trans. Ryan, 1.192: "although minutes before the sky had been marvellously clear"). The breviary versions, however, do not mention the state of the weather before Scholastica's prayer.

35   *snywe.* Gregory in the *Dialogues* mentions only thunder, lightning, and rain, but *hauli* ("hail") is added to this threesome in the *ESEL* St. Scholace 37 (ed. Horstmann, p. 198). The "A" reviser substitutes the more meteorologically spectacular (and miraculous) snow.

        lighte. A variant of the ME verb *lighten* (as in the *ESEL* version: *leiȝten*), one of whose meanings is "to emit flashes of lightning."

35–36   *reyne . . . fyne.* Either the Ashmole scribe or that of his exemplar was unfamiliar with the Southern English strong verb *ryne(n).*, which was being superseded elsewhere by

211

the weak form, *reyne(n)*. The correct rhyme is preserved in other manuscripts: compare the rhymes *rine/fine* in DM.

37–38   Omitted by all medieval versions at this point, whether in Latin or the vernacular, is a lengthy editorializing explanation by Gregory of the exact coincidence of Scholastica's prayer and the miraculous downpour (*Dialogues* 2.33.3). The *SEL* "A" reviser, however, adds instead one of his own characteristic editorializing comments (compare the *SEL* Life of St. Francis, lines 23–24), first to emphasize what a tremendous storm Scholastica's prayers have provoked, and second to exploit the punning possibilities of her name at this climactic moment in the story. *Maister maide* (line 38), a witty oxymoron interpreting *scholastica* (learned female, female teacher) to mean "schoolmaster virgin," and also "maid who is a leader or expert in a profession" (as in, e.g., master-clerk, master-builder, etc.). There is doubtless here a humorous allusion to the science of astronomy and meteorology as Scholastica's academic specialty (*that such weder couthe awynne*, line 38). But the cognomen also may connote "maid who has mastery" (reversing, of course, the medieval norm of gendered hierarchy). Finally, according to the *MED*, *maister* in a compound construction like this seems frequently to carry a pejorative sense, as in *master-lyere*. Thus *maister maide*, while calling attention to Scholastica's miraculous powers, could also be a tongue-in-cheek dig (albeit a good-humored one) at a woman's presuming to behave authoritatively like a man.

47   *Bilef me al one yif thou wolt*. Both the sarcastic humor and mock pathos here are typical of the *SEL*-poet's style, although partly suggested by Gregory's more phlegmatic version in *Dialogues* 2.33.4: "Go now, if you can. Leave me behind" (trans. White, p. 199). This last sentence, which clearly inspired the *SEL*-poet here, is omitted from the account in *LA*.

49–50   A copying error, whereby line 50 has been copied before line 49, was caught, after the fact, by the Ashmole scribe, who has written at the left-hand margin of line 50 the letter "b" and below that, at the beginning of the next line, the letter "a," indicating what should be the correct order, which is printed here. Once again the *SEL* is closer to Gregory (and in this case *LA*) than to the breviaries in detailing the pleasure the two saints take in their further conversation during Benedict's enforced overnight stay.

51–54   All medieval versions, including the *SEL*, omit Gregory's interpretation of the episode at this point (*Dialogues* 2.33.5, trans. White, pp. 199–200), and move directly into the account of Scholastica's death which Gregory reserves for his next chapter, 34. But *SEL* inserts a unique transitional passage whimsically and somewhat audaciously reminiscent of the ancient literary topos of the forced separation of lovers at dawn. See Hatto, *Eos*.

VI

Saint Austin at Compton *(c. 1420–40),*
by John Lydgate

Introduction

A Miracle

John Lydgate's poem relating the miracle at "Compton" performed by St. Austin — Archbishop Augustine of Canterbury[1] — differs from most of the other selections in this volume in being not a complete life of the saint but a single episode from it, or, as Lydgate calls it, a "miracle" (line 404). Miracle stories, frequently illustrating or demonstrating a particular theological problem or ecclesiastical theme, may be extracts from saints' lives proper, or, as in this case, a miracle story attributed to the saint and added to his hagiographical "dossier" long after it was complete. Earlier examples in this volume are the episodes of St. Andrew and the Three Questions (I[b]) and St. Jerome and the Lion (III[b]). Such stories often circulated independently, either as items in large systematic collections of Latin exempla (didactic anecdotes compiled for the use of preachers and writers of theological and devotional tracts),[2] or copied haphazardly, for their intrinsic interest as they came to hand, into the numerous miscellanies of literary or devotional texts surviving from medieval libraries.[3] Some of these hagiographical short stories were rendered into Middle English, usually as whole collections,[4] but occasionally standing alone as does the present work of Lydgate, or the alliterative poem *Saint*

---

[1] The title *The Legend of Saint Austin at Compton*, in McCracken's standard edition (pp. ii, xxv, 193), has no manuscript authority, but has been widely adopted, although usually in shortened form, *St. Austin at Compton* (e.g., by Schirmer, *John Lydgate*, p. 160), which we also use below. Our discussion of Lydgate's poem is rather longer than most of the others in this volume, owing to the complexity of its background and the virtual absence of critical scholarship on the poem or its sources.

[2] Apart from the Marian miracle collections, one of the earliest collections of exempla is the *Dialogue of Miracles* by Caesarius of Heisterbach. See the translation by Scott and Bland. On exempla and Marian miracles, see the Introduction to I(b), above.

[3] E.g., the copy of the Latin Compton legend, henceforth *Narratio*, in Cambridge, Corpus Christi College MS 177, which also included, among many other works or parts of works, a fourteenth-century life of Thomas Becket and Petrarch's story of patient Griselda.

[4] See Cooke's comprehensive survey and bibliography, in *MWME* 9.3268–3328.

213

Erkenwald[5] with which it shares certain plot features and a mutual indebtedness to the legend of Pope Gregory and the Emperor Trajan.[6] Chaucer's Prioress's Tale exemplifies an affiliated genre, the Marian miracle.[7]

St. Austin, Confessor Bishop (feast day May 26)

"Austin" is the common Middle English and early Modern English name of Augustine, archbishop of Canterbury (597–604/05). He was the leader of the Roman missionaries who landed in Kent in 597 to begin the re-establishment of the Christian religion over a century after its retreat, in the face of the advancing heathen Angles, from lowland Britain into the mountains and moors of the extreme West and Southwest. As the first archbishop of Canterbury, and reputedly a worker of miracles, Austin stood fair to become one of the principal saints of his adopted land, like other missionary saints including Denis and Martin in France, Boniface in Germany, Patrick in Ireland, or David in Wales. But for various reasons, although he was honored in medieval English calendars, and enjoyed high status at the ancient Canterbury abbey where he was buried and which came to bear his name, Austin's Canterbury cult never quite managed to win real national prominence. Among the Anglo-Saxons, for example, he was always overshadowed by the real architect of the Roman mission, Pope Gregory the Great, whose first Latin *vita* was composed in Northumberland in the seventh century. By contrast there is no trace of a formal life of Austin, apart from some chapters in Bede's *Ecclesiastical History* that describe the archbishop's mission (largely taken up with his lengthy correspondence with Pope Gregory),[8] until the *Historia Sancti Augustini* composed at Canterbury by the monk Goscelin around 1095, almost half a millennium after Austin's death.[9] It is somewhat surprising, therefore, that an unknown thirteenth-century author chose to give Austin the central role in the legend of the miracle at Compton.

---

[5] See the edition by Peterson. The story of St. Andrew and the devil, which in the *Legenda aurea* and its vernacular derivatives is appended to the apostle's life, originated as a separate tale. See I(b), above, St. Andrew and the Three Questions.

[6] See lines 343–52 of the present text and the corresponding explanatory note, below.

[7] For this and other examples of the genre, see Boyd, *Middle English Miracles of the Virgin*. For additional comments, see the Introduction to I(b), above.

[8] *Bede's Ecclesiastical History*, ed. Colgrave and Mynors, pp. 68–117, 134–45. In Bede's account also, Austin is quite overshadowed by the figure of Gregory, whose life Bede narrates in a long separate chapter at the beginning of Book 2 (pp. 122–35). See most recently Thacker, "In Gregory's Shadow?"

[9] *AS*, Maius 6.375–95 (*BHL* 777). A new edition is in progress by Richard Sharpe.

Introduction to Saint Austin at Compton

The *Narratio* and Its Sources[10]

Preserved in full in nine manuscript copies of the late thirteenth to fifteenth centuries, and in briefer form in several others,[11] the Latin *Narratio* ("narrative") purports to take place during Austin's episcopacy (597–604) while he is on a visit to a village named "Cumeton," supposedly near Woodstock, north of Oxford.[12] It involves a conflict between the parish priest and the local secular lord of the manor, who refuses to pay his tithes[13] (a form of ecclesiastical taxation on his agricultural produce and other income), despite the threat of excommunication (expulsion from membership in the church). After an initial, fruitless attempt to change the layman's mind, Austin begins to celebrate mass for the assembled congregation and issues the customary command for any excommunicated persons to vacate the church. Immediately a hideous corpse rises from a tomb inside the church, leaves the building and takes up a position outside the churchyard for the rest of the service. After Mass, as the terrified congregation looks on, Austin questions the walking dead man, who reveals he was lord of the village in the days of the Christianized Roman-Britons, died excommunicate for failure to pay his tithes, and has been suffering the tortures of the infernal prison-house (presumably Purgatory) ever since. Austin, weeping like everyone else by now, has the cadaver show the way to the grave of the priest who pronounced the original sentence of excommunication; he then resuscitates the dead priest and orders him to scourge the dead lord and absolve him of his sin, after which the layman's corpse

---

[10] In the explanatory notes to *Saint Austin at Compton*, quotations from the Latin legend, *Narratio mirabilis de sententia excommunicationis et beati Augustini Apostoli qualiter resuscitauit duos mortuos*, as three manuscripts entitle it, are from the text in London, British Library MS Harley 105 (from St. Augustine's, Canterbury), as printed in Whatley, "John Lydgate's *Saint Austin at Compton*," pp. 223–27.

[11] Among the abridged versions are two from the fourteenth century: one incorporated in the life of Augustine in John of Tynemouth's *Sanctilogium Anglie* (later printed by Wynkyn de Worde in 1516 as *Nova legenda Anglie*, ed. Horstmann); another in the "Chronicle of John of Brompton," (ed. *AS*, Maius 3.396) a fifteenth-century compilation from fourteenth-century sources, which Walter Schirmer believed, erroneously, to be Lydgate's source for his poem (see note 25, below). While Lydgate may have known the Brompton version (or its exemplar), his main source was the unpublished full version. Some of the evidence for this statement is cited in the notes on the text below. For a fuller discussion, see Whatley, "John Lydgate's *Saint Austin at Compton*," pp. 194–200. On John of Brompton and John of Tynemouth, see Sharpe, *A Handlist*, pp. 220 and 333–34.

[12] See the explanatory note on the text, line 144, below.

[13] "Tithe" is from OE *teoða*, "tenth"; compare Latin *decima*. The Christian system of tithing evolved slowly until by the later Middle Ages it involved a complex system of annual assessments on produce or income from land and livestock, and also from income derived from other modes of production. For an excellent summary, with bibliography, see James A. Brundage's article "Tithes," in Strayer, ed., *Dictionary of the Middle Ages*, 12.62–65.

returns peacefully to his tomb. Austin asks the risen priest if he would like to return to the world and help him with his missionary work. But the priest demurs, preferring the repose of death and his soul's joyful existence with God to the labor and distress of life on earth. Austin wishes him well, consigns him to his tomb once more, receives the penitence and conversion of the present lord of the village, who becomes his disciple, and the story ends.

We know nothing as to where or by whom this legend was composed, and our estimate as to its late-thirteenth-century date is only tentative. The story is almost certainly fictitious, as witnessed not only in its bizarre resuscitations of 150-year-old corpses, but also in its blatant anachronisms. A strict tithing system, such as is presupposed by the actions of the two priests and bishop in the legend, did not emerge until the Carolingian era in Europe, and excommunication for withholding tithes, for example, does not seem to have been a feature of the ecclesiastical scene in England until the later Middle Ages. The *Narratio* also states at the outset that Austin is traveling among the benighted heathen English to convert them to the faith, and yet in Compton itself Christianity is apparently so well established that the missionary bishop has nothing to do but celebrate Mass and adjudicate in a tithes dispute, which he manages to do without the aid of his Frankish interpreters.[14] Given the uneasy fit between the legend and its supposed sixth-century context, it is not surprising that there is no record of it prior to the late thirteenth or early fourteenth century. If there had been any earlier trace of it, Goscelin of Canterbury, hungry for materials with which to expand on what he found in Bede for his *Historia Sancti Augustini*, would almost certainly have used it. Instead, in one of the earliest manuscripts of Goscelin's hagiographic works, the legend had to be inserted by a later (probably fourteenth-century) hand as a supplement to the saint's life proper (London, British Library, Harley MS 105, folios 65–67). Not until the mid-fourteenth century do we find the *Narratio* incorporated into the abbreviated life of Augustine written by John of Tynemouth for his legendary of British saints, *Sanctilogium Anglie*. We can only conclude that rather than being a genuine ancient tradition about Austin, the legend was synthesized some time in the later thirteenth century[15] out of various source materials (discussed below), either to promote Austin's cult, or, as seems more likely, to further the efforts of church authorities (as exemplified in the Lambeth Con-

[14] According to Bede's account (*Bede's Ecclesiastical History*, ed. Colgrave and Mynors, pp. 68–69), Austin and his Italian companions at one point wished to abandon their mission because of their fears of the barbarian Angles. The *SEL* version of Austin's life attributes this trepidation rather to their ignorance of the Angles' language. See DM 1.214, St. Augustine of Canterbury, lines 15–16.

[15] Since it was known to John of Tynemouth in the second quarter of the fourteenth century, the Compton miracle must date from the early fourteenth century or before; at least two of the surviving manuscript copies of the *Narratio* have been judged to be in thirteenth-century hands (those in Oxford, Bodleian Library MS Digby 149, and Dublin, Trinity College Library MS 332); see Marvin L. Colker, *Trinity College Library, Dublin*, 1.672, who dates the hand in the second half of the thirteenth century.

stitutions of 1281) to regularize the use of excommunication against various forms of resistance to church law, and rigorously to enforce the payment of tithes for the support of the parish clergy.[16] For the *Narratio* survives not only appended to or incorporated in copies of the saint's life but also and more frequently as an exemplum in collections of materials intended for preachers.[17] If this was the case, however, the author's creative instincts ran beyond his didactic aim, for the second half of the story turns away from ideas of justice and punishment according to law to focus rather on human and divine compassion and forgiveness, and on blissful indifference to life in the world. The story's apparent ambivalence towards the practice of excommunication for non-payment of tithes is echoed in the reluctance of Chaucer's idealized Parson "to cursen for his tithes" in the General Prologue (*CT* I[A]486).[18]

Unlike many exempla, the *Narratio* is a complex narrative and seems to reflect more than one source tradition. One ultimate source is probably an episode in the late-sixth-century life of St. Benedict of Nursia by Pope Gregory the Great,[19] according to which the corpses of two nuns would leave their graves in a church every time the officiating deacon, just before the Eucharist began, asked non-communicants to depart. This was happening because the nuns had died without repenting of sins for which Benedict had merely threatened them with excommunication. The problem is resolved only after he arranges for prayers to be said on their behalf during Mass and the nuns henceforth lie quiet in their graves. Gregory tells this story ostensibly to illustrate Benedict's holiness by showing the power of his words, even his informal utterances, but the pope also interprets it as reflecting the power given by Jesus to his church, in the person of Peter, "to bind and to loose" (Matthew 16:19).[20] The episode was frequently excerpted in the later Middle Ages, and it stands alone in a variety of contexts quite independent of Benedict, especially in alphabetically organized collections of exempla such as the thirteenth-century

---

[16] Prior to the thirteenth century, incomes from tithes were often diverted to churches outside the parish of their origin or into the hands of layfolk or monasteries. The great attempt to revive and reform pastoral activity in the thirteenth century, after the Second Lateran Council, clearly required a reform of the tithing system so as to provide adequate incomes for the pastoral clergy and their churches. Constable has argued that actual non-payment of tithes by lay people was rarely a problem, rather that tithe disputes were more often unseemly legal struggles to control how the considerable incomes from tithing were to be spent. But this is certainly not the impression gained from late-medieval sermon literature and other documents. See, e.g., Owst, *Literature and Pulpit in Medieval England*, pp. 365–66; *Preaching in Medieval England*, pp. 73–74; and Thomson, "Tithe Disputes in Later Medieval London."

[17] For some examples, see Whatley, "John Lydgate's *Saint Austin at Compton*," pp. 211–12nn50–51.

[18] See the useful note on this line in *The Riverside Chaucer*, ed. Benson, p. 819.

[19] *Dialogues* 2.23, trans. White, pp. 190–91.

[20] Gregory's *Dialogues* contains other anecdotes of forcible ejection of the unworthy from graves in churches: e.g., 4.52–53, trans. Gardner, *The Dialogues of Saint Gregory*, pp. 246–48.

Alphabetum narrationum by Arnold of Liège,[21] and in another more massive preachers' handbook, of the fourteenth century, John Bromyard's *Summa praedicantium*.[22]

Another story that anticipates elements of the *Narratio*, this time from the twelfth century, is not strictly speaking hagiographical at all, but occurs in a more miscellaneous collection of tales, Walter Map's *De nugis curialium*, or *Courtiers' Trifles* (1181–92). Many of these are satirical in nature, but some of them are simply "marvels" (*prodigia*) of a sort commonly found in otherwise serious works of history or topography by contemporary authors. One of Map's *prodigia* provides the closest individual analogue to *Saint Austin at Compton* that I have so far found. He tells how a Northumbrian knight is frightened when visited by the wretched corpse of his long-dead father one summer evening after dinner, but the hellish thing insists it means no harm and bids the son send for the priest. When he arrives, a considerable crowd of people having gathered, the dead man falls at his feet and confesses to unrighteous withholding of tithes (*decimarum iniusta retencione*) during his lifetime, because of which he has been suffering under a general sentence of excommunication pronounced by the priest on all such offenders. As a result of the church's common prayers for the dead, however, and the alms of good people, he has now been permitted to ask for absolution to end his suffering. The priest absolves him and the corpse returns to his grave which closes over him, presumably for good.[23]

One can see easily enough that the anonymous author of the Compton miracle has combined several elements occurring in the Map story (resuscitated corpse, excommunicated for tithe retention in an earlier generation; corpse inspires fear but reassures its interlocutor; crowd of onlookers; priest sent for; ritual absolution; corpse returns to grave), with some of the elements of the earlier story by Gregory the Great (liturgical setting; command forbidding excommunicates from attending Mass; saint's intervention secures peace and reconciliation for the dead). In addition to switching the saint's role from Benedict to Austin of Canterbury, and from nuns to a knight, locating the action in an obscure English village, the author makes the story doubly interesting by dealing with not one but two conflicts over tithing, one in the present, the other in the far-distant past; this in turn means that in order for the dead man to be absolved there must be a second miracle of resuscitation, initiated by the saint when he summons the dead priest to confront the excommunicate. While this doubtless is designed to impress upon the public the efficacy of excommunication even by a lowly parish priest, it also gives the storyteller the opportunity to introduce yet another motif: namely *contemptus mundi*, reflected in the priest's polite rejection of Austin's invitation to serve the church militant, preferring as he does the blissful state of repose that the just enjoy beyond the grave. An early example of this story

---

[21] See the Middle English version in Arnoldus of Liége, *An Alphabet of Tales*, ed. Banks, 1.215–16.

[22] John Bromyard (also John de Bromyarde), *Summa praedicantium*, E.9 (*Excommunicatio*).7, art. 3 (fol. 228r). There is no modern edition of Bromyard's work.

[23] Walter Map, *De nugis curialium*, ed. James., pp. 206–07 (*Distinctio* 2.30).

type is told in the life of an Egyptian abbot, Patermuthius, in the fifth-century collection of desert saints' lives, *Historia monachorum* (The Story of the Monks), an important source of monastic spirituality and exempla throughout the Middle Ages.[24] This provides a rather wry, ironic twist to the ending and seems to further dissipate the didactic force of the earlier part of the story. An exemplum on the dangers of false tithing and the dread power of excommunication turns into a celebration of mercy and forgiveness, the salvation of sinners, and the power of prayer to affect the world beyond the grave.

John Lydgate

John Lydgate (1370?–1451?) was the most prolific and, in his time, the best-known of the early-fifteenth-century English poets who flourished in the generation after Chaucer, Langland, and Gower. Today he is recognized chiefly (and still largely deprecated) for his massive Chaucerian courtly epics, such as his *Troy Book, Siege of Thebes*, *Fall of Princes,* and *Temple of Glass.* But while he was, like Chaucer, a secular court poet with aristocratic patrons, he was also a monk and priest and, as a result, was perhaps better fitted than his master would have been to give voice to the more conventionally devout spirit of the new century. He differed markedly from his illustrious predecessors, for example, by writing a good deal of verse hagiography, including some long and elaborate narrative poems on the Virgin Mary, and the English saints Edmund, Fremund, and Alban.[25] In addition, he wrote a number of shorter hagiographic pieces, including brief versions of the hagiographic legends of George, Giles, Margaret, and

---

[24] Patermuthias is said to have visited a desert monastery stricken by the plague, where the following incident then occurred:

> He went into the house where one of the sick brothers was, and finding him already dead, went up to the bed and prayed and kissed him and asked which he preferred, to go to God, or to continue in the flesh. The brother sat up and said to him, "It is better to depart and to be with Christ. (Phil. 1.23) To live in the flesh is not essential for me." "Then sleep in peace, my child," he said "and intercede with God for me." The brother, just as he was, immediately lay back and died.

The Lives of the Desert Fathers, trans. Russell, p. 84.

[25] Other notable poet-hagiographers of Lydgate's era are Osbern Bokenham and John Capgrave. For editions of Lydgate's works and critical scholarship, see the bibliography by Alain Renoir and C. David Benson in *MWME* 6.1809–20, 2071–2175. On Lydgate's hagiographies, see the critical studies by Schirmer (*John Lydgate*, trans. Keep, pp. 149–72 [on *Saint Austin at Compton*, pp. 160–61]) and Pearsall (*John Lydgate*, pp. 275–92 [on *Saint Austin at Compton*, pp. 279–80]). The standard edition of Lydgate's minor poems, including most of the works referred to below, is that of MacCracken, *The Minor Poems of John Lydgate*.

Petronilla, as well as individual miracles of the Virgin Mary and Austin of Canterbury.[26] When or why he wrote *Saint Austin* is uncertain, but probably in the second quarter of the fifteenth century, i.e., later rather than earlier in his career.[27] Readers of the poem below will quickly see the large contrast in style between its latinate diction and elaborate crafting, aimed at an audience of sophisticated readers, and the homely diction and plain style of the *South English Legendary* lives printed above.

Tithes and Typology

Among the many distinctive features of Lydgate's handling of his Latin source, only the lengthy proem (lines 1–72) will be discussed here, leaving other matters for comment in the notes and elsewhere. Earlier critics have complained that in the proem, as elsewhere in the poem, the narrative line is overwhelmed by the "flamboyance of decoration."[28] Lydgate's language is, admittedly, an obstacle sometimes to rapid reading, but one senses it would present less of a problem to readers more accustomed than we are to the liturgical Latin and biblical culture of the later Middle Ages. His preamble is actually a fascinating meditation on the mysterious relationship between tithing, the Passion, the Eucharist, and salvation. It is worth noting that from the traditional biblical "authorities" for the custom of tithing, Lydgate selects four[29] in particular that are of much wider application than some others, implying from the outset that the legend itself transcends its narrow didactic focus on tithing and excommunication. Rather than highlight the more practical and materialistic Old and New Testament passages on tithing (such as Deuteronomy 14:22–23, Malachias 3:10, Luke 10:7, 1 Timothy 5:18, or 1 Corinthians 9:13–14), Lydgate alludes to four contexts (Cain and Abel, Abraham and Melchisedech, Isaac and Jacob, and Jacob's vision) which, while they were held to have specific meaning for tithing, are also well-known figural "types" or foreshadowings of the central mystery of the Christian faith, the redemption through Christ's body and blood. Thus the story of Abel's sacrificial offering to God (Genesis 4:3–4) was seen in Lydgate's time not only as a

---

[26] Four of these were apparently commissioned: viz., by the armorers' guild of London (George); Lady March (Margaret); St. Edmund's Abbey, Bury (Petronilla); anonymous (Giles). On the possibly "occasional" nature of *Saint Austin at Compton*, see below. For a new edition of Lydgate's poem on St. Margaret, see Reames, et al., *Middle English Legends of Women Saints*, pp. 147–68.

[27] See Whatley, "John Lydgate's *Saint Austin at Compton*," pp. 194–96.

[28] Pearsall, *John Lydgate*, pp. 279–80; compare Schirmer, *John Lydgate*, pp. 160–61.

[29] Readers will discover that the number four is a recurring motif in the poem and, seemingly, an aspect of its structural design. Discounting the poet's *envoi*, the poem amounts to exactly four hundred lines, in 8-line stanzas.

model of devout tithing, as in the well-known Wakefield mystery play, but it was also, more prominently, the first great *type* or *figure*, to use Lydgate's term, of Christ's sacrifice of Himself to God, and of the Eucharist that re-enacts it. Similarly, Melchisedech's offering of bread and wine to Abraham (Genesis 14:18), to which Lydgate devotes his second stanza, is a type of the Eucharist rather than of tithing per se, Melchisedech being regarded as the archetypal priest of God's church. In one of the most familiar and ancient parts of the Catholic Mass, as the celebrant offers the bread and wine to God for consecration just prior to the prayers for the dead, the offerings of Abel and Melchisedech are invoked along with Abraham's offering of his son:

> Moreover we pray that you deign to . . . accept this spotless victim [the "host"], just as you saw fit to accept the gifts of your righteous child, Abel, and the sacrifice of our father Abraham, and the holy sacrifice that your highest priest Melchisedech offered to you.

It is interesting in this respect that Lydgate does not mention Abraham's offering, to Melchisedech, of an actual tithe of his war booty (Genesis 14:20), which was the usual reference point here for the justification of tithing.[30]

The third and fourth parts of Lydgate's biblical "fundacioun" for tithing (lines 29–52) are equally rich in broader meanings, both involving the patriarch Jacob. Lydgate first alludes to Jacob's vision of the heavenly ladder which he saw while sleeping on his pillow of stone (Genesis 28:10–22). Jacob vows to give a tithe of his wealth to God if he is permitted eventually to return home to "his father's house"; but the vision at Bethel was important in Christian doctrine and poetry for various other reasons beside tithing, including the typology of the contemplative life,[31] which the dead British priest eulogizes ecstatically near the end of Lydgate's poem, amusingly transforming Jacob's pillow of "cold stone" into four pillows representing the three spiritual virtues plus the soul's desire for God (lines 369–76). Jacob, as the younger brother who inherited the blessing intended for his elder brother Esau, and who anointed his stone pillow with oil, was also a type of the Christian Church of the Gentiles inheriting the promise forfeited by the Jewish Synagogue. Appropriately, therefore, Lydgate in *Saint Austin at Compton* (lines 49–52), with explicit reference to the mystic importance of bread, wine, and oil, recalls as his final biblical type the blessing Isaac pronounced on Jacob (Genesis 27:27–29). Blind Isaac's blessing, in which he compares the smell of his son to that of a field blessed by God and the dew of Heaven, rich with the promise of corn and wine, was interpreted as "the proclamation of Christ among all the nations," the dew as the Word of God, the rich soil

---

[30] For example, in 1426, the Cambridge University dons who wrote a formal justification of personal tithes, in the complicated case of Friar William Russell, cited Abraham's offering to Melchisedech, not vice versa. See Henry Chichele, *The Register of Henry Chichele* 3.136.

[31] See the explanatory note on *Saint Austin at Compton*, line 374.

as the multitudes of people who hear it, and the corn and wine as the sacrament of Christ's body and blood.[32] By the end of this litany of biblical types, the practice of tithing the fruits of the earth has been subsumed into a larger meditation on the sacrament of the Eucharistic bread and wine, which was used to re-enact Christ's death on the Cross for the salvation of sinful mankind, and of which tithing itself may be seen as a symbol. Tithing is just one manifestation of the cycle of offering and sacrificing that is at the heart of the Christian faith and the economy of redemption and salvation. People give up, sacrifice, part of their incomes to make their own oblation, in effect, of bread and wine to the clergy and church, who are thereby enabled in turn to offer continually to God the Eucharistic prayers and the sacrificial oblation of Christ's body and blood. As Lydgate says himself (lines 14–16), if we sift through all the typology of sacred offerings, we find all of them, and the entire Christian faith, symbolized and foreshadowed in the priest-king Melchisedech's bread and wine. The legendary narrative that follows the preamble, while it is a didactic exemplum on tithing and excommunication, is also a dramatization of the meaning of the Incarnation and Crucifixion, the intersection of divine justice and mercy, which transformed the image of death from that of a fearful, fetid nightmare to a blissful sleep.

The Text

Lydgate's *Saint Austin at Compton* is preserved in six manuscripts, all of which MacCracken collated for his standard edition of the *Minor Poems*. Our edition follows his in taking as the base text Harley 2255, a mid-fifteenth-century collection, possibly produced at Lydgate's own abbey of Bury St. Edmunds, containing mainly religious poetry by Lydgate, with a special emphasis on the shorter hagiographic narratives. We have checked MacCracken's edition against Harley 2255 and found few real errors, but ours is a more conservative rendering of the manuscript than his, rejecting all but two (lines 313 and 390) of his emendations, such as his inconsistent attempts to regularize meter (e.g., by adding final-*e*); we have also omitted his modern stanza numbers and marginal plot summary, along with the subtitle, *Offre vp yowre Dymes*, which is not in the manuscript. Aside from the necessary glossing and notes on meaning and content, and modernizing of capitalization, our main addition to the medieval text is punctuation, where we differ substantially not only from the manuscript but also from MacCracken in places. Our punctuation is simply an attempt to make better sense of Lydgate's syntax.

---

[32] Augustine, *City of God* 16.37, trans. Bettenson, pp. 700–01.

Language

The dialect of the text requires little comment, displaying, like Simon Winter's *Life of Saint Jerome*, typical features of the mixed dialect of the greater London area (i.e., Southeast Midlands) of the mid- to late fifteenth century. However, the Benedictine Lydgate's style is more ornate, his diction altogether richer and more Latinate-French than that of his more ascetic Bridgettine contemporary. *Saint Austin at Compton* abounds in words like *conduite* (line 35, "lead"), *condigne* (line 44, "fitting"), *adverte* (line 71, "notice"), *spectacle* (line 132, "glass"), *emprise* (line 151, "command"), etc., although it stops short of the high "aureate" style found in some of his Marian poetry.[33] Lydgate's syntax is frequently artificial to the point of obscurity, more like Latin than English, in that he often inverts the typical English word order of Subject-Verb-Object, and one sometimes has to hunt for the verb at a considerable distance from its object (e.g., in the first stanza, *ground* in line 2 is the object of *Abel began* in line 5). Occasionally, he imitates the Latin ablative absolute construction (lines 201, 204) and expected verbs and prepositions are sometimes simply omitted (e.g., lines 53, 206). We have therefore provided rather more help in translating lines and sentences than would normally be necessary in a work of the late Middle English period.

Indexed in

IMEV 1875.

Manuscripts

London, British Library MS Harley 2255, fols. 24r–32v.

Previous editions

Lydgate. *The Minor Poems of John Lydgate*. Ed. MacCracken Pp. 193–206.

---

[33] On Lydgate's aureate style, especially in his Marian lyrics, see Pearsall, *John Lydgate*, pp. 262–63, 268–75. See also Lydgate, *Poems*, ed. Norton-Smith, pp. 192–95. Pearsall (p. 280) labels Lydgate's shorter hagiographic narratives "sub-aureate."

VI

Saint Austin at Compton *(c. 1420–40), by John Lydgate, from London, British Library, MS Harley 2255, fols. 24r–32v*

	Lyk as the Bible makith mencioun,	
	The original ground of devout offryng,	*source*
	Callyd of clerkys just decimacioun	*by scholars*
	(In pleyn Ynglissh, trewe and just tithyng),	
5	Abel began, innocent of lyving,	
	Oonly to God for to do plesaunce;	
	Of frut, of beestys, reknyd every thyng,[1]	
	Gaff God his part, tenthe of his substaunce.	*[He] gave*

	Melchisedech, bisshop, preest and kyng,	
10	To Abraham, a prynce of gret puissaunce,	*power*
	For his victorye at his hoom comyng	
	(Whan Amelech was brouht unto uttraunce),	*the land of the Amalekites; destruction*
	Offryd bred and wyn with devout obeisaunce.	
	Of alle oblaciouns figurys out to serche,	
15	On bred and wyn by roial suffisaunce	
	The feith is groundid of al Hooly Cherche.[2]	

	Of good greyn sowe growith up good wheete;	*sowed*
	With gret labour plantyd is the vyne;	
	The tenthe part is to oure Lord mooste meete,	*appropriate*
20	To whos preceptis hevenly and divyne	
	We muste our heedys meekly doun enclyne,	
	Paye our dymes by His comaundementis:	*tithes*

---

[1] Lines 5–7: *Abel, whose life was sinless, began [the practice of tithing: see line 2] / Simply to give delight to God; / Having figured out the sum total of all his produce and livestock*

[2] Lines 14–16: *Sifting through the "figures" (archetypes/typological correspondences) of all kinds of sacrificial offerings, we find that the faith of the entire church rests symbolically on the bread and wine provided by [Melchisedech's] kingly abundance*

Moyses lawe and eek bi the doctryne —   *also; [gospel] teachings*
Foure Evangelistis and too Testamentis.   *two*

25   Fro Melchisedech doun to Abraham —
       To sette of tithes a fundacioun —
       Th'encrees of frute and al that therof cam
       They trewly made there oblacioun.
       Whan Jacob sauh in his avisioun,
30   Tyme that he slepte upon the cold stoon,
       Sauh on a laddere goon angelis up and doun,   *angels walking*
       To God above made his avowh anoon.   *vow*

       This was his vowh, with gret humylité
       Lik his entent, in ful pleyn language:[1]
35   "Lord, yif Thou list to conduite me,   *please; guide*
       Of Thy grace fortune my passage   *let my journey succeed*
       To retourne hoom to myn herytage,
       My fadris hous come therto bytymes,   *to arrive at in good time*
       Of good and tresoure with al the surplusage   *goods; excess*
40   I shal to Thee offren up the dymes."

       Among al frutys in especial
       By a prerogatif excellent and notable,
       In worthynesse verray imperial,   *outstanding*
       Of reverence condigne and honourable,   *fitting*
45   By antiquité in templys custumable,   *In temples according to ancient custom*
       In hooly writ remembryd ofte sithes,   *many times*
       Wyn, oyle and wheete, frutis moost acceptable
       To God above were offryd up for tythes.

       The Patriark of antiquyté,
50   Callyd Isaak, next by successioun
       To Abraham, which with thes frutys thre[2]
       Gaff to Jacob his benediccioun.   *Gave his blessing to Jacob*

---

[1] Lines 33–34: *This was his vow, [spoken] with great humility / Just as his intent [was] humble (i.e., his humble words reflected his inner purpose), in very plain language*

[2] *To Abraham, who with these three fruits (i.e., wine, oil, and wheat)*

St. Austin

The which thre in comparisoun
(Of the moralité whoso takith heed)
55   To preesthood first and kynges of renoun:[1]
Gret mysteries in oyle, wyn, and breed.

Breed and wyn to bisshopis apparteene,
Oyle longith for to anoynte kynges,   *is appropriate*
Offryng is maad of frutys ripe and greene,
60   Of foul and beeste and of al othire thynges;
Breefly conclude: all folk in there livynges   *their*
That trewly tithe with glad herte and face,
Patriarkis, prophetis in ther writynges,
Shal evere encreese with fortune, hap, and grace.[2]

65   And who fro God withhalte his dewté   *whoever withholds from God what he owes*
Lat hym knowe for pleyn conclusyoun
Of warantise he shal nevire the,
Lakke grace and vertuous foysoun,
Of ther tresoure discrece in ech sesoun;
70   To hooly chirche that wil nat pay hys dyme,[3]
Lat hym adverte and have inspeccioun   *notice; consider*
What there befyl in Awstynes tyme.

I meene Austyn that was fro Rome sent
By Seyn Gregory into this regioun,
75   Graciously arryved up in Kent,
Famous in vertu, of gret perfeccioun.
His liff was lyk his predicacioun:
As he tauht, sothely so he wrouhte.

---

[1] Lines 53–55: *For those interested in interpretation, these three [fruits] correspond first to priest-hood and then to renowned kings*

[2] Lines 61–64: *In short the testimony of the patriarchs and prophets promises to increase the good fortune, prosperity, and grace of all people in their livelihoods, who pay their tithes properly with cheerful heart and demeanor*

[3] Lines 67–70: *It is guaranteed that he will never prosper, / [But shall] lack [God's] favor and fertile abundance, / Causing their bounty to diminish with each season; / Whoever will not pay his tithe to Holy Church*

Saint Austin at Compton

	By his moost hooly conversacioun,	*way of life*
80	Into this lond the feith of Crist he brouhte.	

Thoruh al the parties and provynces of the lond *parts*
Of Cristis gospel he gan the seed to sowe,
Unkouth myracles wrouhte with hys hond; *Marvelous*
Worshipped he was bothe of hih and lowe,
85 Withouten pompe grace hath his horn so blowe,
Thoruh his merites, that the hevenly soun.[1]
He callid was, as it is wel knowe,
Cristes Apostil in Brutis Albioun.

He was Aurora whan Phebus sholde arise *the dawn; the sun god*
90 With his briht beemys on that lond to shyne,
Callyd day sterre, moost glorious to devise. *describe*
Our feith was dirkid undir the Ecliptik lyne, *Astronomical equator*
Oure mysbeleeve he did first enlumyne
Whan he outsprad the briht beemys cleere
95 Of Cristes lawe by his parfit doctryne, *perfect*
Thoruh al this lond to make his liht appeere.

This was doon by grace or we were ware, *before; aware*
Of th'Oly Goost by the influence,[2]
Whan foure steedys of Phebus goldene chare
100 List in this regioun holde residence. *Chose*
Who droff the chare, to conclude in sentence,
By goostly favoure of the nyne speerys, *spheres*
Til blissed Austyn by goostly elloquence
Was trewe Auriga of foure gospelleeris? *Charioteer*

105 Or Austyn cam we slombryd in dirknesse *Before*
Lyk ydolastres blyndid in oure siht; *idolators*
Of Cristes feith was curteyned the cleernesse
Tyl *sol justicie* list shewe his beemys briht *"the sun of righteousness"*

---

[1] Lines 84–86: *He was honored by people of high and low rank, because, although Austin avoided worldly display, divine grace had trumpeted his praise, that heavenly sound, on account of his merits*

[2] *By the infusion of the Holy Spirit*

	Of his mercy to clarefye the liht,	*To reveal the light of his mercy*
110	Chace away oure cloudy ignoraunce,	
	The Lord of lordys of moost imperial myht,	
	Tavoyde away our frowarde mescreaunce.	*To dispel; obstinate unbelief*

First, fro the pope that callid was Gregory,
Awstyn was sent (who that list adverte — *whoever cares to take note*
115 Tyme and date be put in memory), *are remembered*
To Cristes feith whan he did us converte.
Our goostly woundys felte as tho gret smerte, *at that time; pain*
Deed was our soule, our boody eek despised, *also*
Tyl Awstyn made us cast of cloth and sherte: *off*
120 In coold watire by hym we were baptised.

Kyng Ethelbert regnyng that tyme in Kent,
Touchyng the date whan Awstyn cam first doun, *To speak of*
Noumbryd the tyme when that he was sent *Reckoning*
By Pope Gregory into this regioun,
125 Yeer of our Lord by computacioun
Compleet five hundryd fourty and eek nyne,
As cronyclers make mencioun,
In ther bookys fully determyne. *calculate*

Thus he began by grace of Goddis hond
130 (Wher God list werche may be noon obstacle), *wishes to work*
By his laboure was cristened al this lond,
Feith of our Lord wex moor cleere than spectacle. *grew; glass*
Whan th'Oly Goost made His habitacle *home*
In tho personys that wern in woord and deede *those; were*
135 By Awstyn tournyd, God wrouhte a gret myracle *converted*
To make hem stable in Articles of the Creede.

But to resorte ageyn to my mateere:
With th'Oly Goost Austyn sett afire *Austin, kindled by the Holy Spirit,*
Gan preche and teche devoutly the maneere
140 Of Cristes lawe abroad in every shire,
Grace of our Lord did hym so inspire
To enlwmyne al this regioun.

| | Of aventure his herte gan desire | *By chance* |
| | To entre a village that callid was Comptoun. | |

145	The parissh preest of the same place	
	Aforn provided, in ful humble wyse	*Previously appointed*
	Besouhte hym meekly that he wolde of grace	*kindly*
	Here his compleynt as he shal devise.	*Hear; describe [it]*
	In pleyn language told hym al the guyse:	*all the particulars*
150	Lord of that thorpe, requeryd ofte sithes	*village; [although] often asked*
	— He ay contrayre t'obeye to th'emprise[1]	
	Of Hooly Chirche — list not paye his tithes.	*would not*

	"Entretid hym lik to his estat,[2]	
	First secrely, next afforn the toun,	*in private; in front of*
155	But al for nouht: I fond hym obstynat,	
	Moost indurat in his oppynyoun,	
	Toold hym the custom groundid on resoun —	*[I] told*
	He was bounde by lawe of oold writyng	*[Namely, that] he was*
	To pay his dymes — and for rebellioun	
160	I cursyd hym, cause of fals tithyng.	*excommunicated him, because*

	"This mateer hool ye must of riht redresse,	
	Requeryng you of your goodlyheede,	*You are required; goodness*
	By youre discrecioun to do rihtwisnesse,	
	Peysen al the cas and prudently take heede	*Weigh; case*
165	That Hooly Chirche have no wrong in deede;	
	Al thyng commytted and weyed in ballaunce,	*[Let] all the evidence be considered*
	Ye to be juge, and lyk as ye proceede	*judge; determine [it]*
	We shall obeye to youre ordynaunce."	

	Hooly Awstyn, sad and wel avised,	*serious and judicious*
170	Kneuh by signes this compleynt was no fable	*Knew*
	And in maneere was of the caas agrised,[3]	
	Fond that the lord was in that poynt coupable.	*[He] determined; guilty [as charged]*

---

[1] *He always refusing to obey the command*

[2] *"[I] pleaded [with] him in a manner befitting his [noble] rank["]*

[3] *And was quite appalled by the facts of the case*

	To reduce hym and mak hym moor tretable,	*reform; amenable*
	As the lawe ordeyned hath of riht,	*justly*
175	Blissid Awstyn, in Cristes feith moost stable,	
	Took hym apart, seyde unto this knyht,	

	"How may this be that thou art froward	
	To Hooly Chirche to pay thy dewtee?	
	Lyk thy desert thou shalt have thy reward;	*According to your deserts*
180	Thynk that thou art bounde of trouthe and equitee	*bound by*
	To paye thy tithes; and lerne this of mee:	
	The tenthe part fro God yif thou withdrawe,[1]	
	Thou muste incurre of necessite	*be liable*
	To been accursyd by rigoure of the lawe."	

185	The knyht, astonyed somwhat of his cheere,	
	"Sire," quod he, "I wol wel that ye knowe	*wish*
	My labour is ay from yeere to yeere,	
	By revolucioun, that the lond be sowe;[2]	
	Afore this peple stondyng heere arowe,	*in rows*
190	By evidence to maken an open preef,	*statement*
	What maner boost that ony man list blowe,[3]	
	I with the nynthe wil have the tenthe cheef.	*sheaf*

	"Sey what ye list, I wyl have no lasse."	*less*
	This was the answere pleynly of the knyht;	
195	Hooly Austyn dispoosid hym to Masse,	
	Ful devoutly and in the peeplys siht,	
	Tornyd his face, comaundith anoon riht	*at once*
	Ech cursyd man that wer out of grace,	*excommunicated*
	Tyme of his Masse that every maneere wiht	*Throughout his Mass; sort of person*
200	That stood accursyd, voyde shulde his place.	*vacate*

| | Present that tyme many creature, | *I. e., in the presence of* |
| | Withoute abood or any long taryeng | *delay* |

---

[1] *If you withhold the tenth part [of your income] from God*

[2] Lines 187–88: *It is always by my labor, without fail, year in, year out, that the land gets planted*

[3] *Whatever kind of boast anyone cares to utter (i.e., regardless of what anyone else says)*

Saint Austin at Compton

Ther roos up oon out of his sepulture   *tomb [inside the church]*
Terrible of face, the peeple beholdyng,   *as the people looked on*
205   A greet paas the chircheyeerd passyng,   *rapidly*
The Seyntuarye bood ther a greet whyle,   *Waited there outside the Cemetery*
Al the space the Masse was seyeng,   *time; being said*
Feerfully afore the chirche style.   *gate*

Withoute meevyng, alway stille he stood;
210   The peeple, feerful in ther oppynyoun,
Almoost for dreed they gan to wexen wood.   *They became almost crazy with fear*
Afftir Masse alle of assent cam doun,   *with [mutual] consent*
To hooly Austyn made relacioun
Of al this caas riht as it was falle.
215   Gaff hem a spirit of consolacioun,   *[He] gave*
Ful sobirly spak unto them alle.

Sad and discreet in his advertence,   *perceptive; awareness*
Sauh by there poort that they stood in dreede.   *[He] saw by their demeanor*
First of alle with ful devout reverence
220   Cros and hooly watir he made aforn proceede
(The crucifix ther baner was in deede),
Blissid Austyn the careyn gan compelle   *corpse*
"In Jesu name, that lyst for man to bleede,   *who chose to bleed for mankind*
What that thu art trewly for to telle."

225   "Disobeisaunt my tithes for to paye,
Of yoore agoon I was lord of this toun,   *A long time ago*
My dewtees I did alwey delaye,
Stood accursyd for my rebellioun,
Made in my liff no restitucioun.   *payment of debts*
230   Geyn thy biddyng I myht no socoure have,   *Against your command*
My cursyd careyn, ful of corrupcioun,
By Goddis angel was cast out of my grave.

"Thy precept was upon ech a side,   *[The power of] your command was everywhere*
Beyng at Masse whil thou were in presence.[1]

---

[1] *For as long as you were present at the Mass*

235	No stynkyng flessh myht in the poorche abyde,	
	I was take up, lad forth by violence.	*led*
	On me was yove so dreedful a sentence	*given (imposed)*
	Of curs, allas! Which to my diffame	*[By] which to my shame*
	Now, as ye seen, for disobedience	
240	Disclaundrid is perpetuelly my name.	*Disgraced*
	"Tyme whan Britouns were lordis of this lond,	
	Hadde the lordship and domynacioun,	
	The same tyme, as ye shal undirstond,	
	Of this village in sothe I was patroun,	*lord*
245	To Hooly Chirche hadde no devocioun,	
	Offte sithe steryd of my Curat	*[Although] many times urged by*
	To paye my dymes, hadde indignacioun,	*[I] had*
	Was ay contrayre, froward, and obstinat.	
	"This hundryd yeer I have enduryd peyne,	
250	And fifty ovir by computacioun;	
	Greet cause have I to moorne and to compleyne	
	In a dirk prisoun of desolacioun	
	Mong firy flawmys, voyd of remissioun."	*devoid of forgiveness*
	And whil that he this wooful tale toold,	
255	Hooly Austyn with the peeple enviroun	*around [him]*
	Wepte of compassioun, as they to watire woold.	*[if] they would [dissolve] into water*
	Austyn gan muse in his oppynyoun	*mind*
	To fynde a mene the sowle for to save.	*means*
	Of this terrible doolful inspeccioun	*At; spectacle*
260	The peeplis hertys gretly gan abave,	*grew disconsolate*
	Whom to behoolde they cowde no coumfort have[1]	
	Al the while the careyn was in there presence.	
	Austin axith yif he knew the grave	
	Of thilke preest that gaf un hym sentence	*on him (i.e., the corpse)*
265	"So long aforn for thy fals tythyng,	
	As we have herd the mateer in substaunce."	

---

[1] *As long as they looked at the corpse, they could not be comforted*

232

"Sothly," quod he, "there shal be no taryeng,
But ye shal have a reconysaunce   *knowledge*
So ye wil digge and doon youre observaunce   *If; rite [of exhumation]*
270 To delvyn up his boonys dul and rude —   *unearth*
Loo! heer he lith, cheef cause of my grevaunce,
So fel a curs he did on me conclude."   *dire; bind*

Austyn fulfilled of grace and all vertu,
As ony pileer in our feith moost stable,
275 The deed preest in name of Crist Jhesu
He bad arise with woordys ful tretable,   *clear and deliberate*
Requeryd hym, by tokenys ful notable,   *Asked*
Yif he hadde, sith tyme that he was born,
Seyn that owgly careyn lamentable,   *Seen*
280 The deed boody that stood hem beforn.

"Sothly," quod he, "and that me rewith soore,[1]
That evir I knewh hym, for his frowardness.
I gaf hym counseil, daily moore and moore,
To paye his tithes, the pereil did expresse.   *[and I] made clear the peril*
285 He took noon heed his surfetys to redresse.   *to repay his arrears*
I warnyd hym many divers tymes,
But al for nouht, I can weel bere witnesse,
Deyed accursyd, rebel to paye his dymes."   *[He] died*

Whan the preest hath toold every deel,
290 With evy cheer and voys most lamentable   *With somber countenance*
Quod Seyn Austyn, "Brothire, thou knowest weel,
Thynk He that bouht us is evir merciable;   *merciful*
By whoos exaumple we must be tretable   *flexible*
As the Gospel pleynly doth recoorde,
295 And for thy part be nat thu vengable
So that with rigoure mercy may accoorde.   *may be reconciled*

"Thynk how Jhesus bouht us with His blood,
Oonly of mercy suffryd Passioun,   *As an act of pure mercy*

---

[1] *"Yes indeed," he said, "and I sorely regret it["]*

For mannys sake was nayled on the Rood,

300   Rive to the herte for oure redempcioun.   *Stabbed*

Remembre how thu dist execucioun   *prosecuted*

Upon this penaunt ploungid in greet peyne.   *penitent*

Withdrawe thy sentence and do remissioun,   *[formally] forgive [him]*

Fro Purgatorye his trowblys to restreyne.[1]

305   "On hym thu leydist a ful dreedful bond,

To thee it longith the same bond to unbynde.

Tak this flagelle devoutly in thy hond,   *scourge (whip)*

On Cristes Passion in this mateere have mynde;

Many exaumple to purpoos thu mayst fynde

310   Of trespasours relesyd of there peyne,   *sinners*

Of Petir, Poule, and Sein Thomas of Ynde,

Of Egipsiacha, and Mary Mawdeleyne,

"Take to mercy for there greet repentaunce,   *Granted mercy (forgiven)*

There was noon othir mediacioun.

315   Thu must of riht yeve hym his penaunce

With this flagelle of equité and resoun,   *justice*

Sette on this careyn a castigacioun   *Inflict; chastisement*

As he requerith kneelyng afor thy face;

Best restoratif next Cristes Passioun   *remedy except for*

320   Is thyn assoylyng for his gret trespace."   *absolution; transgression*

Al this was doon by the comaundement

Of Seyn Austyn, the careyn ther knelyng;

Lord of that village was also there present,

Al the peeple moost pitously sobbyng,

325   From there eyen the teerys distyllyng.

The last preest, reised from his grave,

The tothir corps with bittir fel scorgyng

Assoyled him his soule for to save.[2]

---

[1] *To put an end to his afflictions in Purgatory*

[2] Lines 326–28: *The last priest [of the Britons' time], resuscitated from his grave, / Absolved the other corpse with a bitterly severe whipping / In order to save his soul*

	Oo ded man assoiled hath anothire	*One*
330	(An unkouth caas merveilous texpresse),	*strange*
	Oon knelith doun, requerith of the tothire	
	Pleyn remissioun of oold cursidnesse;	
	Bete with a scorge, took it with meeknesse,	*Beaten; [he] endured*
	Hopyng that Jhesus shuld his soule save.	
335	Seyn Austyn bad him in hast he shuld hym dresse,	
	Thankyng our Lord, ageyn unto his grave.	

	Circumstauncis in ordre to accounte,	
	Of this miracle peised every thyng,[1]	
	Mercy of our Lord doth everythyng surmounte.	
340	To save and dampne He is Lord and Kyng,	
	Hevene and helle obeye to His biddyng,	
	By many exaumple expert in this mateere.[2]	
	Trajan the Emperour for his just deemyng	*judgment*
	Isavid was by meene and the prayeere	*intercession*

345	Of Seyn Gregory, Pope of Rome toun:	
	Cause in his doomys he did so gret riht,	*Because*
	Rigour was medlyd with remyssioun.	*Justice; joined; forgiveness*
	For He that is of moost imperial myht	*He (i.e., God)*
	List advertise in His celestial siht,	*Was pleased to acknowledge*
350	Tween rihte and favour, rigoure and pité,	
	By doom and sentence of every maneere wiht,[3]	
	Mercy of virtues hath the sovereynté.	

	Unto the preest aforn that I you toold	
	Seyn Austyn made a straunge questioun,	
355	To cheese of tweyne, whedir that he woold:	
	To goon with hym thoruh this regioun,	
	The feith of Crist by predicacioun,	
	For his part groundid on scripture,	

---

[1] Lines 337–38: *Putting all the circumstances [of this event] in proper relation, / Weighing every aspect of this miracle [it seems to me that]*

[2] *[As is] proven in many exempla (didactic stories) on this subject*

[3] *With respect to the judging and sentencing of every kind of person*

To doon his deveere of hool affeccioun;[1]
360　Or to resoorte ageyn to his sepulture.　　　　　　　　*grave*

"Fadir," quod he, "with supportacioun　　　　　　　　*[the] help*
Of your benygne fadirly pité,
I you requeere to graunte me pardoun,　　　　　　　　*request*
Unto my grave I may restooryd be;　　　　　　　　*[So that] unto*
365　This world is ful of mutabilité,
Full of trouble, chaung, and varyaunce,
And for this tyme, I pray you, suffrith me　　　　　　　*allow*
T'abyde in reste from worldly perturbaunce.　　　　　　*To wait*

"I rest in pees and take of nothyng keep,　　　　*pay no heed to anything*
370　Rejoisshe in quiete and contemplacioun,
Voyd of al trouble. Celestial is my sleep
And, by the meene of Cristes Passioun,
Feith, hoope, and charité, with hool affeccioun,
Been pilwes foure to reste upon by grace　　　　　　　*pillows*
375　Day of the general resurreccioun,　　　　　　　*[Until the] day*
Whan Gabriel callith t'appeere aforn his face."　　*summons [us] to appear*

"O brothire myn, this choys is for thy beste!
Contemplatiff, fulfilled of al pleasaunce,
I pray to God sende thee good reste,　　　　　　　*to send you*
380　Of goostly gladnesse sovereyn suffisaunce.[2]
Pray for us and have in remembraunce
Al Hooly Chirche in quiete to be crownyd,
That Crist Jhesus dispoose so the ballaunce
That Petris ship be with no tempest drownyd.

385　"I meene as thus: that noon heresye
Ryse in thes dayes, nor noon that was beforn,
Nor no darnel growe nor multeplye,
Nor no fals cokkyl be medlyd with good corn.　　　　*cockle; mingled*

---

[1] Lines 357–59: *To do his utmost, with all his heart, by preaching the faith of Christ as it is grounded in the gospels*

[2] *Supreme fullness of spiritual joy*

Cheese we the roosys, cast away the thorn.
390   Crist boute us alle with His precious bloode: *bought (redeemed)*
To that He bouht us lat no thyng be lorn,[1]
For our redempcioun He starf upon the Rood."   *died*

The knyht, present lord of the same toun,
Thes miracles whan he did se,
395   Austyn axith of hym this questioun,
"Wilt thu," quod he, "paye thy dewté?"   *debt*
He grauntith his axing and fyl doun on his kne,
Moost repentaunt forsook al the world as blyve,   *at once*
With devout herte and al humylité
400   Folwith Seyn Austyn duryng al his live.

lenvoye Go litil tretys, void of presumpcioun!
Prese nat to ferre, nor be nat to bold;   *too far*
This laboure stant undir correccioun,[2]
Of this miracle remembryd manyfold,   *Concerning; in various ways*
405   In many shire and many cité toold.
To you echon to whom I it directe,
Bycause I am of wittis dul and old,
Doth your deveere this processe to corecte.   *Do what you can; narrative*

---

[1] *Let nothing be lost, beyond what He has redeemed for us*

[2] *This [literary] work of mine stands ready to be corrected [by others]*

VI

Explanatory Notes to Saint Austin at Compton *(c. 1420–40), by John Lydgate*

5–8   *Abel began . . . tenthe of his substaunce.* See Genesis 4:3–4. The story of Abel and Cain does not describe their offerings as tithes, but the term is common enough elsewhere in the Old Testament: e.g., Genesis 14:20 (Abraham's tithe to Melchisedech) and Numbers 18:21–29 (the people of Israel are to give their annual tithe of first-fruits to the priestly class of Levites for their sustenance and for sacrifices to God). For a vivid late medieval depiction of the Cain and Abel story as an illustration of just and unjust tithing, see the Wakefield *Mactacio Abel*, in *The Wakefield Pageants*, ed. Cawley, pp. 1–13.

9–14   *Melchisedech . . . figurys out to serche.* Genesis 14:1–24. See the discussion of "Tithes and Typology" in the Introduction to this chapter.

20   *preceptis.* A loaded technical term in this context, since there had been considerable controversy in Lydgate's time and earlier as to whether lay people's payment of personal tithes (on income derived from sources other than agricultural land and produce) to the parish clergy was mandated by God's law (*sub precepto divino*), or whether people were free (*licet unicuique*) to give the tithes to charity instead if they chose. See, e.g., the opening Latin and English documents recording the Archbishop's case against Friar William Russell of London in 1428, Chichele, *Register of Henry Chichele* 3.118–119 (cited above in note 30 of the Introduction).

25–26   *Fro Melchisedech . . . sette of tithes a fundacioun.* Lydgate, having *sette . . . a fundacioun* (i.e., provided one set of Biblical precedents for tithing), continues to offer further authorities in what follows. But his phrase *Melchisedech doun to Abraham* is problematic, since the two were contemporaries. More logical would be "Fro Abel doun to Abraham" or, better still, "Doun fro Melchisedech and Abraham," but the manuscripts concur on the awkward reading.

29–40   *Whan Jacob sauh in his avisioun . . . I shal to Thee offren up the dymes.* Genesis 28:10–22.

238

46–48   *In hooly writ remembryd . . . were offryd up for tythes.* E.g., Deuteronomy 14:23, 18:4; Malachias 3:10; 1 Corinthians 9:11, 13.

49–52   *The Patriark of antiquyté . . . Gaff to Jacob his benediccioun.* See Genesis 27, the story of Isaac, Jacob, and Esau, but there is no mention of oil, only of corn and wine. Jacob does, however, anoint his stone pillow at Bethel (Genesis 28:18).

51   *which.* The relative pronoun seems redundant.

78   *As he tauht, sothely so he wrouhte. Docere verbo et exemplo* (teaching by saying and doing) was a commonplace of medieval hagiography and Christian ethics. Compare Matthew 5:19 and, e.g., Chaucer's Parson in The General Prologue of the *Canterbury Tales*: "first he wroghte, and afterward he taughte" (I[A]497). But Lydgate might also have been prompted by Bede's account, where the missionaries are said to have "in all things practised what they preached" (*Bede's Ecclesiastical History*, ed. Colgrave and Mynors, pp. 76–77).

83   *Unkouth myracles wrouhte with hys hand.* Compare the Latin *Narratio* (line 3): *diuini uerbi semina ex more gentibus erogando* (" as usual sowing the seeds of the divine word among the heathen peoples"). The well-known seed metaphor derives ultimately from the parable of the sower in Matthew 13:1–9, 18–23. Although Bede's account makes it clear that Austin and his followers were performing miracles (*Bede's Ecclesiastical History*, pp. 76–77, 108–09, 136–37), there is no indication that Austin himself undertook any missionary work outside of Kent, except for his ill-fated meeting with the Welsh bishops somewhere in the Midlands (pp. 135–41). Two of his colleagues, Mellitus and Paulinus, successfully established missions in, respectively, the London area and Northumbria (pp. 142–43). Later hagiographers, however, beginning with Goscelin of Canterbury in his *Historia S. Augustini* (end of the eleventh century), ascribe to Austin a variety of wanderings and miracles in other parts of England. The *Narratio* builds on this later legendary tradition, but in doing so creates a blatantly anachronistic situation: for Austin, traveling on a missionary journey, finds at Compton a fully functioning Christian community already in place, complete with a lord of the manor and a disgruntled priest. With some judiciously vague and repetitious narrative later in the poem (lines 129–44), Lydgate manages to suggest that Austin visited Compton after "By his labour was cristened al this lond" (line 131) as part of a second phase in his mission to "preche and teche devoutly the maneere / Of Cristes lawe" (lines 139–40), and to strengthen the faith of the people already converted ("By Awstyn tournyd," line

135). The Compton miracle's divine purpose was "To make hem stable in Articles of the Creede" (line 136).

85–86   *grace hath his horn so blowe . . . the hevenly soun.* In Middle English, "to have one's horn blown" often meant to have one's infamy proclaimed, but Lydgate is clearly using the expression positively to connote a kind of celestial trumpet fanfare bruiting Austin's fame as a holy man.

88   *Cristes Apostil.* None of the biblical apostles was ever credited with preaching in Britain (although the Glastonbury legend of Joseph of Arimathea was a move in that direction), but Bede and most of the English churches awarded the title "Apostle of the English" to Pope Gregory himself. At St. Augustine's, Canterbury, however, whose hagiographic traditions may be reflected here, the title was conferred on Austin. See Thacker, "Cults at Canterbury," pp. 221–46. The apostolic epithet is also used in the title of the *Narratio* in several of the manuscripts.

   Brutis Albioun. According to an early medieval Welsh legend popularized and elaborated by Geoffrey of Monmouth in his *Historia regum Britanniae* or *History of the Kings of Britain* (c. 1136), Britain was originally called Albion, but was renamed in honor of the Trojan prince, Brutus or Britto (great-grandson of Aeneas), who was believed to have colonized the island with his followers in the aftermath of the Trojan war.

89–91   *He was Aurora . . . moost glorious to devise.* *Phebus* and the *day sterre* (lines 89, 91) refer to Christ as the light of the world (compare John 1:4–5) and the sun of righteousness (see below, lines 108–09). Austin is figured here as the dawn, *Aurora*, i.e., the herald of the sun's light. Lydgate found suggestions for these allusions, which are developed with further hybrid classical-biblical imagery in the next stanza (97–104), not in the *Narratio* but rather in the elaborate rhetoric of Goscelin's life of Augustine and in the liturgy for the feast of a Confessor Bishop (such as Austin himself), specifically the readings at Mass drawn from Ecclesiasticus 50, where the high priest himself is compared to the "day star," *stella matutina*. For more details and references see Whatley, "John Lydgate's *Saint Austin*," pp. 215–16.

95   *Cristes lawe.* Lydgate uses the phrase here and later (line 140) to refer to the gospel message, in keeping with the strongly legalistic flavor, and emphasis on due process, of his rendering of the priest's and bishop's encounters with the tithe-breaking laymen. Compare lines 158, 174, 184, and also the opening of the Middle English

poem, *Saint Erkenwald*, lines 33–34: "Now of þis Augustynes art is Erkenwolde biscop / At loue London toun and the laghe teches."

97–104　*This was doon . . . of foure gospelleeris.* The ultimate source of this image of the Church as a *char* (line 101, "car," or "chariot") drawn by four figures representing the Evangelists is Ezechiel's first vision (Ezechiel 1:4–21). Lydgate's question, "Who drove the car?" (line 101), i.e., who preached the gospel before the charioteer (*Auriga*, line 104) Austin, is rhetorical, since the car and the light of the Word were in effect absent from England for 150 years, the bishops of the fugitive Britons doing nothing to convert their heathen supplanters, the English. For further details and references, see Whatley, "John Lydgate's *Saint Austin,*" p. 215n57.

98　*Of th'Oly Goost by the influence.* This sort of inversion of normal word order is typical of Lydgate's aureate, Latinate style. See below, line 107, and many others.

102　*nyne speerys.* The nine crystalline concentric spheres that make up the so-called Ptolemaic conception of the universe widely accepted among learned Christians until the end of the Middle Ages. Here Lydgate seems to equate the combined harmonic influence or "favor" of the spheres with God's grace.

108　*sol justicie.* The original biblical source of this phrase, "sun of righteousness," is Malachias 4:2, shortly after one of the most important biblical passages on tithing, Malachias 3:10–12.

122　*Awstyn cam first doun.* Today we would envisage Austin "coming up" from Italy, northwards towards Britain, but Lydgate may be picturing the Europe of the medieval *mappae mundi* or world maps, in which the Mediterranean was in the middle of the map and Britain below it in the bottom left corner.

126　*five hundryd fourty and eek nyne.* The real date of Augustine's mission to Kent was 597, which was accurately recorded in Bede's *Ecclesiastical History* and the *Anglo-Saxon Chronicle.* The 38-year discrepancy is probably the result of scribal errors in whichever chronicle Lydgate consulted (see line 127), or possibly alludes to some obscure piece of numerological symbolism. The *Narratio* gives no dates, except the 150-year interval between the death of the British priest and Austin's mission.

136　*Articles of the Creede.* Mention of the Creed, which is recited by Catholic Christians, for example, after the reading of the Gospel at Mass, prompts Lydgate's readers to interpret the brief miracle tale that follows as an illustration of the basic truths of the

Christian faith, but especially the eschatological ideas of judgment ("He shall come to judge both the quick and the dead"), mercy ("the forgiveness of sins"), and resurrection ("the resurrection of the body").

144   *Comptoun.* The name in the *Narratio* (line 2) is *Cometona*, from OE *Cumb* ("narrow valley"; compare Welsh *Cym*) + OE *tun* ("village," "town"). There is no Compton in Oxfordshire, but there are several in neighboring Warwickshire. The seventeenth-century antiquary, Sir William Dugdale, in *The Antiquities of Warwickshire*, 1.580–81), identifies the story's locale as Long Compton, close to the Oxfordshire border, with its impressive thirteenth-century church on the road leading to Woodstock and Oxford. Although there are records of late medieval disputes at Long Compton between rival claimants to the tithe income, we are not aware of anything there that could have inspired the legend itself. Moreover, Long Compton is much further from Woodstock than "sex miliariis" (*Narratio*, line 3). Another claimant for the putative location is Combe, Oxfordshire, exactly six miles by road from Woodstock.

146   *Aforn provided. Provide* is used in its ecclesiastical sense, "appoint (someone) to a benefice," i.e., a stipendiary position as a priest. The phrase *Aforn provided* gives the impression that the priest was installed at Compton during the first phase of Austin's mission. See above, note on line 83.

158   *He was bounde by lawe of oold writyng.* In the *Narratio* (lines 23–24) it is Austin who later on formally reminds the lay lord about the *fidelium consuetudines et . . . patrum traditiones* ("customs of the faithful and . . . traditions of the fathers") according to which he must excommunicate him for refusing to pay his tithes. Lydgate has transferred the invocation to the priest and altered it to refer to written law. Tithe payment was hardly a fixed element of church law during the time of Austin himself in the sixth century, but enforcement of tithe payment begins to figure in both ecclesiastical and secular laws from shortly afterwards. The system of paying tithes specifically for the upkeep of the parish church (as opposed to devoting them to poor relief or hospitals) was not formalized in England, however, until the later tenth century, when it becomes explicit in the laws of King Edgar. By 1281 (i.e., probably around the time when the *Narratio* was composed), the Lambeth Constitutions order parish priests to make public and formal pronouncements, four times a year, of sentences of excommunication on everyone in their parishes who, among other offenses, was in arrears with their payments of tithes.

169–76   *Hooly Awstyn . . . seyde unto this knyht.* In this stanza, as in the previous (lines 161–68), Lydgate amplifies the story-line to emphasize legal due process (*compleynt*

[line 170], *caas* [line171], *poynt coupable* [line 172], *lawe* [line 174], *riht* [line 174])
and the care taken by Austin to ascertain the merits of the priest's charges. The *Narratio* (lines 11–12) simply tells how, after hearing the priest's complaint, Augustine
ordered the knight brought before him: "Quod audiens sanctus Augustinus precepit
militem accersiri ante se."

192   *cheef.* Other copies such as London, BL MSS Lansdowne 699 (fol. 37v) and Harley
         4826 (fol. 48r) have the more usual spelling, *sheeff.*

198–200 *Each cursyd man . . . voyde shulde his place.* The sense of line 198, *Each cursyd
         man . . . grace*, is repeated, apparently just to fill out the stanza, at 199–200: *every
         maneer wiht . . . accursyd.*

206   *Seyntuarye.* In late ME, *seyntuarye* can be a synonym for "cemetary" (see *MED
         seyntuarye* 4a); our punctuation avoids the lack of grammatical sense in Mac-
         Cracken's unpunctuated line by assuming that *Seyntuarye* is used in apposition to
         "chircheyeerd" (line 205), and that the adverb *ther* refers forward to "afore the
         chirche style" (line 208). In one Lydgate manuscript, London, BL MS Harley 4826,
         fol. 48v (examined by Robert Upchurch), a later reader added the punctuation we
         have chosen to adopt here. Alternatively, it is possible that, unpunctuated, the dif-
         ficult phrase *Seyntuarye bood* may mean "submitted to the sanctuary," i.e, the corpse
         respected the inviolable space of the church precincts. Either way, he is clearly
         envisaged as standing outside the churchyard. The *Narratio* (line 31) also states that
         he left the *cimiterium.*

213   *To hooly Austyn made relacioun.* The implication is that Austin, absorbed in cele-
         brating Mass at the altar, has not seen what has been happening, since the corpse
         would have left the church at the other end of the building.

221   *The crucifix ther baner was in deede. Baner* is another detail Lydgate found in the
         full Latin *Narratio* (lines 35–36: *precedat nos cum aqua benedicta . . . crucis domi-
         nice vexillum*, "Let the standard of the Lord's cross,with holy water, precede us"),
         but not in Brompton (*sed Crux cum aqua benedicta nos praecedat*, ed. *AS* Maius
         6.396). The image echoes Bede's description of Austin advancing with his monks
         to meet King Ethelbert of Kent for the first time: "But they came endowed with
         divine not devilish power and bearing as their standard a silver cross (*crucem pro
         vexillo*)" (*Bede's Ecclesiastical History*, pp. 74–75). But Austin's formula of con-
         juration (line 223, "In Jesu name, that lyst for man to bleede") is Lydgate's own
         contribution, introducing Christ's personal name and a direct reference to His phys-

ical death on the Cross. This marks a turning point, a shift from emphasis on justice and law towards themes of mercy and forgiveness.

222–24   *Blissid Austyn . . . for to telle.* The infinitive verb *to telle* (line 224) is dependent on *gan compelle* (line 222). Lydgate mingles indirect and direct speech in a way that modern English no longer allows. Another instance is at lines 263–66.

230   *Geyn thy biddyng.* See Austin's command, lines 197–200.

235   *in the poorche abyde.* In the *Narratio* (line 30), the tomb from which the cadaver rises is *in ipso introitu ecclesiae* ("in the very entrance of the church"). Many medieval English parish churches have a roofed porch or vestibule outside the main door leading into the nave. The excommunicated lord's meaning here presumably is that he could not even linger in this outermost part of the building, but was compelled to cross the churchyard and stand at the outermost gate or "style" (see line 208). At Long Compton, as in many other medieval parish churches, the south porch has a medieval sculpted sarcophagus built into its side wall. See the architectural plan in Salzman, ed., *The Victoria History of the County of Warwick*, 5.56.

244   *patroun.* The term here connotes the person who controls the right to dispose of the ecclesiastical benefice attached to the church.

249–50   *This hundryd yeer . . . / And fifty ovir.* The British lord claims to have been suffering in Purgatory for 150 years, i.e., since about the year 399 according to the mistaken dating of Austin's mission as 549 (see line 126 and the accompanying explanatory note). Lydgate transfers the 150-year figure here from Austin's later conversation with the resuscitated priest, perhaps to emphasize the extent of the excommunicate's suffering.

252–53   *a dirk prisoun of desolacioun . . . / Mong firy flawmys, voyd of remissioun.* The equivalent passage in the *Narratio* (lines 54–55) has *animam ad claustra infernalia iugiter cruciandam incendiis emisi* ("I sent my soul to the infernal prison house to be tortured ceaselessly in its fires"). This is another passage linking Lydgate's poem to the full version of the legend rather than to the Brompton Chronicle. But Lydgate adds the phrase *voyd of remissioun* ("devoid of forgiveness"), doubtless an allusion to one of the climactic phrases in the "articles" of the Creed: *in remissionem peccatorum* ("for the forgiveness of sins"). See above, line 136 and the accompanying explanatory note.

264   *un*. MS Harley 2265 and MacCracken's edition have *vn*. The form *un* for the preposition *on* is sometimes found in fifteenth- and sixteenth-century manuscripts.

271   *heer he lith, cheef cause of my grevaunce.* Notice that, despite his excommunicated state, the lord was buried in the privileged interior of the church of which he was patron. The parish priest, however, was buried outside in the churchyard. This social gap between patron and incumbent is emphasized in the *Narratio*, where, by contrast with the knight's durable *mausoleum* in the church porch, the priest's humble tombstone, if he ever had one, has sunk from sight (lines 62–63): *nullum omnino sepulture alicuius indicium apparebat* ("there was absolutely no trace of anyone's grave").

275–76   The word *tretable* (line 276) is used several times in the poem to mean "tractable, amenable, willing to cooperate," but in this and some other instances cited in the *MED* it seems to refer to the clear and precise utterance of prayers and liturgical formulas. Lydgate's handling of this section of the narrative is remarkably brief, completely bypassing the sensational character of the physical revival of the dead priest. Perhaps Lydgate preferred to focus the reader's attention on the urgently needed ritual of absolution. In the *Narratio* (and the Brompton abridgement) the miracle of resuscitation and resurrection is a rhetorical set piece demonstrating the power of Austin's prayer and God's power over life and death, as the dusty remains of the priest's *pauca . . . ossa* ("few bones," lines 66–67) miraculously reconstitute themselves to the onlookers' and the narrator's amazement: *Res stupenda et humanis auribus inaudita! . . . puluerem pulueri aduniri et ossa neruis compaginari; ac sic demum humanum corpus de sepulcro animatum erigi* ("An amazing event and one that human ears have never heard before! . . . Dust combines with dust and tendons join bone to bone, until at last the human body arises [as if] alive from the grave," lines 72–75). Lydgate makes use of this authorial apostrophe later in the poem. See the note on lines 329–30, below.

294   *As the Gospel pleynly doth recoorde.* Matthew 5:7, 7:1–5 and, perhaps, Matthew 5:38–48. Lydgate's line 292, "Thynk He that bouht us is evir merciable," appears to echo the Brompton version of the Compton legend (*Nosti Frater quia misericors est deus*, ed. *AS* Maius 6.396) whereas the *Narratio* (lines 82–83) has Austin invoke a famous psalm verse (*Nosti . . . frater quod miseraciones dei nostri super omnia opera eius*; compare Vulgate Psalm 144:9 [Septuagint]). But Lydgate makes use of this verse later in an important addition to his source narrative. See below, lines 339–52.

296   *with rigour mercy may accoorde.* Lydgate may be alluding here to the eschatological debate and final concord of the "four daughters" of God (mercy and truth, justice and

peace, based on Vulgate Psalm 84:11 and frequently reflected in other works of Middle English literature, e.g., Langland's *Piers Plowman*, C-Text (ed. Pearsall) Passus 20.116 ff., and *The Mary Play* (ed. Peter Meredith), lines 1119 ff. Lydgate elaborates on the *Narratio* here to emphasize the importance of mercy and forgiveness made possible through Christ's suffering and redemption. The warning against "vengeableness" (line 295) is not reflected anywhere in his source. Lydgate offers much sterner advice about *rigour* in his *Defence of Holy Church*, lines 103–05 (ed. MacCracken, *Minor Poems of John Lydgate*, p. 34):

> And Goddys foon manly make to sterue;   *die*
> For any fals feynyd repentaunce
> Of right lat rigour holden the ballaunce.

See also Norton-Smith's edition, pp. 32–33 and his notes, pp. 150–54.

304   *Fro Purgatorye his trowblys to restreyne.* Austin implies, in alluding to Purgatory, that the original act of excommunication was not such as to condemn the offender eternally to Hell itself without possibility of remission. Purgatory is not mentioned in the *Narratio*.

306   *the same bond to unbynde.* Compare Matthew 16:18–19, Jesus' words to Peter, the rock on which "I will build my church, and the gates of hell shall not prevail against it. And I will give to thee the keys of the kingdom of heaven. And whatsoever thou shalt bind (*ligaveris*) upon earth, it shall be bound also in heaven: and whatsoever thou shalt loose (*solveris*) on earth, it shall be loosed also in heaven." On this passage was based the commonplace medieval doctrine of the priestly power to condemn and absolve souls in this life and the next.

309–14   This passage, which has no equivalent in the *Narratio*, is part of Lydgate's apparent effort to focus narrative and theme around the idea of mercy and forgiveness. Austin's list of famous saints who were also "sinners" comprises three male apostles followed by two female penitents. Peter was guilty of so many lapses of faith that it is hard to know which one, if any, is meant here, but best known is his denial of Christ on the eve of the Crucifixion (e.g., Mark 14:66–72) which culminates in his own act of tearful self-recognition. Paul's offense is, of course, his early persecution of Jesus' followers, for which he is struck blind, reproached, and forgiven by God on the road to Damascus (Acts 7:58–60, 8:1–3, 9:1–30). Thomas the Apostle is famous for doubting the resurrection of Jesus (John 20:24–29); according to his apocryphal acts, he later preached the gospel and was martyred in India. Mary of Egypt, according to her medieval *vita*, was a prostitute converted, while on a pleasure trip to Jerusalem, by a vision of the Virgin Mary; she spent the last seventeen years of her life living as a penitent solitary in the desert beyond the River Jordan (see Ward, *Harlots of the Desert*, pp. 26–56). Mary Magdalen is likewise identified in medieval tradition as a prostitute who repented and reformed after the encounter with Jesus related in John 8:1–11. She also was credited with having lived out her life as a desert solitary (see Ward, *Harlots*, pp. 1–25).

313   *Take to mercy*. Literally, "Taken to mercy," i.e., received into or embraced by God's mercy because of their great repentance. In the structure of this sentence it parallels "relesyd" (line 310). See *MED take(n)* 8c.

326   *last*. The meaning is obscure, unless Lydgate means us to assume that the British priest and his lord were of the last generation of Christians before the pagan Anglo-Saxons overran the country. The priest of Compton in Austin's time would therefore be the first to hold the office there since the dead priest himself, 150 years before.

328   *him*. The pronoun is redundant, repeating the object already provided by "tothir corps" (line 327).

329–30   Here Lydgate splices together two phrases from different parts of the *Narratio* (lines 72–73, 88–89): *Res stupenda et humanis auris inaudita* ("an amazing event, by human ears unheard"), which occurs in response to the resuscitation of the dead priest; and *[mortuus] mortuum . . . relaxauit* ("the dead absolved the dead"), which occurs at the present point in the narrative. Lydgate has shifted the emphasis from the miraculous resuscitation to the idea and act of mercy.

337–39   Line 339 itself is a translation of Psalm 144:9 in the Vulgate: *miserationes eius super omnia opera eius* ("his tender mercies are over all his works"), which is quoted in the *Narratio* (lines 82–83) by Austin himself to persuade the dead priest to have mercy on the dead knight's soul. On the Psalm verse as evidence that Lydgate, in his treatment of mercy and justice in the legend of the emperor Trajan (see next note), is alluding here to Langland's *Piers Plowman*, see Whatley, "John Lydgate's *Saint Austin*," pp. 211–14.

343–47   Trajan, the Roman emperor who reigned 98–117, was widely believed in the Middle Ages to have been rescued from damnation (as a pagan) by the prayers and merits of Pope Gregory, who was moved by stories of the emperor's justice as a ruler. In the later Middle Ages some theologians believed that in order for Gregory to "save" Trajan, he must have prayed to resuscitate him and then baptized him. The situation is analogous to that in *Saint Austin at Compton*, where posthumous redemption is made possible by the performance of a sacrament (penance) after the resuscitation of a corpse.

359   *deveer.* From AN *dever* (Modern French *devoir*). Lydgate probably stresses the first syllable here (compare *endeavor*). The word could mean "duty" or "utmost," "what one can." See also line 408.

356–60   Austin is offering the priest the chance to return to the world to help him preach the gospel to the English (as in the *Narratio* [lines 97–99]: *quatinus . . . animas diabolica fraude deceptas ewangelii uerba seminando ad suum creatorem reducas?* ("Do you wish me to pray to the Lord on your behalf that you might come back to us and plant the word of the gospel in order to rescue souls that have been snared by the devil's fraud?"). But Lydgate's rendering is more than usually tortuous.

369   *rest in pees.* Compare the well-known Christian prayer for the dead, *requiescat in pace* ("may he/she rest in peace"), often abbreviated to R. I. P.

373–74   *Feith, hoope, and charité, with hool affeccioun, / Been pilwes foure to reste upon by grace.* We have found no direct medieval source for this delightful image of the four pillows of the contemplative life, which is perhaps intended to balance the four gospels preached by Austin the bishop, embodying the active life. Another of Lydgate's many additions to the narrative, the image appears to conflate the commonplace Christian image of death as a peaceful sleep with the more esoteric association between sleep and mystical contemplation of the divine. See Whatley, "John Lydgate's *Saint Austin,*" pp. 219–20.

375   *Day of the general resurreccioun.* Medieval Christians believed that at the Last Judgment, the end of historical time, all the dead bodies will rise again, to be reunited with their souls for eternity. See the recent study by Bynum, *The Resurrection of the Body*.

377–92   In these two stanzas Lydgate greatly expands on the *Narratio*, in which Austin simply bids the dead priest rest in peace and pray for Holy Church (lines 111–13): *Vade, karissime frater, et per longa annorum tempora quiesce in pace, simulque ora pro me et pro uniuersa dei ecclesia sancta* ("Farewell, dearest brother, and rest in peace the long space of years, and also pray for me and for all the holy church of God"). MacCracken's editing is problematic here. Even though the first stanza clearly echoes some of the language of Augustine's farewell to the priest, Mac-

Cracken omits direct speech marks around the two stanzas, implying that they constitute Lydgate's own authorial address to the priest as a fellow contemplative. Appealing as this idea is, and while it is true that Lydgate is usually careful to identify speakers in this poem, with a judiciously placed "quod he" or other such device, there is clear precedent elsewhere in the poem for the situation here, where two passages of direct speech, from different characters, are juxtaposed without identifying markers. See the beginning of the dialogue between Austin and the corpse of the British lord, lines 223–25 ff.

383 The image of the *ballaunce* here could simply be that of the scales of justice tipping in favor of the righteous (i.e., orthodox) believers by excluding heretics from the church (compare Lydgate's use of the same image in his *Defence of Holy Church*, line 105, quoted in our explanatory note to line 296, above), but the idea of proper balance is also appropriate to the ship metaphor that follows here.

387–88 *darnel . . . cokkyl.* These terms for weeds that invade arable crops, alluding to Jesus' parable of the wheat and the tares (Matthew 13:24–30), refer figuratively to the Lollard heresy. Compare the canceled Epilogue to Chaucer's Man of Law's Tale (*CT* II[B]1182–83). See also Whatley, "John Lydgate's *Saint Austin*," p. 221 and note 70.

401 On the medieval literary topos of the *Lenvoy* (lit., "the sending forth"), whether identified as such, as here and in Chaucer's *balade*, "Fortune," lines 73–79, or untitled (as in Chaucer's *TC* 5.1786–99); see the references provided in the note on *TC* 5.1786 in *The Riverside Chaucer*. Lydgate's appeal for readers to "correct" his work, owing to his own declining powers, is one variation on the so-called affected modesty topos, common in the prefaces and epilogues of medieval writers. Chaucer himself asks John Gower and the enigmatic "philosophical Strode" to correct his *TC* (5.1856–58).

VI

Textual Notes to Saint Austin at Compton *(c. 1420–40), by John Lydgate*

Abbreviations: **H** = British Library, MS Harley 2255, fols. 24r–32v [base text]; **M** = *Minor Poems of John Lydgate*, ed. MacCracken, pp. 193–206.

19	*oure.* So H. M: *our.* Here and in numerous instances below, not recorded in these notes, we have supplied final *-e* after "r" where the scribe uses an "re" abbreviation overlooked by M.
20	*whos.* So H. M: *whose.*
30	*cold.* So H. M: *cold[e].*
65	*dewté.* So H. M: *dew[e]te.*
83	*hond.* So H. M: *hand.*
92	*Ecliptik.* So H. M: *Ecliptic.*
94	*briht.* So H. M: *briht[e].*
96	*lond.* So H. M: *land.*
113	*pope.* So M. H: *pape.* Here, and elsewhere in the text, the word *pope* was erased by a later reader.
177	*froward.* So H. M: *[so] froward.*
205	*greet.* So H. M: *great.*
215	*consolacioun.* So H. M: *consolatioun.*
221	*ther.* So H. M: *their.*
227	*dewtees.* So H. M: *dew[e]tees.*
280	*boody.* So H. M: *body.*
281	*rewith.* So H. M: *rewithe.*
296	*accoorde.* So H. M: *accorde.*
297	*Jhesus.* H: *iheus*; M: *Iesus.*
313	*Take.* So M. H: *took.*
326	*last.* So H. M: *last[e].*
337	*Circumstauncis.* So H. M: *Circumstaunces.*
359	*affeccioun.* So H. M: *affectioun.*
367	*suffrith.* So H. M: *suffrithe.*
373	*affeccioun.* So H. M: *affecioun.*
375	*resurreccioun.* So H. M: *resurrectioun.*

390   *precious*. M: *p[r]ecious; H: pecious*.
396   *dewté*. So H. M: *dew[e]te*.
397   *doun*. So H. M: *doon*.

VII

The Life of St. Francis
in the South English Legendary *(c. 1270–80)*

Introduction

St. Francis (feast day October 4) and the Order of Friars Minor

Francis of Assisi is one of two saints in this volume — the other is Benedict — who were founders of religious orders. Benedict's rule and Benedictine monasticism in one form or another (e.g., that of the Cistercians) dominated the religious culture of the Middle Ages through the twelfth century but began to decline with the rise of the cathedral schools and universities. The Benedictines' preeminent position among the orders was taken over in the thirteenth and fourteenth centuries by the new orders known as friars (from ME and OF *frere*, "brother"), especially the Franciscans and Dominicans.[1]

The Franciscans are named for St. Francis, who was born c. 1182, the son of Pietro Bernardone, a prosperous cloth merchant of Assisi, in Umbria, Italy. In his youth Francis was something of a free-spending playboy and a leader of the city's revelers (he was apparently indulged in this by his parents); he also had knightly ambitions and endured a year as a prisoner of war after a battle between Assisi and the neighboring city-state of Perugia (1202). But according to several thirteenth-century biographers, Francis' extravagance and penchant for role-playing also expressed itself in charitable gestures towards the poor and other social outcasts. In his mid-twenties, after a long illness apparently brought on by his stint in the Perugian prison, he became more introspective, began experiencing religious visions, and in 1204 turned back abruptly from a military expedition to Apulia, where he had hoped to be knighted in the papal forces. Thereafter he became progressively alienated from his former lifestyle and from the moneyed world of his father's cloth business, as he actively if uncertainly sought ways to dedicate himself to a religious life. Finally, the elder Bernardone, after quarreling with his son over some cloth he had appropriated for rebuilding the dilapidated church of St. Damian, lost patience and the two formally repudiated their relationship in the local bishop's court (January or February, 1206), where Francis renounced all his legal claims on the family fortune, dramatically stripped off his expensive clothes and handed them to his father.

---

[1] The standard historical overview of the English religious orders from the tenth century to the end of the Middle Ages is still Knowles, *The Monastic Order in England* and *The Religious Orders in England.*

From then on, at first alone, then with a small band of followers (comprising mainly laymen from in and around Assisi), the formerly popular and fashionable young cloth merchant came to adopt a life modeled (selectively) on that of Jesus and the apostles in the Gospels, devoted to poverty and asceticism, the preaching of repentance, and compassion for the poor and sick (especially, in Francis' case, the lepers). For himself and his followers, Francis coined the name *fratres minori* (the inferior brothers), as a token of their great dedication to the virtues of humility and simplicity, and their utter lack of ambition for the dignities of rank in society or the church. Foreswearing any earthly possessions other than a rough habit and a pair of trousers, with a rope for a belt, and going barefoot even in the depths of winter, they lived in considerable hardship in makeshift shelters at the church of St. Mary of the Angels, at Portiuncula just outside Assisi. They frequently traveled great distances on foot on preaching tours and to work in hospitals. In 1209 Francis wrote a rule for his fledgling order, based closely on Jesus' instructions to His apostles in the Gospels, and succeeded in having it orally approved by Pope Innocent III in 1210 (or 1209). Twenty years later, Francis died at the age of forty-five (4 October 1226), virtually blind, wracked with the pain of the stigmata (Christ-like wounds he had received after a mystic vision on September 14, 1224), emaciated and exhausted by illness, self-privation, the strain of his responsibilities, and continual travel in Italy and abroad (including Spain and Syria). But his small band had already grown into the international Order of Friars Minor, with thousands of members living and working in virtually every country in Europe, drawn from all walks of life but increasingly (and especially north of the Alps) from the ranks of the educated clergy and university faculty. In addition to the Order of Friars Minor, the larger Franciscan movement had also produced an order of nuns, the Poor Sisters of St. Clare (the Second Order), and an order of lay people, the Order of Penitence, or Third Order (the "Tertiaries"). Less than two years after his death Francis was canonized as a saint by Pope Gregory IX, formerly Cardinal Ugolino, Francis' friend and papal "Protector" of the order for several years. Under the energetic supervision of Friar Elias, Minister General of the order, Francis' tomb became the centerpiece of the great new basilica of San Francesco in Assisi, completed by May, 1230.

St. Francis in Historical Context

The Franciscan phenomenon is presented by the hagiographers of Francis' cult (and by some modern biographers) as a unique and providential event, by which God chose an ordinary layman as the vessel of a new outpouring of the Holy Spirit. But in the context of late-twelfth- and early-thirteenth-century ecclesiastical history, Francis' experience can also be seen as the culmination of a well-marked trend.[2] Beginning in the eleventh century, but more frequently in the twelfth, barefoot, unkempt, charismatic itinerant preachers, professing to follow in the footsteps of Christ's apostles, were a recurring feature of the European scene and became a major problem for the church hierarchy by the end of the twelfth century. What all had in common was a dissatisfaction with the opportunities for spiritual life and expression available within existing ecclesiastical and social structures; they also shared a tendency to be critical of the wealth and worldliness of the church, and to deviate in certain ways from orthodox church doctrine. But whereas early itinerants (such as Robert of Arbrissel and Norbert of Xanten) ended up channeling their energies, and shepherding their male and female followers, into new monastic foundations, later representatives remained in the outside world where they often became troublesome to the church hierarchy.

The most notorious were the Catharist heretics of southern France and northern Italy, along with other groups who formed around Peter of Bruis, Henry of Lausanne, Arnold of Brescia, and Waldo of Lyon. Waldo, a rich, married merchant, was moved one day by hearing a street entertainer sing the story of St. Alexis to abandon his secular life; he became a lay preacher, relying on two priest companions for French translations of the Scriptures. Waldo spent much of his life thereafter trying to convince the church hierarchy that he was not a heretic, like the others. Against these last a violent persecution was eventually launched in the form of the infamous Albigensian crusade in which northern knights accompanied monks and other clergy charged with reconverting or purging the recalcitrant heretics. In the midst of this process emerged the figures of two Spanish clerics, Bishop Diego of Osma and his friend, Dominic of Caleruago, a learned and zealous Augustinian canon. They suggested that the heretics needed to be swayed not just by coercion but also by the preaching of orthodox clergy who evinced the same apostolic poverty, simplicity, and zeal that many of the heretics themselves favored. In November of 1206, the same year that Francis broke with his father and adopted a life of poverty and service of the poor, Pope Innocent III sent his Cistercian emissaries on a new mission to the Cathars with instructions to adopt the evangelical approach suggested by Diego and Dominic. The latter, of course, would shortly found the Order of Friars Preachers, the Dominicans.[3]

A few years previously, in 1201, the pope had formally approved the reconciliation and reorganization, into three orders, of a group of religious zealots from northern Italy, the Humiliati, who had been condemned as heretics along with many others by Pope Lucius III in 1184.

---

[2] For an excellent survey, see Brooke, *The Coming of the Friars*, pp. 3–88. For another attempt at contextualization, placing the Franciscans and the Dominicans in relation to the Augustinian Canons and the Cistercians, see Southern, *Western Society and the Church in the Middle Ages*, pp. 240–99.

[3] On Dominic's career and the relation of his order to that of Francis, see Brooke, *Coming of the Friars*, pp. 89–113.

The three orders comprised, respectively, canons serving their own churches, lay people living in separate male and female communities, and married lay people leading normal working lives at home but meeting together on Sundays to hear sermons delivered by members of their congregations. In return for being allowed to pursue their way of life unmolested, the Humiliati observed strict orthodoxy in doctrine and supported the established clergy in combating heresy in their districts. Thus Francis' three orders, and especially the Tertiaries, were anticipated by the Humiliati.[4] In 1208 Innocent III formally approved the reconstitution of another group of suspected heretics, the Poor Catholics, comprising disaffected clerics from Languedoc, when their leader, Durand of Huesca, swore loyalty to the pope and fidelity to orthodox doctrine. In 1210, yet another such group, mainly laymen called the Poor Men of Lyon, under Bernard of Prim, likewise received the pope's approval in return for various loyalty oaths.[5]

Thus the period in which Francis grew up was one of great spiritual ferment, in which the church hierarchy was struggling to find ways to combat a rising tide of heterodox opposition and religious diversity, in which evangelical poverty and the preaching of repentance were leading themes. Francis was only one of a succession of grassroots religious leaders who headed to Rome for papal approval early in the new century. Although the pope and local bishops at times resorted to violence to suppress these proliferating dissident groups, they also saw the value of harnessing the spiritual energy of zealots like Francis who were amenable to being drawn, with their followers, into the structure of the church while retaining the apostolic identity that was evidently so appealing to the general populace. The Franciscans would become one of the papacy's most important and effective tools for implementing the new standards of pastoral care and parish life that were enunciated in the decrees of the Fourth Lateran Council of 1215, and the order's development fell increasingly under the influence of the church hierarchy.

Francis wrote the original rule of his order himself, but the most important revision, the so-called Second Rule of 1223, was a joint composition of Francis and Cardinal Ugolino.[6] In the end, not many years after Francis' death, the order founded by this indifferently educated layman, whose early followers and co-leaders were likewise mainly layfolk, became completely dominated by sophisticated and learned clerics. After 1242, laymen were barred from holding office in the order, and very few were recruited henceforth. At the same time, a succession of adjustments to the rule gradually modified Francis' original ideal that the friars should live in

---

[4] Moorman, *A History of the Franciscan Order*, pp. 41–42.

[5] For a contemporary chronicler's account of the Humiliati and Poor Men as precursors of the Franciscans and Dominicans, see Brooke, *Coming of the Friars*, pp. 201–02.

[6] This is the *Regula Bullata*, approved by Pope Honorius III, who insisted that Francis delete a clause permitting friars to observe the rule literally even if their superiors ordered them to interpret it more loosely for practical reasons (Moorman, *History*, p. 57). In 1230, after Ugolino became pope, he himself issued a further commentary on the rule, making its requirements even less stringent.

abject poverty, physical deprivation, and utter dependence on the charity of the people to whom they strove to bring the Gospel message.

Such changes led to friction within the order between those (the majority) who favored modification of the rule and more flexible interpretations of its strictures (later known as *glossing*),[7] and a minority who clung to what they took to be Francis' original ideals. Eventually, this split would widen and by the end of the thirteenth century the "Spirituals," as the radical conservative wing became known, were more and more subject to persecution and charges of heresy, as the complex problem of clerical poverty and church possessions became one of the most volatile and crucial of the age.[8] But the ideological fissures in the order were already visible during Francis' own lifetime and the decades following his death.[9]

The Middle English Life of Francis discussed and edited below dwells repeatedly on the founding of the Franciscans, on the rule and matters of its observance, and on the physical deprivation and verbal abuse willingly suffered by Francis and his followers. Overall the account seems to display some sympathy with stricter interpretations of the Franciscan way of life, while at the same time endorsing the presence of learned men in the order. This does not necessarily imply Franciscan authorship, but it may well reflect the poet's respect for the zeal, austerity, and learned character of the Franciscans in England in the thirteenth century.[10]

St. Francis in *SEL*

The St. Francis legend seems to belong to the earliest layer of *SEL*, the work of the Z-poet, as represented in the Bodleian manuscript, Laud Miscellany 108 (late thirteenth century). Our working text, however, is taken not from this earliest version but, as in some other chapters of this volume, from the somewhat revised version in another Bodleian manuscript, Ashmole 43, of the early fourteenth century, the language of which is somewhat more "modern" and the text expanded by the addition of several short authorial comments totaling about two dozen lines.[11]

---

[7] Compare the Friar in Chaucer's Summoner's Tale: "Glosynge is glorious thyng, certeyn" (*CT* III [D]1793).

[8] On religious poverty as it affected the medieval monastic and mendicant orders, see Lester K. Little, *Religious Poverty*.

[9] Still the best English account of all this is Moorman's *History*, pp. 53–204.

[10] See Moorman, *History*, pp. 171–74.

[11] These include: lines 23–24 (ironic humor); 41–44 (exegesis); 57–60 (homiletic aside on lepers); 67–72 (exegesis and endorsement of Franciscan order); 189–90 (endorsement of the order); 299–302 (satire on proud "pigasours"); and 317–18 (sarcasm about merchants' lack of fear of the Devil).

For further information on the Ashmole manuscript and its language, see the Introduction to I(a), the Martyrdom of St. Andrew, above.

As explained earlier, in the General Introduction, Jacobus de Voragine's *LA* seems to have become available to the *SEL*-poet after he had completed work on the saints in the first half of the church calendar. Although Francis is an October saint, however, the *SEL* Life of St. Francis was translated not from *LA* but from the *Legenda major*, the full and official Franciscan life of Francis (*BHL* 3017), written by Friar Giovanni Fidanza, better known as St. Bonaventura (henceforth Bonaventure), who at the time was Minister General of the Franciscans.[12] Finished in 1263, in Paris, and distributed to the thirty-four provinces of the order, Bonaventure's *Legenda major* was designated in 1266 as the only authoritative Life of Francis, superseding the two *Vitae* upon which most of it is based, the First and Second Lives by Thomas of Celano, written during the twenty years following Francis' death in 1226.[13] Hundreds of copies of the *Legenda major* were produced for distribution to Franciscan houses during the thirteenth century, and even today there remain over four hundred extant.[14] Modern translations of this and the other lives of Francis, along with a great deal of additional Franciscan literature, including the works attributed to Francis himself, are conveniently collected in the *Omnibus of Sources* edited by Marion Habig, to which frequent reference is made below. The latest critical edition of the Latin text of *Legenda major* is that of Michael Bihl.[15]

Bonaventure organized his *Legenda major* into two parts, the first dealing with the saint's life, the second with his posthumous miracles, which the Middle English poet omitted completely and is therefore not discussed here. Part One is divided into fifteen chapters (I–XV) which Bonaventure explains in his prologue are arranged according to themes, such as poverty, asceticism, humility, mystical devotion to the body of Christ, etc.,[16] but chronology and strictly historical concerns, in typical hagiographic fashion, remain vague throughout the work. Each chapter is further subdivided into sections (with arabic numerals) of varying length and containing one or more episodes. Habig has conveniently provided a comprehensive table (pp. 1638–48) listing the individual episodes as they occur in the successive chapters of the *Legenda*

---

[12] As first pointed out by Carl Horstmann, *ESEL* p. 53n1. See also Manfred Görlach, *Textual Tradition*, p. 195. In our view, the *SEL*-poet may also have been influenced in places by Thomas of Celano's two earlier lives of Francis: see below, the explanatory notes to our edition, lines 273–86 (on "Brother Fly"), and 371–90 (Francis preaching to the birds).

[13] For a critical overview of the early biographical literature on Francis, see Moorman, *History*, pp. 278–94. See also Fleming, *An Introduction to the Franciscan Literature of the Middle Ages*, pp. 32–72.

[14] Marion A. Habig, *St. Francis of Assisi*, p. 626.

[15] Bonaventure, *Legenda Maior*.

[16] Bonaventure identifies the chapter themes in the last section of his Prologue (see Habig, *St. Francis of Assisi*, p. 634).

major and identifying the corresponding sections in Bonaventure's main sources, the lives by Thomas of Celano.

Because the *SEL* Life of St. Francis allows us an unusual opportunity to compare the poet's work with that of his Latin source, we have followed Habig's example and provided in the Table below (pp. 264–65) a detailed breakdown of the sequence of episodes in the *SEL* poem, showing the corresponding source passages in the *Legenda major*, indicated by chapter (Roman numeral) and section (Arabic numeral) as these appear in Habig's translation.

It will be seen that the *SEL*-poet has selected a substantial amount of material from Bonaventure's initial and final chapters and follows them quite closely in places, but he omits a great deal, especially from the middle sections of the *Legenda major*. From chapters I–III, comprising about sixty episodes in Habig's edition, almost thirty episodes reappear in the *SEL* Life of St. Francis. This portion of the Middle English Life, verses 1–228, covers the events of Francis' early life, leading to his conversion and rupture with his father, his time spent repairing churches, then his founding of the order, recruitment of followers, and experiences in Rome securing confirmation of the order and the first rule. The *SEL*-poet seems particularly interested in the order itself, mentioning it in places where Bonaventure does not, and elaborating on it elsewhere. For example, he renders closely the episode from *Legenda major* III.3 in which Francis and his first disciple, Bernard, open a Gospel book at random three times to find passages dictating the basic rules of their new order, after which Francis says to Bernard:

> This is our life and our rule (*vita et regula*) . . . and everyone who comes to join our company (*societati conjungi*) must be prepared to do this. And so, if you have a mind to be perfect, go home and do as you have heard.[17]

This simple sentence is expanded to eight verses in the Middle English version (lines 183–90):

"Thou sucst," quath Seyn Franceis, "her, hou our Lord in a stounde	*see; moment*
Send ous grace up wuch thinge we schulle this ordre founde.[18]	
Up this thre Godspelles, thou sucst, that we habbeth thar verst ifounde,	*Upon these; there first*
We schulle founde oure ordre and up an stronge grounde."	*upon a*
Up this thre Godspell he made his ordre and his reule vorsoth,	
And Frere Menour breketh his ordre that out theragen doth.	*aught (anything); against it*
Noble an ordre it aghte be that so noblich ifounde was,	*a noble order*
Verst thoru toknynge of Jhesu Crist and seththe thoru such cas.	

---

[17] Habig, *St. Francis of Assisi*, p. 648.

[18] *Sends us [the] grace [to know] on what sort of conditions we must found this order*

The *SEL* Life of St. Francis also makes liberal use of chapters XIII–XIV, which focus on Francis' ecstatic vision of the fiery seraph on Monte Alverna, his reception of the stigmata, then his final suffering and death (lines 391–496). From chapters IV–XII, however, comprising some 191 *Legenda major* episodes (almost 60% of the whole work), the *SEL* version uses only seventeen episodes, occupying lines 229–390, of which about thirty lines describe the brothers' missionary life after their return from Rome. The rest recount Francis' colorful contempt for his body (Brother Ass) and for idleness (Brother Fly), and his humble preference for being insulted rather than praised. From the chapter on poverty (VII) only one story appears in the Middle English (of the snake found in a bag of money: lines 303–18), while from chapter VIII, on Francis' piety, the poet recounts only the episodes involving Francis' sympathetic involvement with lambs, sheep, and birds (lines 319–70), to which is added (lines 371–90) an episode, recounted much later by Bonaventure (ch. XII), in which Francis preaches to the birds.

Thus the contents of four whole chapters (IX, X, XI, and most of XII) of the *Legenda major* are almost completely omitted from the *SEL* version. Yet it is in these central sections that Bonaventure most clearly depicts Franciscan spirituality, and the sanctity of Francis himself, in the lush, quasi-erotic vocabulary of affective mysticism (e.g., "the passionate love with which Francis burned for Christ, his Spouse").[19] Omitted also from the Middle English is any mention of the saint's special devotions, his early struggles to tame his sexual urges, his desire for martyrdom and his missionary journey to Egypt, his love of solitude and ecstatic experiences of God's presence, his spirit of prophecy, and his preaching and healing powers. The Monte Alverna vision, with the resulting stigmata, is presented in *Legenda major* as the climax of a long process of spiritual preparation (chs. VIII–XII), ascending steadily from love of God's creatures (inanimate, animal, and human) to love of the Creator. But in the *SEL* Life of St. Francis the saint's climactic vision of the crucified seraph follows directly after his series of droll encounters with the animal world.

Francis' love for animals, recounted several times in *Legenda major*, is interpreted by Bonaventure as reflecting the saint's sense of identity with all beings and things created by God (*Legenda major* VIII.6): hence the well-known language of his *Canticle of Brother Sun* in which sun, moon, stars, wind, air, fire, water, earth, and even death itself, are named as his brothers and sisters. Moreover his uncanny ability to communicate with animals and birds and their obedience to him are explained in terms of the dominion over creatures enjoyed by mankind before the fall, after which the beasts, in Bonaventure's words, "had rebelled against fallen mankind" (*homini iam lapso rebellem*).[20] Through his virtue of compassion or *pietas*, "which subjects all creation to itself," Francis moves, in effect, in an Edenic world,[21] like some unfallen

---

[19] Habig, *St. Francis of Assisi*, p. 698

[20] *Legenda major* VIII.11; Habig, *St. Francis of Assisi*, pp. 697–98.

[21] See also *Legenda major* VIII.1; Habig, *St. Francis of Assisi*, p. 688.

Adam. It has also been suggested that the hagiographer's images of Francis "at peace with all creation" were intended to inculcate in the order's members attitudes of reconciliation and peaceful coexistence, and to allay the factional antagonism disrupting the unity of the Franciscan order.[22]

The *SEL*-poet, however, appears to bypass such concerns, preserving only Bonaventure's explanation as to why Francis was especially fond of lambs: because Christ compared himself to a lamb (in the words of John the Baptist), and because they are "withthoute felonye and mylde as Jhesu Crist" (line 322). Of the eleven animal episodes in *Legenda major* VIII, *SEL* preserves three, concerning the saint's vengeance for a slaughtered lamb, another lamb fond of attending church services, and a flock of noisy birds that interferes with Francis' own liturgical devotions. This is followed immediately in *SEL* with a much later episode, mentioned above, drawn from *Legenda major* XII: Francis preaching to a flock of birds. It is also noteworthy that in addition to these four animal anecdotes (lines 319–90), the Middle English poet has chosen others preceding them (lines 261–86, 303–18) that also involve animals metaphorically, as images for, respectively, the human body (Brother Ass), idleness (Brother Fly), and the devil (serpent in a coin purse). In addition, of the three miracles Bonaventure recounts following the stigmata episode, the only one rendered in the *SEL* Life of St. Francis again concerns animals: the healing of sick cattle with the water from Francis' laundry (lines 439–50). Even the vision of the fiery seraph following the saint's sermon to the birds is linked to the latter by the imagery of wings, of which the seraph has no less than six, duly emphasized by the poet (lines 399–401). Finally, in almost the closing lines of the poem, we are given the story of the flock of swallows that settle on the church roof the night of Francis' death (lines 475–82). The poet's choice of these animal episodes in preference to more exalted stories may be partly a reflection of popular devotion, for, along with the vision of the seraph on Alverna, the episode of Francis preaching to the birds seems to have been a favorite with artists and their patrons, and indeed the poet alludes to the popularity of the stigmata scene in English church murals: "As me such ofte in chirch ipeynt" ("As is often seen painted in church," line 402).[23]

The *SEL*-poet's highly selective treatment of *Legenda major* as a whole is echoed in many of his greatly abbreviated renderings of individual episodes. For example, in the Stigmata epi-

---

[22] Lucille Guilbert, "L'animal dans *Légende dorée*," p. 87 and n. 40 for further references. On the various and changing roles of animals in saints' lives, see, in addition to Guilbert, Sorrell, *St. Francis of Assisi and Nature*, pp. 9–38 and (on Francis' sermon to the birds) 55–68.

[23] Of the four surviving medieval English mural paintings that depict scenes from Francis' life, two depict the stigmata, two the sermon to the birds. Similar preferences are exhibited in surviving English manuscript illuminations. See A. G. Little, ed., *Franciscan History*, chapter 1, plates 1–4 (murals), and chapter 4, plates 8–12 (illuminations), including drawings of each episode by Matthew Paris himself. See also Little's comments, pp. 42–43.

sode (lines 391–424) he eliminates almost entirely the language of fiery love with which Bonaventure evokes the saint's longing for union with Christ through martyrdom, which culminated in his mystical experience on La Verna: e.g., his "unquenchable fire of love for Jesus . . . blazing light of flame. . . . The fervor of his seraphic longing raised Francis up to God and, in an ecstasy of compassion, made him like Christ who allowed himself to be crucified in the excess of his love."[24] *SEL*, on the other hand, attributes the vision to Francis' habit of "deep" and "steadfast . . . thought" (lines 392–93, 397)[25] on the wounds of Christ. Thus the poet reduces the saint's passionate and ecstatic love for Jesus to the level of a popular late medieval devotional practice familiar to his lay audience.[26] But even in this context, his avoidance of any mention of Francis' "love" for Christ is striking, since at the time and later it was a common motif in vernacular meditations on the crucified and wounded Savior. Examples are plentiful among surviving Middle English lyric collections in which Jesus is addressed as "sweet lover" ("lefman, suete") and in other terms borrowed from secular love lyrics, as, e.g., "fayr and fre, / sweetest of alle þynge and ihesu mi suete."[27]

Yet the poet is not always so blandly reductive. As we have pointed out earlier, the *SEL* Life of St. Francis deals quite elaborately with some episodes emphasizing the founding of the Franciscan order, and while it omits entirely Francis' conquest of his sexual urges and his diatribes against women, it dwells on the way he would subject his body, as if it were a pack ass, to harsh extremes of toil and travel (lines 261–72). Another such example is in the episode of the Bending Tree (lines 194–210), where the Middle English version enhances Francis' courage and determination in undertaking the journey to Rome and the saint's own will power is a greater factor than in *Legenda major* (III.8) where it is God's favor and grace, rather than his own willpower, that smooth his path.

For further commentary on the *SEL*-poet's treatment of his source, see the explanatory notes to our text.

Indexed in

IMEV 2899.

---

[24] *Legenda major* XIII.2–3; Habig, *St. Francis of Assisi*, p. 730.

[25] Compare *The Harley Lyrics*, ed. Brook, pp. 57–59, lyric no. 21 (*Iesu, for þi muchele miht*) throughout which the word *think* is used apparently to mean "meditate."

[26] See our explanatory note on the text, line 422.

[27] See Brown, ed., *English Lyrics of the XIIIth Century*, pp. 120–21, lines 12 and 41; p. 123, line 46.

Manuscripts

Oxford, Bodleian Library MS Ashmole 43 (*SC* 6924), fols. 142v–149r.

Oxford, Bodleian Library MS Laud Misc. 108 (*SC* 1486), fols. 41v–46v.

Previous edition

The Early South-English Legendary. Ed. Horstmann. Pp. 53–67. [Based on Laud Misc. 108.; here abbr. *ESEL*]

Table of Correspondences between *SEL* Life of St. Francis and Bonaventure's *Legenda Major*

SEL Life of St. Francis episode	*SEL* Lines	*Legenda Major*
Francis, though a merchant, never refuses requests for alms.	1–6	I.1.
Gives his cloak to a poor knight.	7–11	I.2.
His vision of arms; resolves to become a knight; his journey to Apulia; voice bids him return home.	12–37	I.3.
Beginning of his conversion.	38–40	I.4.
(*poet's addition*)	41–44	
He embraces a leper.	45–50	I.5.
His service of lepers.	51–56	I.6.
(*poet's addition*)	57–60	
Crucifix at church of S. Damian urges him to rebuild the church.	61–67	II.1.
(*poet's addition*)	68–72	
F. sells cloth to raise money for S. Damian.	73–80	II.1.
Hides from his father in ditch; returns to Assisi; imprisoned by his father at home.	81–98	II.2.
Freed by his mother, he returns to the ditch, but is confronted by his father again.	99–108	II.3.
Cited by his father before bishop's court, F. disrobes himself and renounces his father.	109–28	II.4.
F. becomes a beggar at Assisi, and helps rebuild churches of S. Damian and S. Peter.	129–46	II.7.
Begins living in church of S. Mary ("in Desert," i.e. Portiuncula).	147–52	II.8.
Hears gospel of feast of Matthias regarding apostolic life.	153–68	III.1.
Brother Bernard joins F.; the beginnings of the rule.	169–86	III.3.
(*poet's addition*)	187–90	
Brother Giles joins (and three others).	191–93	III.4.
F. resolves to go to Rome to have his order approved; vision of the tree that he bends to the ground.	194–210	III.8.
The order approved by Pope Innocent III (with intercession of Cardinal John of St. Paul; pope's vision).	211–28	III.9.
The hungry brothers fed by a mysterious man (near Spoleto).	229–42	IV.1.
In Assisi, the brothers suffer from lack of food and books.	243–50	IV.3.
They resume residence at "S. Mary in Desert" (Portiuncula); F's preaching, the brothers' love of adversity.	251–60	IV.5.

F. hates idleness; Brother Ass (his own body); Brother Fly, the idler [*expanded by the poet*].	261–86	V.6.
His love of being insulted and of publicly confessing his faults. (*poet's addition*)	287–98 299–302	VI.1–2.
Roadside purse found to contain a snake.	303–18	VII.5.
F's compassion for lambs; curses a sow that killed a lamb.	319–36	VIII.6.
His pet lamb that liked to hear the friars' chanting and knelt during Mass.	337–48	VIII.7.
(*poet's addition*)	349–50	
F. quiets the birds until he finishes reciting his hours.	351–70	VIII.9.
He preaches to a flock of birds.	371–90	XII.3.
The vision of the seraph at La Verna; receives the Stigmata, which he conceals from others.	391–438	XIII.3., XIII.5.
Cure of cattle plague through F's bathwater.	439–50	XIII.6.
Length of his life in the order [*poet changes narrative order*].	451–52	XIV.3.
His suffering; flings himself on bare ground to sharpen the pain and thank God.	453–58	XIV.2.
Has himself brought to S. Mary's church to die (naked on the ground).	459–65	XIV.3.
F. dies after preaching to his brethren and reciting the psalm *Voce mea*.	466–70	XIV.5.
Date and day of his death and burial [*poet changes narrative order here and below*].	471–74	XV.6.
Flock of larks on the night of his death.	475–82	XIV.6. (¶ 4)
Brother Austin's vision and death.	483–95	XIV.6. (¶ 2)
(*poet's closing prayer*)	496	

VII

The Life of St. Francis
in the South English Legendary *(c. 1270–80),*
from Oxford, Bodleian Library MS Ashmole 43, fols. 142v–149r

Seyn Frances, the Frere Menour,   good mon was inough;
In his yonghede marchaunt he was   and to trewenesse drough:[1]
His marchaundise he made al day   in the cité of Assise,   *transacted every day*
Ac in allmesdede and in povere men   he spende his marchaundise.
5 Vor no love of catel,   iwis, he nolde bileve,
Wen eny povere mon him bede good,   bote he him somwat geve.[2]
As he com a day by the wei   he mette bi cas   *one day on the road; by chance*
A knyght that hadde riche ibé,   and apovered was   *been; impoverished*
and wel uvele iclothed ek,   and bcd him som good.   *evilly/wretchedly clothed*
10 Seyn Frances hadde reuthe of him   and a wule astod.   *stopped for a while*
He strupte of his clothes of his rug   and gaf this povere knyght.   *off his back*
Therafter as he lay aslepe   in his bedde anyght,
Him thoghte that a paleis   swythe noble he sei.   *It seemed to him; very*
He escte was that paleis were   that so noble was and hei.   *asked whose*
15 Me sede that it was his   and his knyghtes also.   *Someone said*
Tho this holi mon awok   somwat he thoghte do:
Him thoghte he sei ek in the paleis   knyghtes armes there,   *knights' suits of armor*
And myd a vair crois thoru out   isigned alle were.[3]
Thoghte he, "Our Lord it wole   that ich knyght be,   *wills it (wishes)*
20 And wel feble icham therto   bote ich me bet bisé."[4]
An erl ther was in Apulé   that corteis was and hende;   *Apulia; agreeable*

---

[1] *In his youth he was a merchant and [at the same time] inclined towards virtue*

[2] Lines 4–6: *But in charitable gifts and on poor men he spent (expended) his profits. / When any poor man asked him for charity, certainly he did not refrain, on account of any love of wealth, from giving him something*

[3] *And throughout [the palace] all were inscribed with a fair cross*

[4] *["]I am too puny for such [a life], unless I equip myself better"*

He thoghte be imad knyght of him,[1] thuderward he gan wende.
Ac as wel he myghte habbe ibé atom, thulke travail was vor noght.[2]
Other armes he schulde take wen it were al vorth ibroght.
25 And as he wende toward this erl vorte ben imad knyght,
Our Lord in avision to him com anyght.   *dream (vision)*
"Sei," he sede, "of the lord and of the hine also,
And of the riche and of the povere, wuch mai the mest good do?"[3]
"Bote the loverd," quath the other, "and he that is riche."   *The lord, of course*
30 "Thou haddest almest," quath this other, "ichose uniliche.   *the opposite*
 Vor trust of the hyne, the lord thou vorsoke;
Thou nome uvele thin avision: thou most thee bet biloke.[4]
The armure and the paleis that thou noble iseie
Thou schalt fynde ellesware; thou ne comest noght yut so heie.
35 Thou schalt habbe knyghtes under thee, thulke armes to lede.[5]
Thervore wend hom agen and bithenche bet thin dede." *think of something better to do*
This holi mon, tho he awok, agen wende to Assise
And thoghte al on Jhesu Crist and bilevede his marchaundise.   *gave up*
He bad our Lord nyght and day that He scholde him rede,   *prayed; advise*
40 And His grace him sende and toknynge hou he scholde his lif lede.
Wat were this noble knyghtes that he sei in meting   *these; dream*
Bote Freres Menours and hor ordre that he schulde vorth bringe?[6]
The noble paleis that he isei, that armure was inne,
That was the joie of Hevene that this knyghte scholde wynne.
45 A day this holi mon withthoute Assise drou.   *was riding*
He mette a lolich mesel that grisliche was inough.   *loathsome leper; terrifying*
He bad him som god vor Godes love; Seyn Franceis alighte[7]
And biclupte and custe this mesel as vaire as he mighte.   *embraced and kissed*
Of his selver he him tok and bad him habbe good day.   *gave him some of his silver*

---

[1] *He purposed to be knighted by him*

[2] *But he might as well have stayed home, the effort was for nothing*

[3] Lines 27–28: *"Tell me," he said, " which can do the most good, a lord or a servant, a rich man or a poor man?"*

[4] *You misinterpreted your dream: you must be more careful*

[5] Lines 34–35: *. . . you come not yet to such a lofty position (lit., so high). / You shall have knights under you, to bear those arms (i.e., armor)*

[6] *If not Friars Minor and their order, which he was destined to found?*

[7] *He asked him [for] some charity for [the sake of] God's love; Saint Francis dismounted*

50   Tho nuste he war he was bicome   ne in no stude him ne say.[1]

Tho thoghte he wel ho it was,   and after thulke dede   *Then he realized who it was*

He wep and cride on Jhesu Crist   that He somwat scholde him rede.[2]

And ofte he wolde bi custume   to meseles vare   *go visit lepers*

And seche hem at hor hous,   bote he founde hem elleware,   *find them in their house*

55   And cusse hor honden and hor vet   and hor mouth also,

And geve hem largeliche of his good: bi costume he wolde it do.[3]

So aghte, me thencth, ech man   and nameliche the riche,   *it seems to me*

Vor our Lord hath so ofte be iseie   in hor liche,   *in their (the lepers') likeness*

Vor in non other fourme of monne   me ne may Him so ofte isé.[4]

60   Therwith He dude hem gret honor,   that He wolde hor brother be.

Bi an chirche of Seyn Damyan   Seyn Franceis com gon,

That up the poynte was to valle.   In he wende anon   *was on the point of falling down*

And knelede adoun byvore the Crois,   as he dude wel ofte.

A vois ther spek in the Crois   wel mildeliche and softe:

65   "Franceis," he sede, "Go nou vorth   and arer up myn hous an hei

That thou sucst falle al to gronde   and is al to struid nei."   *seest; nearly all destroyed*

Seyn Franceis, tho the chirche was   dounward so ibroght,   *since*

Wende that our Lord sede therbi: ac therbi nas it noght,[5]

Ac was bi al holi chirche   and bi al cristedom,

70   That his freres scholde upholde   wen the ordre vorth com.   *came into being*

Wel aughte thulke ordre be good,   and uvele ibroght to gronde,   *evil*

Vor with vair toknynge and fale   it was verst ifounde.[6]

Seyn Franceis wende and solde his clothes   and al his other thinge,   *cloths*

And the panes therof nom   and to the chirche he gan bringe.   *pennies/money; took*

75   The prest of the chirche he vond,   the panes he wolde him take   *give*

To rere up the holi chirche,   ac he gan hem vorsake.   *rebuild; refused them (coins)*

He ne dorste noght, vor his fader   ne vor his other frend, he sede,

---

[1] *Then he did not know where he had gone, nor did he see him in any place*

[2] *. . . that He should give him some guidance*

[3] *And give [to] them generously from his goods: by custom (habitually) he would do it*

[4] *For in no other human form [than that of a leper] could one see Him so often*

[5] *Thought that our Lord was talking about that one (the church of St. Damian); but it was not about that one at all*

[6] *For its first founding was heralded by many fair signs and portents*

So much tresour nyme of him,   bote it were bi hor rede.[1]

Seyn Franceis nom that tresour,   tho the other it vorsok,

80   And in a fenestre it leide   and in our Lordes warde it tok.   *window; keeping; entrusted*

Tho the tidynge com to his fader   that he hadde iscold his good,   *sold off his property*

Toward him he wende anon   and vor wraththe was nei wod.   *nearly insane*

Seyn Franceis was iwar of him,   he ne levede noght byhynde,[2]

And wende and hudde him in a diche   that he ne mighte him noght fynde   *hid himself*

85   In the diche wel longe he lay   in honger and in wrechede,

And evere cride on Jhesu Crist   that He him sculde rede.

So longe he was in meseise there   that he vorverde nei,   *misery; nearly died*

That unnethe him couthe iknowe   eny that him isei.[3]

Ate laste in gret meseise   he wende to Assise.

90   That folc, tho hi seie him come,   sore hem gan agrise   *when; were very afraid*

And sede, "Her cometh a wod mon!"   and harlede him wel vaste,

And smyte and pulte her and ther,   and with dynge him caste.

Seyn Franceis eode vorth evere   as him nothing nere.[4]

His fader com also bi cas   and imette him there;   *by chance*

95   He nom and ladde him hom to his hous   and bet him sore inou,   *severely enough*

And bad him bringe hom that good   that he awei drough.   *property; had made off with*

Tho he ne mighte habbe non other good,   he bond him swythe stronge,[5]

So that this holi mon   in prison was wel longe.

Ate laste, the wule his fader   out of toune gan wende,

100   His moder hadde reuthe of him   and broghte him out of bende.   *freed him*

Tho he was out of bende ibroght   he ne levede no leng ther;   *stayed no longer*

He wende to the diche agen   from wan he com er.   *whence; came before*

Tho this godemon com hom,   he ne found him noght there.   *gentleman/man of the house*

He bet his wif sore inough   and escte wer he were.   *beat; asked*

105   To Seyn Damianes chirche   thanene he wende so   *thence*

And founde that tresour al ihol   as he it hadde ido,   *all intact; just as he (Francis) left it*

And seththe he wende to the diche   and founde his sone there.

He escte him vor wat thing   that tresour awei he bere.   *reason*

---

[1] *So much wealth accept from him, unless it were with their consent*

[2] *Saint Francis was anxious about him, he did not remain*

[3] *So that anyone who saw him could hardly recognize him*

[4] Lines 91–93: *And said, "Here comes a madman!" and dragged him quite forcibly, / And smote and pelted [him] here and there and threw dung at him. / Saint Francis kept on walking as if nothing happened*

[5] *Since he could not get any other satisfaction, he tied him up very thoroughly*

Ac tho he sei al then ende   that he lute therof roughte,[1]
110   He nom and ladde him vorth with him   and bivore the biscep him broghte
And bad him, yif he alles wolde   this worldes good vorsake,
That he byvore the biscep therright   up it take.   *give it up (renounce it) at once*
Seyn Franceis myd thulke word   glad and joivol stod;
He gef up ther bivore God   al erthliche good
115   And strupte his clothes of his rug   al to his bare liche,   *body (skin)*
And byvore the biscep tok his fader and bad him be riche.   *handed [them] to*
He sede, "Ichabbe icluped thee 'fader'   evere to this daye,   *I have called you "Father"*
Ac nou it is so ver icome   that nan more I ne may.[2]
Segge ich mot my Pater Noster   henne vorthward iwis,   *I must say; henceforth*
120   And to my Fader holde me   that in Hevene is."   *cling to*
Naked he wende from his fader   byvore hem echon;
After thulke tyme worldliche good   nadde he never non.
A seli uplondisc mon,   that naked isei him go,   *pious peasant*
Gret deol hadde in his horete   of his chele and wo.   *sorrow; heart; cold*
125   He gef him an old mantel   his bones vorte hele.   *to cover*
This holi mon it underveng   to wite him from chele.   *accepted; protect*
His licham he helede therwith   and in meseise inou,   *body*
Agen as he was ibore,   to Assise he drough.   *Back to where he was born*
As he hadde ibé er so riche   and so wel iknowe,
130   A beggare bicom and bad his mete,   therafter in a throwe.[3]
From dore to dore he bad his mete   and wonede him therto;   *accustomed himself*
Some were wrothe vor his dede   and no good nolde him do.
Of the Ordre of Frere Menors   he ne made nothing yute.
He bigon the ordre in poverte inou   and in wel lute prute.   *very little pride*
135   Men of the contreie were   aboute vorte mende   *region; starting to repair*
The chirche of Seyn Damian   that al adonward wende,
Ther as Seyn Franceis hadde ibé   and tresor bilevede there.   *There where*
Tho he non other mighte do   the chirche vorte rere,   *Since; build*
He wende thuder and sore swonc   and ber morter therto   *labored hard*
140   And seththe he eode and bad is mete   wen he hadde ido.   *afterwards; went; finished*
An chirche seththe of Seyn Peter   me rerde ellesware.   *was being built*
This holi mon in his meseise   wel sone was thare,

---

[1] *But when he saw finally that he (Francis) did not care about it at all*

[2] *But now it has come so far (i.e., things have changed so much) that I no longer can [call you father]*

[3] *A beggar [he] became and asked for his food, always [feeling] the pangs [of hunger]*

And drou morter and ston therto   and sore swonc also,

And seththe eode and bad his mete,   tho he hadde al ido.

145   Wen he hurde of eny churche   that owar was to rere,   *was being built anywhere*

Him thoghte evere longe inough   ar he were there.[1]

To Seyn Marie in Desert   ate laste he wende stille

And cride on God nyght and day   that He dude bi him his wille,

And that He geve him grace,   in wuch manere he mighte,

150   His chirche that donward was   best rere up and dighte,[2]

So that God gef him grace   that he there bigan   *[with a result] that*

The holi Ordre of Frere Menors   that saveth mony a man.

In the bygynyng of this ordre,   as our Lord gef that cas,   *brought it to pass*

A mass he hurde a day   that of the apostles was.   *one day*

155   As me rat yut among ous   in the Godspel it sede tho   *as is read still*

That our Lord het His diciples   that hi scholde aboute go,   *commanded; travel about*

That hi ne bere with hem gold ne selver wen hi code over lond,   *in such way that*

Ne bagge, ne twei curtles nother,   ne staf in hor hond,   *nor two coats either*

Ne that hi werrede nathemo   on hem none schon.[3]

160   In this manere our Lord het   the apostles aboute gon.

Tho Seyn Franceis hurde this,   he dude of his scon anon   *took off his shoes*

And porveide that Frere Menors   barvot schulde gon   *ordained; barefoot*

Withthoute bagge and withthoute staf,   withthoute ech thing to spene.

And hose deth eny of this,   he halt noght his ordre, ich wene.[4]

165   In stude of his gurdel ek   with a corde he him bond.   *[leather] belt; rope; tied*

In this manere Freres Menors   schulde go overlond.

Ther bigan Seyn Franceis to don this holi dede

And made the Ordre of Frere Menors   al as the Godspel sede.

Bernard, that was good scoler,   verst to him com

170   And the Ordre of Frere Menors   of his honden nom.   *received at his hands*

He escte at him hou he scholde best   the worlde clanliche vorsake.   *utterly*

Hi wende to Seyn Nicholas chirche;   an massebok hi gonne take;

---

[1] *It always seemed a long time until he got there [i.e., to start work]*

[2] Lines 148–50: *And cried to God night and day that He would grant him his wish / And that He would grant him grace that, in whatever way he could, / He (Francis) best might raise up and adorn His church, which was in decline*

[3] *And that they should never wear shoes*

[4] Lines 163–64: *Without bag and without staff, without anything to spend. / And whoever does any of these things is not observing [the rules of] his order, in my opinion*

271

The boc was iclosed vaste;   Seyn Franceis him bad undo.
He undude the bok al unmundeliche   and the verste that he com to,[1]
175   That was a Godspel that seith   "Yif thou wolt perfit be,
Sul al thi good and gef povere men   and com and siwe me."   *Sell; give [to]; follow*
Al unmundeliche he com efsone   to a Godspel that sede   *in turn*
That me ne scholde nothing by the wei   nother bere ne lede.   *on a journey*
The thridde tyme al unmundeliche   the massebok he wende,   *turned*
180   Tho he com up this Godspel   as our Lord him sende: *came upon*
"Hose wole come after me   he schal himsulve vorsake   *must deny himself*
And his owe rode bere,   and then wei so after me take."[2]
"Thou sucst," quath Seyn Franceis, "her,   hou our Lord in a stounde   *see; moment*
Send ous grace up wuch thinge   we schulle this ordre founde.[3]
185   Up this thre Godspelles, thou sucst,   that we habbeth thar verst ifounde,   *Upon these*
We schulle founde oure ordre   and up an stronge grounde."   *upon a*
Up this thre Godspell he made his ordre   and his reule vorsoth,
And Frere Menour breketh his ordre   that out theragen doth.   *aught (anything)*
Noble an ordre it aghte be   that so nobliche ifounde was,   *A noble order*
190   Verst thoru toknynge of Jhesu Crist   and seththe thoru such cas.   *such [an] event*
Frere Gilis was tho the verste,   that good scoler hadde ibe,   *Giles*
That after Frere Bernard that abit nom,   and seththe other thre.
So that under hem alle were   six freres vorth ibroght.   *all in all; created (inducted)*
And thei this ordre were imad,   iconfermed nas it noght.
195   Seyn Franceis, this holi mon,   tho God then tyme sende[4]
To confermy his ordre aright,   to Rome he wende.   *approve (authorize)*
Ac wel sore he was adrad   leste the pope were
Contrerious agen his ordre,   that he iconfermed nere.[5]
Ac vorth he wende to fonde;   he nolde noght be byhynde.   *try; delay*
200   Ac evere he bad Jhesu Crist   that he moste som grace ifynde.   *could*
Tho thoghte him, in a vision,   that he sei a gret tre,   *then it seemed to him; saw*
So hei that he was adrad   toward the toppe to se.   *high*

---

[1] *He undid the book completely at random, and the first [page] that he came to*

[2] *And carry his own cross, and take the same road as me*

[3] *Sends us [the] grace [to know] on what sort of conditions we must found this order*

[4] Lines 194–65: *And although this order was established, it was not authorized. / Saint Francis, this holy man, when God gave him the time (opportunity)*

[5] *Resistant to his order, [so] that it would not be approved*

And natheles an aunter him dude   and nom therof a bough,[1]

Above in the hexte stude,   and toward him drough.　　　*highest place; pulled [it]*

205　Hit binde al adoun to him,   after his wille inough,　　　*bent; just as he wished*

Vor al that he dradde verst   that it was hei and tough.

Tho this holi mon awok   on his swevene he thoghte longe,　　　*dream*

And therthoru he thoghte   of the pope som grace avonge:[2]

Vor that tre, that was so hei,   lightliche to gronde he drou:　　　*easily*

210　Also he hopede the heie pope   to his wille bringe inou.　　　*In the same way*

To the hei Pope Innocent,   tho he to Rome com,

He bad his religion granti,   to amende Cristendom,

And he wolde his ordre prevy,   and his reule also,

Thoru the Godspel of Godes word,   and therafter do.[3]

215　Tho the pope his reule isei   that heo was clene and good,　　　*it*

And ifounded up the Godspel,   al as he wel understod.　　　*upon*

In his heorte he granted it,   ac noght with mouthe anon,

Vor he moste his cardinals   consely everichon.　　　*consult with*

So that among this cardinals   consell ther was inome:

220　Somme hulde theragen,   and vaste therwith some.[4]

Tho was ther a cardinal,   that biscep was also,

Maister Jon of Seyn Poul   that vaste huld therto.

"Yif we," he sede, "distourbeth him,   agen the Godspel we beth,　　　*hinder/obstruct*

Wen he speketh al up Godes word,[5]   as we wel iseth."

225　In avision to the pope   also anyght it com

That he grantede him his reule   to amendi Cristendom.[6]

So that the pope grantede him   al his reule to do,[7]

---

[1] *And nonetheless he took a risk (made an effort) and grasped a branch of it*

[2] *Because of it (the dream) he expected to obtain the pope's grace (goodwill)*

[3] Lines 211–14: *When he came to Rome, he asked the noble pope Innocent to authorize his form of religion (his religious order), in order to reform Christendom, / And [said that] he wished to prove (validate) his order, and his rule also, / In relation to the Gospel of God's word, and to live according to it (the Gospel)*

[4] Lines 219–20: *As a result a discussion was held amongst his cardinals: / Some held against it, and some firmly in favor*

[5] *Everything he says is according to God's word*

[6] Lines 225–26: *Also, by means of a nocturnal vision, the pope became convinced / That [he should] sanction his rule, so as to reform Christendom*

[7] *As a result the pope granted him [permission] to put all his rule into practice*

And confermede thoru all the court   and gef him more therto.
Tho wende vorth this holi mon   and his freres with him nom,
230   And prechede aboute then Godspel[1]   to amendi Cristendom.
Tho the contrei isei him verst,   gret spech ther was there:[2]
Somme sede that Anticrist   other his disciples it were,   *or*
So that in vele studes   wel lute good hem me sende,[3]
And hi were ofte afyngred sore   as hi aboute wende.   *terribly hungry*
235   Tho that hi come in a stude,   and afyngred were sore,
That some of the freres nadde ithoght   in the ordre ibé nanmore,[4]
Tho com ther a wel vair man   and broghte hem mete inough.
Tho nuste hi war he bicom   ne wudeward he drough,[5]
Tho sei this freres wel   that an angel it was.   *When*
240   The studevastore hi were in hor ordre   vor this holi cas,   *more steadfast*
And bihete God that nevere   vor meseise ne vor wo   *promised*
In the ordre hi nolde   bi hor mighte poverte vorgo.   *deliberately forsake poverty*
So that hi wende in a stude   that was al vorlete,   *And so they went; abandoned*
Biside the toun of Assise   in an olde strete.   *on an old road*
245   In meseise hi were ther inough   and ofte hi wepe sore
Vor defaute of sustinaunce   and vor defaute of bokes more.
Vor hi nadde nanne boc   waron hi mighte loke.   *whereon*
In the Crois hi bihulde al day,   in stude of hor boke,   *instead*
And bede God, yif it were his wille,   som good hem teche,
250   Vor hi nadde non other boc,   ne hi nuste warwith areche.[6]
To Seyn Marie in Desert   thenne hi gonne wende,
As hi bigonne verst hor ordre,   to bringe ther to ende.[7]
Seyn Franceis wende bi the lond   and prechede aboute there.
Men wende, tho hi seie him verst   that of another world he were,
255   Vor he caped evere upard   toward Hevene an hei,
That me wondred and speke therof,   ech mon that him isei.

---

[1] *And preached the Gospel all around*

[2] *When the [people of the] country first saw him, there was a lot of discussion [about him]*

[3] *So that in many places they were given very little charity*

[4] *That some of the friars had considered leaving the order*

[5] *They did not know where he came from or where he withdrew to*

[6] *For they had no other book, and they did not know how to obtain [any]*

[7] *To bring the order to maturity there where they had first begun it*

Mony him huld a truaunt,   of the Develes lore,   *vagabond*

And harled him her and ther   and ofte him bete sore.   *dragged*

This gode mon nom never yeme   ac cride our Lordes ore   *heed; mercy*

260   And war me dude him mest scame,[1]   thuder he drou the more.

Idel nolde he never be,   he ne lovede nothing so lute,

Ne hatede so much, as ese   and idelnesse and prute.   *pride*

"Frere Asse" he clupede his owe flesc, vor thou wost wel an asse,   *called (named)*

Nabbe heo never so lute mete   his travail nys no the lasse,[2]

265   Vor heo is iharled her and ther   and to vile worke ido,   *made to do*

Ipricked and iscourged ek,   and sackes bereth also.

Of wrecchede thing heo is ived,   wen heo cometh therto,   *fed with wretched stuff*

And wel selde icoureied ek: heo nath nother nail ne sco.

And servede so his owe flesc   and clupede it "Frere Asse,"[3]

270   And gef him mete lute inou   and to clothinge lasse,   *gave himself; for clothing*

And prikede him and scourged ek,   and thoroughout the contreie

Harlede him and depe wod   barvot in depe weie.[4]

Wen he sei eny idel man,   that lovede glotenye

And ne travailde noght vor his mete,   he clupede hem "Frere Flye,"   *did not work*

275   Vor the fleye doth non other good   bote fleth ver and ner

And awaiteth wen men goth to mete   other to soper,

And as sone as the dich is iset adoun   heo wole be ate brerde.

Of travail ne kepth heo noght,   bote that heo wel verde.[5]

Wen a man hath al day iswonke,   thei he hadde iswore,

280   He ne schal so sone come to his dich   that heo nele be byvore.[6]

So vareth mony idel man   that no good nele do,   *many [an]*

Bote wen men beth toward the mete   al prest he is therto;[7]

---

[1] *And wherever he was treated most shamefully*

[2] *No matter how little food she may have, she has no less work to do*

[3] Lines 268–69: *And very seldom curried also: she has neither nail nor scourge. / And he treated his own body in the same way and called it "Brother Ass"*

[4] *He dragged himself and trudged barefoot along roads deep in mud*

[5] Lines 277–78: *And as soon as the dish is set down she will be at the edge [of the dish]. / Of work she cares nothing, but only that she should fare (eat) well*

[6] Lines 279–80: *A man who has worked all day, although he might swear [it will be otherwise], / No matter how quickly he sits down to his dinner she (the fly) will be there before him*

[7] *But when people are on their way to dinner all energetic he is for it*

Ate disc hi wolleth as sone be   as hi that habbeth iswonke.

And thenne is al hor werk ido,   habbe hi iyete and idrounke.[1]

285   Then liggeth hi and slepeth   other goth doth som folie.   *lie down; or go [and] do*

Thervore Seyn Franceis clepeth a such man "Frere Fleie."   *such a man*

Of nothing nas this holi mon   so glad as of edwit.   *abuse (reproaches)*

Wen me reprevede his poverte,   he was in gret delit;   *reproved/rebuked*

Wen me clupede him beggar,   other churl, other churles sone,

290   He wolde thonke and be glad: that was ever his wone.   *custom*

"Leve brother," he wolde segge,   "certes thou seist soth.

Iblessed be thou vor thulke word   and alle that so doth!

Peres sone Bernard   it bicometh bi righte lawe.

To here telle of is righte.   Ic aughte be glad and vawe."[2]

295   And wen me preisede of his kunde,   him ne thoghte no delit.   *nature (character)*

Thervore hose him wolde paie,[3]   segge him som edwit.

And bivore al that folc abrod   in his prechinge he sede   *spoke about*

His meseise and his defaute   and ofte his wrechede.   *distress; moral failings*

Wel this prute pigasours   wer hi vare so yute,

300   Hi wricketh and streccheth hem an hei,   hi nute hou go vor prute!

Hem thencth hi nelleth noght go,   ac fle herre then the kute!

Wat, nou wuder thencheth hi?   Al it worth wel lute.

In Puylé Seyn Franceis eode   some tyme overe lond,[4]

So that a pors vol of panes   bi the wei he vond.   *purse full of coins by the roadside*

305   He ne tok no more gome   then to so muche ven.   *heed; than; dung*

His felawe bad him nyme it up   and dele it povere men.   *pick; dole it out to*

"I nele noght," quath Seyn Franceis,   "of other monnes dele."[5]

"Me thencth," quath this frere tho,   "that thou art unvele,   *wrong*

That thou ne lovest noght povere men   wen thou nelt hem do good."

---

[1] *And once they have eaten and drunk, that is all their work done*

[2] Lines 293–94: *[Such abuse] is very fitting, and perfectly lawful, for the son of Peter Bernardone. / It is right for me to hear tell of [such things]. I ought to be glad and happy*

[3] *Therefore whosoever might wish to please him*

[4] Lines 299–303: *These proud pricasours, wheresoever they travel nowadays, / How well they bob up and down and stretch themselves up on high, for their pride, they don't know how to walk! / They seem not to want to walk, but to fly higher than a kite! / What, whither do they think [to go]? They will all come to nothing (lit., very little will come of it all). / In Apulia Saint Francis was walking across country one time*

[5] *"I do not want," said Saint Francis, "to take and distribute something that belongs to others"*

310	This holi mon hurde this and an wule in thoghte stod.	*a while*
	"Thou schalt," he sede, "sone isé wat the panes beth echon."	*soon see*
	He wende and nom up then pors and openede him anon.	*it*
	Tho crep therout an eddre, the grislokes that mighte gon,[1]	
	And the pors al empti was and noght a peny theron.	*therein*
315	That was the Devel of Helle that in fourme of panes lay,	
	Vorte bitraie this holi mon wanne he the panes isay.	*saw*
	Ac natheles ich wene, thei the Devel were al to panes bicome,	
	Yut ich wene this chepmen hem wolde avonge somme.[2]	
	This holi mon Seyn Franceis among ech maner best	*all kinds of animals*
320	Mest he lovede yonge lombron, and honoured hem mest,	*lambs*
	Vor our Lord evenede Him to a lomb thoru Seyn Jon the Baptist,	*likened Himself*
	And vor lomb is withthoute felonye and mylde as Jhesu Crist.	
	And ofte wen men hem wolde quelle fram dethe he hem broghte;	*slaughter; saved*
	With biddyng and faire word ofte he hem boghte.	*pleading; redeemed*
325	In the abbei of Seyn Verecunde a yong lomb he vonde:	
	A souwe astrangelid it a dai and fret in a stounde.	*one day; devoured in a moment*
	Seyn Franceis stod and bihuld: "Among alle bestes," he sede,	
	"Acorsed be thou, luther sowe, that dest such luther dede,	*wicked; [did] do*
	That thi lif be schort and strong and thi deth strong also,	*[So] that; severe; foul (rank)*
330	That nothing ete of thi flesc, wen thou art of lyve ido."	*deprived*
	Tho bigon this sowe, anon as he this word sede,	
	To be vol of scabbes and of other wrechede,	
	That heo orn out al quiture, as al that folc isay.	*she was oozing with pus all over*
	In wrechede and sorwe inou heo deide then thridde day,	*[on] the third*
335	And rotede and stonc foule inou. No best that it isei,	
	Ne revon ne other foul, nolde ene come ther nei.[3]	
	Vor Seyn Franceis lovede lomb, as al that folc isai,	
	On of his frend vor Godes love gef him a lomb a day.	*one day*
	This lomb wolde, yong and old, al day nei him be,	
340	And make with him joie inough wen he him mighte isé.	

---

[1] *Then a snake crept outside, the grisliest (most repulsive) there could be (lit., that could walk)*

[2] Lines 317–18: *But nevertheless I expect, although the Devil were all changed into coins, / I expect these merchants would still accept some of them*

[3] Lines 335–36: *And rotted and stank most foul. No creature that saw it, / Neither raven nor any other fowl, would come near there*

277

Seyn Franceis het this scep a day   wenne it hurde the freres singe
To churche gon at eche tyde   and byleve vor nothinge.
This scep after thulke tyme   selde wolde abide,
Wenne it hurde the freres in the quer,   that it nas at eche tide.[1]

345 Blete it wolde agen hem   vor it ne couthe non other song;   *in response to them; knew*
Wen it seie the freres sitte akné, kneli it wolde among,   *along with them*
And wen the prest sacred ek   kneli it wolde therto,   *consecrated [the Host]*
And inwardliche biholde thuder   as it sei the freres do.   *fervently*
Wel aghte we honouri Godes flesc   wen a such best wolde:

350 A wonder bedmon it was on,   icome to Godes folde.[2]
As Seyn Franceis, this holi mon,   over lond vaste drough,   *diligently traveled*
Wilde foweles smale and grete   honoured him inough.
Vor as he wende in a tyme   to prechi over lond,
An hep of foweles gret inough   in a stude he vond.   *in one place*

355 Hi songe and made noise inou,   everich in his wise.   *each in his own way*
The yut Seyn Franceis to hem com,   hi nolde enes arise.[3]
"Beu frere," quath this holi mon,   "our sostren that beth here
Honoureth God that hem made   ech in his manere.
Right is that we do also,   ar we fram hem gon."   *do likewise, before*

360 Hi bigonne segge hor tyden   among this foweles echon;[4]
Tho made this foweles gret noise   that hi ne mighte noght ihere:
"Sostren," quath this holi mon,   "changeth youre manere!
Beth nou stille and leteth me segge   my tyden and my frere,
And seththe ye mowe after ous,   everich with his ivere."[5]

365 This foweles anon to his heste   stille were also,
And sete and herkenede hor tyden   vorte hi hadde ido.
"Nou sostren," quath this holi mon,   "nou we habbeth ised oure tyden,
Bigynneth youre wen ye wolleth;   ye ne dorre no leng abiden."[6]

---

[1] Lines 341–44: *One day Saint Francis told this sheep to go to church at each of the [canonical] Hours, whenever it heard the friars singing, and not to remain behind for anything. / After that particular occasion, whenever it heard the friars in the choir, this sheep would seldom stay away and miss being at each of the Hours*

[2] *A wondrous clerk it was, come to God's sheepfold*

[3] *When Saint Francis came up to them, they still would not once fly away*

[4] *They began to recite their [breviary] Hours among all these birds*

[5] *And afterwards you may [sing yours], each with your mate*

[6] *["] . . . you need not wait any longer"*

This foweles gonne synge anon,   the leste and the meste:

370   Gret poer he hadde of God   to habbe foweles ate his heste.   *power; command*

This holi mon him wende vorth   to prechi over lond;

A gret hep efsone of foweles   in a stude he vond.   *once again*

He wende vorth among hem: this foweles gonne echon

Aloute to him mildeliche   and honoure him anon.   *bow down*

375   This holi mon atstod an wule   and thoghte hem som god teche,

And as to men of witte   this foweles he gan preche.[1]

"Leve sostren," he sede, "vor Godes love   honoureth youre creaturr,

Vor among alle creatours   ye aughte don Him honur,

Vor he gef you nobleie inough,[2]   wyngen vorte fle,

380   And fetheren to bere you an hei,   wide vorte te,   *to go far and wide*

And mete war ye wolleth alighte,   withthoute ech manere swenche.

He gefth you gret prute and ese   as enymon may thenche.

Ye ne dorre nother delve ne dike,   as mony mon mot do,

And yut ye mowe habbe mete inough,   other mowe noght so."

385   This foweles herkened wel stille,   the wule his prechinge ilaste,[3]

And fram wodes and other studes   thuderward drowe vaste.   *quickly drew near there*

Tho this holi mon hadde ido,   he wende vorth anon,   *finished*

And strokede hem with his longe sleve: hi nolde arise noght on,

Ar he hete hem wende vorth   war hi hadde to done.[4]

390   So sone so the foweles that ihurde   hi wende vorth wel sone.

Seyn Franceis among al other thing,   right at his heorte gronde,   *bottom of his heart*

Ofte thoghte deope inough   in our Lordes wounde.   *meditated on; wounds*

So studevastlich in his thoght   non other thing he nom.[5]

---

[1] Lines 375–76: *This holy man paused for a moment and thought about teaching them something worthwhile, / And he began to preach to these birds as though to intelligent human beings*

[2] Lines 378–79: *For you of all creatures ought to honor Him / For he endowed you with enough [natural] nobility (splendor)*

[3] Lines 381–85: *[*"*]And food where you wish to alight, without any kind of work. / He gives you as much dignity and ease as any one can imagine. / You have no need to delve or dig, as many a man must do, / And yet you may have food enough, [while] others may not." / These birds listened very quietly, while his preaching lasted*

[4] Lines 388–89: *. . . not one of them would take off, / Before he bade them be off to where they needed to be*

[5] *There was no other thing on which he meditated so steadfastly*

So that the Holi Rode tid,   that agen Mielmasse com,[1]

395   Upe the hul of Averne,   as it was our Lordes wille,   *upon*

    Alone in his orisouns   ther he lay wel stille.

    He thoghte on our Lordes wounden   so depe that nas non ende.[2]

    An angel he sei an hei,   right fram Hevene wende.   *coming straight from Heaven*

    Six wyngen, him thoghte, he hadde,   that scynde brighte and wide;[3]

400   Twei stode up above his heved   and twei bi his side,

    And right over the wombe acroys   twei ther were also,   *crossed right over the torso*

    As me such ofte in chirch ipeynt,   hose come therto.[4]

    The armes were along isprad   as hi were on the rode,   *fully extended; as [if]*

    And the vet istreight along,   al urnynde of blode.[5]

405   Thoru the right side he was ismyte   and thoru vet and honde:

    It was, in fourme of an angel,   our Lord, ich undurstonde.

    So gret joie hadde this holi mon   of this noble sighte

    That he was as in another world   and thonkede Godes mighte.

    He nuste wat vor joie do   the wule he this fourme isei.

410   Ate laste it flei agen   into Hevene an hei.   *back again*

    Seyn Franceis was in joie inough   vor the noble sighte,

    And nameliche of our Lordes wounden   that he wilnede day and nyghte.[6]

    He bihuld his owe honden   and his vet also: *own*

    Tho were hi thoru out ismyte   and the nailes theron ido,[7]

415   And his right side wounded ek,   ac wel sore nere hi noght;

    The wounden himsulf he hadde tho   that so much were in his thoght.

    The nailes were blake inough,   the heveden rounde and grete,

    The poyntes were evelong,   as hi were agen ibete.[8]

    Aboute the nailes the flesc stod up,   as it were al toswolle,   *swollen up*

420   As it al aboute were   vor anguisse al tobolle.[9]

---

[1] *Thus on Holy Cross day, which falls just before Michaelmas*

[2] *He meditated with unfathomable profundity on our Lord's wounds*

[3] *Six wings, it seemed to him, he had, which shone bright and wide*

[4] *As is often seen painted in a church, at least by those who go there*

[5] *And the feet stretched straight out, all running with blood*

[6] *And especially [because] of our Lord's wounds that he had wished for day and night*

[7] *In that instant they were pierced through and the nails stuck in there*

[8] *The points were oblong, as [if] they had been hammered back*

[9] *And as [if] around each nail-head it (the flesh) were painfully inflamed*

In this manere we mowe wene   that our Lordes wounden were,
Vor bote ensample of his wounden   in Seyn Franceis nere.[1]
So that this holi mon hadde   our Lordes wounden vyve   *Thus [it was] that; five*
And bilevede on him afterward   the wule he was alyve.   *they remained*
425   The Holi Rode tyd in Septembre   he gan verst this sight isé
And up thulke hul he hadde er   aboute an month ibé.   *on that hill*
Aboute a fourtene nyght   he bilevede after there,
So that evene under al   fourti dawes ther were.   *altogether*
As Moyses up Sinay   was bi olde dawe,   *in ancient times*
430   Fourti dawes in priveté   to se the Olde Lawe,
Also was this holi mon   fourti dawes right   *likewise; exactly*
Up the hul of Averne   to se this holi sight.
So that aboute Myelmasse   verst he wende to gronde
Ac he hudde vaste vet and honde   that me ne seie his wounde.[2]
435   To yer he livede with the wounden   and prechede aboute wide,   *Two years*
And the wounden ourne ofte ablode,   nameliche of the side,[3]
And bibledde his curtel ofte   and his brech also.   *stained his habit with blood; trousers*
Thenne carede he hou he mighte   stilliche awei it do.[4]
Seththe com in the lond ther   a gret qualm of orve,   *epidemic sickness among livestock*
440   That scep and other bestes al day   lye and storve.   *every day lay down and died*
A good mon that hadde muche orf   bed our Loverd vaste,   *cattle prayed; earnestly*
That he ne bynome noght al his good,   ac that som moste ilaste.
Slepynde in a vision   him com thoru Godes sonde
That he nom of the water   that Seyn Franceis wech his honde[5]
445   Other his vet, and therwith   among his bestes sprenge,[6]
And yif ther were to lute,   among other water it menge.   *too little, with; mix it*
This gode mon herafterward   awaited his poynt ofte,   *chance*

---

[1] Lines 421–22: *In this way, we may think about what our Lord's wounds were really like, / For in Saint Francis they were not a mere pictorial image of His wounds*

[2] *But he carefully hid his feet and hands [so] that people could not see his wounds*

[3] *And the wounds often bled, especially from his side*

[4] *He worried a lot as to how he could quietly make it cease*

[5] Lines 442–44: *That [God] not deprive him of all his goods, but that some might be left. / While he was sleeping, it came to him spiritually, as a message from God, / That he should take some of the water with which Saint Francis washed his hands*

[6] *Or his feet, and sprinkle it over his livestock*

And nom of this water stilliche, in priveté wel softe,[1]
And sprend among his owe orf and among other mony on,   *sprinkled [it]; own*
450   And overal war it was bispreng hi were hol anon.   *everywhere*
Seyn Franceis was Frere Menor in the ordre twenti yer
And two yer and almest thre wuke our Lordes woundes he ber.   *weeks*
So that he drough toward the deth and feblede wel vaste.
Him nas unnethe bote vel and bon bileved ate laste.
455   In torment he was strong inough, and wen he was in worste stounde[2]
His lene bones he wolde drawe agen the harde gronde,   *fling against*
Vorte make the more his pyne, and the erthe he custe also,[3]
And thonkede God of alle gode that he him hadde ido.   *for all the good things*
He lay sik and seththe deide, Seyn Franceis this holi mon,
460   In our Levedi chirche ther he the ordre bigon.   *our Lady's (i.e., Virgin Mary's)*
Tho he was the dethe ney, naked he let him do   *near; had himself undressed*
And to the harde erthe al bar naked he lay therto.
He het hem that aboute him were that, after his dethes stounde,[4]
Hi lete him longe ligge so, naked to the gronde,   *They should let him lie*
465   That erthe mighte on erthe deie, vor that were his righte.   *his due*
He bigon to preche his bretheren, up his feble mighte.   *with his failing powers*
Ate laste, tho he sei then Deth and felde him wel strong,[5]
Voce mea he bigan, an saume of evesong.
Al out the saume he sede and huld up his honden heie,   *All the way through*
470   And myd the laste word of the saume he bigan to deie.
He deide twelf hondred yer and six and twenti right
After that God an erthe alighte, in a Setterday at nyght.
Then Soneday he was ibured: he ne verde noght as the riche
That vor bobauns of the world liggeth longe aliche.[6]
475   Tho this holi mon was ded, thei it were by nyghte,
A gret hep of loverkes up the chirch alighte   *flock of larks on the church [roof]*

---

[1] *And took of this water secretly, unobtrusively on his own*

[2] Lines 454–55: *In the end there was hardly anything left of him but skin and bone. / He was in considerable pain, and when he was in a bout of extreme agony*

[3] *To make his pain greater, and the earth he kissed also*

[4] *He instructed them who were around him that, at the hour of his death*

[5] *At last, when he saw Death and felt his might*

[6] *That for [the sake of] worldly pride lie (in state) in the body*

And murie songe allonge nyght[1]   aboute this bodi there,
Tho the soule to Hevene wende,   agé kunde thei it were.[2]
Vor the larke is a fowel   that much loveth light
480   And hereth the day myd hore songe   and ne singeth noght anyght.   *celebrates*
Agen kunde hi songe there   as thei hi hadde in munde   *as though; mind*
Hou muche he was honoured er   with foweles, agen kunde.   *had been honored by birds*
Frere Austyn, that was mynystre   under him ido,   *provincial minister*
Tho this holi mon lay ded   at the dethe lay also,   *close to death*
485   In the lond of Labour   that ver was therbiside.   *far from thereabouts*
Wel longe he lay specheles,   then deth vorte abide,   *waiting for death*
And right as Seyn Franceis deide   ver in another londe,
This frere spac wel mildeliche   and huld up his honde: *spoke very cheerfully*
"Abid, brother, an wule!   Ich come with thee anon!"
490   The freres escte wat it were,   vor hem wondred echon.   *each of them was amazed*
"Bote Seyn Franceis,"[3] he sede, "our fader,   hath ibroght his lif to ende
And is toward Hevene nom   and ichulle with him wende."   *being taken; I shall*
With this word he gan to deie   and his soule al in pes
Wende to the joie of Hevene   with his maister Seyn Franceis,
495   And beth ther bothe two   in joie withthoute ende.
Nou God vor love of hem   ous late thuder wende.   *let us go there*

---

[1] *And sang merrily throughout the night*

[2] *When the soul went to Heaven, although it was against their nature*

[3] *"Saint Francis, indeed"*

VII

Explanatory Notes to the Life of St. Francis in the South English Legendary (c. 1270–80)

Abbreviations: **A** = Bodleian Library MS Ashmole 43 (*SC* 6924), fols. 142v–149r [base text]; **L** = Bodleian Library MS Laud Misc. 108 (*SC* 1486), fols. 41v–46v, ed. Horstmann, *ESEL*, EETS o.s. 87, pp. 53–67; ***LM*** = Bonaventure, *Legenda major*.

1   *Frances*. This form of the saint's name is used once more in the poem (line 10) but beginning with line 47 it is replaced with the more linguistically correct form, *Franceis*, which is closer to the forms used in L: *Franceys, Fraunceys, Fraunceis* (line 1 and *passim*).

         Frere Menour. On the significance of this name for a member of the Franciscan order, see the Introduction to this chapter.

21   *Apulé*. The Apulian knight, unidentified in *LM*, was Walter of Brienne (d. 1202), leader of the papal forces in their war against the German princes (see Habig, p. 563n20). Francis as a young man apparently thirsted for military glory, fought in the battle between Assisi and Perugia (1202), and was taken prisoner. See the conflicting accounts of the Apulian affair by Thomas of Celano in his First Life I.4 (Habig, pp. 232–33) and Second Life I.4–6 (Habig, pp. 364–66).

24   *Other armes*. The poet alludes to the armor of "spiritual warfare," as in Ephesians. 6:10–18, traditionally attributed to monks and popularized in the words of Martin of Tours: *Christi ego miles sum*, "I am a soldier of Christ" (Life of Saint Martin, ch. 4, trans. Hoare, *The Western Fathers*, p. 16).

31   This verse is metrically short, containing only four strong beats instead of the usual seven, although the second half-line was originally regular, with three beats, since *lord* was originally *loverd*, with two syllables, as in line 29, allowing a heavy stress on *thou* (see L, line 29). But I can see no way to wring an extra two beats out of the first half-line in either text.

32–34   *SEL* has omitted Francis' question in *LM*, "Lord . . . What will you have me do?" but has elaborated on God's reply: "Go back to your own town. The vision which you saw foretold a spiritual achievement which will be accomplished in you by God's will, not man's" (*LM* I.3, Habig, p. 637). See also below, explanatory note on lines 41–44.

35   *lede.* See *MED leden* 6(d), where this use of "lead" to mean "carry," or "bear," especially weapons or armor, is seen to be common in ME secular romances.

37–40   These lines express most of the substance of *LM* I.4 (Habig, p. 638), in which Francis is compared to the merchant in the gospel parable who sold everything he had to buy a precious pearl, the kingdom of Heaven (Matthew 13:45–46). But the precise nature of his next move eludes him.

41–44   These two couplets, clarifying the symbolism of Francis' earlier vision, are lacking in the earliest version of *SEL* (for an earlier interpolation by presumably the same reviser, see lines 23–24), and they are not suggested by anything in *LM*. The reviser is here building on his expanded version of God's words to Francis at lines 32–34 (see the note above), where he implies that the arms in the vision are for the future Franciscan friars ("knyghtes under thee," line 35). Here he makes this more explicit. The vision is about the foundation of the Franciscan order, as well as Francis' heavenly reward as its founder. Bonaventure merely says at this point that through this vision God showed Francis "that the kindness he had done a poor knight for love of the supreme King would be repaid with an incomparable reward" (*LM* I.3, Habig, p. 637). Much later in *LM*, however, Bonaventure explains this reward as the Stigmata, the miraculous marking of Francis' body with the "arms" or heraldic symbol of Christ in the form of the bloody wounds in his hands, feet and side. "O valiant knight of Christ! You are armed with the weapons of your invulnerable Leader. They will mark you out and enable you to overcome all your enemies. It is for you to bear aloft the standard of the High King. . . . The very first vision that you saw has now been fulfilled; it was revealed to you then that you were to be a captain in Christ's army and that you should bear arms which were emblazoned with the sign of the cross" (*LM* XII.9–10, Habig, p. 735). For the poem's account of the stigmatization of Francis, see below, lines 413–20.

46   *lolich.* A variant spelling of *lodlich*, loathly (as in L, line 40).

51   *ho it was.* I.e., Jesus, posing as a leper.

53–56 Compare *LM* I.6, Habig, p. 639. *SEL* omits the second part of this chapter of *LM*, in which, among other things, Francis is said to have gone to Rome and, giving away his clothes to one of the many beggars in front of St. Peter's, put on rags and sat among the beggars himself for a whole day, "filled with an unaccustomed joy of spirit" (Habig, p. 640).

57–60 This passage exhorting rich men to remember that Christ is frequently to be found among the lepers is an interpolation of the A reviser. For a well-known example of Christ's supposed appearance in the form of this, the most abject and loathed of medieval humanity, see the Legend of Saint Julian the Hospitaller in *ScL*, lines 409–72 (in VIII, below). Biblical passages that gave rise to such stories include Isaias 53:4 (*et nos putavimus eum quasi leprosum*, "we thought of him as a leper"), and Jesus' parable of Dives and Lazarus (Luke 16:19–31). See Brody, *The Disease of the Soul*, pp. 101–04. The spirit of Franciscan humility and charity is aptly dramatized in this image of the saint embracing the leper. That the friars did not retain this spirit is suggested in the portrait of Chaucer's Friar, among whose many anti-fraternal traits is his studied avoidance of beggars and *lazars* or lepers (General Prologue, *CT* I[A]243–45):

> For unto swich a worthy man as he
> Acorded nat, as by his facultee,
> To have with sike lazars aqueyntaunce.

61 *Damyan*. The church of San Damiano (one of the physician brothers, Cosmas and Damian) was at this time about a half mile outside Assisi.

66 *sucst*. Dialectal variant of ME *sih(e)st*. The "h/c" sound derives regularly from the uncontracted forms of OE *seon* (from **siohan*); the *-h-* of the original stem was retained in the oblique forms until late ME. See also line 402, "such."

   struid. Aphetic form of "destroyed."

72 *toknynge*. The revelation of a future event in symbolic and prophetic terms.

   fale. A variant of ME *fele* (from OE *fæle*) meaning "good," "fitting," or "proper" (compare line 308, "unvele") especially in secular alliterative poetry. Notice the elaborate alliterative patterning of this line.

78–79   The account in *LM* II.1 is more extreme in its depiction of Francis' contempt for money: "In his dislike of money in any form, Francis threw it on the windowsill, and had no more interest in it than if it were dust" (Habig, p. 641).

84   In *LM* Francis hides in a cave, but the ditch certainly makes his misery and deranged appearance more credible.

91   *harlede.* A: *hardlede.* ME *harlen*, "to drag," is of unknown origin.

92   *caste.* See *MED casten*, 1(d), for other examples of the meaning "to throw at."

97   *non other good.* The sense is difficult (but compare *MED god:* 8[e], *have god of*, "receive benefit from"), and the line may be corrupt. L has *non oþur word*, i.e., Francis refused to tell him where the money was (line 83).

103   *godemon.* Used as a title of respect for a householder or husband (compare Nathaniel Hawthorne's *Young Goodman Brown*), but doubtless somewhat ironic here. L has *housebonde* (line 89).

109   *al then ende.* The text may be corrupt, since the usual phrase is *at then ende*, where *then* is the remnant of the OE dative singular (compare *æt þæm ende*) required by the preposition.

112   *up it take.* See *MED taken*, 31a(h), "to give (something) up." *Taken* often means "give" in legal contexts, as here. Compare *LM* I.2.4 (Habig, p. 642): "Now that he had recovered his money, he arranged to have Francis brought before the bishop of the diocese, where he should renounce all his claims and return everything he had." In the Middle Ages, wills and other legal aspects of inheritance and patrimony were not adjudicated by the secular courts but by the church courts, nominally under the bishop.

115–16   In *LM* I.2.4 (Habig, p. 643), Francis on taking off his clothes is found to be wearing a hair shirt, traditional undergarment of the ascetic.

117   *icluped.* The past participle of ME *clepen* (from OE *clipian, geclipod*), in which the stem vowel varies according to the dialect.

122–25   The poem drastically abridges *LM*'s account (II.4, Habig, p. 643) of the clothing of Francis. Bonaventure tells how the bishop embraced Francis with delight after his self-dedication to his new Father, and covered him with his own cloak while his

servants brought the young man an outfit belonging to one of the bishop's farm-
hands. *SEL* retains the farmhand in the *uplondisc mon* (line 123), but uses him to
suppress the bishop's role completely. From this point on, the poem begins to a-
bridge its much lengthier source more frequently and freely, omitting the substance
of the next two chapters of *LM* (II.5–6, Habig, pp. 643–44), in which Francis actually
enjoys being beaten up and left in a ditch by bandits, and then, after begging for a
night's food and shelter at a monastery, goes to Gubbio, gets a cloak from an old
friend and begins to live with and care for the lepers. He also heals a man with an
incurable lesion on his lips by kissing him on the mouth.

126   *underveng.* Compare OE *underfeng,* regular past tense of the verb *underfon.*

138–39 Bonaventure (*LM* II.7, Habig, p. 645) gives the impression that Francis carried out
the repairs on San Damiano, and the other churches mentioned later, virtually on his
own, whereas the poet, more realistically, makes clear that he simply worked as a
laborer for the skilled craftsmen who would be doing the actual renovation.

147   *in Desert.* The third church Francis rebuilt, in which he was to establish his order,
was in the woods just outside Assisi. It was dedicated to the Virgin Mary and called
locally La Portiuncula. The name given here *in Desert* may be due to the fact that
Bonaventure says it was *deserta,* deserted.

151–52 Compare *LM* II.8 (Habig, pp. 645–46): "This was the place where St. Francis
founded the Order of Friars Minor by divine inspiration."

154   The feast of Saint Matthias, February 23 (1208).

155   *me rat.* "One reads," especially as the lection from the Gospel at Mass. *Rat* is a con-
tracted form, from **radet(h),* third singular present tense of *rade(n),* a variant form
of *rede(n),* from OE *rædan.*

156–59 Matthew 10:9–10.

161   The episode is reminiscent of one from the opening of the Life of St. Antony, where
he hears the Gospel being read in church as a divine message to himself: see the
translation in Stouck, ed., *Medieval Saints: A Reader,* p. 58.

164   *ich wene.* This is not just a rhyming tag. The poet's "in my opinion" is a pointed
allusion to the problem of how to interpret the "ordre" or rule of St. Francis: strictly

and literally, or with various kinds of compromising "glosses," which were designed to alleviate the more severe aspects of Franciscan asceticism. On this controversy, between the "Spirituals" and "Conventuals," see the Introduction to this chapter.

169   *Bernard.* Bernard of Quintavalle, from a wealthy Assisi family, is not named as a scholar in *LM*, although in the *Legend of the Three Companions* he has the cognomen "Master," and is known to have been a magistrate of the city. For a detailed account of Bernard and Francis, see Moorman, *History*, pp. 10–11.

174   The sense here is of not picking a place in the book deliberately, but opening it at a random page, as though to let God's providence show Francis which pieces of scripture he needs for guidance. Just as his earlier experience of hearing a crucial piece of scripture echoed that of St. Antony (see explanatory note on line 161), so this act of opening a sacred book at random, looking for divine help, echoes that of St. Augustine, *Confessions* VIII.12 (trans. and intro. Pine-Coffin, p. 178), who in the same context alludes to the St. Antony episode. The Francis legend thus plays an elaborate game with this hagiographic tradition of textual inspiration, aural and written. On the early Christian and pre-Christian context of bibliomancy, see Gamble, *Books and Readers in the Early Church*, pp. 239–40.

175–76   Matthew 19:21. This was the first passage heard by St. Antony in the incident referred to above (see explanatory note on line 161).

177–78   Luke 9:3.

181–82   Matthew 16:24.

183–85   Notice the use of the same rhyme, on *-ounde*, in two successive couplets, and the clever "rich rhyme," *founde/ifounde*. It not only links the couplets, but also puns on the providential connection between the *finding* of the three scriptural passages and the *founding* of the order. The elaborate poetics of this quatrain testifies again to the poet's emphasis on the history and justification of the order as much as on the sanctity of Francis himself. The lines are suggested partly by Francis' short statement in *LM*: "This is our life and our rule" (*LM* III.3, Habig, p. 648), but also by Bonaventure's own statement somewhat later when he mentions the writing of the actual rule (*LM* III.8, Habig, pp. 650–51): "Francis wrote a short, simple, rule of life for himself and his companions. This was based on an unshakeable foundation, the following of the Gospel." But then Bonaventure is careful to say also that "to this he added a limited number of other prescriptions, such as seemed necessary for their life in common." This casual reference masks the deeply controversial nature of the rule and the complex history of its development. The rule referred to here is the so-called "Primitive Rule," approved by Pope Innocent III in 1209 (see below, lines 195ff.). No trace of it remains, but various attempts have been made to reconstruct it from the later First Rule (1221), Second Rule (1223), and Francis' other writings. See Moorman, *Sources*, pp. 51–54, and *History*, pp. 15–16.

188   Perhaps suggested by Francis' words in Bonaventure's *LM* III.3 (Habig, p. 648): "and everyone who comes to join our company must be prepared to do this." But the poet seems especially concerned with proper observance of the Franciscan rule. Compare also above, line 164.

191   The poet's designation of Brother Giles as a *good scoler* flatly contradicts all the Latin sources, in which it is implied that he was a simple and unlearned layman, although he earned a reputation for mystical raptures in later life (Moorman, *History*, pp. 257–58).

192   *other thre*. Silvester (a priest), Peter Catani, and another left unnamed by Bonaventure (*LM* III.4–5, Habig, pp. 648–49).

196   *SEL* omits the substance of *LM* III.6–7 (Habig, pp. 649–50), recounting one of Francis' mystical ecstasies, and the order's first preaching mission (eight friars including Francis going off in pairs in opposite directions). It was after this, when the order comprised a total of twelve, that Bonaventure says Francis composed his rule (1209), and it was this written rule that he took to Rome to be approved by the pope.

        confermy. The *-i/y* infinitive suffix, a weakened form of earlier *-in*, is common in early ME Southwestern texts in verbs of the OE Weak Class II (OE *-ian*), into which class also most loanwords from ON and OF (as here) were attracted. Other, comparable verbs from OF are "granti" (line 212), "prevy" (line 213), etc. One would expect the poet's repeated use of *confermi* to have been prompted by a similar verb in the Latin of *LM*, but Bonaventura uses the verb *confirmare* only once in his account of Francis' trip to Rome, during John of St. Paul's speech reproving the cardinals for doubting the validity of Francis' mission (*cum petat confirmari sibi formam evangelicae vitae*, "because he is only asking us to approve a form of Gospel life"; *LM* III.9, Habig, p. 652), but the Latin verb that is invariably the equivalent of the ME poet's *confermi* is *approbari* (e.g., *LM* III.8: *approbari quae scripserat*; *LM* III.9: *regulam approbari*).

198 *that he iconfermed nere.* The referent of the pronoun *he* is *ordre.* The A scribe's use of the masculine form (which is correct, since the Latin *ordo* and its French derivative are masculine) contrasts with L's *heo* (line 181). The A scribe switches to the feminine pronoun when referring to the "reule." See below, line 215 and explanatory note.

203 *aunter him dude.* See *MED aventure* 3(e).

207–10 In contrast to his earlier misinterpretations of his visionary revelations, Francis is shown here to have become more adept at spiritual understanding: he reads the dream figuratively rather than literally.

215 *heo was clene and good.* The poet refers to the rule as feminine (*heo* = she), and virginal (*clene and good*), in a rare "gendered" usage of grammatical gender (Latin *regula* is feminine, as was *riwle* in early ME). According to Bonaventure, however, it is not the rule but Francis' "wonderful purity of heart" and religious zeal that impress Innocent (*LM* III.9, Habig, p. 652).

218–20 Bonaventure is more specific: "some of the cardinals . . . thought that the rule was too difficult for any human being" (*LM* III.9, Habig, p. 652).

225–28 The poet typically reduces a complex episode to focus simply on the rule of the Franciscan order. He omits completely Francis' elaborate allegory of the marriage of Christ the King and the beauteous spirit of Poverty, "a story which [Francis] had learned from God," and in asserting that the pope's vision was about granting Francis' rule, he sacrifices one of the most famous episodes in the legend: see *LM* III.10 (Habig, pp. 652–53), and Giotto's fresco in the nave of the upper church of the Basilica of Saint Francis, Assisi, where Innocent is shown on the right, asleep in bed (wearing his papal tiara!), while opposite him on the left Francis holds up the falling wall of the Lateran basilica on his right shoulder. See the color reproduction on the front cover of Morello and Kanter, eds., *The Treasury of Saint Francis of Assisi.* Notice how in Bonaventure's scheme of things the pope's vision of Francis holding up the Church balances the earlier one of Francis bending down the papal tree. It is uncertain what significance we should attach to the near suppression of the Lateran episode here in *SEL*'s Life of Francis, while its blatant counterpart in *LA*'s Life of Dominic is retained in detail in the *SEL* version of the latter, lines 84–95 (*ESEL*, ed. Horstmann, p. 280), where Pope Innocent dreams of Dominic rushing to prop up the tottering edifice of the Lateran.

228   *confermede.* Pope Innocent's initial approval of Francis' order was oral and not yet legally binding. Five years later, at the Fourth Lateran Council in 1215, at Francis' urging, the pope formally announced that the Franciscans, like the new Dominicans, were to be considered one of the officially constituted orders of the Church. Moorman, *History*, pp. 18–19, 29–30.

229–42   This episode, illustrating what commitment to the order and to poverty means for the Friars, is partly invented by the poet. In *LM* at this point, Francis decides they should travel from Rome towards Spoleto, "where he determined to preach Christ's Gospel and live according to it" but the episode of the brothers' hunger and the mysterious roadside provider occurs before they reach Spoleto, and there is no mention of preaching, hostile reactions from the people, Anti-Christ, or possible defections (*LM* IV.1; Habig, pp. 653–54). Bonaventure does say that the apparently miraculous provision of food encourages the brothers "never to go back on the promise which they had made to Holy Poverty," however much they might suffer, whereas the ME poet stresses their renewed fidelity to the order as well as to poverty.

238   *war he bicom ne wudeward he drough.* Bonaventure says the friars did not know "whence he came or where he went" (*LM* IV.1, Habig, p. 654), and our footnote gloss takes the ME as a literal rendering of this, but *war he bicom* could also mean "what became of him," and the two clauses could be simply alternative expressions of the same idea.

241–42   *And bihete God . . . poverte vorgo.* The scansion of 242 seems particularly awkward. 242a appears "light" (with only three strong beats at best), and 242b appears "heavy," with four strong beats, if *poverte* is scanned with stress on the first and third syllables. Moving the caesura in 242 so that it follows *mighte* instead of *nolde* would produce the standard four beats in 242a (*In the ORDre hi NOLde BI hor MIGHTe*) and 242b might then be scanned: *POVerTE vorGO.* Compare L (lines 224–25): *And bihieten god þat huy nolden neuere : for miseise ne for wo / In þe ordre bi heore miȝhte : pouerte furgo.* But the A scribe elsewhere (e.g., lines 134, 288) seems to favor the alternative ME pronunciation of *poverte* (often spelled *povert*), with one strong stress on the second syllable, and this may have prompted his particular version of this line. It is unclear what the original version of 241–42 would have been, since neither L's nor A's version is satisfactory.

251   *Seyn Marie in Desert.* I.e., Saint Mary in Portiunculla. See above, line 147.

264   *his.* Except here, where *his* may be either masculine or neuter, the poet uses the feminine pronoun *heo* to refer to the ass throughout this passage.

263–72   This rather repetitious passage is expanded from one sentence in *LM* V.6 (Habig, p. 666): "He used to call his body 'Brother Ass,' as if it were fit for nothing more than hard labor and frequent ill-treatment with a whip, while having only the poorest type of food to live on."

273–86   Again, the ME poet expands at length on a topic that is mentioned only briefly in *LM* V.6 (Habig, pp. 666–67): "If he saw that a friar was given to standing about idle, waiting to be fed by the labor of others, he called him 'Brother Fly,' because he detracted from the good done by others and did no good to himself." In Thomas of Celanos' *Second Life*, chapter CXXI, there is a diatribe against idle friars, which shares some general ideas with the *SEL*-poet (e.g., "working more with their jaws than with their hands . . . Though they do nothing, they consider themselves always occupied. They know the hours of the meals, and if hunger takes hold of them, they complain that the sun has gone to sleep," Habig, p. 492), but the poet's bitter picture of the habits of flies themselves (lines 275–79) seems his own.

293–94   Francis' words here closely follow those in *LM* VI.1, Habig, p. 671: "God bless you my son. What you say is true. That is the kind of thing the son of Peter Bernardone should have to listen to." But Francis (pointedly invoking his mundane identity as the son of a merchant) says this to one of the friars, whom he has ordered to abuse him verbally, to offset the people's praise. The *SEL*-poet's version, in which the people abuse Francis spontaneously, is less artificial, but less faithful to hagiographic tradition: compare the fifth-century *Sayings of the Father* (*Verba Seniorum*), where similar behavior is attributed to Abbot Macarius the Great (Ward, *Sayings of the Desert Fathers*, p. 134).

299   These boisterously satirical lines (aimed at friars who ride rather than walk?), comprising a mono-rhyme quatrain, are apparently the interpolation of the A reviser, although according to Görlach (*Textual Tradition*, p. 194) only two MSS besides A contain the whole quatrain (British Library MSS Cotton Julius A.ix and Egerton 1993; BL Stowe 949 has the first two lines of the quatrain).

303–16   For the source of this episode, see *LM* VII.5, Habig, pp. 682–83. Most of the substance of Bonaventure's chapters V and VI are omitted. Note the caustic interpolation of the A reviser that follows (lines 317–18).

305   *tok no more gome.* "Paid no more heed": the expression is parallel to "nom never
        yeme" (line 259), but using words of Scandinavian origin (ON *taka, gaumr*). The
        epithet *gawmless*, meaning "heedless," "stupid," survives in the Lancashire dialect
        today.

319–36 For Bonaventure's version of this episode, see *LM* VIII.6, Habig, pp. 692–93. The
        poet follows *LM* in prefacing the story of the killer sow with allusions to the lamb's
        New Testament symbolism (see explanatory note on line 321), but Bonaventure
        places the story in the larger context of his virtue of compassion, "which led him to
        devote himself humbly to his neighbor and enabled him to return to the state of
        primeval innocence by restoring man's harmony with the whole of creation" (*LM*
        VIII.1, Habig, p. 688). The *SEL*-poet's description of the sow's death is much more
        graphic than in Bonaventure: "the vicious sow fell sick and after suffering for three
        days it eventually expiated its crime by death. The carcass was thrown into the
        monastery moat where it lay for a long time and became as hard as a board, so that
        even the hungriest animal refused to eat it" (*LM* VIII.6, Habig, p. 693).

321   Compare John 1:29: "The next day, John [the Baptist] saw Jesus coming to him; and he
        saith: 'Behold the Lamb of God. Behold him who taketh away the sin of the world.'"

328   *dest.* The form is present tense, as in *doest.* L has *dudest* (line 305).

342   *eche tyde.* In the early days of the Franciscan order, the brothers, who were laymen,
        had no service books (see above, lines 246–50) or liturgical training, and their simple
        mode of divine worship was improvised by Francis himself. In time, however, as
        individual communities of friars came to have the use of churches and more of their
        members had clerical training, they would devote at least part of their daily routine
        to singing the canonical hours, or services of the Divine Office, at set times of the
        day, like monks in monasteries and canons in secular minsters. The OE word *tid* was
        regularly used for "hour" in this and other senses. The Englishman Haymo of Faver-
        sham, who rose to be Minister General of the whole order, drew up a breviary for the
        use of the Franciscans that was eventually adopted as the official service book of the
        Roman Church. See Moorman, *History*, p. 107.

347   *sacred.* The sheep attended mass as well as the Hours of the Daily Office. It is ironic
        that the *SEL*-poet should allude to one of Francis' intensest religious devotions, to
        the Eucharist, only in this droll context. On the especially visual quality of Francis'

Eucharistic zeal, see Bynum, *Holy Feast and Holy Fast*, p. 99. See also *LM* IX.2, Habig, p. 699.

349   *Godes flesc*. I.e., at the consecration of the Host. L has *sacringe* (line 326).

350   *on*. The pronoun form of *a, an*, here used pleonastically (see *OED one*, B.VI.22).

      folde. Several other MSS, including L (line 327), have *bolde* ("building"), but *folde* ("sheepfold") makes for an amusing play on the literal and figurative meanings of the sheep/shepherd imagery in ecclesiastical contexts (compare Chaucer's Parson, "who kepte well his folde" (*CT* I[A]512), and Milton's *Lycidas* (line 115). This sheep story, with its moral (line 349), is a modified version of *LM* VIII.7 (Habig, pp. 693–94).

356   *The yut*. From OE *þa giet* ("when yet/while").

357   *Beu frere*. Francis is addressing his companion, another friar. This episode, which anticipates the more famous one in which Francis actually preaches to the birds (below, lines 371–90), is based on *LM* VIII.9.

360   *tyden*. Itinerant clergy, whether monks or friars, were supposed to read or recite the canonical *horae* at the appropriate times of day and night even when they were not in church, wherever they happened to be (whereas church service books were often very large, many itinerant clerics had portable, compact breviaries). Compare the monk, Daun John, in Chaucer's Shipman's Tale, who has just finished reciting his early morning "thynges . . . curteisly" in the merchant's garden when the wife encounters him (*CT* VII[B²]91).

364   *ivere*. From OE *gefera*, "comrade," "companion," "wife." L has simply *fere* (line 341). Compare Chaucer's *Parlement of Fowles*, lines 410 and 416.

368   *dorre*. This verb in ME frequently means "need" rather than "dare," through confusion in ME of the OE verbs *þurfan*, "need," and *durran*, "dare." Another instance is at line 383. See also St. Jerome and the Lion (III[b], above), explanatory note on "thurft," line 23.

371–90   The episode that begins here is the only one selected from Bonaventure's chapter on Francis' powers as a preacher and healer (*LM* XII), which begins with the crisis of confidence that preceded one of his preaching missions. Bonaventure tells in detail (*LM* XII.1, Habig, pp. 720–22) how Francis was torn between, on the one hand, the appeal of the contemplative's angelic life of solitary prayer and, on the other hand, the missionary imperative to follow Christ's own model as a preacher and teacher in the world. Francis could not resolve this dilemma himself, but asked for spiritual guidance from (ironically) two contemplatives, Silvester and Clare, who sent word he should devote himself to preaching.

The present episode, the saint's sermon to the birds, is based closely on *LM* XII.3 (Habig, pp. 722–23), which renders the sermon proper as follows: "My brothers, you have a great obligation to praise your Creator. He clothed you with feathers and gave you wings to fly, appointing the clear air as your home, and he looks after you without any effort on your part." The *SEL*-poet's somewhat more elaborate version of this speech (lines 377–84) may be intended as a veiled admonition to the nobility to be thankful to God for their life of ease and privilege. His expansion may have been suggested by the more elaborate version in Thomas of Celano's First Life, I.21 (Habig, p. 278), especially this sentence: "God made you noble among his creatures."

391–93   Bonaventure explains that this intense devotion to Christ's Passion was prompted by another session of bibliomancy, in which Francis asked a companion to open the Gospels three times in succession. Each time the book opened, it did so at the Passion narrative (*LM* XIII.2, Habig, pp. 729–30), indicating to Francis that henceforth until his death he was to imitate Christ's suffering and death just as he has so far imitated his life as a traveling preacher and healer. But the ME poet bypasses the bibliomantic episode and explains Francis' motivation for his La Verna retreat in terms of the familiar late medieval popular devotion to the wounds of Christ (see explanatory note on line 422, below), but using language that notably avoids the imagery of burning love and ecstatic longing that is characteristic of late medieval mysticism in general and of Bonaventure's narrative in particular.

394   *Holi Rode tid . . . Mielmasse.* The Feast of the Exaltation of the Holy Cross falls on September 14, that of St. Michael Archangel on September 29. Referring to feasts in this way to indicate the date of an event was as common in the Middle Ages as giving the month and numerical day (see in III, above, the opening lines of Simon Winter's prologue to his *Life of Saint Jerome*). According to Bonaventure, Francis

had gone up on to Mount La Verna for a forty-day fast in honor of Saint Michael "as was his custom" (*LM* XIII.1, Habig, 729). Bonaventure explains elsewhere (*LM* IX.3, Habig, p. 699) that Francis would fast in solitude for certain forty-day periods during the year, including the period from the Feast of Mary's Assumption (August 15) to that of Saint Michael (September 29). The *SEL*-poet indicates his awareness of this again later, line 426, where he says the vision of the Seraph occurred "aboute an month" after Francis began his fast on the mountain. The vision and the subsequent experience of the Stigmata are said to have occurred on or about Holy Cross Day (*LM* XIII.3, Habig, p. 730). The year was 1224.

395   *Averne.* Bonaventure and Celano call the mountain *Alverna*, so oral tradition among the English Franciscans may explain the ME pronunciation. Line 395a has eight syllables (*Upe* has two) but does not scan properly unless equal stress is placed on the first and second syllables of *Averne*.

398–406   Bonaventure seems to depict a 6-winged seraph holding a cross on which is the crucified figure: "the image of a Man crucified in the midst of the wings, with his hands and feet stretched out and nailed to a cross. Two of the wings were raised above his head and two were stretched out in flight, while two shielded his body" (*LM* XIII.3, Habig, p. 730). But the ME poet does not visualize an actual cross. Rather he pictures the winged being himself with his arms and feet stretched out and pierced "as if they were on the cross" (line 403). Certainly one of the earliest representations of the vision, painted in 1235, less than ten years after the saint's death by one Bonaventure Berlingheri (Church of San Francesco, Pescia), corresponds to the poet's account more than to that in *LM*, showing only the head, and the wounded hands and feet, peeping out from among the elaborately arranged wings (see Morello and Kanter, eds., *Treasury of Saint Francis*, pp. 30, 56). However, in the manuscript drawing by the contemporary English Benedictine artist and writer, Matthew Paris, the winged seraph is nailed to a large cross behind the wings (A. G. Little, ed., *Franciscan History and Legend*, Ch. IV, Pl. 8b). Bonaventure gives a somewhat clearer picture of the seraph in his *Legenda minor* VI.1 (Habig, p. 821), where he states that it was "the seraph that was nailed to the cross although he had wings."

402   *As me such ofte in chirch ipeynt.* The word *such*, "sees," may be a contraction, or simply a scribal misspelling, of the Southwestern dialect *sucth* or *suh(e)th* (compare Midland *sihth*, later *seeth*), the third-person singular of *see(n)*. Compare the second-

person singular form above, lines 183, 185. Most of the Saint Francis paintings that the poet says were plentiful in English churches have not survived. See Little, *Franciscan History and Legend*, pp. 7–11. On the popularity of the scene in medieval art in general, see Frugoni, *Francesco e l'invenzione delle stimmate*.

406   The wording of this verse seems suggested by Bonaventure's phrasing: "[Francis] was overjoyed at the way Christ regarded him so graciously under the appearance of a Seraph" (*LM* XIII.3, Habig, p. 730), but the poet suppresses the metaphysical subtleties that follow. Bonaventure goes on to attribute to Francis a typically Scholastic reservation, that "the agony of Christ's passion was not in keeping with the state of a seraphic spirit which is immortal," i.e., an angel is incapable by nature of experiencing the wounds of crucifixion. But, presumably since the Seraph is especially associated with the fire of divine love, the vision is to be taken as an elaborate sign to Francis that "he would resemble Christ crucified perfectly not by physical martyrdom, but by the fervor of his spirit" (*LM* XIII.3, Habig, p. 731).

411–20   On the late medieval devotion to the wounds of Christ, see below, note on 422. Bonaventure explains that Francis' total love for Jesus involved a desire to imitate him completely, to the point of dying like him as a martyr for the faith: "he longed to offer himself as a living victim to God by the sword of martyrdom; in this way he would repay Christ for his love in dying for us." (*LM* IX.5; Habig, p. 701) More than once Francis actually set out on missionary journeys to Moslem countries, to preach the gospel and, he hoped, suffer martyrdom, but his expectations were frustrated (*LM* IX 5–9; Habig, pp. 701–05). Bonaventure explains that the vision on La Verna, and the Stigmata themselves, were God's way of letting Francis "resemble Christ perfectly not by physical martyrdom, but by the fervor of his spirit" (*LM* XIII.3, Habig, p. 731). See Moorman, *History*, p. 49.

    The ME poet has done his best to convey the gist of Bonaventure's account of the bizarre and much discussed phenomenon of the Stigmata of Saint Francis, differing mainly with respect to the nail-points: "There and then the marks of nails began to appear in his hands and feet, just as he had seen them in his vision of the Man nailed to the Cross. His hands and feet appeared pierced through the center with nails, the heads of which were in the palms of his hands and on the instep of each foot, while the points stuck out on the opposite side. The heads were black and round, but the points were long and bent back, as if they had been struck with a hammer; they rose above the surrounding flesh and stood out from it" (*LM* XIII.3, Habig, p. 731). The earlier biographer, Thomas of Celano, in his First Life (II.3, Habig, p. 309), does not claim that there were actual nails in Francis' hands and feet, but rather that "some small pieces of flesh took on the appearance of the ends of the nails, bent and driven back and rising above the rest of the flesh."

422   *ensample.* Cited by *MED* (*ensample* 2[b]) as meaning "symbol, sign, token," the word here may be used more in the sense of the Latin word *exemplum*, "drawing, picture, sketch." Compare L, where *ansample* is coupled with *schewingue*, vision, manifestation (line 401: *For bote ase a schewinge and Ansaumple : in seint Fraunceyse huy nere*). Bonaventure explains that when he came off the mountain Francis "bore a representation of Christ crucified which was not the work of an artist in wood or stone" (*ferens Crucifixi effigiem, non in tabulis lapideis vel ligneis manu figuratam artificis*) but had been reproduced (*descriptam*) in the members of his body by the hand of the living God" (*LM* XIII.5, Habig, p. 732; compare Exodus 31:18). Francis' stigmata are not a mere image of Christ's wounds, such as a human artist could depict, but a fresh realization of them by God himself, whose handiwork is fleshly reality. Hence the *SEL*-poet's remark that through Francis' wounds people knew what Jesus' wounds were really like. This urge to grasp, and to various degrees experience, the physical reality of the Passion is part of what Duffy (*The Stripping of the Altars*, p. 235) terms "the central devotional activity of all seriously minded Christians" in the later Middle Ages: namely, the devotion to the Passion, and particularly the Five Wounds of Christ, which the poet invokes in lines 422–23. Compare *Sir Gawain and the Green Knight*, lines 642–43: "And alle his afyaunce vpon folde watz in þe fyue woundez / Þat Cryst kaȝt on þe croys, as þe Crede tellez" (p. 232 — "all his faith upon earth was in the five wounds / that Christ received on the cross, as the Creed proclaims"). This kind of devotion was common among clerics in the age of Saints Anselm of Canterbury and Bernard of Clairvaux, but gathered popular impetus through the teachings of the Franciscans and others in the thirteenth and fourteenth centuries. See Duffy, pp. 234–48.

429   Bonaventure does not link Francis to Moses, perhaps because the parallels (each spending forty days on a mountain, having a vision of God and then coming down visibly marked by the experience) would have been so obvious to clerical readers. Since Francis has imitated Christ so faithfully, he inevitably begins to participate in the typology of the Christ figure. Medieval Christianity regarded Moses, giver of the

Old Law, in various ways as a *figura* or *type* of Christ, giver of the New Law. See, e.g., Daniélou, *The Bible and the Liturgy*, pp. 93–95.

434–38   The continual bleeding and staining of Francis' garments, and his anxiety about keeping such things a secret, especially the side-wound, are detailed by Bonaventure in *LM* XIII.3–4 and XIII.8; Habig, pp. 731–32 and 734–35.

439–50   This episode is the first of three miracles (*LM* XIII.6–7) that occurred in succession after the Stigmata episodes. According to Bonaventure they demonstrate that the Stigmata were God's work, but it is ironic that such a sublime event should be validated by such mundane miracles as these, which provide relief from, respectively, an epidemic among cattle, hail stones damaging crops, and the cold of winter that was preventing a poor man from getting a good night's sleep. For the hagiographical topos of the healing power of water that has come into contact with a saint or his or her relics, see Loomis, *White Magic*, pp. 104, 212–13 (for the references).

451   *Frere Menor in the ordre.* Bonaventure says, as he begins the story of Francis' final days, that the saint's death occurred two years after he received the Stigmata, and twenty years "after the beginning of his religious life," which the poet typically renders here in terms of the Franciscan order (*LM* XIV 3, Habig, p. 738). The *SEL*-poet's "and almost thre wuke" (line 452) is deduced from the calendar date of Francis' death which Bonaventura gives somewhat later as October 3, 1226 (*LM* XV.6, Habig, p. 744), roughly three weeks after Holy Cross Day, September 14, on which Francis received the stigmata.

455–58   These lines are based on a specific incident in Bonaventure (*LM* XIV.2, Habig, p. 738) in which Francis, when a well-meaning but simpleminded friar tells him to ask God "to be easier on you," rebukes the friar for daring to find fault with God. He then hurls his wasted body on the floor. Kissing the earth, he thanks God not for all the good things, as in the *SEL* version, but for all the pain, begging that it might be a hundred times worse!

460   *our Levedi chirche.* St. Mary in Portiuncula. See above, lines 147, 251.

464   The emphasis on the body's nakedness in this passage is doubtless intended to recall Job 1:21, "Naked came I out of my mother's womb, and naked shall I return thither."

300

In the context of Francis' own life, the nakedness motif recalls certain key moments in his development, especially his formal abjuration of his earthly father (above, lines 114–21). The *SEL*-poet has bypassed at this point the imagery of martyrdom (as a wrestling contest between naked athletes) evoked by Bonaventure: "so that with all the fervor of his spirit he might struggle naked with his naked enemy in that last hour which is given him to vent his wrath" (*LM* XIV.3, Habig, pp. 738–39). See, however, line 467, where this imagery is suggested. Bonaventure's account of Francis' death is also complicated by various other themes, including the saint's need to feel himself at the end completely devoid of earthly possessions, as "Christ's beggar" who had "kept his faith with Lady Poverty," and who also was imitating Christ who "hung on the cross, poor and naked and in great pain."

465   *his righte.* I.e., it is only right that an earthly thing (his body) should come to its end on the bare earth. This comment is the poet's contribution. The motif of earth returning to earth recalls the familiar prayer recited at the grave immediately after the burial of the dead: *cinis cinerem . . . terra . . . terram et pulvis convertitur in pulverem* (from the *Sarum Ordinal*, ed. Maskell, in *Monumenta Ritualia Ecclesiae Anglicanae*, 1.153); compare the modern version in the *Book of Common Prayer*: "earth to earth, ashes to ashes, dust to dust."

466   See *LM* XIV.5, Habig, p. 740, for the substance of Francis' last sermon to his friars.

468–70   *Voce mea.* Three psalms in the Latin Vulgate include the verse *Voce mea ad dominum clamavi* ("I cried to the Lord with my voice"): 3:5, 76:2, and 141:1. In *LM* XIV.5 it is clear that the psalm Francis sang is 141, because the first and last verses (1 and 8) are also quoted in full (although Habig's translation, p. 740, is misleadingly free). The *SEL*-poet's information (line 468) that this psalm is sung at *evesong* (Vespers) is not in *LM*, and must reflect the poet's own familiarity with the Office. In a thirteenth-century English monastic breviary, Psalm 141 is assigned for singing at Vespers on the Friday after the Octave of Epiphany, as well as at Second Vespers on Holy Thursday (see *Monastic Breviary of Hyde Abbey, Winchester*, ed. Tolhurst, 1.54 and 96; see also Van Dijk, ed., *The Sources of the Roman Liturgy*, 2.59 and 85).

     Both Bonaventure and *SEL* lack the dramatic detail supplied by Thomas of Celano in his Second Life of Francis (chapter CLXIII) that after completing the psalm Francis "exhorted all creatures to praise God . . . he exhorted death itself . . . to give praise, and going joyfully to meet it, he invited it to make its lodging with him. 'Welcome,' he said, 'my sister death'" (Habig, p. 536).

474 *aliche*. From OE *on lice*, "in the body." *Lich* in ME often denotes the body after death. See the *OED* under *lich-gate* and *lyke-wake*.

475–82 This account of the larks episode follows closely *LM* XIV.6, Habig, p. 741, where, however, it is the last of four miraculous signs that accompany Francis' death. The change in narrative order allows the poet to end with the story of Friar Augustine. See next explanatory note.

483–94 The *SEL*-poet ends his life of Francis with the story of Friar Augustine, who was the provincial minister of the Franciscans in Terra di Lavoro (a region near Naples, quite a distance south of Assisi), which the poet renders literally as "land of labor." This type of story, in which someone not present at a saint's death simultaneously witnesses his soul's heavenward flight, is frequent in hagiographic narrative (compare the ending of The Life of St. Benedict in V, above), but the witness' testimony is here particularly forceful because he himself is on his deathbed. The *SEL*-poet may have chosen to put this episode last because the two friars' journey to heaven (line 494) merges neatly with the poet's usual closing prayer (line 496) that he and his readers may take the same journey.

490 *hem wondred*. The verb is here used impersonally.

491 *Bote*. For another instance of this idiomatic use of *but* as an adverb introducing a reply to a question, see above, line 29.

VII

Textual Notes to the Life of St. Francis in the South English Legendary *(c. 1270–80)*

Abbreviations: see Explanatory Notes.

2   *to trewenesse drough*. Compare L (line 2): *to eche treuwenesse drovȝ*. Only *drou* is legible in A, the rest being concealed by tight stitching at the inner margin of the leaf.

13   *swythe*. A: *suyþe*.

15   *knyghtes*. A: *knyȝte*.

84   *he*. A has *me* which could be interpreted "me(n)" but L's reading makes better sense in the context.

88   *isei*. A: *was isei*.

91   *harlede*. A: *hardlede*

101   *leng*. The historically correct form (also *lenge*) of the comparative of the adverb *longe* (OE *lange*). In A a different, probably later, scribal hand has added an *-er* suffix to *leng*, apparently confusing it with the adjective, where the *-er* comparative suffix was historically correct. Compare L (line 87): *he ne bi-lefte no leng þer*.

111   *worldes*. A: *wordles.*

114   *erthliche*. L (line 100): *eorþelich*; A: *erliche.*

122   *worldliche*. A: *wordlich.*

       nadde. The reading in L (line 108) is *ne bod he nevereft non*, "never asked from anyone," but that of A makes better sense.

123   *uplondisc*. L (line 109): *vplondischse*. A: *vplindist.*

127   *therwith*. Altered in A from *ther wis*.

130   *A beggare bicom*. Compare L (line 116): *A beggar he cam.*

134   *prute*. A: *prte*, with superscript *u* added later.

153   *bygynyng*. A: *bygyng.*

163   *staf*. A: *staft.*

165   *bond*. A: *bon.*

171   *worlde*. A: *wordle.*

174   *unmundeliche*. A: *myldeliche*. The A reading, "mildly" (also found in BL MS Cotton Julius D.ix), makes no sense in the context. Although our emendation may be drastic, it seems warranted here. Collation of other manuscripts indicates that the reading

myldeliche is an attempt to find a suitable way out of a puzzle caused by corrupt textual transmission of an unfamiliar or illegible word. Compare also the unsatisfactory readings of British Library MS Egerton 2891: *in vullinge*; Lambeth Palace MS 223: *grepinge* (i.e., "gripping"); the Vernon manuscript (Bodleian Library MS Eng. Poet. a.1 [*SC* 3938–42]): *mundly*; BL MS Stowe 949: *mundlich*. The readings of L, *on-mundliche* (line 159) and *vn-Mundlingue* (lines 162, 164), literally "unmindly," "unminding," i.e., "unintentionally," "unawares," most prob-ably preserve the original reading (the word is found also in other Southwestern texts, such as *Ancrene Wisse* and *Sawles Warde*: see *MED unmindeliche*).

185 *thou sucst, that we habbeth.* A: *he made is ordre : that hi.* Since Francis is still speaking, A's pronouns in the third person are obviously inappropriate. Scribal eye-skip between this line and line 187, each of which begins with the phrase "Up this thre Godspell(es)," has caused the confusion whereby a portion of line 187 has been copied into 185, replacing the original reading. We have supplied this from L (line 170), but it is preserved also in several others from different manuscript groups. The corruption seems to have affected the textual tradition on which both A and BL Cotton Julius D.ix depend, rather than being the fault of the A scribe alone, since the Julius scribe has tried to correct the problem by rewriting the line as follows: *op this þre gospells þat þu hast ferst ifounde* (contradicting Görlach's opinion, *Textual Tradition*, p. 87, that Julius shows no evidence of "conjectural emendation").

206 *tough.* A: *tou.*

228 *gef.* L (line 211): *bi-hiet* ("promised").

243–44 These two lines occur in reversed order in L and with slightly different wording: *Biside þe toun of Asise : feor fram eche strete / huy wenden alle to one stude : þat was al fur-lete* (lines 226–27). Most of the more recent manuscripts follow A's order of lines, but follow L in the stronger wording of the last phrase: e.g., BL Egerton 2891 (fol. 149v): *So þat hi wende to astude : þat was al for lete / Biside þe toun of assise : fer fram eche strete.*

254–56 We have emended some of the personal pronouns in these lines from plural to singular form. In A it is the disciples as well as Francis who were always staring upwards: *Men wende, tho hi seie **hem** verst : that of another world **hi** were, Vor **hi** caped evere upard.* But the plural forms (bold) are plainly wrong, since the public's violent re-sponse is directed at Francis alone in the immediate sequel (see lines 256–60), and both *LM* and L refer only to Francis here also: "To those who saw him he seemed like a man from another world as, with his gaze fixed on heaven where his heart always dwelt, he tried to lift their thoughts on high"(*LM* IV.5, Habig, pp. 656–57). Compare L, lines 237–38: *Men wenden, þo huy seiʒe him furst : þat of an oþur worlde he were / For he capede euere upward*, etc.

278   *Of travail ne kepth heo noght.* This half-line may be short a foot. Compare L (line 261): *Of trauail ne wo ne kep[t]hþ heo nouȝt.*

288   *reprevede.* A: *represede.* The word *repress* is not cited in *OED* until a century later than this, and not in this sense. L (line 271) has *opbraid,* "upbraided."

289–90 A shares with BL MS Cotton Julius D.ix what seems to be a local revision of this couplet. Compare L's more colorful version (similar in Lambeth Palace MS 223 and the Vernon manuscript): *ȝwane Men cleopeden him hoxtare : opur cheorl opur cheorles sone — For port-Men beoth ofte boistouse : and hoxtares [hokerliche?] bi wone* (lines 272–73, "When they called him huckster or churl or churl's son — for townsmen are often coarse tongued and [scornful] as a rule").

292   *so doth.* A: *soþ doþ.* The thorn in *soþ* is marked for deletion. Compare L (line 275): *so dothþ.*

295   *And wen me preisede.* A: *And me preisede.* Compare L (line 278): *And ȝwane men preiseden.*

313   *grislokes.* L (line 292): *fouleste.*

380   *te.* L (line 357) has *seo,* "see" but the ME verb *te(en),* from OE *teon,* is well attested in the sense of "go, travel," which makes better sense here than "see."

387–88 Between these lines A (along with the closely affiliated BL MS Cotton Julius A.ix, and one other manuscript) omits two lines that are well attested in other manuscripts, including L (lines 365–66):

> *And bi-teiȝte heom ihesu crist : and blessede heom ech-on;*
> *he pleide with heom murie I-nouȝ : ase he among heom gan gon*

The omission of the couplet from the common exemplar of A and its affiliates was doubtless caused by eye-skip, since the first line of the missing couplet ends, like A's line 388, with the word *on.*

408   *world.* A: *wordl.*

413   *his owe.* A: *is day owe* (*day* marked for deletion).

416   *wounden.* A: *wouden.*

443   *Godes sonde.* A: *sonde.* We emend here on the basis of several other manuscripts, including L (line 422) and BL MS Stowe 949.

448   *priveté.* The A reviser has substituted this French loanword for the original poet's older native word *huydeles* (from OE *hydels,* hiding-place); see L, line 427.

453   *feblede.* A: *feble.* Compare L (line 432b): *feblischede ful swiþe faste.*

464   *Hi lete.* A: *lete.* The emendation is adapted from L (line 443), *huy leten.*

VIII

The Life of St. Julian Hospitaller in the Scottish Legendary *(c. 1400)*

Introduction

The Legend

The earliest known allusions to Julian date to the late twelfth century and identify him simply as the patron of hospitality: travelers on a journey and far from home pray to him for a comfortable lodging. The expanded legend, further identifying Julian as a parricide, appears to have developed in France during the thirteenth century.[1] The narrative turns on Julian's murder of his own parents, whom he mistakenly takes to be his wife in the arms of a lover. Like Oedipus, Julian in his youth hears this act prophesied and flees his homeland, but, like Oedipus also, his fate catches up with him. Settling in a distant region he prospers and marries, but his parents, wandering the world in search of him, happen by chance on Julian's castle and are welcomed by the wife in his absence. Knowing her husband would wish her to treat the couple with all due honor, she gives them her own bed, and from there events follow their predictably doomed course. As an act of lifelong penance Julian establishes a hospice near a dangerous river-crossing and helps travelers to cross safely. After many years Julian offers warmth and shelter to a leper who, it transpires, is an angelic messenger come to report on God's behalf that Julian's penance has been accepted.

In its most general form, the legend of Julian Hospitaller has many analogues. Similar motifs can be found in myths and legends of diverse origin: the parallel with Oedipus has already been noted; the *Arabian Nights* tells of a father's failed attempt to protect his son from a prophesied death; and Perrault's *Sleeping Beauty* hinges on a similarly fruitless parental effort, though with less fatal consequences. The river crossing, with a passenger who proves to be more than human, occurs in the legend of St. Christopher, where the child transported by the saint grows heavier and heavier, ultimately revealing himself as Christ. No other narrative, however, combines these motifs in the distinctive form in which they are found in the Julian legend, and

---

[1] The most recent discussion of the origins and development of the legend is in Bart and Cook, *The Legendary Sources of Flaubert's Saint Julian, passim.* Also useful is Swan, *The Old French Prose Legend of Saint Julian the Hospitaller*, pp. 1–19. For a comprehensive study of every aspect of the legend's development, de Gaiffier, "La légende de S. Julien l'Hospitalier," is still invaluable.

perhaps the most important significance of the parallels adduced is to suggest their ancient and widespread popularity and, as a consequence, the likelihood that the origin of the Julian legend is more likely to be located in folktale than in history.[2]

The power and popularity of the legend are witnessed, inter alia, by the two great pictorial representations in the stained glass windows of the cathedrals at Chartres and Rouen, executed in the middle of the thirteenth century. The nineteenth-century novelist Gustave Flaubert, who saw the Rouen window, was inspired by the narrative embedded in its thirty panels to create his own fictional representation of Saint Julian, which he published in 1877 in the volume *Trois Contes*.[3] The iconographic tradition, represented in paintings, miniatures, sculpture, and tapestry, as well as in stained glass, makes clear the legend's most memorable features. Julian himself is usually portrayed as a hunter with a sword at his side and a falcon in his hand, reminding the viewer that the prophecy of murder occurred during the course of a deer hunt. Of the two scenes most frequently depicted, the first shows Julian in the act of killing his parents and the second has him carrying the leper across the river to the hospice maintained by Julian and his wife.[4]

---

[2] The following numbers in Thompson, *Motif-Index of Folk-Literature*, are relevant: M343, "parricide prophecy"; N323, "parricide prophecy unwittingly fulfilled"; Q25, "reward for carrying Christ across a stream." See also analogous folktales listed by Aarne, *The Types of the Folktale*, under the headings "Oedipus" (931) and "St. Christopher and the Christ Child" (768). The prehistory of the legend in its most general form has been studied by Schwob, *Spicilège*, pp. 103–20. For a medieval German Oedipus legend, in which the theme is incest rather than parricide and the incestuous one is none other than Pope Gregory the Great, see Hartmann von Aue, *Gregorius, the Good Sinner*, trans. Buehne, and the version by Thomas Mann, *The Holy Sinner*.

[3] That Flaubert saw the window in his native city of Rouen is certain. Teasing out his relationship to and use of the other source materials which he may have utilized for his highly imaginative transformation of the legend is less easy. It is known that he read his friend Langlois' account of the Julian window, as well as a French translation of *LA*, but there has been considerable disagreement as to whether he actually read (or was capable of reading) a manuscript of the thirteenth-century French prose life, which he may have come across during a visit to the Bibliothèque Nationale in 1875 at a time when he was having difficulty with the writing of his own Julian tale. The reader who is interested in this puzzle about the relationship of a great nineteenth-century novelist to the Middle Ages, as well as in the heated opinions of those who have tried to trace the path of his inspiration, may find a detailed and scholarly discussion in Bart and Cook, *Legendary Sources*, pp. 29–93. A recent English translation of Flaubert's *Trois Contes* is *Three Tales*, trans. Krailsheimer.

[4] De Gaiffier, "Julien," pp. 191–200, gives a detailed listing and description of representations of St. Julian found in stained glass windows, paintings, miniatures, sculptures, and tapestries.

Historical Origins

The quest for an authentic historical basis for Julian the Hospitaller and his legend forms part of the great Bollandist project begun in the seventeenth century. Questions about the problem of historical truth in the lives of the saints had arisen as early as the Renaissance, in connection with de Voragine's *LA*, for instance,[5] but beginning in the seventeenth century they took on a new meaning and urgency. The Bollandists, organized by the Jesuit Jean Bolland expressly for the purpose of studying and publishing the lives of saints, continued to honor the devotional impulse that had led to so much uniformity within hagiographical tradition, but the establishment of a critical hagiography became, for them, the single most important task — whence their dedicated attempt to sift out the authentic historical kernel from among different versions of a saint's life and to identify and sometimes discard those for which no such kernel could be found.

In 1643, the published record of their researches began to appear in the multi-volume series known as the *Acta Sanctorum*. The single entry for Julian, which appeared in the second of the two volumes devoted to January saints, is taken from the fifteenth-century chronicle of Antoninus of Florence (*AS*, Ian. 2.974). The apparently straightforward recording of this legend, however, belies the complicated later history of the Bollandists' frustrated attempts to find a factual basis for its main details. From the beginning, the problematic nature of the saint's origin was signaled by the lack of a traditional feast day and the difficulty of locating him securely in a definite country or time period. As David Hugh Farmer succinctly puts it, Julian "has no date, no country, no tomb."[6] During the century following the publication of the January volume of *Acta Sanctorum*, and beginning especially with the efforts of two of Bolland's most famous disciples, Henschenius and Papebroch, the Bollandists engaged in a kind of heroic detective work which they hoped would lead them to the historical Julian. Clues in the form of a Latin manuscript assigning the legend to Provence led to a lengthy correspondence with local Provençal historians, but this did not yield in the end any solid evidence of an authentic localizing tradition. Various other trails, including the attempt to identify a relic in the cathedral at Macerata as the arm of Julian the Hospitaller, were initially pursued in a spirit of hope and excitement, only to conclude in similarly dead ends, and the Bollandists were finally forced to acknowledge that Julian's origins remained enveloped in obscurity.[7] What the reader cannot help admiring in the account of these researches is the passionate desire of the Bollandists to

---

[5] Sherry Reames comments that the sixteenth-century writers Vives and Cano, who attacked *LA*, "treat hagiography explicitly as a branch of historical writing, discussing its deficiencies in chapters devoted to the characteristics of unreliable historians" (*The Legenda Aurea: A Reexamination of Its Paradoxical History*, p. 51).

[6] *The Oxford Dictionary of Saints*, p. 243.

[7] De Gaiffier, "Julien," pp. 146–58.

find an authentic historical figure lying behind the legend, coupled with their painstaking commitment to a scholarship which would not in the end allow them to avoid the conclusion that such a figure did not exist. More recent investigation has only strengthened this conclusion: Julian's name is found in no martyrology (though some versions do provide him with a martyr's death) and, lacking any firm liturgical tie, his very moveable feast day, though officially designated by the Bollandists as January 29, is variably assigned to one of the many other Saint Julians with whom he is regularly confused: Julian of Brioude, Julian of Le Mans, Julian of Rimini, and the Egyptian couple, Julian and Basilissa.[8]

Regardless of his historicity or lack of it, the popular cult centered on Julian Hospitaller must have grown almost as quickly in England as in France. The earliest allusions identifying him simply as the patron of hospitality are widely attested in sources from both countries by the early thirteenth century. Geoffrey Shepherd speculates that his popularity in England was boosted by a confusion with St. Julian of Le Mans, celebrated in England in the twelfth century, probably because Henry II himself came from Le Mans.[9] A few examples will suffice to indicate how familiar the name and reputation of Julian already were at this time. The early-thirteenth-century chronicle of Roger of Wendover (died 1236) alludes to Julian in his report of a vision vouchsafed in 1206 to the peasant Thurkill. The peasant, who has been guilty of not tithing correctly, is taken on a tour of Hell by a guide who first asks Thurkill to find lodging for him and then identifies himself as follows: "For I am Julian the Entertainer [*Iulianus hospitator*] and have been sent on your behalf to show you by divine means certain things that are hidden from men and women in the flesh. Proceed to your house and try to prepare yourself for a journey."[10] Equally compelling is the allusion found in the famous early-thirteenth-century treatise for female recluses, the *Ancrene Wisse*. In the opening of Part VI, "On Penance," one category of the people chosen by God is described metaphorically in terms of good pilgrims:

> [Although] they are in the world . . . [they] always have their hearts toward heaven, as indeed they ought to have. For other pilgrims go with much toil to seek the bones of a single saint, like St. James or St. Giles; but these pilgrims who go toward heaven, they go to become saints themselves, and to find God himself and all his holy saints living in joy, and they all live with him in gladness without end. Surely they find St. Julian's inn, which wayfarers search for so eagerly.[11]

---

[8] De Gaiffier, "Julien," pp. 172–77. Julian is not listed in any of the medieval calendars printed by Wormald, ed., *English Benedictine Kalendars after A.D. 1100*.

[9] *Ancrene Wisse: Parts Six and Seven*, ed. Shepherd, p. 32.

[10] Roger of Wendover, *Flowers of History*, trans. Giles, 2.221.

[11] Savage and Watson, trans., *Anchoritic Spirituality: Ancrene Wisse and Associated Works*, pp. 176–77. In the notes to his edition of parts six and seven of the *Ancrene Wisse*, Shepherd comments that no mention of these saints is made in the sermon by St. Bernard which is the main source for this segment

The *Gawain*-poet and Chaucer attest to the saint's continuing popularity in fourteenth-century England. Sir Gawain, wandering alone in a wild country, glimpses the castle where he will find shelter, and gives thanks to "Jesus and Sayn Gilyan þat gentyle are boþe" (*Sir Gawain and the Green Knight*, line 774). Chaucer portrays the hospitable Franklin as "Seint Julian . . . in his contree" (*CT* I[A]340), and the garrulous eagle exclaims in the *The House of Fame* (lines 1021–23), when he and Geoffrey, after their journey into space, come in sight of Fame's temple,

> Now up the hed, for al ys wel;
> Seynt Julyan, loo, bon hostel!
> Se here the Hous of Fame, lo!

There is no way to ascertain precisely how or when this early tradition began to accumulate the details familiar to us in the parricide narrative. According to one hypothesis, the story may have developed, after the fact, as a means of explaining and providing motivation for a figure around whom a popular cult had earlier developed.[12] Be that as it may, by the mid-thirteenth century the brief Latin epitomes of Bartholomew of Trent, Pierre de Natal, Vincent of Beauvais, and Jacobus de Voragine in *Legenda aurea*, while differing in some details, all present versions of the story in its now familiar form. The precise relationship between the Latin and French versions is particularly difficult to establish in this case. Ordinarily it is the Latin life of a saint that develops first and is subsequently epitomized in compendia like those by the authors named above as well as making its way into the vernacular in various forms. In this case, however, the earliest fully developed Latin *vita* was discovered to be a rather awkward translation of the earliest elaborated thirteenth-century French prose narrative that, it has been argued, may also predate the epitomized versions, suggesting further the legend's links with and possible origin in vernacular folk tradition.[13]

---

of the *Ancrene Wisse*. De Gaiffier, "Julien," pp. 165–66, notes further that the two pilgrimage sites alluded to (Saint-Gilles in Provence and Santiago de Compostela) are precisely those mentioned in the French prose life of Julian.

[12] Bart and Cook, *Legendary Sources*, pp. 7–15, hypothesize a scenario whereby the legend accumulated its various folktale elements in a series of stages. They make no attempt to persuade the reader that this is what actually happened, but their explanation is useful in a general way for understanding the mechanism for such a development.

[13] For references to the Latin versions, see *BHL* 4551 and *BHL NS* 4550v. The most complete listing of manuscripts of the French prose life is in Swan, *Legend*, p. 115. It seems unlikely that the question of origins will ever be finally resolved. De Gaiffier thought he might have discovered, in a manuscript located in Bruges, a Latin text (*BHL NS* 4550v) deriving from a source anterior to the French prose life and he printed this text on pp. 200–19 of his article. According to Bart and Cook, *Legendary Sources*, p. 107, however, "this is probably just an expanded version of the earlier French verse life." While not

The Legend of Julian in *ScL*

Middle English adaptations of the Julian narrative include, in addition to the version printed here from the late-fourteenth-century *ScL*, those in the 1438 *Gilte Legende*, and Caxton's *Golden Legend*, all of which are based directly on the epitome in Jacobus de Voragine's *Legenda aurea*. An earlier ME version, however, that in *SEL* (discussed further below), seems to be independent of *LA*.[14] Although most of the legends in *ScL* are translated from *LA*, and although the Julian chapter is no exception, the author cites his own curiosity about Julian Hospitaller as his motive for narrating this particular legend. That he knew of Julian as a model or type of hospitality, independent of any written source for the legend, is seen in his account of a travelers' custom familiar to him from the days of his youth (lines 7–22). In a brief autobiographical introduction, the poet describes himself as someone who, when young, traveled a great deal in the hope of gaining wisdom from "gud mene" (line 5). The many encounters he had with travelers who invoked St. Julian led him to wish both to learn more about the patron saint of hospitality and to distinguish among the different saints called by the same name. Although W. M. Metcalfe has argued plausibly against a single author for the collection, there is an interesting parallel between the Prologue of the *Legendary*, with its extensive description

---

definitive, Cook's discussion (pp. 8–9) offers the most thorough recent approach to and understanding of the complex issues involved:

> It is reasonable to suspect that the lengthy and detailed Old French Prose Life, one of the principal versions, also had oral or written sources not known to us. Moreover, the Prose Life may possibly be older than the mid-thirteenth century date usually assumed for it. It is one of the very few prose legends in the vernacular to appear in isolation, outside of the collections of such Lives, or 'légendiers,' which date from approximately the middle of the century, and which normally represent groups of translations from existing Latin Lives. No such Latin life is known for Julian, which fact tends to support the notion that his Old French Life is an independent creation older than the *légendiers*, and thus, of course, probably older than Jacobus.

Cook also argues against the evolution earlier proposed by Eugène Vinaver, who assumed that the brief Latin epitomes came first. Vinaver's most interesting point, however, has less to do with answering the chicken-egg question than with folding the legend of Julian into his well-known and still insightful hypothesis regarding medieval romance. Arguing in favor of the significance of formal patterning and against an overly modern dependence on psychological interpretation, he says that "Julian's seemingly natural behaviour carries conviction only when it becomes part of a movement which by its own logic brings about the tragic end" (Vinaver, *The Rise of Romance*, p. 121).

[14] For bibliogaphical references to the Middle English versions see *MWME* 2.597. On the *SEL* version, see also Görlach, *Textual Tradition*, pp. 140–41.

of the author's age and frailty, and his representation of himself here (lines 1–6) also as some-one no longer young.[15]

The long chapter entitled simply "Julian" in Metcalfe's edition, comprising 780 verses, actually covers the lives of five Julians, one of whom, Julian the Apostate, is not a saint at all. *LA* has provided the *ScL*-poet with the primary source material as well as the ordering of all five lives. The first three follow the equivalent passages in *LA* closely, in terms both of the pro-portion of space devoted to each saint, and the details of the representation.[16] The catalogue begins with Julian of Le Mans (identified by some with Simon the Leper) who, following the death of Christ, was ordained the first bishop of Le Mans by the apostles. We are told next of Julian of Brioude, martyred during the Diocletian persecutions, and then of another Julian who, along with his brother Julius, obtained permission from the emperor Theodosius to destroy pagan temples and replace them with churches.[17]

These first three accounts are very brief, while the next, Julian Hospitaller, is narrated at much greater length. Although Jacobus' version of this legend, in *LA*, is similarly much longer and more dramatic than the first three, in the *ScL* version the poet demonstrates the legend's imaginative appeal for him by making additional alterations. As will be seen in the notes, Julian's killing of his parents is, in comparison with the brief and rather laconic account in *LA*, considerably expanded both in detail and emotional intensity. Comparison with the *SEL*'s approach at this point yields a conclusion similar to that proposed in the discussion of the episode of St. Andrew and the Three Questions (see the Introduction to I[b], above). For example, the *SEL*-poet editorializes freely, as in his comment immediately after Julian has slain his parents:

Wonderliche it farþ bi wate . as me may here iseo
Þe þing þat is a man yssape . he ne may neuere vleo[18]

He also takes a far less restrained approach to this scene than the *ScL*-poet, attributing to Julian an extraordinarily vituperative and colloquial outburst in which he calls his wife a whore, and

---

[15] Compare *ScL* Prologue, line 35. For Metcalfe's arguments on the authorship question, see his edition, 1.xxv–xxxii.

[16] See *LA*, chapter 30, ed. Maggioni, pp. 209–17 (trans. Ryan 1.126–30); for Julian Hospitaller in particular, see Maggioni, pp. 212–14 (trans. Ryan 1.127–28).

[17] See the entries in *Butler's Lives of the Saints* for Julian of Le Mans (January 27; *BHL* 4543–50) and Julian of Brioude (August 28; *BHL* 4540–42), 1.183, 3.434. The Julian (brother of Julius) who destroyed temples and built churches in their stead is not listed in *Butler's Lives* (but see *BHL* 4557–58). De Voragine, who sometimes mentions sources, says nothing in this regard about any of the five Julians.

[18] "It is amazing how fate works, as men may see here (i.e., in this case): a man can never escape the destiny that is fashioned for him." From the *SEL St. Julian the Hospitaller*, lines 51–52 (DM 1.34).

her supposed companion both a "gering" ("crude fellow") and a "horling" (lines 46–47, 50). In contrast, the *ScL*-poet, while not excusing Julian's fault, never fails to represent both husband and wife with dignity as well as pathos.

While the *ScL* legend of Julian Hospitaller is clearly based on Jacobus' in *LA*, the poet includes certain narrative details not found in the Latin version. These details suggest, even if they do not conclusively prove, that the author had additional knowledge of the saint, gleaned from either oral tradition or a text related in some way to the French prose life. Detailed commentary on individual passages will be found in the notes to the text.[19]

Julian the Apostate, the well-known Roman emperor (r. 361–63) who rejected the Christianity officially promoted by his uncle Constantine I and the latter's son, Constantius II, makes up the final count of the five Julians. As with Julian the Hospitaller, *ScL* follows closely the details of *LA*'s colorful and largely fictional account of the career of Julian the Apostate, but elaborates greatly in terms of dramatic dialogue.[20] One wonders whether Jacobus' fascination with this sordid and distinctly non-saintly figure may have seemed odd or even somewhat inappropriate to the *ScL* author. Rather than omitting or abbreviating the *LA*'s account, however, he justifies its inclusion by explaining at the outset that it is offered as an example of wickedness, with the aim of restraining others from behaving in a similar manner. Within the legend itself he provides more explicit moral judgments on the conduct of Julian and those surrounding him. A good example of this is the woman who brings her gold to Julian for safekeeping in three pots which she has covered with ash to conceal their contents. Whereas the *LA* account simply states all this as fact, *ScL* provides both motivation and judgment: Julian's subsequent theft of the gold is condemned, but *ScL* lets us understand that the woman's greed makes her partially responsible for her loss. In a final editorial addition, the poet notes drily that no one prays to Julian the Apostate and that no prayers on his behalf will avail. This then allows him to circle neatly back to the "good" Julians to whom one may pray and a final exhortation to the one who is clearly his personal favorite:

. . . namely to that Julyane,	
That for gast has the angel tane,	*as a spirit; taken*
That he for us mak sic prayere	*such*
That we may hafe gud herbry here	*good lodgings*

---

[19] The reader is referred to the Introduction to the episode of St. Andrew and the Three Questions (I[b]) for additional comments on the *ScL*-poet's style, handling of sources, and Scots dialect, as well as information on the unique manuscript of the *Legendary*.

[20] For bibliography and short biographical accounts of Julian the Apostate, the one certainly historical figure in this constellation of Julians, see *New Catholic Encyclopedia*, 8.47, and Berardino, ed., *Encylopedia of the Early Church*, 1.459–60.

And syne in hevine herbryt be	*afterwards*
Amen, Amen, par cheryté. (lines 775–80)	*in charity*

Indexed in

IMEV 4028.

Manuscript

Cambridge, University Library MS Gg.2.6, fols. 169r and 171v–174v. [For the complete *ScL* chapter on the several Julians, see fols. 169r–178r.]

Previous editions

Horstmann. *Barbour's Schottischen Nationaldichters Legendensammlung*. 1.281 and 221–25.

Legends of the Saints in the Scottish Dialect of the Fourteenth Century. Ed. Metcalfe. 1.458–59 and 464–72. [For the complete chapter in *ScL*, see 1.458–80.]

VIII

The Life of St. Julian Hospitaller *in the* Scottish Legendary *(c. 1400),* *from Cambridge, University Library MS Gg.2.6, fols. 169r, 171v–174v,* *as edited by W. M. Metcalfe in ScL 1.458–59 and 464–72*

	Quene that yunge mane I was,	*When*
	I travalyt oft in sere place,	*many (various)*
	Sic thing in my yuthe to lere	*Such*
	Quharewith myn elde I mycht stere.	*With which to guide my old age*
5	And drew me to gud mene, pardé,	
	Thocht lytil thareof be bydyne one me.[1]	
	The travalouris thane custume had,	*then*
	That al day yed ore rad	*walked or rode*
	And for travale ware wery,	*were*
10	Quhene thai come til thar herbry,	*When; to; lodging*
	And namely fra thai mycht it se,	*the moment when*
	Quhethyr that it ware scho ore he,	*Whether; she*
	Hat or hud tak of ore clath,	
	The rycht fut of the sterape rath,[2]	
15	And to Sancte Julyane devotly	
	A Paternoster say in hy,	*Say the Lord's Prayer quickly*
	In hope that al gud herbry suld haf,	*should*
	That in sik wyse it suld crafe.	*such manner; crave (desire)*
	Sic hope into Sancte Julyane	
20	The travalouris thane had tane,	
	As mony men yet are	
	That sammyne oysis here and thare.[3]	

---

[1] Lines 5–6: *I drew near to (i.e., sought the company of) good men, by God, / Though little of it (i.e., of what I learned from them) has remained with me*

[2] Lines 13–14: *[Travelers] removed hat or hood or other garment / [And] quickly [removed] the right foot from the stirrup*

[3] Lines 19–22: *Travelers at that time placed such hope in Saint Julian, / And there are still many men / Here and there who practice the same custom*

	Bot, for that fele ma thane ane	*because many more than one*
	Haly mene are callit Julyane,	
25	I yarnyt to wyt quhilk was he	*yearned to know which*
	Men socht in sic necessyté,	*sought*
	And sa his story I fand al hale,	*so; found; complete*
	As til yow here tel I sall.	*shall*

[Omitted here are lines 29–228, comprising the rest of the poet's Prologue and the legends of Saints Julian of Le Mans, Julian of Brioude, and Julian the Deacon.]

	Yhete in this stoury find we ane,	*Yet*
230	That als wes callyt Julyane,	*also*
	That fadyr and modir bath sleucht,	
	His unwitting: that wrocht hyme wocht.[1]	
	This Julyane wes of nobile kene,	*kin*
	And had mykil warldis wyne.	*worldly joy*
235	And hapnyt hyme in youthhede	*happened [to] him (it came about)*
	That he a day til huntis yede.	*one day to hunting went*
	And quhene he had socht oure the land,	*over (throughout)*
	A gret hart and fare he fand;	*A great and fair hart*
	Thane Julyane rycht besyly	*actively*
240	Folouyt this hart al anerly.	*alone*
	And sa at the laste that best	*beast (creature)*
	Turnyt agane, and mad areste,	*stopped*
	And sad: "Quhy chasis thu me swa,	*said: "Why . . ."; so*
	Wykyt man, that thi fadir sal sla,	*shall slay*
245	And als thi modir of thi hande	
	Sal de be dynt of bytande brand?"	*die by blow of [your] sharp sword*
	Quhene this was sad, he was sary,	
	And dred thai wordis gretumely,	*dreaded (feared) those; greatly*
	That the hart had sad hyme til.	
250	Forthi he dresyt hale his wil[2]	
	To leve the land al prively;	*secretly*
	And as he thocht, he dyd in hy.	*intended; haste*

---

[1] Lines 231–32: *Who, without knowing it, killed both his father and mother: that wrought (i.e., caused) him harm*

[2] *Therefore he completely made up his mind (lit., directed his will)*

Thane one his way sone yed he   *at once*
Furth in a fere cunctré,   *far country*
255   Sa nane hyme knew, na he nane;[1]
Forethi arest thare has he tane.   *dwelling-place; taken*
With his service to wyne gud thane
He thocht, sene he was manly mane.[2]
Thane to the prince of the cunctré
260   Sone he socht; and quhene that he   *sought out*
Wyst quhare he wes and with hyme met,   *Knew where*
Rycht curtasly he has hyme gret,   *greeted*
And sad, "Sir, and it be youre wil,   *said, "Sir, if it . . ."*
Lele service I wald mak you til,   *Loyal; would; to you*
265   And at youre wil tak of yow fe."   *wages*
The prince sad, "Welcume thu be!"
And hyme resavit thankfully,   *received*
And gret gyftis gef hyme in hy.
Thane this Julyane, that was wicht,   *strong*
270   Sa wele in palace and in fycht   *fight (war)*
Enplesit his prince, that he hym mad   *Pleased*
Knycht — sic luf til hyme he had —
And gert hyme wed a yung lady,   *caused (arranged for) him [to]*
That had castel and syngnory.   *estate*
275   Sa that he worth mychtty mane   *became*
Thru gud and prowes that he wane,   *wealth and honor; won*
And lang tyme led gud lyfe,
And gat fare barnis one his wyfe.   *begot fair children*
Bot his fadyre in the mene tyme
280   And his modir in mykil pyne
Lifit, fra tha thare barne tynt,
Fore thai cuth nothir cese na stynt
To sek hyme bath fere and nere.[3]
Tho thai of riches mychtty were,   *Then (at that time)*

---

[1] *Where no one knew him, and he knew no one*

[2] Lines 257–58: *He thought he would be able to win wealth then through his service (i.e., as a knight), since he was a strong man*

[3] Lines 279–83: *Meanwhile, Julian's father and mother lived in great sorrow from [the time when] their son was lost, / So that they could neither cease nor stop / Looking for him both far and near*

285	Bot thareof nathing thai rocht,	*for that; cared*
	Bot al levyt and thare sone socht,	*left everything*
	Waferand fra place to place,	*Wandering*
	Til that it hapnyt thame one case	*to them by chance*
	To that castel ayrly to care,	*early to arrive*
290	That thare sone aucht, and syne his ayre.[1]	
	And that mornyng Julyane was	
	Gane to the feld hym to refres,	*to refresh himself (i.e., exercise)*
	Unhaply in the sythware,	*Unfortunately, in the meantime*
	Lytil before that thai come thare.	
295	And sone the laydy had thame sene,	*immediately*
	And saw thame honest folk and clene,	*recognized them [as]*
	And franyt quhat thare willis ware,	*asked what*
	And quhat thai socht that tyme thare.	*were seeking*
	Fore scho had hard hyre husband tel	*Because; heard*
300	Al hale the case as it befel,	*The story all wholly*
	Thame resavyt scho tendyrly,	*received*
	And, fore thai ware ful wery,	
	Scho gert thare fet be dycht fyrste,	*She first caused their bath to be prepared*
	Syne lad thame in a bed to reste,	*Then laid*
305	And bad thame slepe and mery ma,	*make*
	For scho wald to the chapil ga.	*go*
	And sa scho dyd, and levyt tham, stil	
	Slepand soft at thare wil.	
	And as this thing done was,	
310	Julyane come fra his solas,	*sport (diversion)*
	And forwenyt of his wyf,[2]	
	But areste come belyf,	*Without stopping; quickly*
	Trewand thane foroutyne wene	*Believing; without doubt*
	That scho in hyre bad had bene.	
315	With that the curtyng upe he wavit,	*curtain; lifted*
	And twa lyand has persavyt,	*two lying [there]; perceived*
	That he mysknew, fore thai ware hyd;	*did not recognize; hidden*
	Tharefor gret sorow til hym tyd,	*befell*
	For he wend it had bene sum mane,	*thought*

---

[1] *Which their son owned, and afterwards his heir [would own]*

[2] *And thought beforehand about (i.e., looked forward to being with) his wife*

320	That had his wyf defowlyt thane.	*defiled*
	Forthi of ire he was sa hat,	*with anger*
	That he al resone had forget,	*forgotten*
	And in that wodnes, ore he stynt,	*madness, before he stopped*
	A scharpe swerd owt he hynt.	*took*
325	Thane fadir and modir in that sted,	*place*
	In his wodnes, he slew ded.	*struck*
	And as the ded donne was,	*deed*
	The yunge laydy come fra the Mes,	*Mass*
	And fand hyre lord wrath wondirly;	*found; terribly angry*
330	Thane the cause speryt scho in hy.	*asked; quickly*
	Bot quhene he had hiss wyf sene,	
	Gret wondir put away his tene,	*amazement; anger*
	And sad til hyr: "I pray thee, say,	*[he] said*
	Quhat ware yone twa in myn bed lay?	
335	For I trewit it had bene a fere,	
	Thu had than me fore mare dere."[1]	
	Thane til hyme smyland scho sad,	*to*
	"Thai twa, that tharein I lad,	*Those two*
	Youre fadyre and youre modir are,	
340	That fare has socht you with hart sare.	*[a] sad heart*
	Tharfore I beysit me til es	*busied myself to comfort*
	Thame in althing and to ples."	
	Fra that he had hard this tale,	*When*
	His wit he tynt nere for bale,	*nearly lost for sorrow*
345	And into swonyng fele as ded;	*as [one] dead*
	And scho one hyme fel in that sted.	*place*
	Thane watir one thame men can caste,	*began to*
	And thai ourecome at the last.	*came to (recovered)*
	Thane has scho hyme in armis tane,	*taken*
350	And sad til hyme: "My dere lemmane,	*loved one*
	Quhat amovit you this to fare?	*caused; behave thus*
	Tel me, and nathinge with me spare!"	*spare me nothing*
	Thane sad he: "My laydy gud,	
	Quhat wondir is thocht I be woud?	*though (if); mad*

---

[1] Lines 334–36: ["]*Who were those two lying in my bed? / For I believed that it was a lover, / Whom you held dearer than me"*

320

355 In hart haf I sa mekil wa   *such great woe*
   That myself me byrd to sla;   *I ought to kill myself*
   Preysand with Fortone for to stryf,
   And now has put bath ofe lyf
   Fadir and modir fellounly!¹
360 Allace! That evire borne wes I,
   For to be callit the wykiste   *most wicked*
   Fra suth to north, fra est to weste —
   For of my ded sa cruele
   The warld sal nevire cese to tel.
365 Allace! I thocht nocht fore to thryfe,
   With Fortone quhen I began to strife.
   I gaf na treutht that it suld be
   Suth, the hart had sad til me;²
   And now fulfillyt has in dede
370 The thing that I sa sare cane dred;   *bitterly did fear*
   Tharefore I levyt kithe and kyne, *For that reason I left kindred and family*
   And yet this wrak is falline in.   *vengeance is coming to pass*
   Tharefore farewele, systir swet;
   For with thee sal I nevire met,   *meet*
375 Bot ay . . . nycht and day,   *always*
   Til Jhesu Criste, that mychttis may, *who can perform mighty acts*
   My pennance tak and rew of me!" *Accepts my penance and has pity on me*
   Thane wes gret pité fore to se
   How his wyf hyme in armis hynt,   *took*
380 Gretand sa fast that scho na stynt,   *Weeping so hard*
   And sad til hyme: "Swet lord dere,
   Quhat, wene ye to leve me here?   *think*
   Na, forsuth, it beis nocht swa,   *in truth; will not be*
   Bot quhare thu gais, I sal ga,
385 And wa with thee thole als wele³
   As evire I tholyt welth or wele,

---

¹ Lines 357–59: *I tried to struggle against Fortune, / And now I have cruelly deprived both my father and mother of life (lit., put both [out] of life)*

² Lines 365–68: *Alas, I should not have expected to succeed, / When I began to strive with Fortune. / I did not believe that what the deer had said to me would come true*

³ Lines 384–85: *But whither thou goest, I shall go, / And suffer woe with thee as well*

	And of thi pane partenare be,	*pain partner*
	As I of joy has bene with thee."	
	A new dysese thane can he tak,	*distress*
390	Seand his wyf sic sorou mak;	
	Na hyre purpos he chang ne mycht	
	Nothir for prayere na for mycht.	
	Thane passyt thai furth, waverand,	*wandering*
	A gret revire til thai fand,	
395	Quharein fele drownyt ayre and lat,	*Wherein many; early and late*
	For thare was nothir bryg na bat.	*bridge nor boat*
	Thane he and scho, that mychtty ware	
	Of gold and silvir, wald nocht spare,¹	
	Bot ane hospytale mad but were	*without doubt*
400	One the bank of that rivere,	
	Quharin al that had nede	*Wherein*
	Thai herbryt wele, and can tham fede.	*lodged*
	And al that wald the watir pas —	*wished to cross over the water*
	For he mekile man and stark wes —	*great; strong*
405	Quhene thai come nycht or day,	
	He bare thame oure but delay.	*over without*
	And tharewith als in chastyté	
	Devotly lifyt his wyf and he.	
	And quhene thai lang had led sic lyf	*such*
410	Thankful to God, he and his wyfe,	*Pleasing*
	It hapnyt hyme al wery	
	In til his bed a nycht to ly,²	
	Quhene sa gret falline wes the snaw,	
	That nane mycht the yerd knaw,	*recognize the courtyard*
415	And wele gret was the frost withal.	*so great*
	About mydnycht he hard ane cal	*heard someone call*
	Ful pytuisly one hyme be name,	*by*
	And gretand sad: "Ryse, Julyane,	*weeping*
	And oure this watir thu bere me	*over*
420	That in poynt is to peryst be!"	*Who am about to perish*
	Thane Julyane na dwelling mad,	*tarrying*

---

¹ Lines 397–98: *Then he and she, who were rich / In gold and silver, would spare nothing*

² Lines 411–12: *It happened [that] he (i.e., Julian), very weary, / Lay down in his bed one night*

	Bot furth he rane but abad,	*without delay*
	And fand a yunge barne in that stede,	*young child; place*
	That fore cald nere wes ded;	*cold nearly*
425	For he wes myssele and sare seke,	*leper and grievously ill*
	And ilke bale cane uthyre eke,	*each trouble increased the other*
	That Julyane hyme bethocht	*So that Julian thought to himself*
	That he the watir pas wald nocht	*cross over*
	With this chyld, til he warmyt ware.	
430	Forthi sone he hynt hyme thare,	*Therefore; took*
	And to his ostel has hyme borne,	*hostelry; carried*
	And mad a fyre sone hyme beforne.	
	Bot, fore na fyr he mycht mak,	
	The child na kyndly het cuth tak.[1]	
435	Thane for dowt the barne suld spil,	*fear; die*
	He mad a bed and bare hyme til,	*carried*
	And happyt hyme ful tendirly,	*covered*
	And wele lang tyme let hyme ly.	
	And quhen cummyne wes the day,	*come*
440	Julyane come quhare he lay,	
	And fand hyme yet lyand clede,	*clothed*
	As he had lad hyme in his bede.	*laid*
	He bad hyme ryse, fore it wes day,	
	Gyf he had hast of his way.	*If he was in a hurry to be on his way*
445	The chyld semyt than fere mare clere	*far more bright*
	Thane is the sowne in myd yere,	
	That wes before al myslary	*[riddled with] leprosy*
	And gret seknes ful ugly.	*[because of his] great illness*
	For of his face come a leme	*ray of light*
450	As it had bene a sonebeme.	*As [if]*
	With that he passit ful rath in Hevine,	*rose quickly into Heaven*
	And til his hoste sad in swet stevine:	*said; voice*
	"Gud Julyane, God has send me	
	To comfort and to say to thee,	
455	That thi pennance sa thankful is,	*acceptable*
	That He til thee al hale this myse	*completely; sin*

---

[1] Lines 434–35: *But, despite any fire that he could make, / The youth could take no natural warmth from it*

323

	Forgyfine has quyt and fre.	*altogether and freely*
	And alsa bad me sa to thee,	*say*
	That thu sowne, and thi folow bath,	*soon both you and your spouse*
460	Sal til Hyme cum in Hevine ful rath,	*Heaven*
	Quhare ye sal bruk the gret blyse,	*enjoy*
	That He as grantyt til al his,	*has*
	And namely for thu set thi wil	*especially because*
	Til herbry al that come thee til.	*shelter*
465	Forthi thai at in name of thee	*they that*
	Askis herbry, sal herbryit be,	
	And be wele esyt at the lest,	
	Suppos thai haf nocht plesand fest."[1]	
	The angel than of his sycht	*from*
470	Vanyst, and he with al mycht	*Vanished*
	Lowyt fast God of His bounté,	*Praised greatly; goodness*
	That let hyme sa His angel se.	
	Sancte Julyanc than and his wyf	
	To God led thai sa thankful lyfe —	
475	That thare dedis sa wele can stere	
	The lytil tyme that tha lifit here —	
	That one a day and in ane houre[2]	
	Thai deyt, and til oure Saveoure	
	Sa quemful, that, rycht as thai twa	*[Were] so pleasing*
480	Has tholyt here bath wele and wa,	*experienced*
	Sa togydyre He thame brocht	
	Til His gret blyse, that falis nocht.	*fails*
	The quhilk fore His debonare wil	*through; gracious*
	He grantyt us al to cum til.	*may He grant*

---

[1] Lines 465–68: *Therefore those who ask lodging in thy name shall be sheltered, / And at the least made comfortable, / Although they may not have a delightful feast*

[2] Lines 474–77: *Led a life so pleasing to God — / Who guided their deeds so well / [During] the little time that they lived here — / On one [and the same] day and at one [and the same] hour*

VIII

Explanatory Notes to the Life of St. Julian Hospitaller in the Scottish Legendary *(c. 1400)*

1–28   This introduction is original to our author. The recitation of the Lord's Prayer (line 16) is widely associated with the cult of Julian Hospitaller (de Gaiffier, p. 167). A late-twelfth-century Latin chronicle of the Percy family (London, BL MS Royal 7.A.III) provides the most expansive account of practices associated with the saint, confirming the details offered here by the *ScL*-poet as forming part of a popular and long-standing British tradition. According to the Percy chronicle, every prudent Englishman, "when about to set out on a journey which involves spending even a single night from home, makes a point, before he crosses his threshold, of saying a Paternoster, accompanied by a prayer to St. Julian for protection against ghostly and other foes by the wayside, both for man and beast and for goods and chattels, and that he may securely take his ease at his inn or wheresoever he may find hospitality on his travels." The anonymous monk who compiled this chronicle goes on to report on the disastrous consequences which befell William de Percy, a vassal of William the Conqueror, who, following a successful war against Scotland, arrogantly refused to take part in further prayers to Saint Julian. One after another of his holdings were burned or otherwise destroyed as Percy traveled homewards until finally he repented and asked pardon of St. Julian, whereupon good fortune once again attended him. See Gilson, "St. Julian the Harbinger," 304–12.

22   *sammyne*. This Northern variant of ME *same*, here meaning "the same [thing, practice]," may be influenced by the OE adverb *samen/somen* (together).

        oysis. The *oy* diphthong is a common spelling in later Northern ME and Middle Scots to indicate the Anglo-Norman *u* in verbs like *use*, *refuse*, *pure*, etc., which is often represented by linguists as *ü* and in ME as *iu*, *eu*, *ew*, etc. Note also the *-is* suffix, common in Northern ME and Scots in the present plural.

29–228 *ScL* first lists the five Julians whose legends are to be narrated (lines 29–40), and then offers accounts of Julian of Le Mans (lines 41–62), Julian of Brioude (lines 63–142) and Julian the brother of Julius (lines 143–228), following the order of *LA*.

325

231–32   *sleucht, / . . . wocht*. The apparent false rhyme here is more likely the fault of the scribe than the poet, who probably wrote *sleucht / weucht*. The stem vowel *-eu-* in *sleucht* ("slew," more usually *sloh* in ME), results from leveling from, or analogy with, the preterite plural and past participle forms of the verb, *sleughen/sleuchen* (this Northern pronunciation eventually predominated further south: hence Modern English *slew*). The rhyme-word in line 232, *wocht*, corresponds (apart from the final *-t*) to the common ME word *woh/wogh*, "harm, injury," but the variant *weuch* is recorded elsewhere in Middle Scots, and the poet doubtless originally wrote *weucht* to rhyme with *sleucht*. The intrusive final *-t* added to both words is common in this manuscript after *-ch-* (compare "thocht," "though," line 6; compare also "treuht," line 367).

232   *His unwitting*. This phrase (here meaning, in effect, "with his unwitting") is quite common as an absolute construction with the possessive in late ME and Scots. Compare also *ScL* Placidas, line 531, "& nereby, his vnwittand, / his sonnis twa were duelland" (ed. Metcalfe, 2.84), and Chaucer's The Franklin's Tale, "Unwityng of this Dorigen at al, / This lusty squier . . . / Hadde loved hire best of any creature" (*CT* V[F]936–37, 939).

233–34   *kene, / . . . wyne*. This sort of rhyme pair (pronounced *ken-wen*) is common in Northern ME and Scots texts, where short *i*, especially before a nasal consonant, was pronounced more like short *e*.

246   *bytande brand*. Where Jacobus de Voragine in *LA* says simply, "you . . . are going to kill your father and mother" (trans. Ryan, 1.127), the Scots poet adds something close to an old English kenning with the alliterative expression *bitande brand*. *Brand* in Old English meant "flame," but by virtue of a flame's "shining" property, it was also used to indicate a sword.

248   *gretumely*. A Scots dialect word. See the comments on *ScL*'s vocabulary in the Introduction to I(b), above.

259–78   This passage embellishes and alters the equivalent passage in *LA*: "Having reached a very remote region he took service with a prince, and carried on so manfully in wartime and peacetime that the prince dubbed him a knight and gave him a widow, a noblewoman, in marriage, with a castle as dowry" (trans. Ryan, 1.128). Julian's entry into feudal service affords the Scots poet an opportunity to invoke the conventions of romance, and he not only expands and dramatizes the negotiations between Julian and the prince, dwelling on the former's prowess, but also further transforms the widow into a *yung lady* (line 273) and then endows Julian with a family: *And gat fare barnis one his wyfe* (line 278).

281   *tynt*. The verb *tyne*, *tine* (from ON *tyna*) is common in Northern and Midland ME, but thereafter is confined to Scots. It is cognate with OE *teona* ("grief/pain").

284   *thai of riches mychtty were*. These riches, which mean nothing to Julian's parents in comparison with the loss of their son, form part of a series of reflections on the meaning and use of wealth and power original to this text. In the lines just before this passage we saw the romance-like emphasis on Julian's rise to power in his new domain. In a later section the couple use their accumulated wealth to build the hospital which will become their means of enacting penance for Julian's sin, thus allowing the poet to have his cake and eat it too: he develops the story in a way that embraces the values and conventions of secular romance up to a point, but at the same time he suggests the limited value of worldly goods, with the further implication that they are most appropriately used for acts of charity.

289–90   *care, / . . . ayre*. The rhyme here is good; *care* (pronounced approximately as in Modern English) is simply a Scots spelling of ME *cayre* (from ON *keyra*, "to drive/ ride").

290   *ayre*. The heir is not mentioned in *LA*.

292   *Gane to the feld hym to refres*. *LA* says only that "As it happened, Julian was away" (*a castro casu recesserat*, ed. Maggioni, p. 212; trans. Ryan, 1.128). The Old French prose version says quite explicitly that Julian has gone out hunting, and much is made of the parallelism between his earlier hunting activities and his return to the pursuit of this sport after his marriage. The Scots version seems to fall somewhere in between, mentioning that Julian has gone off to rest or relax (*hym to refres*) in the fields. It seems at least possible that the poet has hunting in mind, though he has not chosen to make this explicit.

298   Metcalfe indicates, through a set of ellipsis marks between lines 298–99, that he thinks something has been missed out here, namely, the statement in *LA* that the wife "realized that they were her husband's father and mother" (trans. Ryan, 1.128). This is certainly possible but it could as easily be the case that the Scots poet thought the inference was obvious enough not to need being made explicitly.

303   *fet be dycht.* The correct translation of this phrase is far from clear. It has no equivalent in *LA*, which says only that "she welcomed them cordially and, for love of them, left her husband's bed to them and slept in another room" (trans. Ryan, 1.128). The most obvious meaning for *fet* is "feet," but this makes little sense here with *dycht* ("prepared/provided/dressed"). If, however, we take *fet* to mean a tub filled with hot water (see *MED fet*, 1a), not only does the phrase make more sense, but it parallels an episode in both the French prose and French verse versions of the legend, where the wife offers the couple baths which had earlier been prepared for her husband and herself (for the prose, see Bart and Cook, p. 127; for the verse, see lines 3264–67, ed. Tobler, "Zur Legende vom heiligen Julianus," p. 149). An alternative would be to define *fet* as "festive meal." The early epitomized Latin version of Bartholomew of Trent (1244) says that the couple was well received and refreshed (*bene recepti et refecti*), while the later Bruges manuscript printed by de Gaiffier mentions giving them a meal (*cenam*) as well as a bath (de Gaiffier, p. 169 and pp. 212–13). In the French prose version, after the couple has bathed, Julian's wife *lor aporta a mengier* (Bart and Cook, p. 127). All three versions, in other words, offer some support for a tradition which spoke of a welcoming meal; however, while the *MED* gives *fete* as meaning a feast or banquet, the spelling *fet* is not listed as a possibility, so this is perhaps a less likely alternative than the bath.

303–04   *fyrste, / . . . reste.* The original rhyme pair was probably *freste* (a variant form of *first*) and *reste*.

311   *forwenyt.* This verb is not recorded elsewhere in ME or OE. Metcalfe (*ScL* 3.292) suggests translating *forwenyt* as "unexpected," which he links to OE *wenan*, to "think" or "expect," taking the prefix *for-* as a negative intensifier. He also emends the manuscript's *of his wyf* to *to his wyf*. But in the OE (and ME) verbs where *for-* is thus used (e.g., *fordon*, "kill"; *fordruncen*, "drunk"), it is not a simple negative, meaning *un-*, and Metcalfe's hypothetical verb would mean something more like "regret" (as in ME *forthinke*), or even "expect the worst," neither of which is remotely appropriate here. It seems simpler to interpret *for-* as the widely attested temporal prefix *for(e)*, with almost adverbial force (accent on *for-* as well as *wen-*) and *wenyt* as the simple past tense of *wene(n)*, and to retain the manuscript reading *of his wyf*. The line would thus mean literally: "and he thought beforehand about his wife," i.e., he was anticipating being with his wife (in bed). Metcalfe's emendation, substituting *to* for *of*, is also unnecessary. The direct object of *wenan* in OE is frequently in the genitive case, although this is rare in ME, but constructions with various prepositions, including *of* as well as *to*, occur (which is understandable since the verb was used more and more as a simple synonym of *think*). If the poet's meaning here is that

328

Julian was thinking about making love to his wife, it makes his fury at finding her in his bed with another, as he thought, even more understandable and parallels the poet's effort throughout this episode to humanize Julian's terrible crime. See also below, note on lines 320–26.

315   *curtyng.* Apparently the bed envisaged by the Scots poet was of the deluxe kind (later called a "four-poster"), enclosed on all sides with drapes for privacy and warmth. A famous illustration (c. 1460) of such a bed, with the *curtyng upe . . . wavit*, is in *King René's Book of Love*, ed. Unterkircher, trans. Wilkins, folio 2 (plate on p. 17).

320–26   Jacobus' unexpressive statement that Julian believes he has found *uxorem cum adultero suo* ("his wife and her lover"), followed by the equally bland *silenter extracto gladio ambos pariter interemit*, "silently drew his sword and killed them both" (*LA*, ed. Maggioni, p. 213; trans. Ryan, 1.128), is amplified here first by the more idiomatic rendering of Julian's suspicion that someone had *defowlyt* (line 320) his wife, and then by the lengthy portrayal of his anger and loss of reason which, if they do not justify the deed, represent it as more humanly comprehensible.

337–92   The *ScL*-poet devotes over fifty lines to the scene of Julian's reaction to the discovery that he has murdered his parents, a major expansion of *LA*'s brief paragraph (trans. Ryan, 1.128). The dramatic qualities of the scene, evidently viewed by the poet as the emotional center of the legend, are heightened by the following added details: the wife's expression, to Julian, of her joy at the arrival of his parents (lines 337–42), a nice piece of dramatic irony under the circumstances; her subsequent fainting (line 346: the double faint is also found in the French prose version, but only Julian is said to have "nearly fainted" in Jacobus' narrative); the wife's taking Julian in her arms to comfort him (lines 349–50, 378–81); and Julian's added sorrow over the sight of his wife's distress (lines 389–90). The wife's protestation to Julian that *quhare thu gais, I sal ga* (line 384: possibly echoing Ruth 1:16) forms part of a much more extended focus on the mutuality of the couple's tender concern for one another.

353–72   The Scots poet alludes to *Fortoun* in line 357, and again in line 366, as a personified representation of fate. Boethius' sixth-century work, *The Consolation of Philosophy* (frequently translated into medieval vernaculars, e.g., by Chaucer) was enormously influential in popularizing this conception of Fortune as a (female) figure who controls one's earthly destiny, however hard one may strive against it (although the goal of Boethius' work is to teach indifference to Fortune's earthly blows by the cultivation of moral virtue and the desire for union with God). The equivalent segment of *LA* neither uses the word nor dwells on Julian's reaction to his fate at such length:

Ecce, impletum est uerbum cerui, quod dum uitare uolui, miserrimus adimpleui,
"Behold, the word of the stag has been fulfilled; what I wished to avoid, most miser-
able, I have fulfilled" (ed. Maggioni, p. 213; my translation). Julian's lament on
Fortune concludes at line 372 with a verse of moving poetic simplicity: *and yet this
wrak is falline in*. The standard English work on Fortune is still that of Patch, *The
Goddess Fortuna in Medieval Literature*.

357   *Preysand*. Scots *preyse*, with its ME equivalent *prese/prece*, is a variant form of
         press (pronounced approximately as if to rhyme with Modern English *race*).

397–98   See the note to lines 284–85, above. *LA* makes no mention of the couple's wealth at
         this point.

407–8   There is no vow of chastity in *LA*. This is the strongest single piece of evidence for
         the poet's knowledge of other traditions as seen by a comparison with the French
         prose version, which states that the couple vowed never to have "carnal relations"
         with one another: *Andui ont voé a Dieu que ja mes n'avront charnel conpaignie en-
         semble* (Bart and Cook, p. 131).

414   The great fall of snow that makes the courtyard unrecognizable is a nice northern touch
         on the part of our Scots poet. The French prose speaks of a great and horrible storm,
         but without giving details, while Jacobus says simply that it was a freezing night.

423ff.   The Scots poet refers to the visitor as a *yunge barne* in line 423 and subsequently as
         a *child*, in lines 429, 434, and 445. Curiously, and despite Ryan's translation, which
         uses the words "man" and "stranger" to describe the visitor, *LA* in fact never uses a
         noun, introducing him as a voice (*uocem*), and then as "one near death from the
         cold" (*gelu deficientem*), and thereafter referring to him only in pronominal form as
         ipsum or *ille* (ed. Maggioni, p. 213). All the other versions I have read describe him
         initially as a leper, without reference to age. Where, then, does the idea of a child
         come from? In one branch of the Julian tradition in French the stranger reveals
         himself as Christ rather than an angel, and perhaps knowledge of this tradition has
         led our poet to make a connection with St. Christopher, who transports a child who
         grows heavier and heavier until he finally reveals himself to be the Christ. I have not
         found anything comparable in other Middle English versions; *SEL*, for example,
         stays closer to the tradition in identifying the visitor as a "man" and a "grislich
         mesel" (see *SEL* St. Julian the Hospitaller, lines 109ff., DM 1.36).

447–48 The general sense of this couplet is clear enough — namely, that the child had been greatly disfigured by leprosy and sickness — but the syntax seems corrupt or incomplete. One solution would be to emend *al* (line 447) to *of*, in which case one might translate: "who before, from (lit., of) leprosy and great sickness, had been very ugly."

459 *folow*. I.e., *fellow* (OE *feolaga*, one who lays down money in a common cause), which does not often have the sense "spouse," and then mainly in Northern texts.

485–780 As in *LA*, the account of Julian the Apostate takes up the remainder of the text. For the blessing in the final lines, by means of which the poet returns himself and the audience to Julian Hospitaller, see the Introduction to this chapter.

VIII

Textual Notes to the Life of St. Julian Hospitaller in the Scottish Legendary (c. 1400)

Abbreviations: **MS** = Cambridge, University Library, MS Gg.2.6, fols. 169r, 171v–174v

1   *Quene.* MS: *wene.* The initial letter *Q* is wanting. A space was left at the beginning, presumably for a capital which was never added.

229   *Yhete.* MS: *Hete.* Space is left for a large capital *Y,* signaling the beginning of the account of Julian Hospitaller.

244   *sal.* MS omits.

246   *be.* MS: *but.*

254   *in.* Metcalfe's emendation, *into,* is not necessary to the sense (ME *in* often means "into") but does make for better scansion. The poet, however, should not be held to a strict standard of metrical regularity.

273   *a yung.* MS: *and a yung.*

275   *mychtty mane.* Metcalfe emends to *a mychtty man,* perhaps to improve the meter. That the indefinite article *a* is not necessary for sense or idiom is evident from lines 258 ("sene he was manly mane") and 277 ("And lang tyme led gude lyfe").

288   *thame.* MS omits.

321   *Forthi.* MS: *For.*

327   *as the ded.* MS: *as he ded.*

343   *hard.* Metcalfe emends to *had hard,* to regularize the meter, but the poet is just as likely to have accented *he* and *hard* with a pause (at the caesura) between them, thus: **Fra** that **he / hard** this **tale.** See also below, line 368.

359   *fellounly.* MS: *fellouny.*

368   *sad.* Metcalfe unnecessarily emends to *had sad,* regularizing the meter.

375   *ay.* Metcalfe's emendation (*ay sal I*) fails to solve the problem in this sentence, which lacks a main verb, not just an auxiliary, and does not need to repeat the personal pronoun from line 374. Although *LA* has "never shall rest until," the context here requires something like *ay sal dre,* "ever will endure/suffer (i.e., be a penitent), until Jesus . . . accepts my penance."

388   *with thee.* MS: *with he.*

407   *tharewith als.* MS: *with als.* The MS reading is clearly wrong. The simplest emendation is to substitute *withal* ("moreover") for *with als* ("with also"), as noted by Met-

calfe (3.292), but because it produces better sense and scansion the emendation adopted here is that of Horstmann, *Barbour's des schottischen nationaldichters Legendensammlung*, 1.224.

420   *That*. MS: *Thai*.
429   *this*. MS: *his*.
435   *spil*. MS: *spiel*.
469   *angel than of*. MS: *angel of [?] than of*.
476   *lifit*. MS: *lif*.
479   *rycht as*. MS: *rycht*.

Bibliography

Aarne, Antti. *The Types of the Folktale: A Classification and Bibliography*. Trans. and enl. Stith Thompson. Second revision. Helsinki: Suomalainen Tiedeakatemia, 1981.

Abrams, M. H., et al., eds. *The Norton Anthology of English Literature*. Seventh ed. 2 vols. New York: W. W. Norton, 2000.

Acta Sanctorum. See Bolland.

Adamnan of Iona. *Life of St Columba*. Trans. Richard Sharpe. Harmondsworth, UK: Penguin Books, 1995.

Aitken, A. J. "The Language of Older Scots Poetry," In *Scotland and the Lowland Tongue: Studies in the Language and Literature of Lowland Scotland in Honour of David D. Murison*. Ed. J. Derrick McClure, with foreword by A. J. Aitken. Aberdeen: Aberdeen University Press, 1983. Pp. 18–49.

Aldhelm. *Aldhelm, the Prose Works*. Trans. Michael Lapidge and Michael W. Herren. Cambridge, UK: D. S. Brewer, 1979.

————. *Aldhelm, the Poetic Works*. Trans. Michael Lapidge and James L. Rosier. Cambridge, UK: D. S. Brewer, 1985.

Altaner, Berthold, and Alfred Stuiber. *Patrologie: Leben, Schriften u. Lehre d. Kirchenväter*. Eighth ed. Freiburg-im-Breisgau: Herder, 1978.

Amélineau, E., ed. and trans. *Contes et romans de l'Égypte chrétienne*. Collection de contes et chansons populaires 13. Paris: Ernest Léroux, 1888.

Amt, Emilie, ed. *Women's Lives in Medieval Europe: A Sourcebook*. New York: Routledge, 1993.

Ancrene Wisse: Parts Six and Seven. Ed. Geoffrey Shepherd. London: Thomas Nelson, 1959. [See also Savage and Watson, 1991.]

Andrew, Malcolm, and Ronald Waldron, eds. *The Poems of the Pearl Manuscript: Pearl, Cleanness, Patience, Sir Gawain and the Green Knight*. Rev. ed. Exeter: University of Exeter Press, 1996.

Arnoldus of Liège. *An Alphabet of Tales. An English 15th Century Translation of the Alphabetum narrationum of Étienne de Besançon*. Ed. Mary Macleod Banks. EETS o.s. 126–27. London: Kegan Paul, Trench, Trübner and Co., 1904–05.

Ashley, Kathleen, and Pamela Sheingorn. *Writing Faith: Text, Sign & History in the Miracles of Sainte Foy*. Chicago: University of Chicago Press, 1999.

Athanasius. *The Life of Antony and the Letter to Marcellinus*. Trans. Robert Gregg. New York: Paulist Press, 1980.

Aufhauser, J. B. *Das Drachenwunder des heiligen Georg in der griechischen und lateinischen Überlieferung*. Byzantinisches Archiv 5. Leipzig: B. G. Teubner, 1911.

Augustine, bishop of Hippo. *Confessions*. Trans. and intro. R. S. Pine-Coffin. Harmondsworth, UK: Penguin Books, 1961.

———. *Concerning the City of God against the Pagans*. Trans. Henry Snowcroft Bettenson. Intro. David Knowles. Harmondsworth, UK: Penguin Books, 1972.

Auster, John. *Poems, with Some Translations from the German*. Edinburgh: W. Blackwood, 1819.

Ælfric of Eynsham, abbot. *The Homilies of the Anglo-Saxon Church: The First Part, Containing the Sermones catholici or Homilies of Ælfric*. Ed. and trans. Benjamin Thorpe. 2 vols. London: The Ælfric Society, 1844–46.

———. *Ælfric's Lives of the Saints: Being a Set of Sermons on Saints' Days Formerly Observed by the English Church*. Ed. Walter W. Skeat. 4 vols. EETS o.s. 76, 82, 94, 114. London: N. Trübner and Co., 1881–1900; rpt. 2 vols. London: Oxford University Press, 1966.

———. *Ælfric's Catholic Homilies: The Second Series: Text*. Ed. Malcolm Godden. EETS s.s. 5. London: Oxford University Press, 1979.

———. *Ælfric's Catholic Homilies: The First Series: Text*. Ed. Peter Clemoes. EETS s.s. 17. London: Oxford University Press, 1997.

Bibliography

Æthelwold, bishop of Winchester. *Regularis Concordia anglicae nationis monachorum sancti-monialiumque*. Ed. and trans. Thomas Symons. London: Thomas Nelson, 1953.

———. *Die angelsächsischen Prosabearbeitungen der Benediktinerregel*. Ed. and trans. Arnold Schröer. Bibliothek der angelsächsischen Prosa 2. Kassel: G. H. Wigand, 1885–88; rpt. Darmstadt: Wissenschaftliche Buchgesellschaft, 1964.

Bart, Benjamin F., and Robert Francis Cook. *The Legendary Sources of Flaubert's Saint Julien*. University of Toronto Romance Series 36. Toronto: University of Toronto Press, 1977.

Bately, Janet. "Those Books That Are Most Necessary for All Men to Know: The Classics and Late Ninth-Century England, a Reappraisal." In *The Classics in the Middle Ages: Papers of the Twentieth Annual Conference of the Center for Medieval and Early Renaissance Studies*. Ed. Aldo S. Bernardo and Saul Levin. Medieval & Renaissance Texts & Studies 69. Binghamton, NY: Center for Medieval & Early Renaissance Studies, 1990. Pp. 45–78.

Bateson, Mary. *Catalogue of the Library of Syon Monastery, Isleworth*. Cambridge: The University Press, 1898.

Battifol, Pierre. "La Légende de Sainte Thaïs." *Bulletin de littérature ecclésiastique* 5 (1903), 207–17.

Baugh, Albert C., and Thomas Cable. *A History of the English Language*. Third ed. Englewood Cliffs, NJ: Prentice-Hall, 1978.

Beau, A. *Le culte et les reliques de Saint Benoît et de Sainte Scholastique*. Montserrat: Publicacions de l'Abadia de Montserrat, 1980.

Bede. *Bede's Ecclesiastical History of the English People*. Ed. Bertram Colgrave and R. A. B. Mynors. Oxford: Clarendon Press, 1969.

Benedict, abbot of Monte Cassino. *The Rule of St Benedict*. Trans. Justin McCann. London: Sheed and Ward, 1976.

———. *RB 1980: The Rule of St. Benedict in Latin and English with Notes*. Trans. Timothy Fry. Collegeville, MN: Liturgical Press, 1981.

Bennett, J. A. W. *Poetry of the Passion: Studies in Twelve Centuries of English Verse*. Oxford: Clarendon Press, 1982.

Bennett, J. A. W., and G. V. Smithers, eds. *Early Middle English Verse and Prose.* Second ed. Oxford: Clarendon Press, 1968.

Benskin, Michael, and Angus McIntosh. "A Medieval English Manuscript of Irish Provenance." *Medium Ævum* 41 (1972), 128–31.

Berschin, Walter. *Biographie und Epochenstil im lateinischen Mittelalter.* 4 vols. Quellen und Untersuchungen zur lateinischen Philologie des Mittelalters 8–10, 12. Stuttgart: A. Hiersemann, 1986–2001.

Bestul, Thomas H. *Texts of the Passion: Latin Devotional Literature and Medieval Society.* Philadelphia: University of Pennsylvania Press, 1996.

Bibliotheca hagiographica Latina. See Bollandists.

Bjerre-Aspegren, Kerstin. *The Male Woman: A Feminine Ideal in the Early Church.* Ed. René Kieffer. Acta Universitatis Upsaliensis, Uppsala Women's Studies, A; Women in Religion 4. Stockholm: Almqvist & Wiksell International, 1990.

Blair, Peter Hunter. *The World of Bede.* New York: St. Martin's Press, 1971; rpt. Cambridge, UK: Cambridge University Press, 1990.

Blake, N. F. "Wynkyn de Worde: The Later Years." *Gutenberg-Jahrbuch* (1972), 128–38.

Bodleian Library. *A Summary Catalogue of Western Manscripts in the Bodleian Library at Oxford.* Oxford: Clarendon Press, 1895–1953.

Boenig, Robert, trans. *The Acts of Andrew in the Country of the Cannibals: Translations from the Greek, Latin, and Old English.* Garland Library of Medieval Literature 70, ser. B. New York: Garland Publishing, 1991.

Bokenham, Osbern. *Legendys of Hooly Wummen.* Ed. Mary S. Serjeantson. EETS o.s. 206. London: Oxford University Press, 1938; rpt. Woodbridge, UK: Boydell & Brewer, 1997.

———. *A Legend of Holy Women: Osbern Bokenham, Legends of Holy Women.* Trans. Sheila Delany. Notre Dame, IN: University of Notre Dame Press, 1992.

Bolland, Johannes, et al., eds. *Acta Sanctorum.* 68 vols. First ed. Antwerp; Brussels: Société des Bollandistes, 1643–1940.

Bibliography

Bollandists. *Bibliotheca hagiographica Latina antiquae et mediae aetatis ediderunt Socii Bollandiani.* 2 vols. Subsidia hagiographica 6. Brussels: Société des Bollandistes, 1899–1901; *Novum Supplementum,* ed. H. Froz. Subsidia hagiographica 70. Brussels: Société des Bollandistes, 1986.

Bonaventure. *Legenda Maior Sancti Francisci.* Ed. Michael Bihl, O. F. M. *Analecta Franciscana* 10 (1926–41), 555–626.

Bonner, Gerald, David Rollason, and Clare Stancliffe, eds. *St. Cuthbert, His Cult and His Community: To AD 1200.* Woodbridge, UK: Boydell Press, 1989.

Booth, Wayne C. "Irony and Pity Once Again: *Thaïs* Revisited." *Critical Inquiry* 2 (1975/76), 327–44.

Boyd, Beverley, ed. *The Middle English Miracles of the Virgin.* San Marino, CA: Huntington Library, 1964.

Bremond, Claude, Jacques Le Goff, and Jean-Claude Schmitt. *L'"Exemplum."* Typologie des Sources du Moyen Age Occidental 40. Turnhout: Brepols, 1982.

Breviarium ad Usum Insignis Ecclesie Eboracensis. Ed. Stephen Willoughby Lawley. 2 vols. Surtees Society 71 and 75. Durham, UK: Andrews & Co., 1880–83.

Breviarum ad Usum Insignis Ecclesiae Sarum. Ed. Francis Procter and Christopher Wordsworth. 3 vols. Cambridge, UK: Cambridge University Press, 1879–86; rpt. Farnborough, UK: Gregg, 1970.

Bridget of Sweden, Saint. *Revelaciones.* Ed. Birger Bergh, Hans Aili, et al. 7 vols. Samlingar utgivna av Svenska Fornskriftsällskapet, Ser. 2. Latinska skrifter 7. Uppsala and Stockholm: Almquist & Wiksell, 1967–92.

———. *The Liber Celestis of St Bridget of Sweden: The Middle English Version in British Library MS Claudian B.i, Together with a Life of the Saint from the Same Manuscript.* Vol. 1 (Text). Ed. Roger Ellis. EETS o.s. 291. Oxford: Oxford University Press, 1987.

The Bridgettine Breviary of Syon Abbey, from the Ms. with English rubrics F. 4. 11 at Magdalene College, Cambridge. Ed. Arthur Jeffries Collins. HBS 96. London: HBS, 1969.

Brody, Saul. *The Disease of the Soul: Leprosy in Medieval Literature*. Ithaca, NY: Cornell University Press, 1974.

Bromyard, John. *Summa praedicantium*. 2 vols. Basel: Johannes Amerbach, ca. 1484.

Brooke, Rosalind B. *The Coming of the Friars*. Historical Problems: Studies and Documents 24. London: G. Allen and Unwin, 1975.

Brown, Carleton, ed. *English Lyrics of the XIIIth Century*. Oxford: Clarendon Press, 1932.

Brown, Carleton, and Rossell Hope Robbins, eds. *The Index of Middle English Verse*. New York: Columbia University Press, 1943.

Brown, Peter. *The Cult of the Saints: Its Rise and Function in Latin Christianity*. The Haskell Lectures on History of Religions n.s. 2. Chicago: University of Chicago Press, 1981.

—————. *Society and the Holy in Late Antiquity*. Berkeley: University of California Press, 1982.

—————. *The Body and Society: Men, Women, and Sexual Renunciation in Early Christianity*. New York: Columbia University Press, 1988.

Butler, Alban. *Lives of the Saints*. Ed. and rev. Herbert Thurston and Donald Attwater. 4 vols. London: Palm Publishers, 1956.

Buttrick, George Arthur, ed. *The Interpreters' Bible*. 12 vols. New York: Abingdon Press, 1952–57.

Bynum, Caroline Walker. *Holy Feast and Holy Fast: The Religious Significance of Food to Medieval Women*. Berkeley: University of California Press, 1987.

—————. *The Resurrection of the Body in Western Christianity, 200–1336*. New York: Columbia University Press, 1995.

Cabrol, Fernand, and Henri Leclercq, eds. "Georges (Saint)." In *Dictionnaire d'archéologie chrétienne et de liturgie*. 15 vols. Paris: Letouzey et Ané, 1907–53.

Caesarius of Arles. *The Rule for Nuns of St. Caesarius of Arles*. Trans. and intro. Maria Caritas McCarthy. Washington, DC: Catholic University of America Press, 1960.

Bibliography

Caesarius of Heisterbach. *The Dialogue on Miracles*. Trans. Henry von Essen Scott and C. C. Swinton Bland. Intro. G. G. Coulton. 2 vols. London: G. Routledge and Sons, 1929.

Capik, Gloria Ann. "La Vie de Thais: Prolegomena." Ph.D. Dissertation: University of Chicago, 1986. *DAI* 47.7 (1987), p. 2604A.

Carey, Hilary. "Devout Literate Laypeople and the Pursuit of the Mixed Life in Late Medieval England." *Journal of Religious History* 14 (1987), 361–81.

Cassian, John. *Conferences*. Trans. Colm Luibhéid, intro. Owen Chadwick. New York: Paulist Press, 1985.

Cavallera, Ferdinand. *Saint Jérôme: sa vie et son oeuvre*. Spicilegium Sacrum Lovaniense: Études et documents 1–2. Louvain: Spicilegium Sacrum Lovaniense, 1922.

Caxton, William. *The Golden Legend, or Lives of the Saints*. Ed. F. S. Ellis. 7 vols. in 4. London: J. M. Dent, 1900; rpt. New York: AMS Press, 1973.

Chambers, E. K. *The English Folk-Play*. Oxford: Clarendon Press, 1933; rpt. 1969.

Chaucer, Geoffrey. *The Riverside Chaucer*. Third ed. Gen. ed. Larry D. Benson. Boston: Houghton Mifflin, 1987.

Chichele, Henry. *The Register of Henry Chichele, Archbishop of Canterbury, 1414–1443*. Ed. E. F. Jacob. 4 vols. Oxford: Clarendon Press, 1938–47.

Chitty, Derwas J. *The Desert a City: An Introduction to the Study of Egyptian and Palestinian Monasticism under the Christian Empire*. Oxford: Basil Blackwell, 1966.

Clark, Elizabeth. *Jerome, Chrysostom, and Friends: Essays and Translations*. Lewiston, NY: Mellen, 1979.

Colgrave, Bertram, ed. *Two Lives of Saint Cuthbert: A Life by an Anonymous Monk of Lindisfarne and Bede's Prose Life*. Cambridge, UK: Cambridge University Press, 1940; rpt. 1985.

Colker, Marvin L. *Trinity College Library, Dublin: Descriptive Catalogue of the Mediaeval and Renaissance Latin Manuscripts*. 2 vols. Aldershot, UK: Scolar Press, 1991.

Colledge, Edmund. "*Epistola Solitarii ad Reges*. Alphonse of Pecha as Organizer of Birgittine and Urbanist Propaganda." *Mediaeval Studies* 18 (1956), 19–49.

Conner, Patrick W. *Anglo-Saxon Exeter: A Tenth-Century Cultural History.* Woodbridge, UK: Boydell Press, 1993.

Cross, James E. "Saints' Lives in Old English: Latin Manuscripts and Vernacular Accounts: *The Old English Martyrology*." *Peritia* 1 (1982), 38–62.

————, and Thomas D. Hill, eds. *The Prose Solomon and Saturn and Adrian and Ritheus.* McMaster Old English Studies and Texts 1. Toronto: University of Toronto Press, 1982.

Curtius, Ernst Robert. *European Literature and the Latin Middle Ages.* Trans. Willard R. Trask. Bollingen Series 36. Princeton, NJ: Princeton University Press, 1953, rpt. 1973.

Cusack, Pearse Aidan. "St. Scholastica: Myth or Real Person?" *The Downside Review* 92 (1974), 145–59.

Cutler, John L., and Rossell Hope Robbins, eds. *Supplement to the Index of Middle English Verse.* Lexington: University of Kentucky Press, 1965.

Daniélou, Jean. *The Bible and the Liturgy.* Notre Dame, IN: University of Notre Dame Press, 1966.

Davies, Stevan L. *The Revolt of the Widows: The Social World of the Apocryphal Acts.* Carbondale: Southern Illinois University Press, 1980.

D'Evelyn, Charlotte. "The Scottish Legendary." In *MWME* 2.419–22, 557–58.

————. "Instructions for Religious." In *MWME* 2.460–63.

————. "Saints' Legends." In *MWME* 2.553–649.

De Hamel, Christopher. *Syon Abbey: The Library of the Bridgettine Nuns and Their Peregrinations after the Reformation: An Essay, with the Manuscript at Arundel Castle.* Otley, UK: Smith Settle, 1991.

Delany, Sheila. *Impolitic Bodies: Poetry, Saints, and Society in Fifteenth-Century England: The Work of Osbern Bokenham.* New York: Oxford University Press, 1998.

Bibliography

Delehaye, Hippolyte. *Les légendes grècques des saints militaires*. Paris: Librairie Alphonse Picard, 1909; rpt. New York: Arno Press, 1975.

———. *The Legends of the Saints*. Trans. Donald Attwater. Fourth ed. New York: Fordham University Press, 1962.

———. *Les passions des martyrs et les genres littéraires*. Second ed. Brussels: Société des Bollandistes, 1966.

de Vogüé, Adalbert. "La rencontre de Benoît et de Scholastique: Essai d'interprétation." *Revue d'histoire de la spiritualité* 48 (1972), 257–273.

———. "The Meeting of Benedict and Scholastica: An Interpretation." *Cistercian Studies* 18 (1983), 167–83. [Translation of de Vogüé, 1972.]

Di Berardino, Angelo, ed. *Encylopedia of the Early Church*. Trans. Adrian Walford, with a foreword and bibliographic amendments by W. H. C. Frend. 2 vols. Cambridge, UK: James Clarke, 1992.

Didi-Huberman, Georges, Riccardo Garbetta, and Manuela Morgaine. *Saint Georges et le dragon: versions d'une légende*. Paris: A. Biro, 1994.

Dobbie, Elliott Van Kirk, ed. *The Anglo-Saxon Minor Poems*. Anglo-Saxon Poetic Records 6. New York: Columbia University Press, 1942.

Dorn, Erhard. *Der Sündige Heilige in der Legende des Mittelalters*. Medium Aevum, Philologische Studien 10. Munich: Wilhelm Fink Verlag, 1967.

Doyle, Ian. "Publication by Members of the Religious Orders." In *Book Production and Publishing in Britain 1375–1475*. Ed. Jeremy Griffiths and Derek Pearsall. Cambridge, UK: Cambridge University Press, 1989. Pp. 109–23.

Duffy, Eamon. *The Stripping of the Altars: Traditional Religion in England, c. 1400 – c. 1580*. New Haven, CT: Yale University Press, 1992.

Dugdale, Sir William. *The Antiquities of Warwickshire*. Second ed. 2 vols. London: J. Osborn and T. Longman, 1730.

Dunbar, William. *The Poems of William Dunbar*. Ed. W. Mackay Mackenzie. London: Faber and Faber, 1932.

Dunn-Lardeau, Brenda, ed. *Legenda aurea, sept siècles de diffusion: actes du colloque international sur la Legenda aurea, texte latin et branches vernaculaires à l'Université du Québec à Montréal, 11–12 mai 1983*. Montreal: Bellarmin, 1986.

———. *Legenda aurea — La légende dorée (XIIIe–XVe s.): Actes du Congrès international de Perpignan (séances "Nouvelles recherches sur la Legenda Aurea")*. Moyen français 32. Montreal: Ceres, 1993.

Dutschke, C. W., with the assistance of R. H. Rouse and Sara S. Hodson et al. *Guide to Medieval and Renaissance Manuscripts in the Huntington Library*. 2 vols. San Marino, CA: The Library, 1989.

The Early English Versions of the Gesta Romanorum. Ed. Sidney J. H. Herrtage. EETS e.s. 33. London: N. Trübner and Co., 1879; rpt. London: Oxford University Press, 1962.

The Early South-English Legendary or Lives of Saints. I. MS. Laud. 108, in the Bodleian Library. Ed. Carl Horstmann. EETS o.s. 87. London: N. Trübner & Co., 1887; rpt. Woodbridge, UK: Boydell and Brewer, 2000.

An East Midland Revision of the South English Legendary: A Selection from Ms. C.U.L. Add. 3039. Ed. Manfred Görlach. Middle English Texts 4. Heidelberg: Carl Winter, 1976.

Eddius Stephanus. *The Life of Bishop Wilfrid*. Ed. Bertram Colgrave. Cambridge, UK: Cambridge University Press, 1927; rpt. 1985.

Elliott, Alison Goddard. *Roads to Paradise: Reading the Lives of the Early Saints*. Hanover, NH: University Press of New England, 1987.

Elliott, J. K., ed. *The Apocryphal New Testament: A Collection of Apocryphal Christian Literature in an English Translation*. Oxford: Clarendon Press, 1993.

Ellis, Roger. *Viderunt eam filie Syon: The Spirituality of the English House of a Medieval Contemplative Order from Its Beginnings to the Present Day*. Analecta Cartusiana 68. Salzburg: Institut für Anglistik und Amerikanistik, 1984.

Étienne de Bourbon. See Stephanus de Borbone.

Bibliography

Eusebius. *The History of the Church from Christ to Constantine*. Trans. and intro. G. A. Williamson. Harmondsworth, UK: Penguin Books, 1965; rev. and ed., with a new intro., Andrew Louth, 1989.

Felix. *Felix's Life of Saint Guthlac*. Ed. Bertram Colgrave. Cambridge, UK: Cambridge University Press, 1956; rpt. 1985.

Finucane, Ronald C. *Miracles and Pilgrims: Popular Beliefs in Medieval England*. Totowa, NJ: Rowman and Littlefield, 1977.

Flaubert, Gustave. *Three Tales*. Trans. A. J. Krailsheimer. Oxford: Oxford University Press, 1991.

Fleming, John V. *An Introduction to the Franciscan Literature of the Middle Ages*. Chicago: Franciscan Herald Press, 1977.

Fontenrose, Joseph. *Python: A Study of Delphic Myth and Its Origins*. Berkeley: University of California Press, 1959.

France, Anatole. *Thaïs*. Trans. Robert B. Douglas. Intro. Raymond Weaver. New York: Macmillan, 1929.

Freire, José Geraldes. *A versão latina por Pascásio di Dume dos Apophthegmata patrum*. 2 vols. Coimbra: Instituto de estudos clássicos, 1971.

Fros, Henryk. *Bibliotheca Hagiographica Latina Antiauae et Mediae Aetatis. Novum Supplementum*. Subsidia Hagiographica 70. Brussels: Société des Bollandistes, 1986.

Frugoni, Chiara. *Francesco e l'invenzione delle stimmate: Una storia per parole e immagini fino a Bonaventura e Giotto*. Turin: G. Einaudi, 1993.

Furnivall, Frederick J., ed. *Early English Poems and Lives of Saints, with Those of the Wicked Birds Pilate and Judas*. Berlin: A. Asher, 1862.

Gaiffier, B. de. "La légende de S. Julien l'Hospitalier." *Analecta Bollandiana* 63 (1945), 145–219.

Gamble, Harry Y. *Books and Readers in the Early Church: A History of Early Christian Texts*. New Haven: Yale University Press, 1995.

Gayet, Albert. *Antinoë et les sépultures de Thaïs et Sérapion*. Paris: Société française d'éditions d'art, 1902.

Gerould, Gordon Hall. *Saints' Legends*. Boston: Houghton Mifflin Co., 1916; rpt. Folcroft, PA: Folcroft Press, 1969.

Gibbs, Henry Hucks, ed. *The Life and Martyrdom of Saint Katherine of Alexandria, Virgin and Martyr*. London: Nichols and Sons, 1884.

Gilson, Julius P. "St. Julian the Harbinger and the First of the English Percys." *Archaeologia Aeliana*, third ser. 4 (1908), 304–12.

Gneuss, Helmut. *Handlist of Anglo-Saxon Manuscripts: Revised Preliminary List of Manuscripts Written or Owned in England up to A.D. 1100*. Medieval and Renaissance Texts and Studies 241. Tempe: Arizona Center for Medieval and Renaissance Studies, 2001.

Golding, Brian. *Gilbert of Sempringham and the Gilbertine Order, c.1130–c.1300*. Oxford: Clarendon Press, 1995.

Görlach, Manfred. *The South English Legendary, Gilte Legende and Golden Legend*. Braunschweiger anglistische Arbeiten 3. Braunschweig: Institut für Anglistik und Amerikanistik, 1972.

———. *The Textual Tradition of the South English Legendary*. Leeds Texts and Monographs n.s. 6. Leeds: University of Leeds, School of English, 1974.

———. "Middle English Legends, 1220–1530." In Philippart, 1994–. Vol. 1. 1994. Pp. 429–85.

Goscelin of Canterbury. *Historia Maior Sancti Augustini episcopi Cantuariensis*. In *Acta Sanctorum*. Maius 6.375–95.

Gower, John. *The English Works of John Gower*. Ed. G. C. Macaulay. 2 vols. EETS e.s. 81–82. Oxford: Clarendon Press, 1900–01; rpt. London: Oxford University Press, 1957.

Gregory of Tours. *Glory of the Martyrs*. Trans. and intro. Raymond Van Dam. Translated Texts for Historians, Latin Series 3. Liverpool: Liverpool University Press, 1988.

Gregory the Great. *The Dialogues of Saint Gregory, Surnamed the Great: Pope of Rome & the First of That Name*. Ed. Edmund Garratt Gardner. London: Philip Lee Warner, 1911.

————. *Dialogues*. Ed. Adalbert de Vogüé. 3 vols. Sources Chrétiennes 251, 260, 265. Paris: Editions du Cerf, 1978–80.

————. *The Life of St. Benedict*. Trans. Hilary Costello and Eoin de Bhaldraithe, with commentary by Adalbert de Vogüé. Petersham, MA: St. Bede's Publications, 1993.

————. "Life of St. Benedict" (*Dialogues* 2). Trans. White, 1998. Pp. 161–204.

Gretsch, Mechthild. "Æthelwold's Translation of the 'Regula Sancti Benedicti' and Its Latin Exemplar." *Anglo-Saxon England* 3 (1974), 125–51.

Grimm, Jacob. "The Devil and His Grandmother." In *The Complete Grimm's Fairy Tales*. Intro. Padraic Colum. New York: Pantheon Books, 1972. Pp. 563–66.

Gripkey, Sister Mary Vincentine. *The Blessed Virgin Mary as Mediatrix in the Latin and Old French Legend prior to the Fourteenth Century*. The Catholic University of America Studies in Romance Languages and Literatures 17. Washington, DC: Catholic University of America, 1938; rpt. New York: AMS Press, 1969.

Guilbert, Lucille. "L'animal dans *Légende dorée*." In Dunn-Lardeau, 1986. Pp. 77–89.

Habig, Marion A., O. F. M., ed. *St. Francis of Assisi: Writings and Early Biographies: English Omnibus of the Sources for the Life of St. Francis*. Trans. Raphael Brown et al. Fourth rev. ed. Quincy, IL: Franciscan Press, Quincy College, 1991.

Hadley, D. M., ed. *Masculinity in Medieval Europe*. London: Longman, 1999.

Hagiographica: Rivista di agiografia e biografia della Società internazionale per lo studio del Medio Evo latino. Turnhout: Brepols, 1994–.

Hamer, Richard, ed. *Three Lives from the Gilte Legende: Ed. from MS B. L. Egerton 876*. Middle English Texts 9. Heidelberg: Carl Winter, 1978.

Hamer, Richard, and Vida Russell, eds. *Supplementary Lives in Some Manuscripts of the Gilte Legend*. EETS o.s. 315. Oxford: Oxford University Press, 2000.

The Harley Lyrics: The Middle English Lyrics of Ms. Harley 2253. Ed. G. L. Brook. Publications of the University of Manchester 302, English ser. 26. Manchester: Manchester University Press, 1948.

Hartmann von Aue. *Gregorius, The Good Sinner*. Trans. Sheema Zeben Buehne. New York: Frederick Ungar, 1966.

Hatto, A. T., ed. *Eos: An Inquiry into the Theme of Lovers' Meetings and Partings at Dawn in Poetry*. London: Mouton, 1965.

Haubrichs, Wolfgang. *Georgslied und Georgslegende im frühen Mittelalter: Text und Rekonstruktion*. Theorie-Kritik-Geschichte 13. Königstein: Scriptor, 1979.

Head, Thomas, ed. *Medieval Hagiography: An Anthology*. New York: Routledge, 2001.

Heffernan, Thomas J. "The Authorship of the 'Northern Homily Cycle': The Liturgical Affiliation of the Sunday Gospel Pericopes as a Test." *Traditio* 41 (1985), 289–309.

———. *Sacred Biography: Saints and Their Biographers in the Middle Ages*. New York: Oxford University Press, 1988.

———. "Orthodoxies Redux: The *Northern Homily Cycle* in the Vernon Manuscript and Its Textual Affiliation." In *Studies in the Vernon Manuscript*. Ed. Derek Pearsall. Cambridge, UK: D. S. Brewer, 1990. Pp. 75–87.

———. "Dangerous Sympathies: Political Commentary in the *South English Legendary*." In Jankofsky, 1992. Pp. 1–18.

The Hereford Breviary. Ed. Walter Howard Frere and Langton E. G. Brown. 3 vols. HBS 26, 40, 46. London: [Henry Bradshaw Society], 1904–15.

Hill, Joyce. "Saint George before the Conquest." *Report of the Society of the Friends of St George and the Descendants of the Knights of the Garter (Windsor Castle)*, 6/7 (1985–86), 284–95.

———. "Ælfric, Gelasius, and St. George." *Mediaevalia* 11 (1989 for 1985), 1–17.

Hoare, Frederick Russell, ed. and trans. *The Western Fathers: Being the Lives of SS. Martin of Tours, Ambrose, Augustine of Hippo, Honoratus of Arles, and Germanus Auxerre*. New York: Sheed and Ward, 1954.

Hollis, Stephanie. *Anglo-Saxon Women and the Church: Sharing a Common Fate*. Woodbridge, UK: Boydell Press, 1992.

Horstmann, Carl. "Die Evangelien-Geschichten der Homiliensammlung des Ms. Vernon." *Archiv* 57 (1877), 241–316.

———. "Prosalegenden." *Anglia* 3 (1880), 293–360.

———. *Altenglische Legenden: Neue Folge, mit Einleitung und Anmerkungen*. Heilbronn: Henninger, 1881.

———, ed. *Barbour's des schottischen Nationaldichters Legendensammlung nebst den Fragmenten seines Trojanerkrieges*. Heilbronn: Henninger, 1881–82.

———, ed. *Nova legenda Anglie: As Collected by John of Tynemouth, John Capgrave, and Others, and First Printed, with New Lives, by Wynkyn de Worde, A.D. mdxui*. 2 vols. Oxford: Clarendon Press, 1901.

Howard-Johnston, James, and Paul Antony Hayward, eds. *The Cult of Saints in Late Antiquity and the Middle Ages: Essays on the Contribution of Peter Brown*. Oxford: Oxford University Press, 1999.

Hrotsvitha, abbess of Gandersheim. *Hrotsvithae Opera*. Ed. Helena Homeyer. Paderborn: Ferdinand Schöningh, 1970.

———. *The Plays of Hrotsvit of Gandersheim*. Trans. Katharina M. Wilson. New York: Garland, 1989.

Hughes, Andrew. *Medieval Manuscripts for Mass and Office: A Guide to Their Organization and Terminology*. Toronto: University of Toronto Press, 1982.

Hulst, Cornelia Steketee. *St. George of Cappadocia in Legend and History*. London: D. Nutt, 1909.

Hutchison, Ann. "Devout Reading in the Monastery and in the Late Medieval Household." In *De cella in seculum: Religious and Secular Life and Devotion in Late Medieval England: An Interdisciplinary Conference in Celebration of the Eighth Centenary of the Consecration of St. Hugh of Avalon, Bishop of Lincoln, 20–22 July, 1986*. Ed. Michael G. Sargent. Cambridge, UK: D. S. Brewer, 1989. Pp. 215–37.

Jacob, E. F. *The Fifteenth Century 1399–1485*. Oxford: Oxford University Press, 1961.

Jacob's Well: An English Treatise on the Cleansing of Man's Conscience. Ed. Arthur Brandeis. EETS o.s. 115. London: Kegan Paul, Trench, Trübner & Co., 1900.

Jacobus de Voragine. *Legenda aurea. Vulgo historia Lombardica dicta*. Ed. Th. Graesse. Third ed. Osnabrück: Otto Zeller, 1890; rpt. 1969.

———. *Three Lives from the Gilte Legende: Ed. from MS B. L. Egerton 876*. See Hamer, 1978.

———. *The Golden Legend: Readings on the Saints*. Trans. William Granger Ryan. 2 vols. Princeton, NJ: Princeton University Press, 1993.

———. *The Golden Legend: Selections*. Ed. Christopher Stace. London: Penguin Books, 1998.

———. *Legenda aurea: Edizione critica*. Ed. Giovanni Paolo Maggioni. 2 vols. Rev. ed. Millennio Medievale 6, Testi 3. Florence: SISMEL, Edizioni del Galluzzo, 1998.

James, M. R. *Descriptive Catalogue of the Manuscripts in the Library of St. John's College, Cambridge*. Cambridge, UK: University Press, 1913.

———, and C. Jenkins. *Descriptive Catalogue of the Manuscripts in the Library of Lambeth Palace: The Medieval Manuscripts*. Cambridge, UK: Cambridge University Press, 1932.

Jankofsky, Klaus P. "Entertainment, Edification, and Popular Education in the *South English Legendary*." *Journal of Popular Culture* 11 (1977), 706–17.

———. "*Legenda Aurea* Materials in *The South English Legendary*: Translation, Transformation, Acculturation." In Dunn-Lardeau, 1986. Pp. 317–29.

———. "National characteristics in the portrayal of English saints in *The South English Legendary*." In *Images of Sainthood in Medieval Europe*. Ed. Renate Blumenfeld-Kosinski and Timea Szell. Ithaca, NY: Cornell University Press, 1991. Pp. 81–93.

———, ed. *The South English Legendary: A Critical Assessment*. Tübingen: Francke, 1992.

Jerome. *St Jerome: Letters and Select Works*. Trans. W. H. Fremantle et al. In *A Select Library of the Nicene and Post-Nicene Fathers of the Christian Church*. Ed. Philip Schaff and Henry Wace. Second Ser. 6. 1893; rpt. Grand Rapids, MI: Eerdmans, 1979.

———. *Sancti Eusebii Hieronymi Epistulae*. Ed. Isidorus Hilberg. 3 vols. Corpus Scriptorum Ecclesiasticorum Latinorum 54–56. Vienna: F. Tempsky, 1910–18.

Johann, von Neumarkt. *Schriften Johanns von Neumarkt unter Mitwirkung Konrad Burdachs, herausgegeben von Joseph Klapper*. 4 vols. Vom Mittelalter zur Reformation, Forschungen zur Geschichte der deutschen Bildung, 6. Berlin: Weidmann, 1930–35.

John of Tynemouth. *Sanctilogium Anglie*. See Horstmann, *Nova legenda Anglie*.

Jones, Charles W. *Saint Nicholas of Myra, Bari, and Manhattan: Biography of a Legend*. Chicago: University of Chicago Press, 1978.

Kaftal, George, with Fabio Bisogni. *Iconography of the Saints in the Painting of North East Italy*. Saints in Italian Art 3. Florence: Sansoni, 1978.

Karras, Ruth Mazo. *Common Women: Prostitution and Sexuality in Medieval England*. New York: Oxford University Press, 1996. [See especially chapter 6, "Saints and Sinners," pp. 102–30.]

Keiser, George. "Patronage and Piety in Fifteenth-Century England: Margaret, Duchess of Clarence, Symon Wynter and Beinecke MS 317." *Yale University Library Gazette* 60 (1985): 32–53.

———. "St Jerome and the Brigittines: Visions of the Afterlife in Fifteenth-Century England." In *England in the Fifteenth Century: Proceedings of the 1986 Harlaxton Symposium*. Ed. Daniel Williams. Woodbridge, UK: D. S. Brewer, 1987.

Kelly, J. N. D. *Jerome: His Life, Writings, and Controversies*. London: Duckworth, 1975.

Ker, N. R. *Medieval Libraries of Great Britain: A List of Surviving Books*. Second ed. Royal Historical Society Guides and Handbooks 3. London: Offices of the Royal Historical Society, 1964.

Kieckhefer, Richard, and George Doherty Bond, eds. *Sainthood: Its Manifestations in World Religions*. Berkeley: University of California Press, 1988.

King René's Book of Love (Le cueur d'amours espris). Ed. F. Unterkircher, trans. Sophie Wilkins. New York: George Braziller, 1975.

Kirschbaum, Engelbert, and Günter Bandmann, eds. *Lexikon der christlichen Ikonographie*. 8 vols. Rome: Herder, 1968–76.

Knowles, David. *The Religious Orders in England.* 3 vols. Cambridge, UK: Cambridge University Press, 1948–59; rpt. 1979.

———. *Saints and Scholars: Twenty-Five Medieval Portraits.* Cambridge, UK: Cambridge University Press, 1962.

———. *The Monastic Order in England: A History of Its Development from the Times of St. Dunstan to the Fourth Lateran Council, 940–1216.* Second ed. Cambridge, UK: Cambridge University Press, 1963.

———. *Great Historical Enterprises: Problems in Monastic History.* London: Nelson, 1963.

Kotzor, Günter. *Das altenglische Martyrologium.* 2 vols. Bayerische Akademie der Wissenschaften, Philosophisch-Historische Klasse, neue Folge 88. Munich: Bayerische Akademie der Wissenschaften, 1981.

Kruger, Steven F. *Dreaming in the Middle Ages.* Cambridge, UK: Cambridge University Press, 1992.

Krumbacher, Karl. *Der heilige Georg in der griechischen Überlieferung.* Abhandlungen der königlich bayerischen Akademie der Wissenschaften, Philosophisch-philologische und historische Klasse 25.3. Munich: Königlich Bayerische Akademie der Wissenschaften, 1911.

Laborderie, Oliver de. "Richard the Lionheart and the Birth of a National Cult of St George in England: Origins and Development of a Legend." *Nottingham Medieval Studies* 39 (1995), 37–52.

Lamont, Stewart. *The Life of Saint Andrew: Apostle, Saint and Enigma.* London: Hodder and Stoughton, 1997.

Langland, William. *Piers Plowman: The C-Text.* Ed. Derek Pearsall. Exeter: Exeter University Press, 1994.

Lapidge, Michael. "A Tenth-Century Metrical Calendar from Ramsey." *Revue Bénédictine* 94 (1984), 326–69.

———. "Surviving Booklists from Anglo-Saxon England." In *Learning and Literature in Anglo-Saxon England: Studies Presented to Peter Clemoes on the Occasion of His Sixty-Fifth*

Birthday. Ed. Michael Lapidge and Helmut Gneuss. Cambridge, UK: Cambridge University Press, 1985. Pp. 33–89.

———, ed. *Anglo-Saxon Litanies of the Saints*. HBS 106. London: Boydell Press, 1991.

Lawrence, C. H. *St. Edmund of Abingdon: A Study in Hagiography and History*. Oxford: Clarendon Press, 1960.

———. *Medieval Monasticism: Forms of Religious Life in Western Europe in the Middle Ages*. Second ed. London: Longman, 1984.

The Lay Folks' Catechism, or the English and Latin Versions of Archbishop Thoresby's Instruction for the People. Ed. Thomas Frederick Simmons and Henry Edward Nolloth. EETS o.s. 118. London: Kegan Paul, Trench, Trübner, and Co., 1901.

Leclercq, Jean. *The Love of Learning and the Desire for God: A Study of Monastic Culture*. Trans. Catharine Misrahi. New York: Fordham University Press, 1961.

Lees, Clare A., ed., with the assistance of Thelma Fenster and JoAnn McNamara. *Medieval Masculinities: Regarding Men in the Middle Ages*. Minneapolis: University of Minnesota Press, 1994.

Legends of the Saints in the Scottish Dialect of the Fourteenth Century. Ed. W. M. Metcalfe. 3 vols. Scottish Text Society first ser. 13, 18, 23, 25, 35, 37. Edinburgh: W. Blackwood and Sons, 1896; rpt. London: Johnson Reprint, 1968.

Legg, J. Wickham, ed. *The Sarum Missal*. Oxford: Clarendon Press, 1916; rpt. 1969.

Le Goff, Jacques. *The Birth of Purgatory*. Trans. Arthur Goldhammer. Chicago: University of Chicago Press, 1984.

Levison, Wilhelm. *England and the Continent in the Eighth Century: The Ford lectures Delivered in the University of Oxford in the Hilary Term, 1943*. Oxford: Clarendon Press, 1946.

Lewis, Katherine J. *The Cult of St Katherine of Alexandria in Late Medieval England*. Woodbridge, UK: Boydell Press, 2000.

Liszka, Thomas R. "The *South English Legendaries.*" In *The North Sea World in the Middle Ages: Studies in the Cultural History of North-Western Europe*. Ed. Thomas R. Liszka and Lorna E. M. Walker. Dublin: Four Courts Press, 2001. Pp. 243–80.

Little, A. G., ed. *Franciscan History and Legend in English Mediaeval Art*. British Society of Franciscan Studies 19. Manchester: Manchester University Press, 1937.

Little, Lester K. *Religious Poverty and the Profit Economy in Medieval Europe*. Ithaca, NY: Cornell University Press, 1978.

Loomis, C. Grant. *White Magic: An Introduction to the Folklore of Christian Legend*. Mediæval Academy of America Publication 52. Cambridge, MA: Mediæval Academy of America, 1948.

Lorris, Guillaume de, and Jean de Meun. *The Romance of the Rose*. Trans. Charles C. Dahlberg. Princeton, NJ: Princeton University Press, 1971.

Lydgate, John. *The Minor Poems of John Lydgate*. Ed. Henry N. MacCracken. Vol. 1. EETS e.s. 107. London: K. Paul, Trench, Trübner and Co., 1911.

———. *Poems*. Ed. John Norton-Smith. Oxford: Clarendon Press, 1966.

MacDonald, Dennis Ronald. *The Acts of Andrew and the Acts of Andrew and Matthias in the City of the Cannibals*. Texts and Translations 33. Christian Apocrypha Series 1. Atlanta: Scholars Press, 1990.

———. *Christianizing Homer: The Odyssey, Plato, and the Acts of Andrew*. New York: Oxford University Press, 1994.

Mâle, Emile. *Les saints compagnons du Christ*. Paris: P. Hartman, 1958.

Mandeville, Sir John. *The Travels of Sir John Mandeville*. Trans. C. W. R. D. Moseley. Harmondsworth, UK: Penguin Books, 1983.

Mann, Thomas. *The Holy Sinner*. Trans. H. T. Lowe-Porter. Harmondsworth, UK: Penguin, 1961.

Mannyng, Robert of Brunne. *Handlyng Synne*. Ed. Idelle Sullens. Medieval & Renaissance Texts & Studies 14. Binghamton, NY: Medieval & Renaissance Texts & Studies, 1983.

Bibliography

Map, Walter. *De nugis curialium: Courtiers' Tales*. Ed. and trans. M. R. James. Rev. ed. C. N. L. Brooke and R. A. B. Mynors. Oxford: Clarendon Press, 1983.

Markus, R. A. *Gregory the Great and His World*. Cambridge, UK: Cambridge University Press, 1997.

Matzke, John E. "Contributions to the History of the Legend of St. George with Special Reference to the Sources of French, German, and Anglo-Saxon Metrical Versions." [I] *PMLA* 17 (1902), 464–535; [II] 18 (1903), 99–171.

———. "The Legend of St. George: Its Development into a *Roman d'Aventure*." *PMLA* 19 (1904), 449–78.

McCann, Dom Justin. "Early English Verses on St. Benedict." *The Downside Review* 41 (1923), 44–56.

McClendon, Muriel C. "A Moveable Feast: St. George's Day Celebrations and Religious Change in Early Modern England." *Journal of British Studies* 38 (1999), 1–27.

McIntosh, Angus, and M. L. Samuels. "Prolegomena to a Study of Medieval Anglo-Irish." *Medium Ævum* 38 (1968), 1–11.

McIntosh, Angus, M. L. Samuels, and Michael Benskin, eds., with the assistance of Michael Laing and Keith Williams. *A Linguistic Atlas of Late Mediaeval English*. 4 vols. Aberdeen: Aberdeen University Press, 1986.

McKerrow, Ronald Brunless. *Printers' and Publishers' Devices in England and Scotland, 1485–1640*. Illustrated Monographs 16. London: Chiswick Press, 1913.

McMahon, Katherine G. "Scholastica — Not a Wife!" In Jankofsky, 1992. Pp. 18–28.

McNamara, JoAnn. "Cornelia's Daughters: Paula and Eustochium." *Women's Studies* 11 (1984), 9–27.

———. *Sisters in Arms: Catholic Nuns through Two Millennia*. Cambridge, MA: Harvard University Press, 1996.

———, and John B. Halborg. *Sainted Women of the Dark Ages*. Durham, NC: Duke University Press, 1992.

McNamara, JoAnn, and Suzanne F. Wemple. "Sanctity and Power: The Dual Pursuit of Medieval Women." In *Becoming Visible: Women in European History*. Ed. Renate Bridenthal and Claudia Koonz. Boston: Houghton Mifflin, 1977. Pp. 90–118.

Meale, Carol M. "Laywomen and Their Books in Late Medieval England." In Meale, 1993. Pp. 128–58.

———, ed. *Women and Literature in Britain, 1150–1500*. Cambridge Studies in Medieval Literature 17. Cambridge, UK: Cambridge University Press, 1993.

Middle English Dictionary. Ed. Hans Kurath et al. Ann Arbor, MI: University of Michigan Press, 1952–2001.

Migne, J.-P, ed. *Patrologia Latina*. 221 vols. Paris: Garnier Frères and J.-P. Migne, 1844–80.

Millett, Bella, and Jocelyn Wogan-Browne. *Medieval English Prose for Women: Selections from the Katherine Group and Ancrenne Wisse*. Oxford: Clarendon Press, 1990.

Mirk, John. *Mirk's Festial: A Collection of Homilies*. Ed. Theodor Erbe. EETS e.s. 96. London: Kegan Paul, Trench, Trübner and Co., 1905; rpt. Woodbridge, UK: Boydell and Brewer, 1997.

Mombrizio, Bonino. *Sanctuarium seu Vitae Sanctorum*. Ed. A. Brunet. Second ed. 2 vols. Paris: Albert Fontemoing, 1910.

The Monastic Breviary of Hyde Abbey, Winchester: Mss. Rawlinson Liturg. e. 1*, and Gough Liturg. 8, in the Bodleian Library, Oxford. Ed. and intro. John Basil Lowder Tolhurst. 6 vols. HBS 69–71, 76, 78, 80. London: Harrison and Sons, 1932–42.

Moorman, John R. H. *The Sources for the Life of S. Francis of Assisi*. Foreword by A. G. Little. Manchester: Manchester University Press, 1940.

———. *A History of the Franciscan Order from Its Origins to the Year 1517*. Oxford: Clarendon Press, 1968.

Morello, Giovanni, and Laurence B. Kanter, eds. *The Treasury of Saint Francis of Assisi*. Milan: Electa, 1999.

Morrissey, Jane. "Scholastica and Benedict: A Picnic, a Paradigm." In *Equally in God's Image*: *Women in the Middle Ages*. Ed. Julia Bolton Holloway, Constance S. Wright, and Joan Bechtold. New York: Peter Lang, 1990. Pp. 251–57.

Mussafia, A. "Studien zu dem mittelalterlichen Marienlegenden." *Sitzungsberichte der Kaiserlichen Akademie in Wien, Philologische-Historische Klasse*, 113 (1886), 917–94, 115 (1887), 5–92.

The Myroure of Oure Ladye: Containing a Devotional Treatise on Divine Service, with a Translation of the Offices Used by the Sisters of the Brigittine Monastery of Sion, at Isleworth, during the Fifteenth and Sixteenth Centuries. Ed. John Henry Blunt. EETS e.s. 19. London: N. Trübner and Co., 1873.

Narratio mirabilis de sententia excommunicationis et beati Augustini Anglorum Apostoli qualiter resuscitauit duos mortuos. Ed. E. Gordon Whatley, "John Lydgate's *Saint Austin at Compton*." Pp. 223–27.

Nau, François. "Histoire de Thais: Publication des textes grecs inédits et de divers autres textes et versions." *Annales du Musée Guimet* 30.3 (1903), 51–112.

New Catholic Encyclopedia. 18 vols. New York: McGraw-Hill, 1967–88.

Nightingale, John. "Oswald, Fleury and Continental Reform." In *St. Oswald of Worcester: Life and Influence*. Ed. Nicholas Brooks and Catherine Cubitt. London: Leicester University Press, 1996. Pp. 23–45.

The Northern Homily Cycle: The Expanded Version in MSS Harley 4196 and Cotton Tiberius E VII. Ed. Saara Nevanlinna. 3 vols. Mémoires de la Société néophilologique de Helsinki 38, 41, 43. Helsinki: Société néophilologique, 1972–84.

An Old English Martyrology. Ed. George Herzfeld. EETS o.s. 116. London: Kegan Paul, Trench, Trübner, and Co., 1900; rpt. New York: Kraus Reprint, 1973.

Ordinale Exon[iensis]: Exeter Chapter Ms. 3502 collated with Parker Ms. 93. With two Appendices from Trinity College, Cambridge Ms. B. XI. 16 and Exeter Chapter Ms. 3625. Ed. John Neale Dalton, G. H. Noble, et al. 4 vols. HBS 37–38, 63, 79. London: Harrison and Sons, 1909–40.

Ortenberg, Veronica. *The English Church and the Continent in the Tenth and Eleventh Centuries: Cultural, Spiritual, and Artistic Exchanges*. Oxford: Clarendon Press, 1992.

Owst, Gerald Robert. *Preaching in Medieval England: An Introduction to Sermon Manuscripts of the Period c. 1350–1450*. Cambridge, UK: The University Press, 1926; rpt. New York: Russell & Russell, 1965.

————. *Literature and Pulpit in Medieval England: A Neglected Chapter in the History of English Letters & of the English People*. Cambridge, UK: The University Press, 1933; rpt. Oxford: Basil Blackwell, 1966.

The Oxford Classical Dictionary. Ed. Simon Hornblower and Antony Spawforth. Third ed. Oxford: Oxford University Press, 1996.

The Oxford Dictionary of Saints. Ed. David Hugh Farmer. Second ed. Oxford: Oxford University Press, 1987.

The Oxford English Dictionary. Ed. James Murray et al. 12 vols. and Supplement. Oxford: Oxford University Press, 1933.

Palladius, bishop of Aspuna. *Palladius: The Lausiac History*. Trans. Robert T. Meyer. Ancient Christian Writers 34. Westminster, MD: Newman Press, 1965.

Pantin, W. A. *The English Church in the Fourteenth Century*. Notre Dame, IN: University of Notre Dame Press, 1963.

Parker, Roscoe E. "A Northern Fragment of *The Life of St. George*." *Modern Language Notes* 38 (1923), 97–101.

Passio sancti Andreae apostoli. In *Acta apostolorum apocrypha*. Ed. Richard Adelbert Lipsius, and Max Bonnet. 2 vols. Leipzig: H. Mendelssohn, 1891–1903.

Patch, Howard R. *The Goddess Fortuna in Medieval Literature*. Cambridge, MA: Harvard University Press, 1927.

Pearsall, Derek. *John Lydgate*. Charlottesville: University of Virginia Press, 1970.

Petersen, Joan M. *The Dialogues of Gregory the Great in their Late Antique Cultural Background*. Toronto: Pontifical Institute of Mediaeval Studies, 1984.

Bibliography

Philippart, Guy. *Les légendiers latins et autres manuscrits hagiographiques*. Typologie des sources du Moyen Age occidental 24–25. Turnhout: Brepols, 1977.

————, ed. *Hagiographies: Histoire internationale de la littérature hagiographique, latine et vernaculaire, en Occident, des origines à 1550*. Turnhout: Brepols, 1994–.

Pickering, O. S. "The Southern Passion and the Ministry and Passion: The Work of a Middle English Reviser." *Leeds Studies in English* 15 (1984), 33–56.

————. "South English Legendary Style in Robert of Gloucester's *Chronicle*." *Medium Ævum* 70 (2001), 1–18.

Pollard, A. W., and G. R. Redgrave, et al. *A Short-Title Catalogue of Books Printed in England, Scotland, and Ireland, and of English Books Printed Abroad, 1475–1640* Second ed. Rev. and enlarged. 3 vols. London: Bibliographical Society, 1976–91.

Poncelet, A. "Miraculorum B. V. Mariae quae saec. VI–XV latine conscripta sunt index postea perficiendus." *Analecta Bollandiana* 21 (1902), 241–360.

Prieur, Jean-Marc, ed. *Acta Andreae*. 2 vols. Corpus Christianorum, Series Apocryphorum 5–6. Turnhout: Brepols, 1989.

Pseudo-Augustine of Hippo. [*Epistola*] *Augustini Hipponensis Episcopi ad Cyrillum Jerosolymitanum Episcopum de Magnificentiis Beati Hieronymi*. In *PL* 22.281–89.

Pseudo-Cyril of Jerusalem. [*Epistola*] *Cyrilli Jerosolymitani de Miraculis Hieronymi ad Sanctam Augustinum Hipponensem*. In *PL* 22.289–326.

Pseudo-Gennadius of Marseilles. *Vita Sancti Hieronymi Presbyteri*. In *PL* 22.175–84.

Pseudo-Sebastian of Monte Cassino. *Vita Divi Hieronymi*. In *PL* 22.201–14. [See also Mombrizio.]

Quasten, Johannes, et al. *Patrology*. 4 vols. Westminster, MD: Christian Classics, 1986–92.

Quentin, Henri. *Les martyrologes historiques du Moyen Âge: Étude sur la formation du martyrologe romain*. Paris: Victor Lecoffre, 1908.

Rader, Rosemary. *Breaking Boundaries: Male/Female Friendship in Early Christian Communities.* New York: Paulist Press, 1983.

Rauer, Christine. *Beowulf and the Dragon: Parallels and Analogues.* Rochester, NY: D. S. Brewer, 2000.

Reames, Sherry L. *The Legenda aurea: A Reexamination of Its Paradoxical History.* Madison: University of Wisconsin Press, 1985.

———. "Mouvance and Interpretation in Late-Medieval Latin: The Legend of St. Cecilia in British Breviaries." In *Medieval Literature: Texts and Interpretation.* Ed. Tim William Machan. Binghamton, NY: Medieval & Renaissance Texts & Studies, 1991. Pp. 159–89.

———, and Deborah Vanderbilt. "Hagiography." In *Medieval England: An Encyclopedia.* Ed. Paul E. Szarmach, Teresa Tavormina, and Joel Rosenthal. New York: Garland, 1998. Pp. 333–36.

Reames, Sherry L., ed., with the assistance of Martha G. Blalock and Wendy R. Larson. *Middle English Legends of Women Saints.* Kalamazoo, MI: Medieval Institute Publications, 2003.

Rice, Eugene F. *Saint Jerome in the Renaissance.* Baltimore: Johns Hopkins University Press, 1985.

Riches, Samantha J. E., and Sarah Salih, eds. *Gender and Holiness: Men, Women, and Saints in Late Medieval Europe.* London: Routledge, 2002.

Riddy, Felicity. "Women Talking about the Things of God." In Meale, 1993. Pp. 104–27.

Ridyard, Susan J. *The Royal Saints of Anglo-Saxon England: A Study of West Saxon and East Anglian Cults.* Cambridge, UK: Cambridge University Press, 1988.

Roberts, Alexander, and James Donaldson, eds. *The Ante-Nicene Fathers: Translations of the Writings of the Fathers Down to A.D. 325.* Rev. ed. A. Cleveland Coxe. 10 vols. New York: C. Scribner's Sons, 1911–26.

Robertson, Duncan. *The Medieval Saints' Lives: Spiritual Renewal and Old French Literature.* Lexington, KY: French Forum, 1995.

Rochelle, Mercedes. *Post-Biblical Saints Art Index: A Locator of Paintings, Sculptures, Mosaics, Icons, Frescoes, Manuscript Illuminations, Sketches, Woodcuts, and Engravings,*

Created from the 4th Century to 1950, with a Directory of the Institutions Holding Them. Jefferson, NC: McFarland, 1994.

Roger of Wendover. *Flowers of History: Comprising the History of England from the Descent of the Saxons to A. D. 1235, formerly ascribed to Matthew Paris.* Trans. J. A. Giles. 2 vols. Bohn's Antiquarian Library. London: H. G. Bohn, 1849.

Rollason, D. W. *Saints and Relics in Anglo-Saxon England.* Oxford: B. Blackwell, 1989.

Rosenthal, Constance L. "The Vitae Patrum in Old and Middle English Literature." Ph.D. Dissertation: University of Pennsylvania, 1936.

Rosweyde, Heribert, ed. *De vita et verbis seniorum libri x, historiam eremiticam complectentes.* Antwerp: Plantin, 1615.

Rousseau, Philip. *Ascetics, Authority, and the Church in the Age of Jerome and Cassian.* Oxford: Oxford University Press, 1978.

Rubin, Miri. *Corpus Christi: The Eucharist in Late Medieval Culture.* Cambridge, UK: Cambridge University Press, 1991.

Russell, Norman, trans. *The Lives of the Desert Fathers: The Historia Monachorum in Ægypto.* Intro. Benedicta Ward. London: A. R. Mowbray, 1981.

Saint Erkenwald. Ed. Clifford Peterson. Philadelphia: University of Pennsylvania Press, 1977.

Salzman, L. F., ed. *The Victoria History of the County of Warwick.* 8 vols. London: Institute for Historical Research, 1949; rpt. London: Dawsons of Pall Mall, 1964–69.

Samson, Annie. "The South English Legendary: Constructing a Context." In *Thirteenth-Century England.* Vol. 1. Ed. Peter R. Coss and Simon D. Lloyd. Woodbridge, UK: Boydell Press, 1986. Pp. 185–95.

Sarum Ordinal. Ed. William Maskell. In *Monumenta Ritualia Ecclesiae Anglicanae.* Second ed. 3 vols. Oxford: Clarendon Press, 1882.

Savage, Anne, and Nicholas Watson, trans. and intro. *Anchoritic Spirituality: Ancrene Wisse and Associated Works.* Classics of Western Spirituality. New York: Paulist Press, 1991.

Scanlon, Larry. *Narrative, Authority, and Power: The Medieval Exemplum and the Chaucerian Tradition*. Cambridge, UK: Cambridge University Press, 1994.

Schirmer, Walter F. *John Lydgate: A Study in the Culture of the XVth Century*. Trans. Ann E. Keep. Berkeley: University of California Press, 1961.

Schulenberg, Jane Tibbetts. "Strict Active Enclosure and its Effects on the Female Monastic Experience (ca. 500–1100)." In *Medieval Religious Women*. Vol. I: *Distant Echoes*. Ed. John A. Nichols and Lillian Thomas Shank. Kalamazoo, MI: Cistercian Publications, 1984. Pp. 51 86.

———. "Female Sanctity: Public and Private Roles, ca. 500–1100." In *Women and Power in the Middle Ages*. Ed. Mary Erler and Maryanne Kowaleski. Athens: University of Georgia Press, 1988. Pp. 102–25.

Schwob, Marcel. *Spicilège*. Paris: Mercure de France, 1896; rpt. 1960.

The Scottish Legendary. See *Legends of the Saints in the Scottish Dialect of the Fourteenth Century*.

Severs, J. Burke, and Albert E. Hartung, gen. eds. *A Manual of the Writings in Middle English, 1050–1500*. 10 vols. to date. New Haven, CT: Connecticut Academy of Arts and Sciences, 1967–. [Severs is gen. ed. for vols. 1–2; Hartung is gen. ed. for vols. 3–.]

Severus, Sulpicius. *Dialogues* and *Life of St. Martin*. See Hoare, *Western Fathers*.

Shailor, Barbara A. *Catalogue of Medieval and Renaissance Manuscripts in the Beinecke Rare Book and Manuscript Library, Yale University*. Vol. 2: *MSS 251–500*. Medieval & Renaissance Texts & Studies 48. Binghamton, NY: Medieval & Renaissance Texts & Studies, 1987.

Sharpe, Richard. *A Handlist of the Latin Writers of Great Britain and Ireland before 1540: Additions and Corrections, 1997–2001*. Publications of the Journal of Medieval Latin 1. Turnhout: Brepols, 2001.

Sheingorn, Pamela. *The Book of Sainte Foy*. Philadelphia: University of Pennsylvania Press, 1995.

Shippey, T. A. *Poems of Wisdom and Learning in Old English*. Cambridge, UK: D. S. Brewer, 1976.

Bibliography

Sigal, Pierre-André. *L'homme et le miracle dans la France médiévale (XIe–XIIe siècle)*. Paris: Les Éditions du Cerf, 1985.

Sorrell, Roger D. *St. Francis of Assisi and Nature: Tradition and Innovation in Western Christian Attitudes towards the Environment*. New York: Oxford University Press, 1988.

The South English Legendary: Edited from Corpus Christi College Cambridge Ms. 145 and British Museum Ms. Harley 2247, with Variants from Bodley Ms. Ashmole 43 and British Museum Ms. Cotton Julius D. IX. Ed. Charlotte D'Evelyn and Anna J. Mills. 3 vols. EETS o.s. 235–36, 244. London: Oxford University Press, 1956–59.

Southern, R. W. "The English Origins of the Miracles of the Virgin." *Medieval and Renaissance Studies* 4 (1958), 176–216.

———. *Western Society and the Church in the Middle Ages*. Pelican History of the Church 2. Harmondsworth, UK: Penguin Books, 1970.

Sparks, H. F. D. "Jerome as Biblical Scholar." In *The Cambridge History of the Bible*. Vol. 1: *From the Beginnings to Jerome*. Ed. Peter R. Ackroyd and Christopher Francis Evans. Cambridge, UK: Cambridge University Press, 1970. Pp. 510–41.

Speculum Sacerdotale: Edited from British Museum Ms. Additional 36791. Ed. Edward H. Weatherly. EETS o.s. 200. London: Oxford University Press, 1936.

Sperk, Klaus, ed. *Medieval English Saints' Legends*. English Texts 6. Tübingen: M. Niemeyer, 1970.

Stancliffe, Clare. *St. Martin and His Hagiographer: History and Miracle in Sulpicius Severus*. Oxford: Clarendon Press, 1983.

Stephanus de Borbone. *Stephani de Borbone Tractatus de diversis materiis predicabilibus: Prologus, prima pars De dono timoris*. Ed. Jacques Berlioz and Jean-Luc Eichenlaub. Corpus Christianorum Series Latina, Continuatio Mediaevalis 124. Exempla Medii Aevi 1. Turnhout: Brepols, 2002.

Stouck, Mary-Ann, ed. *Medieval Saints: A Reader*. Readings in Medieval Civilizations and Cultures 4. Peterborough, ON: Broadview Press, 1999.

Strayer, Joseph R., ed. *Dictionary of the Middle Ages*. 13 vols. New York: Charles Scribner's Sons, 1982–89.

Swan, Carolyn Taylor. *The Old French Prose Legend of Saint Julian the Hospitaller*. Tübingen: Max Niemeyer Verlag, 1977.

Taft, Robert F. *The Liturgy of the Hours in East and West: The Origins of the Divine Office and Its Meaning Today*. Collegeville, MN: Liturgical Press, 1986.

Talbot, C. H., ed. and trans. *The Life of Christina of Markyate: A Twelfth Century Recluse*. Oxford: Clarendon Press, 1959.

Thacker, Alan. "Cults at Canterbury: Relics and Reform under Dunstan and His Successors." In *St Dunstan: His Life, Times and Cult*. Ed. Nigel Ramsay, Margaret Sparks, and Tim Tatton-Brown. Woodbridge, UK: Boydell Press, 1992. Pp. 221–46.

———. "Memorializing Gregory the Great: The Origin and Transmission of a Papal Cult in the Seventh and Early Eighth Centuries." *Early Medieval Europe* 7 (1998), 59–84.

———. "In Gregory's Shadow? The Pre-conquest Cult of St. Augustine." In *St Augustine and the Conversion of England*. Ed. Richard Gameson. Stroud, UK: Sutton, 1999. Pp. 374–90.

Thomas de Cantimpré. See Vet, Wouter Antonie van der.

Thompson, Anne B. "Shaping a Saint's Life: Frideswide of Oxford." *Medium Aevum* 63 (1994), 34–52.

———. "The Legend of St. Agnes: Improvisation and the Practice of Hagiography." *Exemplaria* 13 (2001), 355–97.

———. *Everyday Saints and the Art of Narrative in the South English Legendary*. Aldershot, UK: Ashgate, 2003.

Thomson, J. A. F. "Tithe Disputes in Later Medieval London." *English Historical Review* 78 (1963), 1–17.

Thompson, Charlotte. "Paphnutius and the Cultural Vision." In *Hrotsvit of Gandersheim: Rara Avis in Saxonia? A Collection of Essays*. Ed. Katharina M. Wilson. Ann Arbor, MI: MARC Publishing Co., 1987. Pp. 111–25.

Bibliography

Thompson, Stith. *Motif-Index of Folk-Literature: A Classification of Narrative Elements in Folktales, Ballads, Myths, Fables, Mediaeval Romances, Exempla, Fabliaux, Jest-books, and Local Legends*. Rev. ed. 6 vols. Bloomington, IN: Indiana University Press, 1966.

Tobler, A. "Zur Legende vom heiligen Julianus." *Archiv* 102 (1899), 109–78.

Townsend, David. "Hagiography." In *Medieval Latin: An Introduction and Bibliographical Guide*. Ed. F. A. C. Mantello and A. G. Rigg. Washington, DC: Catholic University of America Press, 1996. Pp. 618–28.

Tubach, Frederic C. *Index exemplorum: A Handbook of Medieval Religious Tales*. FF Communications 86.204. Helsinki: Suomalainen Tiedeakatemia, 1969.

Upchurch, Robert K. "The 'Goed Fyn' of Saint Alexius in a Middle English Version of his Legend." *Journal of English and Germanic Philology* 102 (2003), 1–20.

Van Dam, Raymond. *Saints and Their Miracles in Late Antique Gaul*. Princeton: Princeton University Press, 1993.

Van Dijk, Stephen Joseph Peter, and Joan Hazelden Walker. *The Origins of the Modern Roman Liturgy: The Liturgy of the Papal Court and the Franciscan Order in the Thirteenth Century*. Westminster, MD: Newman Press, 1960.

Van Dijk, Stephen Joseph Peter, ed. *The Sources of the Roman Liturgy: The Ordinals by Haymo of Faversham and Related Documents (1243–1307)*. 2 vols. Studia et documenta Franciscana 1–2. Leiden: E. J. Brill, 1963.

Vauchez, André. *Sainthood in the Later Middle Ages*. Trans. Jean Birrell. Cambridge, UK: Cambridge University Press, 1997.

Vet, Wouter Antonie van der. *Het Biënboec van Thomas van Cantimpré en Zijn Exempelen*. The Hague: Martinus Nijhoff, 1902.

Vinaver, Eugène. *The Rise of Romance*. Oxford: Oxford University Press, 1971.

Vogel, Cyrille. *Medieval Liturgy: An Introduction to the Sources*. Rev. and trans. William George Storey and Niels Krogh Rasmussen, with the assistance of John K. Brooks-Leonard. Washington, DC: Pastoral Press, 1986.

365

Voigts, Linda Ehrsam. "A Handlist of Middle English in Harvard Manuscripts." *Harvard Library Bulletin* 33 (1985), 5–96.

von Dobschütz, Ernst, ed. *Das Decretum Gelasianum de libris recipiendis et non recipiendis.* Texte und Untersuchungen zur Geschichte der Altchristlichen Literatur third ser. 38.4. Leipzig: J. C. Hinrichs, 1912.

Waddell, Helen, trans. *The Desert Fathers: Translations from the Latin with an Introduction.* London: Constable & Co., 1936.

Wærferth, of Worcester. *Bischofs Waerferths von Worcester Übersetzung der Dialoge Gregors des Grossen über das Leben und die Wunderthaten italienischer Väter und über die Unsterblichkeit der Seelen.* Ed. Hans Hecht. 2 vols. in 1. Bibliothek der angelsächsischen Prosa 5.2. Leipzig: G. H. Wigand, 1900–07; rpt. Darmstadt: Wissenschaftliche Buchgesellschaft, 1965.

The Wakefield Pageants in the Towneley Cycle. Ed. A. C. Cawley. Manchester, UK: University of Manchester Press, 1958.

Walter, Christopher. "The Origins of the Cult of St. George." *Revue des Études Byzantines* 53 (1995), 295–326.

Wansbrough, J. H. "St. Gregory's Intention in the Stories of St. Scholastica and St. Benedict." *Revue Bénédictine* 75 (1965), 145–51.

Ward, Benedicta. *Miracles and the Medieval Mind: Theory, Record, and Event, 1000–1215.* Philadelphia: University of Pennsylvania Press, 1982.

———, trans. *The Sayings of the Fathers: The Alphabetical Collection.* Cistercian Studies Series 59. Rev. ed. Kalamazoo, MI: Cistercian Publications, 1984.

———. *Harlots of the Desert: A Study of Repentance in Early Monastic Sources.* Kalamazoo, MI: Cistercian Publications, 1987.

Waters, Claire. "Symon Wynter, *The Life of St. Jerome.*" In *Cultures of Piety: Medieval English Devotional Literature in Translation.* Ed. Anne Clark Bartlett and Thomas H. Bestul. Ithaca, NY: Cornell University Press, 1999. Pp. 141–63 (translation), 232–49 (edition).

Weber, Robertus, et al., eds. *Biblia sacra iuxta Vulgatam versionem.* Fourth ed. Stuttgart: Deutsche Bibelgesellschaft, 1994.

Bibliography

Weinstein, Donald, and Rudolph M. Bell. *Saints and Society: The Two Worlds of Western Christendom, 1000–1700*. Chicago: University of Chicago Press, 1982.

Wells, J. E. *A Manual of the Writings in Middle English, 1050–1400*. New Haven: Yale University Press, 1916.

Welter, J.-Th. *L'exemplum dans la littérature religieuse et didactique du Moyen Âge*. Paris: E. H. Guitard, 1927.

Whatley, E. Gordon, ed. and trans. *The Saint of London: The Life and Miracles of Saint Erkenwald: Text and Translation*. Medieval & Renaissance Texts & Studies 58. Binghamton, NY: Medieval & Renaissance Texts & Studies, 1989.

————. "John Lydgate's *Saint Austin at Compton*: The Poem and Its Sources." In *Anglo-Latin and Its Heritage: Essays in Honour of A. G. Rigg on his 64th Birthday*. Publications of the Journal of Medieval Latin 4. Ed. Siân Echard and Gernot R. Wieland. Turnhout: Brepols, 2001. Pp. 191–227.

White, Carolinne, ed. and trans. *Early Christian Lives*. London: Penguin Books, 1998.

Whiteford, Peter, ed. *The Myracles of Oure Lady*. Middle English Texts 23. Heidelberg: Carl Winter Universitätsverlag, 1990.

Whiting, Bartlett Jere, with the collaboration of Helen Wescott Whiting. *Proverbs, Sentences, and Proverbial Phrases from English Writings Mainly before 1500*. Cambridge, MA: The Belknap Press of Harvard University Press, 1968.

Wilson, Stephen, ed. and intro. *Saints and Their Cults: Studies in Religious Sociology, Folklore, and History*. Cambridge, UK: Cambridge University Press, 1983.

Winstead, Karen A. *Virgin Martyrs: Legends of Sainthood in Late Medieval England*. Ithaca, NY: Cornell University Press, 1997.

————, ed. and trans. *Chaste Passions: Medieval English Virgin Martyr Legends*. Ithaca, NY: Cornell University Press, 2000.

Winter, Simon. "*Symon Wynter, The Life of St. Jerome*." Ed. and trans. Claire Waters. In *Cultures of Piety: Medieval English Devotional Literature in Translation*. Ed. Anne Clark

Bartlett and Thomas H. Bestul. Ithaca, NY: Cornell University Press, 1999. Pp. 141–63 (translation), 232–49 (edition).

———. "Life of St. Jerome." In Hamer and Russell. Pp. 321–65, 511–13. [Based on MS Lambeth 72.]

Wogan-Browne, Jocelyn. "The Virgin's Tale." In *Feminist Readings in Middle English Literature: The Wife of Bath and All Her Sect*. Ed. Ruth Evans and Lesley Johnson. London: Routledge, 1994. Pp. 165–94.

———. *Saints' Lives and Women's Literary Culture c. 1150–1300: Virginity and Its Authorizations*. New York: Oxford University Press, 2001.

———, and Glyn S. Burgess, eds. *Virgin Lives and Holy Deaths: Two Exemplary Biographies for Anglo-Norman Women*. London: J. M. Dent, 1996.

———, et al., eds. *The Idea of the Vernacular: An Anthology of Middle English Literary Theory, 1280–1520*. University Park: Pennsylvania State University Press, 1999.

Wolpers, Theodor. *Die englische Heiligenlegende des Mittelalters: eine Formengeschichte des Legendenerzählens von der spätantiken lateinischen Tradition bis zur Mitte des 16. Jahrhunderts*. Tübingen: M. Niemeyer, 1964.

Woodward, Kenneth L. *Making Saints: How the Catholic Church Determines Who Becomes a Saint, Who Doesn't, and Why*. New York: Simon and Schuster, 1990.

Wormald, Francis, ed. *English Kalendars before A.D. 1100*. HBS 72. London: [Harrison and Sons], 1934.

———, ed. *English Benedictine Kalendars after A.D. 1100*. HBS 77, 81. London: Harrison and Sons, 1939–46.

Glossary

Included here are common Middle English words and forms that are not always translated in the marginal glosses and footnotes. [**N** = Northern/N. Midland dialect and Scottish.]

abid(e), abit *wait, wait for*

afyngred *hungry, famished* (from **ofhungered**)

als *also, as*

amorwe *next day, on the morrow*

and *and; an* (Anglo-Irish); *if* (when introducing a clause)

an, ane (N), **one, oo, oon** *a, an; one; on*

ano(o)n *at once, immediately*

ar, er, or *before*

assay *test, prove*

ay *ever, always*

ayen(st) *again; against; back; towards; in anticipation of*

bad(e) *asked, asked for, prayed for; ordered, told*

bath(e) (N) *both*

be(n), beo *be; been*

best(e) *beast, animal*

beth, beoth *are*

bi, be, by *by; about; over*

bileve, beleve *believe; remain* (intransitive); *abandon, leave behind* (transitive)

bivore, byvore *before*

boght(e), aboghte, boughte, bouhte *redeemed*

bond *bound*

bon(e) *bone; prayer, request (boon)*

bot(e), but *but; without, except; only; unless*

cam, com(e) *came*

can(e) *did* (N); *can; know how to*

certes *without doubt, truly*

clepe, clupe *call, name;* **clupe** *called*

chere, cheer *look, appearance, manner*

cheese, chese(n) *choose*

chele *cold, chill*

clupe ⟹ **clepe**

couthe, cuth *could; knew how*

dei(e) *die*

dome *judgement, sentence, opinion (doom)*

don *do;* **destou, dostow** *thou dost, you do;* **dude** *did;* **do, don(n)e, ido** *done, finished, made, put, destroyed*

dorre *needed*

dorst(e) *"durst," dared*

dred(e) *fear, doubt*

drogh(e) (N), **droughe** *drew; drew near, approached, went; pulled*

ech(e), yche *each, every; any*

echon(e) *everyone, each one*

eft *again*

ek *also*

eode, yede Preterite of **ga(n)**

er *before, earlier*

everich, everichon *each one*

eyen, eyin, ewyne *eyes*

fa(y) »» **fo**

fend(e) *fiend, devil*

fer(e), ferd *fear*

fo, fa(y) *enemy, foe*

fol *foolish; fool; full*

fond(e) preterite of **find**

fonde *tempt, test*

for(e)thi *therefore*

forte *(for) to*

full *full; very*

ga(n) *go, walk*

gan (sing.), **gonne** (plu.) *began; did* (often as an auxiliary to form the preterite of other verbs)

gert (N) *arranged for, had something done*

gode *god; God; good*

gonne »» **gan**

gud (N), **gode** *good*

gyf, gyve, yef, yif, yyf, yyff, yfe *if*

gyfe, gyff(e), gyve, yef, yeve, yive *give*; **gaf, gafe, gaff, yef, yeve** *gave*

habbe, haf(e) *have*

hal(e) (N) *whole, complete*

hard »» **here, hure**

hem *them*

heo *she* (see also **scho**)

her *here*

her(e), hure *hear;* **herd, (i)hurde, hard** (preterite) *heard*

herie *praise*

het(e), heght (N) *ordered; was called*

heved *head* (n.); *to behead* (vb.)

hey *high*

hi, hy *they*

hir(e), hyre, her(e) *her; their*

hit *it*

hor(e) *their, of them; whore*

hose *whoever* (lit. *who so*)

hure »» **here**

i-, y- In most instances the prefix **i-** or **y-** (from OE **ge-**) denotes the past participle or verbal adjective (e.g., **ido** *done*), and sometimes certain forms of the finite verb. All such forms are glossed alphabetically under the stem verb.

ic, ich *I* (frequently elided with auxiliary verbs, e.g., **ichabbe** *I have*, **ichulle/icholle** *I will*, for **ich wolle**).

ilk (N), **ilkon** *each, every, each one*

inou(gh), inow *enough*

iwis, ywis *truly, certainly*

kund(e) *nature, kind*

(i)laste *lasted*

lefe, (i)leve *dear* (adj.); *life; leave; stay*

lere *teach*

let *ordered, arranged for* (with infinitive of action)

levere *rather*

list(e) *pleases, is pleased to, wishes to; was pleased to, chose to*

lore *teaching, learning*

loverd(e) *lord*

lute *little*

me *me, to me; one* (impersonal pronoun), *people in general*

370

mekil, mickle (N), **much** *much; great*
  (adj.), *numerous*
mid, myd *with*
mo *more*
moste *must; could; was allowed*
mote *may; have leave to*
mowe *may; be able, might*

nabbe ne + habbe
nadde ne + hadde
nas ne + was
nede, neode *need*
nel(l)e(th) ne + wille(th)
nere ne + were
nolde ne + wolde
nom(e), neme *took* (see **nyme**)
nost ne + wost
nother *neither*
nuste ne + wuste
nyme, nime *take*

of(e) *of; off; for*
one See **an, ane**
ony *any*
oo(n) ⇒ **an**
or ⇒ **ar**
orisoun *prayer*
other *other, others; or*
ous *us*

pane ⇒ **pyn(e)**
perfit, parfit, perfyt *perfect*
pistel(l), pistil, pystel *epistle, letter*
povere, pur (N) *poor*
preve, prevy *prove*
preve, prive(y) *private, intimate*
prevely, prively *secretly, privately*
pyn(e), pane (N) *pain*

quath ⇒ **quod**
quha (N) *who*
quham (N) *whom*
quhare (N) *where*
quhat (N) *what*
quhilk (N) *which*
quic *alive, living*
quod, quath *said*

red(e) *advice, counsel, plan; read* (vb.)
repreve *reprove; reproof*
rode, rood *cross*

sa (N) *so; say*
sad ⇒ **sede**
sai ⇒ **sei**
sall, ssel (both N) *shall, must*
scho (N), **schou, schow** *she*
scholde, schulde, suld (N) *should, must*
schow *show*
schrift *confession*
se(e), isé *see;* **seth, seith, iseth, iseoth**
  see (pres. plu.); **(i)sei(e), (i)sey(e),**
  (i)sai, (y)say, ysey *saw, seen*
segge, sa (N), **say** *say;* **seist** *(you) say;*
  seith *says;* **sede, ised, sad** (N), **sayd,**
  sayde *said*
sek *sick, ill*
seththe ⇒ **siththe**
sic, sik *such*
siththe, seththe, suththe *after,*
  afterwards
socht (N) *sought*
sonde *providence* (lit., *sending*)
sone *soon, at once, immediately; son*
soth(e) *truth, fact*
soth(e)ly, sothes *truly, certainly*
ssel ⇒ **sal**
stede, stude *place*

Glossary

sto(u)nde, stunde *hour, space of time*
stude ⇒ **stede**
stynt *stopped, ceased*
sulf *self*
sunne *sin*
suththe ⇒ **sittthe**
swithe, swythe *very; greatly*
swonc, iswonke *labored*
syne *after, afterwards*

ta (N), **take** *take, give;* **tok(e)** *took;*
  take, tane (N) *taken*
thai (N), **thay, thei** *they; those*
tham(e) (N) *them*
thane (N) *then*
thei *although* (see also **thai**)
then *than; then; that, the* (definite
  article/demonstrative in oblique cases)
thenc(h)(e), thynke *think, intend,*
  consider; seem
thenne, thens *thence*
theos, thes, this *these*
ther(e) *there; where; their*
tho, tha (N) *when; then; those, they*
thoght(e), thocht Preterite of **thenc**
thoru(gh) *through*
thud(d)er *thither*
thulke, thilke *the same, the very same*
til(l) (N) *to*
trow(e) *believe, trust*
twa (N), **twei(e)** *two*

unnethe *scarcely, hardly*
up *up; upon*
uthyre (N) *other*

vair *fair*
vall(e) *fall*
vare *fare, travel*

vast(e) *fast*
ver *far*
verst, virst *first*
very, verie, verray *true*
veryly *truly*
vet *feet*
vol *full*
vond *found*
vor *for* (preposition and prefix)
vorte *to*
vorth *forth*

wald(e) ⇒ **wolde**
war(e) *where; were* (N)
was (N) *whose*
wat *what* (see also **quhat**)
waxe, wexen; wex (preterite) *grow*
wende *go, make one's way; went*
wene (vb.) *think, expect, consider* (vb.);
  wene (N) *doubt* (n.)
wep(e) *wept*
wer *where*
wes *was*
wile, wule *while; once*
wit, wyt *know;* **wost** *you know;* **wat**
  knows; **wist, wuste** *knew*
wode *wood*
wol(e) *will, wish, intend;* **woltou** *wilt*
  thou, do you wish; **wolde, wald** (N)
  would, wished
wonde *wound(s)*
wone *place; custom, habit* (n.); **wone**
  dwell; (vb.) **(i)woned, wont**
  accustomed
wost ⇒ **wit**
wule ⇒ **wile**
wuste ⇒ **wit**

yaf, yef, yeve ⇒ **gyfe**

yat, yet(e) *gate*

yche ➻ **eche**

yed(e) ➻ **eode**

yeet, yut(e) *yet*

yef, yeve, yive ➻ **gyfe** (*give*)

yef, yif, yyif ➻ **gyf** (*if*)

yere, yeer *year*

yong(e), yung(e) *young*

yore *your*

The Assembly of Gods: Le Assemble de Dyeus, or Banquet of Gods and Goddesses, with the Discourse of Reason and Sensuality, ed. Jane Chance (1999)

Thomas Hoccleve, *The Regiment of Princes*, ed. Charles R. Blyth (1999)

John Capgrave, *The Life of St. Katherine*, ed. Karen Winstead (1999)

John Gower, *Confessio Amantis*, Vol. 1, ed. Russell A. Peck; with Latin translations by Andrew Galloway (2000); Vol. 2 (2003); Vol. 3 (2004)

Richard the Redeless and *Mum and the Sothsegger*, ed. James Dean (2000)

Ancrene Wisse, ed. Robert Hasenfratz (2000)

Walter Hilton, *The Scale of Perfection*, ed. Thomas Bestul (2000)

John Lydgate, *The Siege of Thebes*, ed. Robert Edwards (2001)

Pearl, ed. Sarah Stanbury (2001)

The Trials and Joys of Marriage, ed. Eve Salisbury (2002)

Middle English Legends of Women Saints, ed. Sherry L. Reames (2003)

The Wallace: Selections, ed. Anne McKim (2003)

Richard Maidstone, *Concordia (The Reconciliation of Richard II with London)*, ed. David R. Carlson, with a verse translation by A. G. Rigg (2003)

Three Purgatory Poems: The Gast of Gy, Sir Owain, The Vision of Tundale, ed. Edward E. Foster (2004)

William Dunbar, *The Complete Works*, ed. John Conlee (2004)

Chaucerian Dream Visions and Complaints, ed. Dana M. Symons (2004)

Stanzaic Guy of Warwick, ed. Alison Wiggins (2004)

Siege of Jerusalem, ed. Michael Livingston (2004)

Other TEAMS Publications

Documents of Practice Series:

Love and Marriage in Late Medieval London, selected, translated, and introduced by Shannon McSheffrey (1995)

Sources for the History of Medicine in Late Medieval England, selected, introduced, and translated by Carole Rawcliffe (1995)

A Slice of Life: Selected Documents of Medieval English Peasant Experience, edited, translated, and with an introduction by Edwin Brezette DeWindt (1996)

Regular Life: Monastic, Canonical, and Mendicant Rules, selected with an introduction by Douglas J. McMillan and Kathryn Smith Fladenmuller (1997); second edition, selected and introduced by Daniel Marcel La Corte and Douglas J. McMillan (2004)

Women and Monasticism in Medieval Europe: Sisters and Patrons of the Cistercian Reform, selected, translated, and with an introduction by Constance H. Berman (2002)

Medieval Notaries and Their Acts: The 1327–1328 Register of Jean Holanie, introduced, edited, and translated by Kathryn L. Reyerson and Debra A. Salata (2004)

Commentary Series:

Commentary on the Book of Jonah, Haimo of Auxerre, translated with an introduction by Deborah Everhart (1993)

Medieval Exegesis in Translation: Commentaries on the Book of Ruth, translated with an introduction by Lesley Smith (1996)

Nicholas of Lyra's Apocalypse Commentary, translated with an introduction and notes by Philip D. W. Krey (1997)

Rabbi Ezra Ben Solomon of Gerona: Commentary on the Song of Songs and Other Kabbalistic Commentaries, selected, translated, and annotated by Seth Brody (1999)

John Wyclif: On the Truth of Holy Scripture, translated with an introduction and notes by Ian Christopher Levy (2001)

Second Thessalonians: Two Early Medieval Apocalyptic Commentaries, translated with an introduction by Steven R. Cartwright and Kevin L. Hughes (2001)

The Glossa Ordinaria *on the Song of Songs*, translated with an introduction and notes by Mary Dove (2004)

Medieval German Texts in Bilingual Editions Series:

Sovereignty and Salvation in the Vernacular, 1050–1150, introduction, translation, and notes by James A. Schultz (2000)

Ava's New Testament Narratives: "When the Old Law Passed Away," introduction, translations, and notes by James A. Rushing, Jr. (2003)

History as Literature: German World Chronicles of the Thirteenth Century in Verse, introduction, translations, and notes by R. Graeme Dunphy (2003)

To order please contact: MEDIEVAL INSTITUTE PUBLICATIONS
Western Michigan University
Kalamazoo, MI 49008–5432
Phone (269) 387–8755
FAX (269) 387–8750

http://www.wmich.edu/medieval/mip/index.html

Medieval Institute Publications is a program
of The Medieval Institute, College of Arts
and Sciences, Western Michigan University

Typeset in 10.5 pt. Times New Roman
with Times New Roman display
Manufactured by McNaughton & Gunn, Inc.—Saline, Michigan

Medieval Institute Publications
College of Arts and Sciences
Western Michigan University
1903 W. Michigan Avenue
Kalamazoo, Michigan 49008-5432
www.wmich.edu/medieval/mip/

 WESTERN MICHIGAN UNIVERSITY